P9-CBF-915

The Aesthetics of Violence
in Contemporary Media

The Aesthetics of Violence
in Contemporary Media

Gwyn Symonds

continuum

2008

The Continuum International Publishing Group Inc
80 Maiden Lane, New York, NY 10038

The Continuum International Publishing Group Ltd
The Tower Building, 11 York Road, London SE1 7NX

www.continuumbooks.com

Copyright © 2008 by Gwyn Symonds

All rights reserved. No part of this book may be reproduced, stored in a retrieval system, or transmitted, in any form or by any means, electronic, mechanical, photocopying, recording, or otherwise, without the written permission of the publishers.

Library of Congress Cataloging-in-Publication Data
Symonds, Gwyn.
The aesthetics of violence in contemporary media/Gwyn Symonds.
    p. cm.
Includes bibliographical references and index.
ISBN-13: 978-0-8264-2987-2 (hardcover: alk. paper)
ISBN-10: 0-8264-2987-4 (hardcover: alk. paper)
1. Violence in mass media. 2. Mass media–Aesthetics. 3. Mass media–Audiences. I. Title.

P96.V5S96 2008
303.6--dc22   2008021979

Typeset by Newgen Imaging Systems Pvt Ltd, Chennai, India
Printed in the United States of America

"When I first viewed my own movie, *Thelma and Louise*, with an audience and the shooting occurred, the audience cheered and I was stunned because I had expected a completely different reaction. I had hoped for a stunned reaction from the audience of realization that this character had just sealed her fate in a very horrible way. But, instead, they burst into applause."

(Callie Khouri, screenwriter)

Contents

Prologue

"I don't keep rules," he said, gesturing to the black cap on his head with "No rules" logoed on it. I stood at the front of the class contemplating my next step. The adolescent student rocked his chair casually onto its back legs and tapped a wooden ruler with increasing loudness on the desk, using it with almost no break in the rhythm to sweep paper and a pencil onto the floor. He then snapped the ruler in half with two hands. The three other students in the room stopped work to watch in anticipation. Another ruler was split. "If you're not going to do the work then you can sit at your desk until you are ready, but there is no other choice for now," I said. "Let me know when you're ready to work." I continued to teach, ignoring the intermittent rocking and the snapping of a third ruler. Incrementally, he stopped rocking and, forming his hand into the shape of a gun, casually imitated a repeated firing motion, aiming it at me. He cocked his hand and fired, smiling and carefully watching for some reaction on my part. He got it. "That's not appropriate classroom behavior. Be a sensible idea to stop it, thanks. How about taking a few minutes to think about it?" Casually, he raised his hand and *fired* again saying, "F___ing bitch."

The most striking aspect of this interaction between the student and me is the communicative symbolism of the encounter. The student forming his hand into the shape of a gun was a symbolic message to me of the anger and aggression he was feeling, and was perceived by me as such. Neither the student nor I saw the gun gesture as a threat that would be actualized with a real gun; it was symbolic aggression, symbolic violence. While the threat spilled into verbal aggression and was preceded by destruction of property, the symbolism is embedded in the experience as it happens, enabling violence to be ritualized. There is a whole cultural discourse behind that hand/gun gesture which, while the student may not have been aware of it, makes the gesture a symbol available to him to communicate to me his opposition to, and rejection of, the authority I symbolized as a teacher in the education system I worked for. The individual's encounter with violence occurs with reference to a larger discourse of textual representation. The student had probably never seen an actual gun cocked in that way, but he would have seen such a gesture simulated innumerable times on television, in video games or at the cinema. It is probably true that children have been playing make-believe games with fingers as guns well before the current mass media age in true "cowboys and Indians" fashion. But, in the class-room incident described, the gesture was not made for a game but to communicate, albeit in an antisocial manner, something the student felt. Symbol and communica-tion, were both embedded in a physical, violent gesture that proclaimed the textuality of violence.

I have had a real gun pointed at me in the innocuous northern suburbs of a housing commission home in Melbourne as the decade of the '50s turned over into the '60s and took my childhood with it. In the context of personal peril, mediated by memory, I mostly recall the emergence of the symbolic from the actual event. I have no memory of the exact day but, apart from the type of gun it was, I remem-ber the details vividly: my drunken father weaving unsteadily on his feet, the slurred speech and the threatening chuckle as he talked about having some *fun*, and the slowly raised gun that, in my terror, seemed to be the size of a cannon. Though it must have happened in seconds, my fear perceived it all in dreadful, agonizingly slow motion. The barrel of the gun seemed to take endless minutes to inch its way up until it was pointed at my chest. All I could see was the hole at the end of the barrel and all I could feel, apart from paralyzing fear, was the slow trickle of urine down my legs as I wet myself, convinced he was going to kill me. I could not move my legs to run and there seemed to be endless time to wait for the sound of the shot. When it came, loud and predictable, my legs gave way from under me and I sat down in the urine puddle at my feet. I stayed on the ground shaking and crying. At some point, my mother called the police. They came and left after giving my father a warning, finding no evidence of a gun. I slipped back into that state of constant dread, in which I lived, as I waited for the next time I would be attacked.

The next day, I found the bullet hole in the wall behind where I had stood. The police had accepted my father's story that he had not fired any gun. I lived in that house until I was seventeen and, on more than one occasion, I ran my fingers over that hole to reassure myself that the experience had happened. While I had no doubt it had, the failure of anyone, particularly the police, to act to protect me was unnerving. It was as if my own very real experience of the incident was not tangible enough for the truth of it to be accepted. I found the hole in the wall symbolically comforting. It was proof beyond what I had felt, beyond my own terror, and beyond the words with which I had tried to tell the police and my mother about what had happened, that the shocking episode had been given some place in the scheme of my life that I could not, at the time, have put into words. Precisely because I was not believed, I was reassured by that hole as a symbol, as well as hard evidence, of the reality of the violence I had endured. Eventually, as time passed, it just became a nick in the wall that I rarely noticed but for the longest period I *always* knew it was there and ritualized its presence further by brushing my fingers over it as I walked past. Touching the hole was a way of congratulating myself that, amazingly, I had survived and that, paralyzing terror to the contrary, the threat embodied in the bullet was, in the end, just a hole in the wall. As a wife who witnessed the murder of her husband has perceptively described her sense of the murder scene, "It's just walls, doors and some grass . . . it's we who lay the emotion over the top of it."[1] I was a passionate *Star Trek* fan (the original series) as a child and thought the rudimentary special-effect sound and light of the Federation starship crews use of the hand held phaser weapons on the show was exciting. I had no problem, despite my encounter with a real weapon, thinking so. Special-effects violence was a different context entirely. I enjoyed the television battles in which they were used. Up on the screen the phasers were used to fight the bad guys, were never pointed at children, and did not look at all real. In the text of *Star Trek*, violence had a moral force and did not terrify me as actual violence had.

During the Gulf War I was living in Jerusalem, Israel, with my four children who were of primary school age or younger. When the air raid siren sounded, announcing a Scud attack from Iraq, I would join the rest of the country in entering the sealed room that each household had prepared in advance, sealing the door behind us around the edges with tape and, with my then husband, putting gas masks on my children and myself. As the minutes ticked by, we would wait for the all-clear on the radio from the army spokesperson who would announce the end of the attack and when it was safe to remove the masks and exit the room. Despite my childhood history of violent abuse, it began as a surreal experience of violence for someone who, having grown up in Australia and converted to Judaism prior to moving to Israel, had no experience of war. It was disconcerting to hear the protective but still ominous boom of a Patriot missile battery that was placed in suburban proximity to us as it fired in response to attack. In the early days of the war when it was not clear whether Iraq would use chemical warheads or not, fear was created as much by the initial uncertainty of that possibility, as much as it was by the immediate threat of being hit by a missile. It is difficult to stay in a heightened state of alert for lengthy periods to a threat that is so impersonal as a missile. As the attacks, the sirens, the entrance into the sealed room, and carrying your gas mask everywhere with you became a part of everyday life for weeks on end, this experience of violence on a national scale became, on a personal level, a part of daily routine.

My family and I were lucky in that no missile ever landed near us, though we saw the ever-present results of Scud missiles hitting other areas on the television news. The threat and the consequences were real. Yet, in the sealed room during an attack—with my children playing or reading in gas masks, or drowsily protesting having to put the masks on if an attack came in the middle of the night—the experience took on a sense of routine much like any other. The schools were closed initially but eventually reopened and I packed the kids lunches and their gas masks. If you were caught out shopping during an attack you found the nearest store with a sealed area and put on the gas mask you had with you. Or you ignored the attack altogether and just kept going about your business with the kind of reckless abandon that living with routine threat encourages. Finally, the needs and routines of the daily round assert themselves over the threat of destruction and, while you never underestimate the reality of that threat permeating daily life in a nation that is on a war footing and regularly under attack, you come to accept it, give it a place in your life, normalize its presence, and go on. It was no longer surreal and, at times, was pushed to the periphery of daily life.

However, the actual experience resonated in a media transformation of what others and I were experiencing. During an interview with CNN that replayed on Israeli media, a spokesman for the Israeli government of the day, Binyamin Netanyahu, was answering a question when an air raid siren sounded. In a dramatic, and no doubt, a public relations gesture, he excused himself to the American interviewer, explained what was happening, put on his gas mask, and continued with the interview. What had become a routine experience to me, as I watched someone play out the public drama of putting on the mask, redirected my view of what I had come to accept as a part of my daily life, to a point of reference on a television screen, and to an ideological level on a global stage. More than the actual act of having to use a mask whenever the country was attacked, Netanyahu doing it shocked me into recognizing that this was not supposed to be a *normal* state of existence. The drama and symbolic impact of Netanyahu's gesture was not lost in the international media follow-up in the press and other televised reports as it became a media story. The impact of the televised donning of the gas mask within Israel itself was similar to the shock value it had outside the country. The Israeli public, like myself, seemed as much surprised by the larger than daily life portrayal of the response to threat being played out on a televised stage when it had been given its place in the sealed rooms of their homes. Like so much of the violence that occurs in Israel, the attacks, at least partially, had become something the country lived with. The representation of that violence to others in a televised media context framed the lived experience as news and a public relations exercise. Up there on the television screen, beamed around the world via CNN, the act of putting on the gas mask became something other than it was when we did it at home while under attack—a virtual act in a political and ideological space. As an individual, I was aware of the transition, even if the exact border between my own experience and the televised version of it was not necessarily something I could easily articulate. But I knew that the context of my experience of violence, and its meaning, had been changed by its virtual reframing as televisuality. Nevertheless, transformed as it was in a media text, the authenticity of the experience was not lost to myself and the rest of the country. After all, Israelis had been donning their gas masks in the same attack as Netanyahu.

Introduction

In fact, there are many uses of the innumerable opportunities a modern life supplies for regarding—at a distance ... other people's pain.

(Susan Sontag)[2]

The question is not why am I using so much violence, but why are others not? Human beings are violent. Stephen Hawking once said he was sure there was life on other planets, and it would be hostile.

(Paul Verhoeven, film director)[3]

There is no quicker way to get audience or reader attention in narrative than to beat up or kill someone. The pervasiveness of the representation of violence, making it the lifeblood of contemporary storytelling and exceeding the rate of its occurrence in reality,[4] indicates that it may be close to impossible to define human behavior aesthetically in text without using it. Callie Khouri, the screenwriter for *Thelma and Louise* (1991) has said a gun in a scene is the instrument that "you can take out and totally change the course of everything."[5] Violence can generate gripping action and character development. Beyond that incontrovertible statement it is necessary to tread warily when generalizing about the representation of violence. Unless it is viewed on a continuum of authenticity—ranging from indexical representation of actual events to more stylized and fictional genres—violence in contemporary text appears to be a contradictory discourse. The collapsing towers of the World Trade Center billowing smoke on CNN, the two high school students at Columbine emerging as poster boys for the debate for gun control in the documentary *Bowling for Columbine*, honor killing as hoax in Norma Khouri's fictionalizing of memoir in *Forbidden Love: A Harrowing True Story of Love and Revenge in Jordan*, the camera panning over a prosthetically constructed forensic crime scene in television's *Law & Order*, Tony brutally carrying out a Mafia hit in *The Sopranos*, *Buffy the Vampire Slayer* punning and dusting vampires to save the world while she goes to high school, the Bride in the *Kill Bill* films improbably slaying countless enemies standing between her and vengeance, the relentless flaying of Christ's body sending chunks of flesh flying in *The Passion of the Christ*, or a frustrated Homer choking a recalcitrant Bart in *The Simpsons* are all different contexts framing a meaning for

1

the word "violence." My book will engage with that contradictory variety in its journey across a vast and complex narrative landscape and bring clarity to that overview by examining the degrees of visceral authenticity in such representations.

Assessing the degree to which viewers and readers react with a visceral response to violence on the screen or page invariably depends on how authentic or realistic they perceive it to be. Such an assessment is problematized by violence being used in narratives whose messages about its use are profoundly at variance with one another. Violence is represented as something to be deplored or seen as a necessary evil. It is liberally resorted to by heroes but excoriated as criminal when used with equal liberality by villains. It is the catalyst to the restoration of order and to rampaging social implosion. It is delighted in as "butt-kicking" and technically brilliant special effects but is also used to repel audiences with such graphic physicality that it makes the viewer want to turn away from the screen. It is used to save worlds spectacularly in fictional wars but decried when it reduces the innocent to collateral damage in news reports. It is the road to redemption in storytelling as well as the road to perdition. It is embraced as fundamental to narrative and rejected as gratuitous. It is documented as brutalizing fact and praised as extravagantly imaginative fantasy. Above all, it is funny, even though there are images of it that make audiences and readers weep. In that contradictory plethora, Stathis Gourgouris's question about the incidence of actual violence in the United States could also be asked about the texts that represent it to Western audiences generally: "No doubt, violence in the United States is self-evident, but what does this mean exactly? . . . how does it become perceptible and for whom?"[6]

In answer, I argue that by viewing the contexts of the textual representation of violence on a continuum, from the indexical to the most stylized, it is possible to examine the ways in which texts that use violence make claims to, or convince their audience of, the authenticity of their representation of the experience. It is also possible to see the degree of distance separating some representations of violence from anything to do with actual, real-life violence. Using such a continuum, I can productively generalize about the use of violence without straying too far from the unique detail in texts which give weight to generalization. It also allows explication of the ways in which the texts reflect cultural anxieties about violence and about what the authenticity of their representation might mean to audiences and readers as they accept or reject, enjoy or decry violence in text. The degree and nature of violence portrayed, the look of the blood or the sound of the blow landing on flesh, is often seen to have affective impact because it is graphically represented. While that claim is certainly true, definitions of what constitutes the graphic quality of images of violence and the role played in that affective impact by the relationship of the graphic to actual violence outside the text has been little examined. Viewed on a continuum from the indexical to the fantastical, the range of uses to which violence is put in narrative is revealed to also be a discourse about how authentically it is being portrayed.

For the purpose of my book, the term "authenticity" is not used to describe some objective experience of its representation, though a case for an indexical relationship between image and the violent event is made in Chapter 1, which examines the live television transmission of the events of September 11, 2001. Authenticity is used to describe an aspect of the reception of violence, a cultural concern with what is realistic or true about its representation. This concern can be found within the texts themselves when claims are made for the truth of the narrative (as in the True Crime genre discussed in Chapter 3). It can be found in the perceptions of audiences when there is anxiety about how much violence is portrayed (as in the controversy surrounding the use of violence in Mel Gibson's *The Passion of the Christ*, discussed in Chapter 7). It is particularly notable when the text relies on audience expectations that generic conventions promise something actual about the lived experience of violence (as in the documentary forms examined in Chapter 2). Alternatively, it is the transformation of violence to decrease authenticity that characterizes generic conventions representing far from indexical forms of violence. Such texts distance audiences from the real-world implications of the trauma of violence so that they are free to enjoy being entertained by it. This transformation is particularly captivating in exciting action film fight sequences, which are the topic of Chapter 6.

By examining a range of texts on a continuum from the more indexical images of violence to the stylized forms that vary in their capacity to disturb audiences, I will argue that the affective impact of violence in a text depends on a degree of audience or reader belief or disbelief in the visceral authenticity of its telling. Such believability, in turn, is directly a product of collective cultural anxieties about violence in the community, even as it feeds back into those anxieties. Affective impact on audiences and readers is also a product of the way texts work to use or deflect those anxieties when violent scenarios are textualized. The degree of authenticity is a reflection of a text's distance from the lived experience of violence "out there" beyond the screen or page. In addition, the use of violence in text often depends on a textual playing with claims to authenticity to encourage believability in the experience of violence that is the subject. Examining the fascinating range of texts about violence reveals a cultural equivocation about the actual experience itself and about the authenticity of its graphic portrayal when it is perceived as authentic enough to disturb audiences and readers.

The debate over the ill-effects of violence in the media, for example, is a reflection of that equivocation and centers on whether or not it has antisocial effects[7] even as, concurrently, its use in text is viewed as entertaining. However, public acceptance of its entertainment value is qualified by public anxiety that leads to censorship and rating systems.[8] Along with censorship laws and rating systems, the debate over the ill-effects of violence in the media is the most prominent symptom of this moral and cultural anxiety about the authenticity of the representation of violence in text. I will not engage in the ill-effects debate per se but my book is a precursor to that engagement, which requires that we define how individual or generic texts actually represent violence.[9] It is a precursor to that debate in that it attempts to describe and contextualize selected representations of violence as a necessary step that must be taken prior to researching effects on behavior. This essential step is often neglected in the public debate over the ill-effects of violence, where the differences between images, and therefore the possibility that they might have different effects, is rarely recognized.

Cultural anxieties about texts with violent content embody public unease about violence itself that texts, to varying degrees, authenticate for aesthetic impact.[10] Robert McKee has said that, along with emotional authenticity or "behavioral credibility" in character development and convincing logic in plot development, authenticity in narrative depends on the use of the selective "telling detail,"[11] which allows the audience's imagination to supply the rest and accept the experience as credible. In his view, it is the intrusion of the filmmaker's technique as a part of that detail that can shatter believability. This intrusion is particularly noticeable when trying to make violence appear graphic, whether or not the graphic image is forensically actual. Given that the audience also brings personal interpretation to the creation of credibility, the degree of what is seen as believably authentic in the representation of violence cannot be decided outside a discussion of the aesthetic impact of individual texts, or groups of texts that share the same aesthetic conventions, on a continuum. Censorship or rating bodies and participants in the ill-effects debate, for example, often use the term graphic or nongraphic violence to make distinctions but rarely with any attempt at contextualizing with clarity how those distinctions actually work. For the purposes of my book, the word "graphic" denotes visually vivid and explicit detail that appears so in context. Such vividness and explicitness can be the effect of a representation's relationship to indexical reality but also to the intensity of its visual impact as a function of its content and the photo-realistic or hyperrealistic effects of textual mediation. The degree of indexicality the representation has with historical examples of actual violence is one way affective impact on readers and audiences can be heightened.

While graphic details in the representation of fictional violence can cause less desensitized audiences of a film to turn away from the screen or to provoke public calls for stricter censorship, there remain distinctions to be made between that effect and the viewing by audiences of violence in real time that they know to be nonfictional, as in television live-from-the-scene reporting. At the far end of the continuum from that indexicality where graphic violence is at its most stylized and the representation of violence can be turned primarily into an aesthetic pleasure— as the way people are hurt on screen becomes a production value defined by virtuosity in special effects re-creation—we find violence that often deflects audience response away from the revulsion that violence in actuality would inevitably cause.[12] However, it is also at that end of the continuum that audience revulsion toward images of violence can be the product of an exaggeration of actual violence that is hyperreal rather than forensically authentic. It is not my aim to cover all textual possibilities about violence on the continuum. Rather, my discussion will alight at various points of interest to reveal shared cultural understandings and beliefs about violence that the seemingly contradictory discourse about it can obscure if it is not viewed in this way. I accept the problem as defined by the following questions from Michael Kowalewski:

> Is violence an action or the cause of that action? Is violence an emotion or the result of that emotion? Is it a crime or a disease? And if a disease, what kind: mental or physical? Is it an individual behavioral aberration or a culturally determined reflex? The bewildering array of sociological, psychiatric, judicial, physiological, religious, political, and anthropological answers to questions like these do not, perhaps, affect our practical usage of the word or our ordinary conception of violence. They should, however, effectually erode any firm certainty we may have in thinking about what violence is and how we know about it.[13]

Thus, no objective or overarching dictionary definition of violence is assumed in my argument outside individual or generic textual contexts.[14]

However, despite the contradictions inherent across any broad view of a range of texts, reader and viewer trust or distrust in the textual authenticity of the violent experience is cued by a text's discrete place on a continuum, ranging from violence that has a visceral indexicality[15] up to its most fantastical imagining in the frivolities of the spectacular. It is a continuum following a linear movement from the lived experience of violence at one end, as it becomes text at the point of origin of the act, through to various forms of textualization that incorporate increasingly larger elements of manipulation and illusion for affective impact. At the latter point on the continuum, textualization gradually becomes totally fictional and hyperreal with the most stylized relationship to the lived experiences of violence. There are also points along the continuum where violence is used to explore aspects of lived experiences other than the violence that is the content of the text, such as when it is used for polemic or metaphorical storytelling.[16] The authenticity of the representation of violence in a text is modified by ideological framing of content, the technology and production values of the medium used, and the aesthetic aims of its presentation. Isolating some of those factors along a continuum enables contextualization of the way an audience belief in a text's representation of the violent experience is modified by decreasing indexicality and increasing fantasy.

My aim is not simply to determine the truth of any textual discourse about violence but rather to bear in mind Francesco Casetti's dictum, in reference to film spectatorship, "that when considering the truth *of* a discourse one must think of a truth *as* a discourse."[17] As Casetti also points out, the spectator does more than remain present in front of the text; if the spectator can be manipulated, he can also resist: "Ultimately, the film needs a spectator, as much because the facts it presents requires supplement as because its progression requires continual motivation and reception."[18] The significance of audience perceptions of the authenticity or inauthenticity of the representation of violence at any point on the continuum is an ongoing concern of the analysis of the texts under discussion. Audience affective biases, audience familiarity with the conventions of the text, the ways in which texts aesthetically target audience response and pleasure, and the role audience expectations play in interaction with the text are all aspects of audience response that inevitably form a part of the discussion of violent texts. It is in accordance with Annette Hill's view that "the significance of real experience emerges as central to understanding fictional violence"[19] that, as an undercurrent to my discussion, I refer to the field of audience reception to give empirical context to textual violence. Hills' empirical research reveals the degree to which audience self-awareness of response; the significance of the viewing environment; the impact of gender, physical, and emotional response; and of anticipation of outcomes and visual effects, all impact on the way representations of violence in fiction are viewed. The consideration of the representations of violence in that dynamic and often contradictory framework illuminates interpretation of text and subtext. While Hills concludes that there are a range of responses to watching violence "which are activated by the consumer, not by the movies themselves,"[20] the individuality of that response is activated by specific textual contexts. Textualization can reflect the use of violence as a drawcard or as a launching pad to hold the viewer's attention. However, violence as a commodity does not preclude the audience taking meanings of personal significance from it or bringing his or her own subtext to the viewing and reading of the text that uses it.[21]

Texts about violence are inextricably shadowed by the strength of those perceived links to violence in the world outside the text from which they draw their degree of authenticity from a backdrop of real experience. Even the animated boulder splattering the Coyote's body to the canyon floor, when a trap for his prey, the Road Runner, backfires, relies for its comic effect on the audience's conviction that "Ouch, that's gotta hurt!" It deflects that recognition along the continuum of authenticity, making it fantastical, by allowing the Coyote to come out from under and walk away unhurt, if "concertinaed." However, the humor of his frustration, the comic effect of his self-destructive, Sisyphean attempts to finally silence the "Beep, beep" of his prey, depends on audience beliefs about violence and its links with human suffering. It depends on a shared perception among viewers that violence in lived experience is potentially fatal, suspended though its consequences are in this animated context. Viewer distress in the face of news reports on actual violence, for example, and viewer laughter at the Coyote's existential fate as the victim of the violent traps he sets for the Road Runner, stem from that same source. Both reactions are mutually dependent on the collective knowledge of the annihilating impact of violence on the subject that is born out of collective lived experience. It is the mode of textualization, the context that frames and creates varying degrees of audience perception that the violence is authentically portrayed. It is the aesthetic of textualization that determines whether the audience/reader weeps or laughs, views the violence with delight and aesthetic pleasure, or finds its representation morally bereft. It is the degree of distance from the lived experience of violence encouraged by the textual context that determines whether the reader or viewer will be amused or revolted, pleasurably entertained or disturbed.

The dominant public debate about violence in the media, over issues of censorship or the ill-effects on readers and viewers of exposure to representation, reflects anxiety about how graphically and realistically these texts represent it. The closer the texts link to an actual event, the more it disturbs an audience or reader with its affective sense of lived authenticity. A report in *Time* magazine on the horrors of genocide in the Sudan, reporting on the rampaging, government-supported Janjaweed fighters murdering Darfurian children, affectively unsettles the reader with its description of deplorable violence toward an innocent as a prelude to arousing reader outrage:

> For Darfurians like Melkha Musa Haroun, the horrors they have witnessed will never fade. After an attack last year she fled with her four children and spent eight months hiding from the Janjaweed, walking from village to village until she found refuge in a camp. Now, one year later, she recalls watching Janjaweed fighters on a rampage deciding whom to kill. A fighter unwrapped swaddling cloth and rolled a newborn baby onto the dirt. The baby was a girl so they left her. Then the Janjaweed spotted a 1-year-old boy and decided he was a future enemy. In front of a group of onlookers, a man tossed the boy into the air as another took aim and shot him dead. "It was the worse thing I ever saw," Haroun says softly, casting her eyes downward as she hugs her baby tightly to her breasts.[22]

The report provokes a visceral disturbance of reader repose and equanimity through the contrast between indifference to life and the maternal nurturing of it—the horror unsettles even across the safe distance that time, space, and textual mediation places between the reader and the actual event. It engages reader empathy and trust in the authenticity of the text's narrative about violence primarily because it is described as an account of an historical, physical experience of violence. Paradoxically, textual mediation that creates a safe distance from the experience (the reader is getting it third hand and on the page) exists side by side with the vivid recreation of the brutal indifference to the value of a young life, so casually dispatched, that is also a product of the techniques of textual mediation. The account is representative of all violent texts because its impact relies on a collective under-standing of the effects of lived violence that is born out of a shared history of violent conflict in intimate and public spaces. Unless the report is a hoax, the violence did not take place only on the page, the boy really died and—even mediated through the reporter's rhetoric and the subjective recall of an eyewitness—that indexicality shocks more than if the account were distanced by placing it further along an expressive continuum as a fictional fantasy. Nevertheless, it also allows the reader a safely mediated textual experience of violence from a distance.

The report is also representative of all texts about violence because its degree of authenticity provokes moral engagement or disengagement with the use of violence that is its subject and with how graphically the violence is described. The text has a view on the violence and the reader will have a view of the text's stance on it. The textualization of the experience in the *Time* report provokes the desire in the reader to morally engage with the experience of violence it represents or with the morality of the text's stance on it. "It was the worse thing I ever saw"—eyewitness shock at seeing the actual violence parallels the reader's more muted rejection of the act in response to a textualized "seeing" of the "horrors." It is a given of the cultural and social response to violence that one is appalled by its antisocial, nonculturally sanc-tioned uses and, sometimes, with the boundaries of textual exploration. Lambert Zuidervaart is probably right that theoretical discussion of artistic truth "has fallen on hard times."[23] Nevertheless, the use of violence in fictional texts, in particular, is often framed by audience expectations that its artistic use will disclose something about the experience of violence so that it is also relevant to consider whether "[a]uthenticity is a matter of mediated expression that is imaginatively disclosive."[24]

Each chapter will have an ongoing concern with the implied or assumed interac-tion of texts about violence and their audiences created by claims to authenticity. Ideological and moral judgment of the subject of violence is most prominently dis-played in the discourse of legal texts but it is never far from the concerns of texts on violence and the public debate about their reception. The resources of society are geared to preventing and dealing with violence as crime, punishment, rehabilita-tion, prevention, treatment, moral judgment, and conflict resolution. Texts emerging from these categorizations cover a landscape of scientific, behavioral, psychoana-lytic, sociological, moral, and media fields. The use of, or interplay with, such categorizations in imagined fictional and nonfictional texts in popular culture leads to a two-way fertilization and, oftentimes, a mesmerizing imaginative discourse that creates the panorama of what is recognized as violence and how it is judged by the public, even if it is fictional. It is those texts with an indexical relationship to actual violence that are likely to rely the most on public anxieties about violence to create their affective impact. The text of judgment embodied in the outcome of a trial, for example, assumes an authentic forensic recreation in a disciplined accounting of violence done to the body in order to convict but it, too, shares in a more generalized tone of collective moral outrage. In sentencing remarks reported in the press from the New South Wales District Court, in Australia—in the trial of a perpetrator in the gang rape of a sixteen-year-old girl in a home invasion in Sydney in 2004—a judge expressed that larger cultural discursive visceral response to a court narrative of actual violence:

> In sentencing Steven Aslett on Thursday to 24 years jail, with a non-parole period of 17 years, NSW District Court judge Michael Finnane said it was a "particularly brutal home invasion" . . . In the space of two hours, the men "plundered, pillaged and raped" committing a crime that "any civilised human being would find appalling," the judge said. . . Judge Finnane said Steven Aslett, although led by his uncle, "was prepared to wound a 16 year-old, tiny girl without any mercy or any regard for human feelings" . . . The judge, who has described Dudley Aslett as a "cold, callous, vicious and extremely dangerous criminal," said he had not seen a victim with such severe injuries in his 35 years in the law."[25]

"Appalled," the judge claims to speak for the broader collective of "any civilized human," for the law, and from his personal observations over 35 years of experience in viewing the vicious side of human behavior. As with the report on the Sudan, this text is representative of violent texts on the most unsettling end of the discourse continuum about the subject of violence, when the narrative is a report of an actual occurrence. They represent violence as a textual struggle to make sense of a primal viciousness teetering at the limits of explication. They reflect an intrinsic desire, occurring across a broad continuum of cultural discourses about violence, to decry the act of brutal transgression, and its infliction on the body. In the legal judgment, the physicality of rape as the wounding of a tiny young girl sanctions the outrage at violence. That discourse of disciplinary judgment and legalese contains rape as a crime but, nevertheless, cannot easily contain that outrage. As S. Caroline Taylor notes, the legal system codifies in its text the moral values of the social ethos outside its courtrooms[26] and public horror at violation of the body by the violent act is reflected in the legal discourse that includes the judge's remarks. Fictional texts also seek to engage with this horror and it is not surprising that films and television often reflect that legal and social encounter with violence in a range of police and forensic procedurals and True Crime stories.

There is movement in and out of the text by the viewer or reader as a part of the need to find moral ground and understanding. Intrinsic to textual response is the desire to bear witness to trauma and suffering. Texts bear the burden of the violent act as an individual *and* collective experience.

In the aftermath of the September 11 attacks on the World Trade Center and the Pentagon, Americans started talking. And we kept talking for days afterwards.

The telling and the retelling came from a need, if not a compulsion, to give testimony to what we saw and experienced—to make sense of the incomprehensible, to transform the surreal into the real, to connect with others in a time of utter bewilderment and dislocation, to somehow fix in the mind a national trauma of ineffable dimensions. Not only did we turn to one another, but we were glued to the media, which provided a continual stream of information and acted as communal, albeit virtual, site for the bearing of witness, where we could measure our own responses against those of journalists, critics, writers, and artists. This communal witness bearing gave birth to our common perception of the event as historical reality, the accepted judgment of mainstream culture—one that artists will later embrace or subvert, transgress, and reimagine.[27]

As Donna Harkavy notes in discussion of both the communal and the artistic response to the American national trauma of September 11, discourse about violence incorporates the interaction between individual sense-making and collective knowledge about the degree of authenticity of the violent experience conveyed by the text that represents it. Being "glued" to the text is, in the context of sharing, measuring, and exploring outside the text, an attempt to determine authenticity and to fix meaning in the mind. Thus Chapter 1 will argue the common perception of 9/11 as "historical reality" was more a product of the event forming the text than the other way round.

That argument does not deny that the collective cultural view of the authenticity of the violence in a text is in a problematic relationship with the factual because, textually speaking, violence is also a spectator sport, a commodity produced for entertainment. The average viewer, as Todd Gitlin notes, is not "likely to mistake the TV image of a corpse for an actual cadaver," but viewer/reader reception of a violent text as entertainment is often in conflict with a degree of authenticity in the textualization of the experience because

we do demand something from our images, even if they are "almost real." We expect them to heighten life, to intensify and focus it by being better than real, more vivid, more stark, more *something*. We want a burst of feeling, a frisson of commiseration, a flash of delight, a moment of recognition—so that's what it's like when your boyfriend sleeps with your sister, when you lose a patient in the emergency room, when you're voted off the *Survivor* island. We depend on these images to imagine the great elsewhere: "realistic" presences that point, say, to the real ruins of the World Trade Center, or fictions that gesture toward a real world where attendants wheel patients into operating rooms.[28]

The further a violent text is placed along a continuum of representation from the recording of an actual event—as in the case of live broadcasts of the World Trade

Center's destruction or the delayed, reported actuality of the Sudan article—toward the symbolic and the fictional, the more tenuous is its grip on an indexical sense of the lived violent experience as technology creates illusion, fantasy, and spectacle. However, while the pixilated splatter in the computer game installments of the videogame *Grand Theft Auto* franchise[29] engages far less with the lived experience of violence, nevertheless, continually advancing technology has increased the visceral, photorealistic nature of the graphic. As a result, censorship ratings reflect the perception that digitally created violence provokes anxiety about its interaction with the lived experience of violence outside the screen—even when the special effects aesthetic of the text does not create a representation of actuality that is forensically authentic.

Textualization partakes of the recognition that violence infringes on lived safety, on the safety of textual distance, and on textual categorization, just as it resists categorization in lived experience. Nick Giovanni contemplates violence within and across the racial divide, acknowledging the ease with which a desire to distinguish between oppressor and oppressed can take comfort from the categorization of acts of violence:

> When you leave your domicile in the morning, and sometimes even when you stay there all day, there is the ever-present fear of assault whether physical or mental. There is something about, well, life that makes you nervous. In many respects the violence of some whites is the easiest to take because it is physical and immediate. It hurts but if you survive you can categorize it, and therefore dismiss it, by saying "white folks." The violence, both physical and mental, that Blacks do to ourselves is more difficult. That violence takes away safety. The violence of child abuse, wife beating, drug taking is much harder to codify because somehow we victims feel we have brought this on ourselves.[30]

The less personalized the violence the easier it is to face. In the experience Giovanni describes there is violence "out there" and violence "in here." Even if the act is the same, the impact is easier for him to deal with as an Afro-American when it is clearly associated with its expected source of a white Other. It is harder to deal with when it is too close to home and violates his shared circle of ethnic or cultural safety. Placing the violence, categorizing it, naming a perpetrator that is not "us" but Other, keeps it at a distance, so it can be dealt with in familiar ways that are acceptable to the psyche. But, when the attacker is "us"—for Giovanni this is when it is black on black violence—the attempt to make sense of it is more fraught. Giovanni's text is itself a protective barrier *and* a channel through which readers can contemplate a neighborhood and ethnic experience that is not their own. All texts considered here provide textual surface genre categories that encourage increasingly safe textual distances along a continuum to contemplate lived violence but it is only a matter of degree. In that sense, textualization can involve depersonalization, with the viewer able to relax into the fact that the story is not about him or her. However, the safety net provided by textual distance is perpetually under threat from the text's potential for the representation of authentic violence that exists at the heart of any convincing illusion—even if there is no indexicality with an actual event.

When the textual experience of violence is highly graphic it can infringe on the comfort of a safe textual distance, even when the event portrayed is fictional. When the text containing violence is at its most manipulated in the fictional, the audience can perceive authenticity and viscerally respond as graphic imagery crashes through the spectator comfort zone. Speaking in an extras feature on the DVD of the film *Irréversible*[31] of the complex, multilayered special effects used to create the violence in the film, the special-effects coordinator, Rodolphe Chabrier, has described the way in which the graphic, fatal beating of a character with a fire extinguisher was digitally authenticated. Using a range of techniques—including 3D imaging, CGI (computer generated images), matte painting, graphic design, editing, morphing, composing, software used to show vibration and motion blur to modify filmed acting, make-up, prosthetic latex masks, and dummy heads—the film creates a graphic stomach-churning scene for the filmed sequence. He describes the shooting of two scenes with the actor, Albert Dupontel. One with the actor holding a fire extinguisher cut in half which allowed him to "hit" the other actor without touching him. The other shot with the use of a real fire extinguisher and the hitting of a motionless latex dummy filled with "blood." Chabrier notes the aesthetic allure visually created by the process of layering the CGI effects for the blood on the face:

> This is an interesting bit in which only the bruising and blood effects are visible. The face appears little by little, marked by blood. It's quite a strange but beautiful effect.[32]

The CGI effect he describes is one of a slowly emerging, bloodied human facial features morphing out of a technological void as the face vibrates in response to unseen blows, a pulsating red form partially delineated against a black screen that becomes more disturbing and more aesthetically pleasing for the viewer at the same time. The aesthetic pleasure of the digital remains embodied in the noncorporeal space of the shiny technological ether, to be transformed when the special effects are completely layered to explode into the violent visual horror of the final filmed sequence—as the character crushes the face of an unresisting, prone body into a hideous pulp. Knowledge of this textual manipulation reveals that the process that creates the experience of violence embedded in technological illusion does not always subvert the desire to look away from its perceived authenticity. The sequence depends on manipulation to create an effect that undermines the safety of textual fantasy, challenging the act of watching by pushing the viewer to associate the beating with the painful collective knowledge of the lived experience of the brutal which the text needs, as much as it does the technology, to authenticate its effect and its story.

In the same film, a real-time, nine minute graphic rape scene in a blood-red urban tunnel, done in one long take, breaches fantasy time to challenge the comfort of viewer expectations that the camera will protectively cut away after making a familiar plot point about the brutality of rape. The unflinching camera stays until the end, forcing the viewer to stay longer in the illusion than feels comfortable, destroying the pretence that cinematic mediation implies that it is always safe to look. Well into the rape scene, a bystander enters and exits the scene at the far end of the tunnel, failing to assist the victim and disappointing viewer anticipation that character intervention might end the violence and, along with it, viewer discomfort. Disturbingly, viewer comfort is only restored after the attack culminates with the brutal bashing of the victim's face in addition to the rape; forcing the audience to recognize that while it may have thought that it had plumbed the depths of viewer tolerance for the portrayal of believable violence with the rape itself, the filmmaker knows otherwise. It is not surprising reviewers were upset:

> It's hard to imagine a more unpleasant film than *Irréversible*, a tale of sexual and physical violence that pulls out all the stops in attempting to shock its audience. The new film by French filmmaker Gaspar Noé—whose last feature, *I Stand Alone*, boasted a 30-second warning countdown before its graphic finale—is determined to rub our noses in the horrid realities of life.[33]

Nicholas Schager's review is responding to the intrusion of the screen violence into the viewer's personal temporal space that the distance created by the mediation of the screen generally guarantees will not be violated. Perhaps he is also missing the film's attempt to do what Paul Schrader, the screenwriter and director, has stated is the only acceptable justification for the use of violence in film—to indulge the need for the vicarious experience of violence while undermining it:

> I think *The Wild Bunch* is a great film because it understands how deeply sick it is, and let's you know how sick it is; so it not only exploits your vicarious need for violence, but undermines it at the same time. I think films that analyze violence in that way are entirely justified.[34]

Such a viewing experience aims to unsettle as well as entertain.

Of course, the closer the viewer or reader comes to a perspective that pricks audience comfort, as *Irréversible* does or, alternatively, to a perspective of the perpetrator which implicates the audience's shared humanity with violent impulses portrayed in the text, the more audience perceptions of authenticity overwhelm textual barriers. In her discussion of the artist Sue Williams' *Irresistible*,[35] a rubber sculpture of a prone battered woman curled up like a fetus on the floor—forcing the observer into the position of the perpetrator towering above the form—Harkavy notes:

> Not for nothing did the artist place a sign next to the sculpture when it was first exhibited asking "sadistic" viewers to refrain from further abusing the figure, a request not heeded by all who came into the gallery.[36]

Lifelike, naked, one eye closed from bruising, a hand holding her cheek, bruises and shoe prints on the body, with legs bent close to a fetal position, the sculpture of the body of the woman is also covered in the words of the perpetrators' justifications for battering the female form: "Look what you made me do" and "I think you like it." The exposure of the female body on the gallery floor clearly discomfits because it implicates the observer simply by the prone figure's proximity; discomfiting because one sees what the perpetrator saw—vulnerability to attack. As Harkavy notes, with the shrinking of textual and spatial distance, some visitors to the gallery could not resist and became a perpetrating audience. Lived experience merged with the authenticity of the text as, presumably, visitors to the gallery put the boot in. The spectator space, in a sense, became participant space.

While not easily discernible, it is possible to detect that movement from the lived experience of violence into text, as a participant transitions to spectator and back again, in autobiographical renditions of violent events, which recognize what is and is not authentic to textual recreation.[37] Gail Bell, as the subject of her own textual transition from the lived experience of violence in *Shot: A Personal Response to Guns and Trauma*, characterizes the way in which being shot—anonymously in the back, as a teenager of 17 in 1968 in Sydney—was itself the propulsion for the making of text, for the transformation of the intimate violence done to her life into multiple narratives:

> Being shot propelled me, temporarily, into a hyper-real world peopled with policemen, doctors, nurses, journalists, photographers and, most unexpectedly, into the collective consciousness of Sydney citizens, who responded by sending me hundreds of cards and enough flowers to brighten an entire hospital.[38]

For Bell, publication of the event to others in the media made over a personal experience of violence into the "hyper-real." The event catapulted her simultaneously into other texts that made her a changing subject in different stories that relied on her own for an authentic starting point to other narratives. Every police, medical, or newspaper report gave another narrative perspective until she was a character in a collective story told to multiple audiences by people she had never met, such as the anonymous Sydney well wishers learning about her from the media who cast her in the role of an object of sympathy.

Her published book is itself an added layer to that textuality as she tries to understand, three decades later, how that event changed her and the future course of her life. The shocking novelty of the unexpected violence propelled her into a search for meaning as surely as the physical impact of the bullet pushed her forward as it struck. Through multicontextual perspectives on the physiology of being shot—in newspaper reports, police investigations, legal procedures and hospital and surgical treatments—on its psychological trauma—filtered through interactions with family, her fallible memory and shared experiences with other victims of crime—and on the mechanics of firing a gun and gun culture—"the business of killing"[39] in war, police work and the euthanasia of animals—Gail Bell retraces her own transformation from "pre-shot" to "after-shot." The book is a textual identity transformation giving Bell and the reader the pre-book, during-book, and after-book Bell. Her identity as textual subject is changed by the physical and emotional price paid for the journey of writing about the experience, as there was to be paid for the event itself:

> My accident was a private tragedy with no epic or heroic dimension, no meaning other than the obvious, no consequences other than the expected, yet glinting in the distance are some of the warning signs survivors of all tragedies glimpse. The loss of language to tell your story once you return from hell, the learning of silence when you've tried, no matter how understatedly, to describe your experience and in response been asked to keep your horrors to yourself, to stop frightening old people and children. The willful forgetting. The act you perfect of fitting in again and being as you were before it all happened. Since I opened that box of old papers, I've suffered an acuteness of the senses, and a consistent pain in my back, in an area roughly approximating the quadrant affected in the shooting. It's been a dull, sub-clinical manifestation, there but not there, both noticeable and endurable.[40]

The authenticity of the violent experience is relived by the body as a memory with physical symptoms and mirrored pain, even though the pain is still a phantom event: "there but not there." The re-creation is inextricable from the textualized journey begun when "I opened that box of old papers" from the time of the event. Despite her disclaimer that there is "no meaning other than the obvious," the physical, mental, emotional, and compositional act of will her book embodies as she searches for understanding uncovers the complexity beneath the "obvious." There is a final clarity about the possibilities of arriving at a "meaning unambiguous in the right context": "SHOT is a NEAT, well-balanced word, its short vowel-sound as penetrating as the act itself, its meaning unambiguous in the right context."[41] The meaning of the experience of violence to her, the point of her literary journey is the book itself. The text offers a clarity of perception that roots itself in an authenticity of representation uncovered as the short, sharp "penetrating" bluntness of the event's making over of her life and embodied in the book's blunt title, *Shot*. Just as the "loss of language to tell your story" is reversed through the text, the event itself can also be reclaimed from its loss in the hyperreal years ago to regain personal meaning.

The discursive strategy of Bell's memoir is one that seeks to bridge the gap between memory and the authenticity of the experience; to make sense of an experience that grew out of the immediate trauma but which "changed over time from a single ugly encounter to a state of perpetually remembering and reliving aspects of the day itself":

> With a gun pointed at her head, Lisa anticipated her life coming to an end— compounded with the big imponderables, why me, why now when I am not ready, and even more basic fears, like will it hurt, will I suffer? What happens when the curtain comes down? With each second of her ordeal she was tormented with a new fear? ... There is time for imaging many different outcomes: pain, mutilation, bleeding, dying quickly or slowly, and, beyond yourself, children growing up without their mother, parents losing a daughter, a husband losing a wife.[42]

Bell is describing the experience of another victim of violence who had a gun held to her head. Just prior to the anticipated violent event, possible outcomes are called up as images of lived futures, traumatized predictions engendered by terror. The experience is both lived in the present yet, at the same time, viewed from outside that frame from the perspective of a still to be lived and unknown future. In discussing her own experience, Bell describes the transition from teenager to "a victim of violent crime," from a state of being before to the one after of the "not-dead," from safety to an eternally watchful awareness of being alive, of surviving: "The shift was existential and irreversible."[43] Her shift into a life state she calls one of hyperawareness, equivalent to "canine bristle,"[44] is the physical manifestation of that imaginative awareness that all encounters with violence set in train and which are never erased from the way life is subsequently lived. Such shifts transform identity with a spontaneity and immediacy that leaves fear in the place of actual threat. Bell's text, shaped and distanced by memory from her own precipitating violent injury, while it can only partially relive the event, still vividly "bristles" with an authentic awareness of its trauma. While memory can suppress authenticity, text can reclaim, recreate, and reinvigorate it. The event can be found again, faced, and exorcised, with life strengthened against the endemic trauma violence engenders.

I accept that it *is* a complex matter to untangle *exactly* the degree to which images and symbols gain their potency from actual experience or are engaged in recreating and shaping it in textualities. Nevertheless, the textual contexts embodying images of violence are a particularly fertile field in which to undertake an exploration of the virtual, for example, as the advent of technological innovation in image transmission has always been associated with violence as content. Initially, at least, the impact of the virtual image on reality was aggressive and shocking: "The moment high-speed photography was invented, making cinema a concrete possibility, the problem of the paradoxically real nature of 'virtual' imagery was in fact posed."[45] Karl French, in his introduction to *Screen Violence,* describes how the 1903 movie *The Great Train Robbery* contained the image of a firing gun pointed directly at the audience as the target. Audiences who saw the movie at the time were apparently startled by their perspective-as-target and, momentarily at least, forgot that it was a simulated and not a *real* experience. While that confusion can only have been for an instant, the audience *was* looking down the barrel of a gun in "the cinema's first example of truly gratuitous violence."[46] From its beginning, as Jake Horsley notes, the popular media staked its claim to the violent as spectacle and the viewer of the simulation was intentionally visually assaulted: "Cinema, from its very first moments, was, like a blow to the retina that broke right through to the brain, an intrinsically aggressive . . . and *violent* medium."[47] Looking down the barrel of the gun people were not able to sit passively in their seats. Horsely calls it "art-as-terrorism."[48] However, as Susan Sontag asks about the shock value of photographic violence, "How else to get attention for one's product or one's art"[49] without it? If commodification types the viewer as voyeur ("there is shame as well as shock in looking at the close-up of a real horror"[50]) it also types the viewer as seeking an aesthetic that makes meaning from the violence that is endemic to the human condition.

1

"Violence at the Speed of Live":[51] The Televirtuality of 9/11 and Rebuking the Frame of (Re)Presentation

Well, wherever you are in the world today, or in the United States, the landscape of New York City has just changed and one has to assume that thousands of lives have been extinguished.[52]

(Peter Jennings, ABC news anchor on 9/11)

Any sense of real audiences encountering real texts in real situations is squeezed out of the frame by the burgeoning rhetoric of the simulacrum.

(John Dovey)[53]

I watched the screen in stunned amazement as a mighty architectural icon was ripped from its structural base, exposing twisted steel and the flimsiness of the cultural belief that powerful capitalist icons cannot be destroyed. It was a delightful special-effects disaster extravaganza as the mighty Golden Gate Bridge was lifted up by the evil Magneto at the head of his mutant army and realigned as a causeway to Alcatraz island in the battle climax to film *X-Men 3: The Last Stand*.[54] Like the rest of the audience, I could safely indulge myself in the imaginative wholesale destruction of the film's finale because I knew the heroes would win out in the end. Plot certainty and the safety of the simulacrum reassured pleasure; it was fiction. However, it is a lack of total immersion in the safety of the textual mediation of violence that accounts for audience anxieties in the face of images of death and destruction that have an indexical relationship with actual events. Jean Baudrillard has described the cultural triumph of the virtual text over reality as "the murder of the real,"[55] which he argues has deprived us of historical events. I would argue that within that ironically posed crime scene indexical authenticity can be found at the beginning of the continuum of texts about violence in the live recording of

19

events as they cross the border from the lived experience into representation in televised text. The most discussed iconic[56] example in recent history of such broadcasts is, undoubtedly, the attack on the World Trade Center (WTC) on September 11, 2001 (9/11). It is at that point of live transmission on the continuum that the authenticity of violence as a lived experience most defies textualization and challenges the simulacrum, even as it relies on the virtual text for the communication of its historical authenticity. While Baudrillard's ironic theoretical point of view has contributed to a postmodern recognition that mediation of image is a more complex discourse than a viewer looking at a screen representing a reality outside it, nevertheless, it is my contention that violence in text at that point of interaction with lived experience resists the abolition of the real.

Baudrillard has noted that the murder of the real is a far from perfect crime and has left room for the possibility that there are bits of the real still out there: "as in the best detective novels, the crime is never perfect."[57] However, his caveat has been glossed over in much postmodern critique of the hyperreal. Violence, in particular, is not always experienced, read about, or viewed with equanimity as if it were a nonauthentic experience without historical reality. When a live recording of it enters the living room its authentic actuality breaks down illusions about the affective safety of virtual mediation of the experience. A closer analysis of the television content of the representation of 9/11 is required to replace generalizations about the technological determinants of the virtual medium that conveyed those shocking images where 2749 people died, including 340 fireman and 60 policeman involved in rescue attempts. Such an examination reveals a visceral authenticity created by its temporal indexicality and historical reality, which had an affective impact that is not simply defined by the simulacrum. At the beginning of the continuum of the viewing experience of violence it is important to remember that "[v]iewers are continuously probing the boundaries among different levels of reality and image and among the various elements that constitute depiction, representation and visualization."[58] The content of the televisual representation of the events of 9/11 interrupted the flow of the hyperreal for its audiences and resurrected historical authenticity. I am in agreement with Bill Schaffer when he says:

> The cinematic metaphors evoked around the event of September 11 ... cannot be sufficient, at least, not from the perspective of those of us interested in thinking about the *specificity* of the moving image in general, and of its different forms in particular, to simply find here yet another *example* of already established metaphors and concepts, proving, yet again, the universal compass of the postmodern critique of universality.[59]

As David Bordwell reminds us "theoretical concepts that guide our inquiries should be treated as hypotheses, delicate enough to respond to fluctuations in the material."[60]

Definitions of the postmodern simulacrum should not be exempt from that challenge. Analysis of the television broadcast as a real-time live news transmission reveals it as having a strong narrative authenticity about violence, placing it near the beginning of the continuum as a minimally mediated, contemporaneous record of devastation in which historical indexicality challenged its virtual textual framing.

The televised events of 9/11 were extraordinary violence in an iconic real that was not plotted to end with the aesthetic neatness and filmic flourish of the good guy winning before the screen fades to black. Prefiguring cinematic disaster movies proved to be an imaginative shortfall for many viewers looking at a screen through a camera pointing at that plane flying into the WTC because outside the frame New Yorkers could look out of their windows and see the same thing happening off screen. The photographer George Weld, who lived within naked eye view of the WTC, had taken a "before"[61] photo of the view he had of the towers from his apartment building. His view, caught in the photographic frame, is strikingly similar to many of the views broadcast on television—simply minus the smoke. His "9/11"[62] photo is similar but smoke-filled as he walked toward the towers leaving his apartment behind. His photographs, before and after, at some minimal level, have the forensic indexicality of what he saw with the naked eye before he framed it with his camera. In his discussion of the video of the Los Angeles Police Department police beating of Rodney King, Bill Nichols has described this "indexical whammy" of a signifier that is a "rebuke" to the "simulacrum," as often intrinsic to violence in texts:

> Representations of violence often have this effect. They cry out for response; they retain the power to produce visceral effect. This is even more true when what we see, the imagistic signifiers, bear an indexical relation to an event that occurred before the camera and that we take to be an historical event, not a staged, scripted or re-enacted one.[63]

In the case of the broadcasts of 9/11, the viewer was not completely cocooned by other textual signifiers from the actuality of the event. If, as Michael Schudson has noted, "All news stories are stories, but some are more story-like than others"[64] and remind us of fictional forms, it does not mean that the audience sees or responds to them as only fictional.

The iconicity of 9/11 has been defined by its televised images above and beyond the television news obsession with violent deaths and injuries,[65] proverbially noted in journalistic parlance as "if it bleeds, it leads" and aptly described by Jean Seaton as the experience of vicarious carnage and horror.[66] The images of the attack on the WTC on 9/11 have been described as trapped in the televisuality of a global simulacrum, as cinematic representations of a violent event viewed live that had the hyperreal and fiction as a referent. Critics like John Frow could characterize the event as being prefigured by film *and* critical theory of the virtual, as if it "might have been written by Hollywood, or by Baudrillard."[67] To quote Baudrillard himself:

> In all these vicissitudes, what stays with us, above all else, is the sight of the images. This impact of the images, and their fascination, are necessarily what we retain, since images are, whether we like it or not, our primal scene. And, at the same time as they have radicalized the world situation, the events in New York can also be said to have radicalized the relation of the image to reality ... the terrorist act in New York has resuscitated both images and events.[68]

According to Baudrillard, the news reporting of the September 11 attacks on the WTC on outlets like CNN and the NBC and ABC networks in the United States, which were broadcast globally, rescued virtual imagery from the banality plaguing the simulated "real-time" transmission of nonevents and transformed the attack into an "image-event."[69] For Baudrillard, the image consumed the event in a virtual fiction that transformed its reality. It was public fascination with the preexisting fictional imaginings of disaster, given an extra "frisson" by real violence, which accounted for this iconicity: "Something like an additional fiction, a fiction surpassing fiction."[70] Paul Virilio noted in his discussion of the events in *Ground Zero*[71] that some TV viewers initially thought the WTC attacks were a disaster movie before the discovery that it was being reported live on several channels told them it was not. He views the initial confusion as symptomatic of ocular meltdown, using a millisecond of confusion to argue ongoing loss of the real on a global scale.

This characterization of the images of 9/11 was partly a product of the cinematic textual techniques framing them—particularly filmic editing incorporating split screens, striking camera angles, and lingering, repeated images of the towers being struck and collapsing—and of a sense of déjà vu experienced by critics, viewers, and eyewitnesses accustomed to the disaster movie genre. Norman Mailer eloquently depicts the effect as, "Our movies came off the screen and chased us down the canyons of the city."[72] Baudrillard, ironically provocative as ever, described this fictionalization of the event as a "Manhattan disaster movie,"[73] a transformation of reality *and* televirtuality by images that prefigured the event through previous cinematic fascinations:

> And in this singular event, in this Manhattan disaster movie, the twentieth century's two elements of mass fascination are combined: the white magic of the cinema and the black magic of terrorism; the white light of the image and the black light of terrorism.[74]

The cinematic form of the live image, the recognized conventionality of the image experience, was seen as overwhelming the authenticity that might have been more sustained in raw footage if it had not been "eerily familiar."[75] For Slavoj Zizek:

> [T]he question we should have asked ourselves as we stared at the TV screens on September 11 is simply: *Where have we already seen the same thing over and over again?*[76]

And yet, while I would not want to deny the extensive impact of the visual imagery on the frame of the virtuality of the event, it has to be asked: what about the rest of the narrative? The above responses seem to define the text as only visual, with little regard to the audio aspects of the text. Where are the televised voices that accompanied the images in the arguments for or against textual authenticity? Inclusion of the audio puts into question both the analogy with the disaster movies as a descriptor for viewer shock, and for the nature of the "frisson" that Baudrillard posits as a responsive companion to the transformation of the historical event by virtuality. It is necessary to ask, was the image as cinematic in its impact on audience reception as commentators like Baudrillard assert?

Déjà vu and the Inadequacy of Fantasy

The analogy made with Hollywood disaster movies was based on the special effects such films use to display their spectacles of violent destruction and on the prescience of terrorist narratives in the genre. J. Hoberman, in a *Village Voice* article typically entitled *Made In Hollywood: How Movies Foretold the New Reality*, outlined at the time of 9/11 the global cinematic backdrop that critics like Baudrillard would have had in mind:

> Thus the déjà vu of crowds fleeing *Godzilla* through Lower Manhattan canyons, the wondrously exploding skyscrapers and bellicose rhetoric of *Independence Day*, the romantic pathos of *Titanic*, the wounded innocence of *Pearl Harbor*, the cosmic insanity of *Deep Impact*, the sense of a world directed by Roland Emmerich for the benefit of Rupert Murdoch.[77]

Hoberman wittily lists cinema's various visualizations of the foe as terrorist Other:

> For Hollywood, this "unspecified enemy," in Deleuze and Guattari's phrase, was variously visualised as Euro-terrorists in *Die Hard* (1988), narco-terrorists in *Die Hard 2* (1990), neo-Nazi terrorists in *Die Hard With a Vengeance* (1995), homegrown terrorists in *Under Siege* (1992), "international" terrorists in

Under Siege 2 (1995), extraterrestrial terrorists in *Independence Day* (1996), dino-terrorists in *The Lost World: Jurassic Park* (1997), Russian terrorists in *Air Force One* (1997), Bosnian terrorists in *The Peacemaker* (1997), and Islamic terrorists in *True Lies* (1994), *Executive Decision* (1996) and *The Siege* (1998).[78]

Kenneth Jackson, of the New York Historical Society, noted a month after the attack that while heavy visual documentation made it an "event for which there is no exact parallel"[79] there was still a visual precedent in film, which showed that "the highjackers weren't the first people to target The World Trade Center."[80] For Jackson, it was the towering, immense stature of the building as a geographical reference point for New Yorkers from all vantage points in the city and the vastness of its floor space—the 109th floor so large that an airplane hitting it at high speed could strike it and not come out—its architectural straight-up-ness that "belittled" the buildings around it, which linked the WTC to the preferred monolithic targets for destruction in Hollywood disaster movies (*The Towering Inferno* in the 1970s comes to mind.)

However, initial cinematic déjà vu does not adequately account for the iconicity of 9/11's virtual representation. Habituation to such special-effect imagery and stock villains did not lay the imaginative groundwork for the unmitigated shock and emotionality with which Americans, in particular, viewed the images as a representation of actual events.[81] It was not long into the event before viewers found that the "the question of the moving image's fidelity to the real did not arise."[82] It is to the inadequacy of fantasies of violence as a precursor to the reality of the event, rather than to its prefiguring of it, that one is more likely to infer the shock. As Timothy Gray points out, "there was a kind of innocence in Hollywood's depiction of terrorism . . . mostly they were a slobbering sadistic group who threatened mayhem, but would get blown away before any serious damage occurred, that is, before any of the principal actors got killed."[83] It is always clear who the good guys and the bad guys are, it is "them" and "us." Imaginative, vigilante violence in such movies was not, as Ray Green notes, "violence with consequences, something rarely dramatized in the exploding funhouse of American movie culture."[84] Gregg Kilday is right when he says that while the television images of 9/11, "the ferocious fireballs, the pancaking structures, the shattered humans emerging like ghostly wraiths from the choking clouds of smoke were . . . eerily familiar" due to special-effects technology, "the horrifying reality made the usual fantasies in which the industry traffics pale."[85] As Steven Zani reminds us, citing Laurie Anderson's apt description, disaster in such movies gives the viewer the ironic satisfaction of seeing the "hubris of mankind" in its architectural and technological achievements brought low. We know the Titanic will sink, or buildings will be blown up, and the more spectacularly the better:

When the Titanic sinks it's spectacular, it sinks expensive technology, money, power and savoir faire. It's a perversely satisfying experience, like blowing up the White House in "Independence Day."[86]

Like kicking over sandcastles at the beach, the disaster movies are not traumatic viewing. Violence and destruction in them is inevitable, expected, satisfying, and exciting. It is why audiences go to see them. They are also fundamentally optimistic with plots that end in survival and the restoration of threatened systems or rebuilding.[87]

The resulting Hollywood fear that 9/11 images would kill the audience desire for disaster as entertainment, expressed by the industry postponing the release of selected blockbusters right after the attack,[88] has not come to fruition. It is precisely because the disaster movie is recognized as entertainment fantasy and viewers appreciate them for the pleasures of their imaginative spectacular conventions that, post 9/11, they are as popular as ever. At 6:38 a.m. local time[89] on *Today in LA* with a live feed from NBC in New York, in response to Katie Couric's questioning if there could have been a warning of the attack, Larry Johnson, a former State Department official being interviewed, draws a distinction between fantasy and reality: "it's only in the movies that you get the advance warnings."[90] For American citizens at least, watching the WTC implode was not "fun."[91] It was the disjunction between previous fantasies and the authenticity of the event that was disturbing, not fantasy's prescience.[92]

At first glance, the occasional eyewitness account that utilised the cinematic effect analogy would seem to support Baudrillard's analysis. Judy Woodruff, a CNN reporter described the plane hitting the Towers in cinematic terms because

> the actual airplane hitting the building, it was surreal. As we looked at it, we thought it was something out of a movie; it just didn't seem real. The airplane just came in at a tilt, we heard the scream of the plane, then a crack, crack, crack, boom, boom, boom, and the plane just disappeared. You didn't see the plane anymore, and then you saw the blow out from the other side. (3:18 p.m.)[93]

The description even comes with sound effects. However, it is important not to equate statements of initial disbelief and momentary shock, made in the struggle for descriptive analogy to make sense of experience, with immersion in the virtuality of the event as Baudrillard defines it, experienced from inside the imaginary hyperreal. James Brandon, a kidnapped journalist in Iraq, made a similar analogy in retelling the experience of being pistol-whipped, threatened, and a gun held to his head as his captors played Russian roulette with his life in a sequence of mock executions: "The first time, I didn't know the weapon wasn't loaded. It felt surreal . . . like a bad film." He calls it a *bad* film because that cinematic imagery exists as an analogy for, but is disconcertingly out of synchronization with, the terror he is experiencing: "At that point, after hours of fear, all I could think was: they are going to kill me."[94] The nature of an analogy is that the similarity is partial and not a one-to-one correspondence. Brandon's sense of the filmed reality is that it is an imaginative experience made irrational when juxtaposed with the reality of his own terror which, when using what he knows of those films as a referent, feels like a horribly surreal existential joke. What is clear from Woodruff's and Brandon's use of the analogy with movie experiences is how it was only a limited signifier for what they were going through. "It looked *like* a movie," as so many eyewitnesses, journalists, and viewers described it, is the language of similitude not referential interchangeability.

The Audio of the Image

The most unsatisfying aspect of the utility of the cinematic analogy as a descriptor of the televised event is that it ignores the part of the spectacle that was embodied in news presentation practices that were a "discourse unfolding in duration," to use Margaret Morse's phrase.[95] There is a particular contribution from television media to a socially represented or shared knowledge, a contribution that Joseph Reser and Steven Muncer have termed social "sense-making"[96]—the classification, the unfolding, and the interrelating of explanatory abstract concepts surrounding an event. In the live presentation of television news the reception is only partially cued by visual imagery. The absence of recognition of the role of the news format—the hours of "talk" that swirled around those images—from theoretical assessments elevating the role of the visual is startling. It is as if the event was televised in complete silence. A visit to *The Sonic Memorial Project* Web site,[97] an archive of audio traces and artefacts from 9/11 that had first person significance in forming the experience, memories, and meaning of the event for members of the public making sound contributions to the Web site, is a reminder that audio, as much as image, can inform personal and collective memory.

The Mexican director Alejandro González Iñárritu, in his contribution to the film collection *11'09"01: 11 September*[98] dramatically returns the audio to representation by a stark and spare use of the images. Iñárritu keeps the screen black for most of the film, interspersing brief, flashed images over a soundtrack. The iconic collapse of the towers is no longer than an image of a few seconds in the film, mirroring the brevity of the actual collapse itself. The film begins with a ritualized litany in a non-English language over a black screen and an occasional thud. Periodically, there is a brief flash of something falling and, as the flashes break the black with increasing frequency and slightly more detail, it becomes clear that they are the bodies of people jumping or falling to their deaths from the towers.[99] Underlying the black and the flash of images, as the litany is drowned out, is the sequential introduction of the day—routine broadcasts of the weather prior to the event, the sound of the plane engine, crash sounds, and eyewitness cries of "Oh my God ... there's another one ... I don't believe this"—building into a cacophony of commentary, including phone calls to answering machines from victims in the towers and planes expressing their love for family members. Eventually, the film arrives at the sound of the towers collapsing and suddenly cuts to a close-up in silence as the collapse is completed. Horrifying as the image is, it is distinctly less so without the sound—just as the thud of a body hitting the pavement is inextricably a part of the excruciating violence of the image of the bodies in freefall down the side of the towers.

Many of the sounds and voices in the Iñárritu film were a part of the broadcast from networks like CNN on 9/11, of actual live presentation of events as they happened, or in the constant repackaging of it in reports and stories. Iconicity was undoubtedly a result of sheer repetition; the images of the towers burning were everywhere. There was constant "re-racking"[100] of images—such as the moment where Aaron Brown, the CNN anchor, requests the rerunning twice of the plane hitting the second tower sourced from PAX TV footage. He directs the viewer where to look so they can "absorb" what happened: "if we can re-rack and show it again so you'll know where to look. You'll see the plane first in the lower left side of the screen" (5:36 p.m.). Sometimes this repacking seems to occur just to fill an informational void—a repetitiveness that increased as the actual time of the attack and collapse of the towers receded. The network obsession with the images,[101] along with a glut of them in print,[102] certainly contributed to their ubiquitous iconicity. The deluge of print distribution of those images of the burning towers suspended in the memorial stillness of the photographic frame seared the event into collective memory. Such photographic artifacts may have contributed to the subsequent theoretical discussion of the images as if they were frozen in space and time—as if they were photographs in a silent void—rather than one part of an audiovisual moving image in an unfolding news narrative.[103]

Disarray evident in presenter responses to unfolding events, conflating the viewers and presenters into a shared spectator space, reveals how uncinematic it felt to view news characterized by emotional and subjective narrative that placed journalists as event participants. The normally dispassionate tone of anchors like Aaron Brown or Paula Zahn on CNN, or the assured confidence of Matt Lauer and Katie Couric on the NBC *Today* show, was strikingly modified in broadcasts on 9/11 by expressions of disbelief and confusion. This discourse undermines the expected presentation hierarchy of the authoritative anchor voice, powerfully contributing to a visceral sense of the authentic violence of the event overwhelming the boundaries of the media frame. Instead of authoritative confirmation by anchors/announcers on-air, the viewer hears the incredulous, shocked, uncertain responses of presenters within a narrative flow of equally shocked and uncertain eyewitnesses. As Jean Bourdon has pointed out, neglect of what is vococentric about the television news medium is not unusual in critical analysis,[104] but to neglect it here is to miss its centrality as confirmation for the viewer of the visual indexicality of the event. Morse has perceptively described the American network news format of direct address to the viewer, through the personality of the anchor, as promoting the appearance of real-time "liveness" in packaged images that simulate "the paramount reality of speaking subjects exchanging conversation in a shared space and time."[105] As Morse notes, the anchor functions as a point of sincere direct engagement with the viewer, a reference point orienting interpretation in a hierarchical discourse shifting between sound bites that form tiers of virtual conversation. Conversations occur between the anchor and other presenters who are not necessarily physically present in the same geographical space, or between reporters and interviewees in the field, or with designated experts invited to comment on events. While the viewer may infer meaning from these conversations, he or she is excluded from this "restrictive discursive system" that "drastically reduces the number and kind of subjects who can speak for themselves to a wider public."[106] In a presentation hierarchy that puts the anchor at the top, Morse places the viewer at the bottom.

The tone of anchor direction, as well as the stance of commentators, plays a role in this establishment of hierarchy. Anne Foster recalls National Public Radio host Bob Edwards' calm, respectful but shocked voice announcing the collapse of the first tower as a part of her audio memory of that first day.[107] While radio is a medium that emphasizes the voice, vocal impact from anchors/presenters who commented on the transmitted images on television as the event happened cannot be assumed to be negligible. Audience habituation to news packaging informs viewer expectations that simultaneous transmission and reception of presentation of news will portray conventions of accumulative information gathering even when packaging is supplanted by real-time "live" events. The interplay of authoritative journalistic voices incorporates the image, "live" or prepackaged, as a part of that unfolding. On 9/11 the televised image rarely appears in silence or dead air but it is surrounded by information uncertainty. At 8:49 a.m.[108] on CNN, even though the building is on fire after the first plane hits, it is mentioned that the reports that a plane struck the building are unconfirmed. An eyewitness, Sean Murtagh, a CNN producer who happened to be in the area, reports that he saw what he *thinks* is a 737 jet going into the WTC around the 80th floor and not coming out and that there is smoke billowing out of the building. At 8:56 a.m. an eyewitness, identified as Jeanne Yurman, living near to the towers in Battery Park, says by telephone that she heard what she thought was a sonic boom, her TV went out, and that, from her window, she saw that "debris started falling, I couldn't believe what I was watching." At 9:01 a.m., CNN crosses to a New York affiliate WABC for another eyewitness account from a Winston Mitchell: "It's almost like the plane probably went through, *I'm not sure.*"

Even more startling, at one point, the attentive viewer knows more than the traditionally authoritative anchor. At 9:06 a.m., as Mitchell is talking, with the tower live on screen, the second plane hits the south tower of the WTC. The reporter talking to the eyewitness is unaware of that event, though it is clear to the viewer watching, and he simply mentions it as a second fire and shortly after refers to the first plane as the "first accident" when distinguishing between the two explosions. This combination of announcer disbelief and the viewer having knowledge not yet transmitted by the anchor in the context of "live" transmission is a radical discourse upheaval.[109] The presentational hierarchy of news discourse that places the viewer as subject to encoded informational flow collapses as encoding lags behind and the viewer takes on the encoding role directly from the image:

> The only quantitative information available was the exact time of each specific incident, and this was repeated ad infinitum—as if by chanting this mantra the anchorperson's role as informed and authoritative individual could be maintained.[110]

The delay in recognizing that terrorism is the cause further reinforces this. At 9:06 a.m., CNN rerun footage of the second plane and the reporter speculates that it might be some navigating system or electronic fault that could have caused two planes to crash into the buildings. At 9:10 a.m., Ira Furman, a former National Transportation Safety Board spokesman, is asked "What can you make of what we have just seen?" and "expert" reportage finally catches up with simultaneous viewer perceptions:

> That's absolutely inexplicable. There shouldn't be any aircraft in that area, much less something heading what looked like deliberately for the World Trade Center Tower . . . a second occurrence within a few minutes is beyond belief.

At 9:18 a.m., it is reported that the Associated Press are saying that the FBI in Washington is investigating whether the crashes are the result of "foul play" and, at 9:25 a.m., that, according to an unnamed official, it "appears to be an act of terrorism." At 9:30 a.m., the Presidential statement is televised confirming this but still with the use of the word "apparent."

The effect of this verbal commentary of information in flux—with events happening too fast for facts to be immediately clarified—is disconcerting in the context of the usually authoritative, hierarchical format that characterizes the conventions of news presentation, both packaged and "live." It is also disconcerting in the context of aspects of network conventions which manufacture certainty and try to make newsworthy events out of nonevents. By around 9:36 a.m., Aaron Brown is in New York reporting against distant shots from 30 blocks away: "We also have reports of a thousand injuries, that is unconfirmed . . . driving in, it is extremely chaotic." At 9:42 a.m., against a shot of the WTC burning, Brown questions Chris Plante, a CNN producer, of reports of a fire at the Pentagon:[111]

> Arriving at the Pentagon, a short time ago, there was a huge plume of smoke, which continues to rise from the west side of the Pentagon. The plume of smoke is enormous, it's a couple of hundred yards across at its base, it is billowing into the sky hundreds of yards. It is impossible for me to say from this side of the building whether the building itself is on fire or up in flames or exactly what caused this.

Announcing the suspension of all civilian air travel, Brown notes that "people are trying, people in government, police forces, fire departments are trying to figure out what exactly is going on." As he speaks the screen is split between a close-up, with the camera angled so both towers can be seen, and a distance shot with smoke billowing and then cutting back to a medium distant shot. This shot then changes to a split screen with one shot of the WTC and live from the Pentagon with smoke rising from the building. The juxtaposition of such images against journalistic uncertainty, devoid of the basic rhetoric of authoritative spin, and the fragmented informational narrative would not have provided already shocked viewers with much informational or ideological scaffolding to cushion that shock.

Much later in the day, at 2:19 p.m., Woodruff, in reporting on a phone call from the highjacked plane that went down in Pennsylvania to an emergency dispatcher, acknowledges the piecemeal nature of facts coming out: "That's just one more piece of the story, the many, many stories that we are pulling together as we watch these developments." This journalistic uncertainty in the context of "live" transmission is a part of a broader range of voices that modify the traditionally authenticating roles of witnesses and experts in news discourse. At 1:21 p.m. Brown interviews former U.S. Ambassador Richard Holbrook and asks for an historical context for "the enormity of what has taken place":

> Well, I think your coverage has made it more clear than anything else. Although, despite the superb efforts you've made, it hasn't yet become fully evident to your viewers what would be evident to any of us, like myself, who worked in the World Trade Center (I was there in the last bombing, as I mentioned earlier) that the number of people in that area, including the Chamber Street subway stop which goes right under the World Trade Center, means that the dimensions of it exceed, by a factor of probably a hundred, any previous incident, including Oklahoma city and the previous World Trade Center, in American history . . . I think CNN is the first real glimpse that the viewers

have had into how dangerous this is. If the Taliban shelters Osama Bin Laden, as they do, and if Osama Bin Laden is responsible for this, as I think almost everyone is going to suspect, then the Taliban must be held equally responsible for what has happened today.

It is striking that, even though he is brought in as an expert on terrorism, his information value is simply as a bystander with first-hand knowledge of the building. Rather than fulfilling his designated role as "expert," Holbrook is simply one bystander among many as his words are played over scenes of billowing smoke and destruction. Holbrook's evaluation of CNN's coverage strengths as "more clear than anything else," of its weaknesses ("it hasn't yet become fully evident to your viewers") and of the partial nature of what is shown as a "glimpse" into possible causes, feels like an accurate assessment of what the broadcast process up until this point allows the viewer to know. The polished veneer of access to information that is the promotional promise of corporate news broadcasting consistently fractures.

Emotions and the Breakdown of Narrative Authority

In addition to the lack of confirmation of information, news on 9/11 was characterized by the unusually emotive responses of anchors and reporters to the events as they happen. There is research that acknowledges the professional trauma that comes with covering violent events[112] but it is not common to hear personal responses of trauma and shock so prominently displayed on air in news reporting. Anchors and journalists acknowledged personal difficulties in processing what they were seeing and hearing, while intermittently returning to the more dispassionate professional narrative of information gathering and the confirmation of facts. At 10:00 a.m. the south tower collapses and the screen splits with one side the tower and another all billowing smoke as Brown comments emotively: "that is about as frightening a scene as you will ever see." Shortly after this we get the first view of the iconic shot from the ground level of the tower collapsing and people running from the billowing smoke and ash behind them. As the north tower collapses,[113] viewed from the distance, Brown responds:

> Good Lord! There are no words ... this is just a horrific scene and a horrific moment ... [and after a report that there were people jumping from the windows prior to the collapse] ... It is just one of those awful moments that you need to look at for a minute or two to absorb exactly what has happened. Two of the most recognisable buildings in the city of New York have been attacked and both of them have collapsed.

The anchor, the authoritative encoding focal point in conventional news presentation, expresses shock and discourse disorientation: "There are no words." Personal and visibly emotive responses were not confined to CNN. Donohue notes CNBC's Geraldo Rivera saying, "I have no answers for my children when they worry that a plane will fall from the sky . . . I have no answers for them."[114] While Rivera's remarks have a composed rhetoric to them that is not the same as the more spontaneous remarks by Brown, such remarks feed into the discourse of "live" event transmission as the disruption of conventional encoding practices. In a discussion of Romanian television broadcasting the revolution in 1989, Morse acknowledges that conventional televisual hierarchies can disintegrate under "live" transmission when broadcasts "open into the unknown" and the duration of time reasserts itself against the packaging of the image:

> The televisual events in Romania were presented "live" and in duration, not in the "real time" that simulates duration of American television. Processed and compressed, computer-generated, and packaged images and stories control the flow of time and are "live" only by virtue of their simultaneity of transmission and reception . . . but do not open into the unknown.[115]

Urgency and consternation in the face of what is unknown drives presentation in the televisuality of 9/11. Intermittently, the business of reporting continues—shortly after 10:37 a.m. the reports come in of a 747 plane crashing in Pennsylvania,[116] of the collapse of part of the Pentagon, and at 10:48 a.m. there is a split screen of New York and Washington. At 11:00 a.m.—increasing factual certainty transforms into more dramatic news rhetoric—the caption on screen now reads *America Under Attack*. But personal bluntness still breaks through the veneer of news jargon—when Mayor Guiliani is asked, "What should New Yorkers do?" he replies:

> Urge them to remain calm, to remain at their place of business unless they're in Lower Manhattan. By that I mean, south of Canal Street. If you're south of Canal Street, get out.

The uncharacteristic bluntness of this directive from an official is in keeping with the language of crisis that permeates the narrative that breaks through the clichés of news broadcasting.

By 11:14 a.m. on-air speculation begins about Osama Bin Laden and there is extensive recapping by the network of what are now confirmed events. In essence, rerunning images of the towers collapsing and President Bush's earlier speech; updated timelines of events in both New York and Washington; information on air travel cancellation, the White House and Pentagon evacuations, and the closing of state offices; and pictures of the Pennsylvania crash site. However, all of this is punctuated by ongoing emotive declarations similar to Brown's. The reporter Judy Woodruff, recapping from Washington, speaks as much as a viewer/listener as an authoritative voice:

> Aaron we've been listening to your reporting and the people you have been talking with, I have to say, in stunned silence. None of us have ever seen anything close to the magnitude of these horrific events of this morning.

Later, Brown (at 2:03 p.m.) will again acknowledge the difficulty of a journalistic response and of comprehension: "It is the enormity that's a little bit hard to get our arms around right now." At 5:13 p.m. an interview is played with *USA Today* journalist Mike Walter, who saw the plane crash into the Pentagon. After giving a description of the crash he is asked what went through his mind as he saw it.

> You know, I've asked that question of a million people and, you know, the only thing that I . . . I just kept uttering it over and over again, "Oh my God, Oh my God, Oh my God, I can't believe this." And I think that's what goes through your mind is that you just can't believe that something like this could happen. And yet, I was sitting there listening on the radio to the accounts of what happened in New York, I'd just listened to the President and you'd think as a journalist I'd put two and two together and think . . . and it didn't even occur to me . . . And the toughest thing for me right now is I've got a 14-year-old daughter and a lot of her friends have parents who work in the Pentagon. And I just talked to her on the phone and those kids are going through agony tonight. They don't know if they're okay, so it's tough. I mean this really hits home.

Walter is less a reporter than a nonprofessional bystander in this report, acknowledging how little his journalist professionalism is of use to him. The typicality of news presentation breaks down under spontaneity of journalistic response and insight that is anecdotal and intimately confessional. Commentary was offered as personalized discourse in which professionals reduced themselves to rattled viewers in a disturbance of news rhetoric—contributing to the reading of the event by the viewer as profoundly distressing even when the images of destruction or attack were not on screen.

The uncertainties of information and emotive professional responses were not confined to CNN. When I, as a researcher, revisited the event through a tape of coverage on *Today in LA* on NBC, it was poignant to hear the announcer start the broadcast at 5 a.m. LA time with "A peaceful morning to you." It is a reminder that the impact of the attack was inevitably as shocking in its unexpectedness to those reporting it as a part of their own professional routine, as well as to those viewing it. When the show switches to the initial attack as *Breaking News*, confusion is evident and it is described as a "high-rise fire" occurring "somewhere in Manhattan." Even when it is identified as the WTC, details are uncertain and the reporters acknowledge this, saying that they are passing information on to the viewers as they are receiving it. At 6:03 a.m. they cross over to the NBC *Today* show in New York with Matt Lauer and Katie Couric. Jennifer Overstein reports in initial disbelief:

> Matt . . . it looks like a movie. I saw a large plane like a jet go immediately, headed directly into the WTC, it just flew into it . . . I watched the plane fly into the World Trade Center . . . I couldn't believe my eyes.

Despite hearing this from an eyewitness, Lauer is confused, saying the plane doesn't look like a jet. He says the towers look like they are leaning but probably are not and then says they are getting reports that they are leaning. At 6:09 a.m. Katie Couric places herself as a viewer watching a "completely shocking video." Like us, she is not seeing out the window but through a screen:

> Well, of course, this is, as we've said, completely shocking video, and a shocking turn of events. And we've been talking here that the first incident, one might surmise that it was some kind of accident. And then to have a second . . . the question of terrorist activity has to surface.

Shortly after that, the reporter Jim Miklaszewski (6:38 a.m.) at the Pentagon reveals the lack of information that comes from being both in and out of the action:

> I don't want to alarm anybody right now but, apparently, it felt, just a few moments ago, like there was an explosion of some kind here at the Pentagon. We have a window that faces out toward the Potomac, toward the Kennedy Center. We haven't been able to hear or see anything after the initial blast. I just stepped out in the hallway, security guards were herding people out of the building and I saw, just a moment ago as I looked outside, a number of construction workers who've been working here, have taken flight . . . I heard no sirens going off in the building, I see no smoke. But the building shook for a couple of seconds, the windows rattled and security personnel are doing what they can, momentarily, to clear this part of the building. Again, I have no idea whether it was an accident, or what is going on. We're gonna try to find those details and get them to you as soon as possible.

In terms of factual detail, the report is uninformative because the reporter is, like the viewer, out of sight of the event. However, he displays a careful avoidance of untoward speculation in his report that is the typically nonemotive care with detail that maintains formal journalistic conventions. Tom Brokaw (6:57 a.m.), on the other hand, when commenting on the hijacked flight from Boston, is less circumspect: "Did the highjackers get control, did they shoot the pilot? It boggles the mind beyond our ability to figure out what was going on."

Across all networks under discussion here, speculation was often tentative and, eventually, contributed to the accumulation of accurate knowledge of the events once it was confirmed over time. However, the emotional variety of journalistic responses, ranging from the perceptive to the confused, reflected varying access to accurate sources and professional anxiety, paralleling perhaps, the more tragic confusion of people outside the frame of the screen:

> The survivors of the first plot to bring down the Twin Towers, the botched attempt in 1993 that left six dead, had a great advantage over their colleagues. When the first explosion came, they knew to get out. Others were paralyzed by the noise, confused by the instructions.[117]

The shock and bewilderment that saturated verbal coverage and the journalistic confusion about detail amplified the sense of the collective shock the images themselves created. With eyewitnesses and, occasionally, the viewer better informed than the announcers and journalists, it is the fallibility of the media in response to pressure of events that stands out. The distinctive self-implication by journalists in words that acknowledge they are affected participants in the events, while understandable, breaches the conventional dispassionateness and gravitas of television news protocol and draws attention as much to its emotive tone as its informational content.

From what we know about events in hindsight, the information gathering worked with varying levels of efficiency across networks. There is an ebb and flow to the confirmation of information, interspersed with periods of ambivalence, despite the fact that incremental informational clarity emerged over time. Interactive talk undermined the conventional discrete roles of anchor, field reporters, experts, and eyewitnesses reducing them to mutually involved participants in a media discourse that undercuts the usual hierarchy of presentation.[118] The fact that, for the presenters-as-participants, the attack is on American soil at times gave CNN coverage a parochial tone that was less that of a global media outlet than a localized network. A *Time* report a few days later records the similar confusion in bystander reactions to the first plane hitting the WTC's north tower:

> People thought it was a sonic boom, or a construction accident, or freak lightning on a lovely fall day; at worst, a horrible airline accident, a plane losing altitude, out of control, a pilot trying to ditch in the river and missing.[119]

The 9/11 Commission Report[120] records that there was also confusion across the U.S. government system at the time of the attacks. Both the political system on Federal, state, and local service level, and the population in general were in the throes of trying to accommodate the extraordinary occurrence with difficulty and mistakes were made. The media embodied and reflected the social and political confusion and early ambivalence of information flow that was not only its own. It reflected the cultural, social, and political shock of the United States as a national entity.

As William O'Rourke noted shortly after the attacks, while services and reporting did not exactly keep pace with events, nevertheless

> television has performed a service during the first dreadful days. It has had a story as large as its appetites. Television did what it does best—it shows. And though what is merely told trails fitfully behind, more of that will catch up, in time.[121]

"Violence at the speed of live," the camera pointed at an event as it occurs, feeds viewer expectations of being shown the event "live" but the definition of that in terms of proximity to the event is ambivalently perceived. What it often amounts to is "in the vicinity" of the camera, or in "virtual attendance" within the limitations of the televised frame. It promises the enhanced knowledge of a bystander with access to other bystanders at multiple vantage points that will lead to an unfolding of knowledge about the event. While it is not to be confused with the experiential knowledge of a place in the ring, that promise of a ringside seat is not only determined by what is seen. The fact that the shock of the WTC attack was embedded in media practices that, temporarily at least, were factually lacking and emotive, promoted anxiety about the image that reinforced their horrific visuality. Ultimately, information, while on time-delay, emerged. There were times when the visual was the source of the confirmation of information for the viewer and others when it was not enough without the clarification of the audio. It may be ironic that the instantaneity of the "live" is often less informative than the traditional journalistic print practices of simply building up an accumulation of some basic factual information over time and then putting them on screen. No bystander, even an eyewitness to the event, had the whole picture. No viewer of the global images could have followed the informational plot with the picture on mute.

The (Im)Perfection of the Virtual and the Assumption of Global Homogeneity

Nevertheless, the concept of "showing" cannot so easily shake off the theoretical anxiety about the construction of reality raised by the cinematic descriptions of the representation of 9/11 violence on television. Postmodernity is characterized by the fetishization of information. Expectations raised by theoretical uses of the term "information" still harbor an unacknowledged adherence to a linear and homogenous view of transmission and reception as storage and retrieval. Reporting in television news programs has been traditionally based on utopian concepts of accuracy, bias, and objectivity, on the access to raw footage,[122] and on the belief that competing points of view could be represented in balanced and "fair" ways.[123] Such a view has not been jettisoned by journalists, despite poststructuralist deconstructions of the ideologies shaping news reporting—where editing, the selection of sources, decisions about what is newsworthy, and language all shape the values of news narrative.[124] Such a belief in objective truth is expressed by the documentary-maker of *Control Room* reporting on Al-Jazeera and American CentCom media reporting from Iraq:

> I went with a lot of curiosity, and I thought if I was around people who were trying to get at the truth, journalists, I might get close to it, too.[125]

Such a view has been found to be theoretically problematic, as Stuart Allen has noted, because the ideological encoding of the discourse is not necessarily decoded as the preferred reading and can be modified by the dynamics of production itself:

> The encodification of hegemony, conditional as it is upon contending processes of transformation and incorporation for its renewal, always risks coming unravelled.[126]

The question is: whether the broadcast transmission of 9/11 produced information chaos, as Baudrillard suggests is often the case, or whether it provided a flood of information that never reached resolution but, nevertheless, existed on a somewhat linear path—which John Ellis describes is an open-ended "working through" in which information is "continually worried over until it is exhausted."[127]

For Baudrillard, the act of producing events and broadcasting them in "real-time" precludes absolute meaning because "they can have all possible meanings" and are "lost in the void of information," receiving

> an artificial gravity, where, after being flash frozen politically and historically, they are restaged transpolitically, in real—that is to say, perfectly virtual—time.[128]

In my view, Baudrillard's claim seems unsatisfactory because the analysis of the audio of the 9/11 news broadcasts raises questions about the perfection of the virtual and reveals the possibilities of its fracture under the pressure of the indexical violent event. The belief in the all encompassing explanation of the perceptual dominance of the image over the real, ultimately, has within it a similar tendency to desensitize us to what can be known with certainty in meaning and of the way we are the creators of virtuality as well as being shaped by it. Daniel Chandler more accurately describes the process of interaction with mediated information, virtual or otherwise:

> All of these features—selectivity, transparency, transformation and reso-nances—are associated with every process of mediation. And such features and processes exist in dynamic interaction. Traditional academic disciplines attempt to fit the practices of everyday life into frameworks which are primar-ily socio-cultural, psychological, linguistic or technological. But, against the tide of academic specialization, I would suggest that those who seek to explore processes of mediation should attempt to move as readily as possible between such interpretative frames . . . Such frame shifting is essential for gaining insights into the "ecology" of processes of mediation in which we are all inex-tricably enmeshed—in which our behavior is not technologically determined, but in which we both "use tools" and can be subtly shaped by our use of them.[129]

Information is not simply transmitted but interacted with and the information flow is not one way. That interaction is not simply about the technology or the tool but, as Chandler diagrams in his persuasive article, about the ecology of the inter-action between the roles, tasks, practices, and attitudes that surround the use of the technology. This interaction resonates in a range of contexts and frames that cannot summarily be lumped together but need to be accounted for in analysis of any virtual text.

Baudrillard's ironic use of the phrase "Manhattan disaster movie," wittily pro-claims a less than full immersion in his own argument and raises a deeply serious skepticism about virtuality. Theoretically, however, that irony runs the risk of encouraging a tendency to sweeping critical assumptions about the homogeneity of virtualities and of the deterministic perfection of its impact. Thus, for Virilio, technologically determined information systems, the optics of the global, is "audio-visual derealization" which he describes as

> that ever great sophistication of technical perception which was to lead to the—no longer natural, but artificial—selection of the ocular imagery of man. An audiovisual derealization as a result of which the worldly public . . . would end up believing what it would not touch and could not have "seen."[130]

His belief that the "sophistication of technical perception," seeing through audiovi-sual media, can be contrasted with a vaguely defined "natural" ocular perception that preceded our current state of ocular trauma overgeneralizes. It is a statement about global perceptions at accelerated speeds based on the untenable assumption that all audiences are united in their homogeneity. As the second plane hit the WTC in "live" transmission, on-air reporting succumbed to a temporary informational paralysis brought on by the certainty of the authentic historical physicality of the attack. That certainty, however, was still in the context of a fundamental *uncertainty* about the ideological, political, and social implications of the event for the public viewing it (implications which continue to be debated). Succumbing to fear and shock in the face of the unknown "other," information was in an interpretative state of flux for announcers and viewers alike. However, it was not ocular confusion about the authentic indexicality of the violent event itself.

There are unacknowledged assumptions about the global homogeneity of viewer reception in the theoretical cinematic analogy that also undermines its utility as a descriptor of a virtual monolithic receptive vision. As Colin Sparks reminds us, in a timely analysis of some of the assumptions operating in theories of globalization, theory can be limited by its conceptualizing as a generalization of Western trends.[131] Despite quoting Paul Klee's words about images in art where "those who, in looking at them, produce half the pictures,"[132] Virilio seems to deny this possibility to the postmodern television viewer simply because of the accelerated reduction of time and space between subject and object. The use of the cinematic analogy, if it is to be used, must account for the possibility of multifarious reception embedded in a complicated multicultural global response. The film editor Walter Murch points out that

> cinema is, by definition, a theatrical, communal experience for the audience as well as the authors, but one in which the play remains the same each time it is shown. It is the audience's reactions that change.[133]

As Louis Spence notes, even in America itself viewing the event on TV may have promoted an illusion of contemporaneous national experience that was not likely to last:

> Seeing events happening in the present, what George Gerbner has called "instant history" . . . for a short while, it may have seemed as if our collective remembering, our shared past, provided a sense of national identity, even if our individual political views, class, or cultural backgrounds had made us seem very different before.[134]

Images can be transmitted globally, but we do not interpret them globally—mass transmission is not the same as homogeneous mass reception.

Some of the excerpts in the film *11'09'01: September 11: A Collective Film* offer idiosyncratic views of September 11 and are dramatic evidence for the deconstruction of this theoretical misapprehension of receptive homogeneity. Samira Makhmalbaf, directing the Iranian segment, gives a localized perspective of the burning towers through the uncomprehending eyes of children in a village of a third-world country that does not turn to Hollywood cinema to find its iconicity.[135] A teacher rounds up Afghani refugee children, squelching mortar with their bare feet for a bomb shelter of bricks before school, for a lesson on what she calls an "important global incident." She has trouble rounding them up as they are assisting the villagers who see the outcome as a threat to their survival: "Hurry up! America wants to bomb Afghanistan! Let's build a shelter." The teacher promises them books if they will come to school, pointing out they may as well come as "you can't stop atomic bombs with these bricks." She asks the children if they know what has happened: "Children, important news. A big incident took place in the world. Who knows anything about it?" The uncomprehending children refer to the events that have tragic importance in the life of the small village: "Someone dug a well and two people fell in and died." Another child says her aunt was buried up to her neck in Afghanistan and stoned to death, and a third offers the fact that a flood came and caused many deaths. The exasperated teacher says that two planes hit the WTC towers. Recognizing that in a mud brick village what a tower is needs definition, the teacher points to the smoking chimney of the brick kiln through the window to illustrate.

In reply to the teacher's question as to whether the children know who destroyed the towers a child answers "God," and the children start to debate this, despite the teacher's call for the children to first participate in a minute of silence in memory of the dead. The children's ages and cultural and religious beliefs frame their comprehension and their enthusiasm for their own preoccupations overrides their ability to relate to the tragedy of others ("Does God kill? Does he kill? God hasn't got airplanes."), as do their childish interactions ("Excuse me, he's spoiling the silence") and the wry innocence of their logic:

Girl: God's not crazy enough to kill people.
Boy: It's none of your business. God can do what he wants.

Unable to get a memorial silence for an event that has no meaning for them, the teacher tries illustrating its tragic import with a description of one person's attempt to call for help from under the rubble with a mobile phone. However, she again faces that cultural and technological divide from the West when she finds herself needing to explain to her charges what a mobile is. In a last attempt to get her moment of memorial the teacher takes the class to stand at the base of the kiln chimney outside: "Look at the chimney. Think of all those people in the towers who died under the rubble." While the children shield their eyes from the bright sun as they look up a boy asks: "What do we do if we want to talk?" The teacher answers: "Just bite your lips and look at the chimney." The last frame is of the camera below the level of the children, panning up at the smoking chimney of the brick kiln.

The kiln is the film's metaphor for the burning towers and it powerfully illustrates that the televised images have no global blockbuster meaning in this village. Iconicity lies in the kiln of a mud brick factory. The global impact is dwarfed by their own localized concerns. In the Israeli offering in the collection, which portrays their citizens dealing with their own terrorist incident, the nearest reference point is not a disaster movie but their own experiences of terrorism. Gianpaolo Baiocchi, in his discussion of Brazilian television coverage of 9/11, says that while networks there initially just streamed CNN with no translation, and only occasional voiceover commentary in Portuguese, by 2 p.m. local contextualizing had already begun, with coverage seeking to know what the event looked like to a Brazilian shoeshine worker in New York, for example.[136] As Susan Sontag notes, there is a kind of "provincialism" in reading too much into the globalization of the spectacle:

It universalizes the viewing habits of a small, educated population living in the rich part of the world. . . It assumes that everyone is a spectator . . . There are hundreds of millions of television watchers who are far from inured to what they see on television. They do not have the luxury of patronizing reality.[137]

Global audience reception of the visuals of 9/11 was not dominated by the preferred readings of the Western simulacrum or by its film imagery. Worldwide, there were culturally distinctive responses to the authenticity of the global violent event.

The discourse about the authenticity of the "live" violent event, subsumed as it is into the larger debate about the nature of reality on-screen, is also one about why the viewer watches, about the nature of the desire to be present via the screen. The documentary filmmaker Ken Burns characterizes the artistic gaze drawn to such a great event as demanding "our complete presence and attention."[138] In that respect, the "live" news transmission of 9/11 shares one of the core assumptions of reality television, that the audience believes it needs to know. As Bob Simon, a journalist for the American version of *60 Minutes* has pointed out: "We talk about this need to know. People do not have a need to know immediately. It's a need that's been created by the possibility of knowing."[139] Spectacular and sensational violence in news presentations evidenced in its more "flamboyant production aspects"[140] in shows as far apart in approach as *Hard Copy* and *60 Minutes,* has a closer relationship with the contrivances of reality TV than with that of the cinema. Defining the cinematic analogy, along with the concept of "virtuality" itself, as interchangeable only with the visual, ignores the audio, the range of voices that punctuated the glossy, visual constructedness of the "image-event." If watching the towers collapse on screen exemplified the desire to be present as Burns defines it, audiences were more horrified than excited to find they *were* present. What television gave access to was the stark violence of the images of the event in an ocean of responding voices struggling with participation as well as observation under the unique pressures of the "live" transmission of occurrence—revealing both the strengths and weaknesses of television journalism as a source of information in times of crisis. The primal impact of the visual and the virtual, and its use to justify aspects of theories of globalization, at least in the case of 9/11, needs to be modified with a more specific analysis of the text itself.

When Baudrillard characterized the image-event as a "Manhattan disaster movie," placing it in a loop of signifiers, he assumed an easy transition from lived experience into text. Yet it is difficult, if not impossible, to relocate permanently, or for long, to the hyperreal and to leave lived experience behind, as anyone knows who blinks as they leave the darkened cinema and strives to retain the feelings evoked by a movie. Gail Bell's alienation from the hyperreal texts into which her trauma mutated, mentioned in the introduction, is also a testimony to this complex relationship text has with the lived experience that launches it. Bill Nichols notes that the video of the LAPD police beating of Rodney King has iconic and visual affectiveness because it is a recording where "the historical referent once again cuts through the inoculating power of signifying systems to turn our response to that excess beyond the frame."[141] For Nichols, the brutal viciousness of the image of King being beaten was a product of what was viewed in it *and* of how it signified the reality outside the frame: "Rodney King, as a signifier for this larger array of events that so massively exceeded his own body and his own experience, bursts beyond the frame of the spectacle" to become a part of the larger debate about public policy and racism in American society provoked by the riots his beating led to.[142] The iconicity of that beating depended on the indexicality of the image to the wider social context of the subsumed violent racism in the guise of law enforcement for which it was a symptom, and from which it exploded into the media text.[143]

> The relation of signifier to referent cannot be displaced by endless chains of signifiers and the signifieds we forge to accompany them. We wince, we gasp; we experience this brutal event with moral outrage.[144]

The historical actuality of the violent event marks the text and burns its timeless authenticity into collective memory. Putting back the audio into the televirtuality of 9/11 reveals in the extraordinary assertion of language and live action over the simulacrum that there is a case for affective impact on any given viewer being shaped by a more complex discourse than the primacy of the image.

The Chairman of the American Commission of Inquiry into the government response and intelligence failures leading up to and following the attack, Thomas H. Kean, bluntly noted: "This was a failure of policy, management, capability and, above all, a failure of imagination."[145] While Kean was not commenting on the link with images of disaster in the movies that preceded 9/11, I think his comment is closer to the nature of that connection than postmodern theory, which has elevated cinematic visuality above all else as a signifier of iconicity. It is not that cinematic imagination prefigured the event, but that it spectacularly failed to do so in any meaningful sense that was not shattered by the historical reality of the event itself. Paul Harvey, in his practical and useful overview of postmodern theory reminds us that in 1984 Jameson viewed postmodernism as originating in a perceptual short-fall against a changing experience of space and time. He accepts at face value Jameson's remark that

> [w]e do not yet possess the perceptual equipment to match this new kind of hyperspace ... in part because our perceptual habits were formed in that older kind of space I have called the space of high modernism.[146]

I am more in agreement with Scott Bukatman that

> the ultimate effect of the electronic refiguring of the world remains indeter-minate; the boundaries of the new technological powers are still uncertain while all ontological categories are seemingly up for grabs.[147]

The broad elevation of the image as the determinant for specific textual experiences denies that complexity. While it is axiomatic "that people create their own fears out of the imagination of possible horrors," as Andrew Stathern and Pamela J. Stewart go on to add "when actual horrors take place ... these in turn feed into the world of the iconic imagination."[148] The door to the simulacrum is wide open to the world outside the virtual frame.

In the case of the audience viewing televised broadcasts of 9/11, what was heard and seen was the struggle to make meaning in the face of the devastating social and political impact outside the television screen for Americans finding a war tak-ing place inside their borders. It is the tone of shock and bewilderment in the journalistic voices, the indexical authenticity of lived experience outside the screen, which breaches virtuality. The event reached through the text to shatter the distance between it and the normally insulated viewer.[149] As Dominic Wells points out: "a great 'Outland' cartoon has the heroes whooping and cheering in front of some TV shootings, only to become sombre indeed when it dawns on them that they're watching, not an action film, but the news."[150] Ron Burnett also notes, while images are a means by which the world is visualized when patterns of interaction with them are disrupted, as they were on 9/11, "a great deal of what happened was beyond the images":

> The images were powerful, but they were not enough as people looked for social contexts in which they could share their pain and shock at the events

with others. Images of suffering have this dual effect of distance and closeness and are examples of the frailty of communication as well as its strength.[151]

Ultimately, while watching the broadcast on 9/11, the shock for the American viewers lay in the discovery that it was not in the virtual representation of violence but on the destroyed streets amongst a devastated New York citizenry that they actually lived.

2

"We Can't Believe It's Not Butter": Polemical Violence and Faking Authenticity

Audiences are attracted to the hoax and by the very success of the hoax—by the ability of the maker to produce a perfect illusionistic imitation.[152]

If you want to make good, believable, useful documentaries or reality videos, you have to get over the idea that you can suck reality into a camera and blow it back at your audience.[153]

While the first chapter argues for "a qualified realism of the image,"[154] this is not to deny that symbolic use of indexical images is problematic.[155] It becomes more problematic when texts are found further along the continuum of authenticity than the simultaneous transmission of a spontaneous indexical event such as 9/11. Nonfiction texts, which make documentary claims to representing reality as the basis for making polemical arguments about violence, are of particular interest in that context. Sliding along the continuum from contemporaneous transmission of the observed violent event, it is not possible to discuss nonfiction texts making rhetorical claims about violence without finding that issues about the authenticity of their claims become a part of the discussion. The documentary accuracy of the texts is something the texts lay claim to as nonfiction and audiences expect them to have a lingering indexical, if often vaguely defined, relationship with actual events. This expectation persists despite audience acceptance that the events are being edited for meaning. This expectation of some degree of authentic representation of actuality plays a central role in audience reception of the texts and in audience acceptance or rejection of the texts' views about violence.

This chapter examines the textual construction of violent "realities" licensed by the nonfiction hybrids of reality television, popular documentaries, and best-seller personal revelations that seduce with a degree of fakery to sustain the claims to authenticity of their polemics about violence. It examines the film *Series 7: The Contenders*[156] which uses a violent premise to polemicize about the violence reality

TV does to authenticity. I also discuss Michael Moore's *Bowling for Columbine*[157] and Norma Khouri's *Forbidden Love: A Harrowing True Story of Love and Revenge in Jordan*,[158] both of which manipulate factual authenticity to polemicize about violence. As *Series 7* satirizes with regard to reality TV, *Bowling for Columbine* reveals in its documentary methodology and *Forbidden Love* draws attention to through the public excoriation of the author for her hoaxing of her readers, the claims made for the representation of reality in text raises questions about the authenticity of the texts themselves as well as about the authenticity of the representation of the violence that is their subject. All three texts have violence in their content and all have provoked critical discussion about the nature of fakery or the hoaxing of the viewer/reader when authenticity is made suspect by editorial manipulation of nonfiction. They are texts that uniquely serve as a point of focus for issues raised about the representation of violence and the representation of authenticity. They are also examples of how elements of "faking it" can exist in the textual mix with elements audiences are willing to accept as ambiguously authentic. Indeed, it could be said that the attraction of the texts under discussion for their audiences and readers is as much a product of their interest in the tension between manipulation and actuality as it is a product of an interest in the subject of violence itself. Nostalgic or not in the postmodern context, audience belief in documentary reality, existing in a contradictory relationship with an acceptance of manipulation, is what powers audience engagement with these kinds of texts.

While the word documentary[159] is still being used to describe traditional nonfiction formats, examples must almost be placed individually on the continuum of authenticity posited, even though they form a cluster that includes traditional documentaries, mockumentary, and reality TV. As Susan Murray points out in her appropriately titled article *I Think We Need a New Name for It*, contemporary genres of nonfiction often provoke subjective analysis that is based on unacknowledged critical stances embedded in values about commercialization versus social and cultural worth—a rhetorical struggle to keep entertainment and more canonical and culturally valued texts on different planes.[160] Such denigration is particularly a part of the critical reception of what is seen to be fake about reality TV. Instead of defining degrees of fakery and authenticity when placing them on the continuum, I would argue it is more illustrative to recognize that claims to authenticity made by the texts exist in concordance with a dependence on fakery that defines the uniqueness of the texts' approach to their storytelling or polemic. Such texts are uniquely welcomed and enjoyed by an audience willing to go along with a degree of hoaxing and to live with ambiguity about the authenticity of how "real" the representation may be. For consumers of such texts, drawing meaning from them does not require a rigid definition of a fictional and nonfictional divide.

The belief that a text conveys "reality" is a powerful cultural force when it comes to perceptions of violence. As Franklin Zimring, quoting W. I. Thomas observes,

"If men define situations as real, they are real in their consequence."[161] Commenting on the high level of the concern in American society in the 1990s about crime and violence, he delineates how perceptions of crime became an empirical factor in public debate. Government legislation was influenced by the perception of a crisis in youth violence, whether or not that perception was borne out by known facts. He offers convincing insight into the rhetorical themes of the "crisis": the viciousness of the "new breed" of offenders, the "revolving door" of justice, the retributive view of youth as "adult offenders" that characterized the shared imagery of the American debate (often reported in the press) on the feared "coming storm" of a crisis in youth violence. The violent juvenile offender was not only the subject of changes to the legal system in the United States but also the "symbol that justifies the reorientation of the legal system toward young offenders in general, if not toward an even broader segment of the youth population."[162] The textualization of juvenile crime led to youthful offenders being made "the delinquent archetype of the current generation" and "the poster child"[163] for public perceptions and for the way American governmental process acted to manage public policy on crime. The poster stereotype was both text *and* an empirical factor with consequences for social and ideological change. The actual occurrence of juvenile crime was effectively subsumed into a symbolic discourse with power over the public domain. The perceived authenticity in the stereotype was powered by the lived experience of fear of violence engendering the discourse that reflected it.[164] In that sense, a rhetorical stereotype that was itself a product of authentic public fears in turn became a force that shaped political decision-making. It was a classic example of the porous fluidity that exists between text and actuality, which inevitably muddies the waters of discussion about authenticity in the representation of violence.

Series 7: The Contenders

The fact that audiences are willing to believe in the reality aesthetic is supported by the contemporary popularity of reality TV. Perceived authenticity, or the promise of it, is the pleasurable allure for contemporary audiences of the texts that claim to document reality like *Big Brother* or *Survivor*. As audiences find themselves watching texts with "sliding and evolving expectations"[165] of authenticity, the critical debate over such hybrid documentary genres has also embodied anxieties about identity, expressed as the publicly private. Popular fascination with crime and violence in reality TV or documentary television formats in American shows like *Cops* (or the Australian equivalents such as *The Force* and *The Code: Crime and Justice*) and *America's Most Wanted* or Australian formats like *Sensing Murder* (which followed the attempts by psychics to solve crimes) provoke a critical interest in drawing the line between entertainment and the more minimally varnished journalistic and nonfiction reflections on the subject of violence. It is the journalistic reports, rather than reality TV incarnations, which resonate in the public arena as raising issues of social and political importance but the distinction is not absolute.

The inevitable editing for effect behind the claims made by reality TV is excoriated as the satirical subject of *Series 7: The Contenders*, which uses the absurdity of violence as a produced commodity to parody, as exploitive illusion, the idea that reality TV gives access to authentic experience. The film is a comic indictment of audiences who are portrayed as willing dupes in their fascination with representations that are manipulated spectacle. The film's characters are conscripted to be contestants in a last-man-standing competition in which the reigning champion has to eliminate (literally by killing them) every other competitor to win:

> Six strangers, brought together by the luck of the draw. In a game without rules. Where the only prize is the only prize that counts. Your life.

Series 7 is a satirical answer to Salmon Rushdie's question about reality TV: "if we are willing to watch people stab one another in the back, might we not also be willing to actually watch them die?"[166] The false claim that no constructedness exists in reality television is the main target: "Everything you are about to see is real. Real people, in real danger, in a fight for their lives"—despite the fact that

> having constructed a violent game show premise that has nothing to do with the everyday lives of its contestants, the programme's links to any "reality" is purely rhetorical.[167]

Spoofing the idea of responsible production behavior with the segue, "Due to the graphic nature of the following program viewer discretion is advised," *Series 7* is relentless in targeting every aspect of the gamedoc[168] format typified by *Survivor* and *Big Brother*.

Much of the enjoyment of the film's satire comes from viewer familiarity with the conventions of the reality TV genre. The voiceover commentary of the hyped-up television promotional spot is brilliantly lampooned in the mellifluously exaggerated portentousness of

> [e]verything on the line and nothing can be taken for granted. One winner. Showdown. The season finale is coming up.

The 24-hour surveillance in the show trumpets technology at the service of the presentation of uncut reality: "State of the art transmitters and global positioning systems help us to bring you the real story as it unfolds." Yet, production rules condition behavior ("The rules are as simple as life and death") and game score-keeping creates the statistics that matter ("This narrows the field to three"). Audience pseudoinvolvement in the fate of the participants is used as a promotional hook: "Can she survive another round of vicious, deadly opposition. And can we take it?" Suspense is milked from the vapidly mundane: "We've burned hours of videotape to capture Jeff's waking moments." The latter claim is accompanied by a long pause of dead air and a shot of an unconscious contender in a hospital bed after a suicide attempt with a massive, black camera apparatus looming over his upper body. There is the promise of revelation ("It's homecoming for our reigning contender as her secrets are revealed."), the pathos of confession ("In a moment of tenderness, our reigning contender lets down her guard."), and the promotion of competition as pseudopersonal challenge ("Is Jeff ready to face the future, alone?"). It is insinuated that "real" personal relationships are being dramatically propelled forward because of encounters on the show ("Will Dawn be able to eliminate Jeff or will her feelings for him get in the way?") and that personal adversity is being overcome ("It's amazing that Dawn is up at all. She's still weak after giving birth only hours ago."). The voiceover stereotypes participants as a conduit for audience empathy and support ("Dawn Legato, mother, hero, contender") in clichéd action ("These cats don't have nine lives"). A video game form of suspense ("One mistake and it's Game Over") ramps up a sense of participant pseudoperil. Comically, reality TV violence is offered as a feel-good conduit for personal therapy: "Sometimes, it's like, you're just so angry and so confused and all you can think to do is go out and kill someone," transforming Dawn, contestant and a soon-to-be mother, into the Dirty Harry of reality TV: "I just gotta do what I gotta do. I gotta take care of what I gotta take care of." War is reduced to the metaphor for a game show: "I guess it's like being in a war mentality. It's kill or be killed."

The film opens with a pregnant Dawn Legarto, the current champion, walking into a convenience story and matter-of-factly shooting a rival contender in the head, splattering blood everywhere. The act comically reveals the way the televised game has blended into the "real" world outside the show in the film. The convenience store clerk is concerned with what is to be done with the body and not with the fact that a murder has been committed and Dawn nonchalantly moves from killing to making a mundane enquiry about a purchase before she leaves:

Dawn: (taking the dead man's gun) Do you have any bean dip?
Clerk: (Hands in air) All we have is what's out.
(As Dawn starts to leave) Hey! What about the body?
Dawn: Just let them deal with it.

Dawn is a celebrity and the production staff of the show she is on will clean up the mess. Following the introductory murder we are given a "Previously on the Contenders" sequence to remind us of Dawn's motivation. She speaks directly to the camera, to the cameraman who has posed the unheard question, and to the show's audience: "All I can allow myself to think about is my baby." Action is recapped through the rerunning several times of her murder of the convenience store customer and the promotion of the show as producing reality-game history: "With ten kills in only two tours she's been unstoppable. Now, one month before the birth of her child, just five lives stand between her and her freedom." She exits the store with her shopping bag, resigned but determined: "I try not to think about it too much because I just have to get through this," walking past onlookers who do not look surprised or afraid. The bystanders are not witnesses to a crime but the audience and, as a billboard erected on a visit to the champion's hometown proclaims with its "Good luck Dawn," they are also fans. While satirizing it, the film shows the way in which television fakery nevertheless intrudes into the experience of the real world of fan emotional involvement:

> The merging of realism with reality TV is a condition of our experience of the world, even if it is at odds with the common epistemological framework that generally keeps them apart.[169]

The fans in the film are straddling the border between being audience members and participants in the reality illusion.

The gun-toting, pregnant Dawn, unlike the audience in the film, is aware she is exploited by the cynical commercialism at the core of reality TV production. When asked about her feelings on seeing an ex-boyfriend, who is now a contestant that she has to kill, she replies sarcastically:

> Well, I'm really excited to see him because I have to kill him. That really excites me. I always wanted to kill my friend and now I get the chance to do it.

Even in the absurd world of reality television, some things are more absurd than others. She is aware of the typecasting superficiality of media-manufactured celebrity and "quick-fix fame"[170] when she says "What did they call me in the paper the other day? Bloody Mama? Christ!" However, it is a fame that she herself exploits in the cryptic way she introduces herself on the phone in the self-confident assumption of celebrity shorthand: "This is Dawn, of Dawn and Jeff." The absurdity of looking for privacy when participating in a reality TV show is comically pointed out when Dawn, having shot a competitor, solicitously tells the cameraman to leave the wife to her grief: "Can you please give the woman some privacy?" Ironically, other characters object to the voyeurism they participate in. In Jeff's first, hesitant video confession he looks directly at the camera in a close-up and fails to deliver self-exposure:

> **Jeff:** I'm not exactly sure what you're looking for . . . what is it that you want me to say? Do you want me to say something for your program or something?

Cameraman: Look at me. Tell Dawn whatever you want to tell her right
(off camera) now.
Jeff: (He looks at the camera and then looks away and down.)
I can't do this anymore. I think.

His vulnerability is undercut, however, by the lingering uncertainty of his "I think." In another dryly comic scene, Dawn's water breaks just as a rival contestant and emergency room nurse, Connie, is about to kill her. Connie is forced to call 911 and assist with the birth to save the life of "an innocent baby."

Connie: (holding a gun on Dawn) I got a woman here, a contender,
ready to give birth.
911 Operator: Okay. Is there a camera on?
Connie: Yes. Two cameras.

First the camera, then the ambulance and, if Connie has her way, it will be followed with the death of Dawn at her hands in front of the camera after the birth.

Camera-induced performance is revealed as the insincerity of sincerity—undercutting, retrospectively, the vulnerability we thought we might have perceived in the video confession by Jeff above—when Dawn, on a visit to her hometown, is hugged by a niece who says, "I saw you on TV. I love you." The artificiality of that "love" comes from its dependence on a fan relationship with the on-screen portrayal of Dawn and not the "real" Aunt, whom she has not seen since she was a baby. The effect is chilling when, as the niece hugs Dawn, she looks directly at the camera in a knowing way—a sophisticated complicity in exploitative intent that is all the more disturbing because it is on the face of a child. When the show operatives come to get a young woman picked by lottery to compete in the show her mother protests, "No, not my baby, you can't do this," but the woman tells her mother not to answer for her and looks at the camera, pleased and seduced by the chance to be on television. The hypocrisy of televised emotion is at its most farcical when Connie engages in a parody of a church confession after killing a competitor by injection. Her droll litany of sins, inclusive of the trivial, "I accuse myself of being impatient with one of my patients," and the ridiculous, "I had impure thoughts about a television personality," ludicrously excludes her act of murder. Even in this satirical world it is hard not to agree with Dawn's assessment of Connie that "this nurse has gotta be stopped, she's a fuckin' psycho!" Connie is the exaggeration of a Jerry Springer Show milieu characterized by the expression of identity in spaces

filled by voices proclaiming and celebrating their own 'freakishness,' articulating their most intimate fears and secrets, performing the ordinariness of their own extraordinary subjectivity.[171]

Connie is the excess of an already outlandish subjectivity.

Yet, that subjectivity has its seductive pathos, even though the audience of *The Contenders* in the narrative and, by implication the audience of *Series 7* the film, are given warnings of manipulation and fakery. Franklin, a contestant eliminated by Connie in a mall shootout, warns the other contestants:

> Everything you people believe is bullshit! It's high time the American public should be allowed to know what I know, what I've known for a long time. The show is a fake.

However, perversely, the farce gives us affective moments of poignancy, encouraging the viewer to care about the fate of Dawn and Jeff. It is the oddly affective quality of moments in the film that mimics the constructed allure of reality television itself, when the audience *chooses to believe* and trusts that the "real" emotions of "real" people are at stake, and reacts empathically. This is true of Jeff's confessional moments where he shows uncertainty in front of the camera, and of parts of the rekindling of the preshow relationship between Dawn and Jeff. As Dawn says: "Seeing Jeff opened up this whole other part of me that I know nobody on this show has ever seen." However, the immediate voiceover exploitation of this emotion ("Is Dawn ready to extinguish an old flame?") reminds the viewer that this is reality television and the possibility of sincerity is always in question.

The effect of this interplay between satire and pathos in the film parallels the mixture of cynicism and identification with which researched audiences reveal themselves as responding to reality television. Mark Andrejevic describes how some fans of *Big Brother* felt they were getting a slice of life, while others had a "savvy" audience response created by the voyeuristic online "live" feed of *Big Brother* (supplementing what was aired on television). The "live" feed was a promise to online fans that they would have insider knowledge of the "truth of its artifice"[172] because they could compare the unedited version with the televised one:

> The live feeds enhanced the promise of access to the real by offering viewers the unedited content from which the nightly broadcast segments were constructed. The result of this access was to foreground the production process itself, and thereby to allow online viewers to thematize the way in which the show was being manipulated and produced even while billing itself as "reality" TV ... However, *Big Brother* helped show how the promise of demystification could be co-opted as a marketing strategy. If part of the appeal of the show was precisely the way in which it allowed viewers to see through the promise of reality, this served, paradoxically, as one more savvy promise of access to reality: "You, the Internet viewers can see the 'real' truth of 'reality' TV": the way in which we edit the show in order to manipulate reality.[173]

Andrejevic contrasts the positivist approach of audiences who expect shows to give reality in a kind of social experiment versus a postmodern approach that cynically accepts the inevitability of contrivance: a situation that "both exploits and defers the desire for authenticity."[174] He argues that the acceptance of illusion in slick production values of shows like *Survivor* are aspects of that kind of reflexivity, exposing its own artifice through its invocation of pseudotribal archetypes while promising real interactions. Surveillance in this genre, and the interest in being subjected to surveillance, is inevitably concomitant with the loss of belief in the access of representation to an authentic referent.

> In the register of reality TV, the savvy awareness of contrivance coincides with the brutal "reality" of survival at all costs. It is perhaps not coincidental that the current trend in reality television is increasingly toward various forms of borderline torture that guarantee the "reality" of the emotions portrayed . . . On the one hand, we know all this is contrived; on the other, we seem to demand more and more punishing contrivances in the hopes of squeezing out a bit of authenticity—of real emotion (fear, anxiety, pain, etc.).[175]

For Andrejevic, however, acceptance of the inevitability of contrivance is not liberation through demystification but "a fetishisation of mediation itself—the savvy reduction of reality to mediation with no remainder"[176] and a form of impotent complicity with deception.

Undoubtedly, the exploited participants share this complicity. The director of *Series 7*, Daniel Minehan, has described the kind of "self-consciousness" he required of actors performing reality show participants "acting."

> The idea was that people on these shows play the part they think they're supposed to play. *Oh, she's the Bitch. He's the Uptight Born-Again Christian.* As it turns out, all I had to do was remind people that there was a camera in the room, and that it would be a character in *Series 7*. That naturally gave the performances the self-consciousness that I wanted.[177]

Richard Hatch confirms this view as a *Survivor* winner; calling the role he played as a contestant a "game face," a strategy, and not who he was.[178] He performed the part as a strategy and a role and thus would have made himself complicit in the manipulation in return for fame and fortune. Yet, for some fans in Andrejevic's study, awareness of manipulation of the story for marketing purposes did not preclude a sense of trust that something authentic about the contestants still emerges. The acceptance of the fact that putting a nonprofessional actor in front of a camera will nevertheless lead to "acting" was not seen (perhaps also to be read as theatrical "scene") as precluding subjective authenticity in role-playing that exists in an undefined grey area between unguarded self-presentation and professional acting.[179] Perhaps this is a level of self-awareness (or non-self-awareness) that the contestants, producers, critics, and audiences would not be able to finally untangle from performance, certainly not with enough nuance to remove all traces of ambiguity from authenticity.

For Minehan, pointing a camera at a participant does violence to authenticity:

> To me, invasion of privacy is a form of violence. I'm very ambivalent about it. Having produced this stuff, I know the power of bringing a camera into somebody's house. People will do almost anything you ask when you're there with a camera crew. Now, it would be puritanical of me to point a finger and say, "This is a bad thing," because people are complicit with it. But, I do hope *Series 7* points out that anti-social aspect—the *brutality* of these shows.[180]

The choice made by participants to compete suggests issues of privacy may be a moot point. If audience and participants share complicity in the hoax the question then follows: is whether, as Andrejevic argues, the genre is simply mediation that deprives the audience of any access to authenticity. *Series 7* certainly rejects the possibility of an unscripted, unguarded moment in the reality TV hoax. In the series finale of *The Contenders* Jeff and Dawn declare their love for one another and resolve to break the rules, escape from the show's grip, and recover Dawn's baby who has been removed by the producers for its own safety (and for the pathos of watching Dawn's pain). With all other contenders eliminated, the audience is promised "the ultimate battle," as Dawn and Jeff face off like two urban gunfighters in the empty, "undisclosed location" of a sports stadium reminiscent of a *Mad Max* Thunderdome. Sensationalism and faux-suspense ("Will Dawn be able to eliminate Jeff or will her feelings for him get in the way?") and claims that even Jeff's sexuality is in play ("Can Jeff really change from an ex-gay pacifist to a fierce contender?") parodies the commodification of contestant free will. Dawn and Jeff turn their guns on the cameramen rather than each other and demand that the cameras be turned off, following a declaration of freedom from manipulation and exploitation:

Dawn: Jeffrey, let's not do this. They're fucking with us. Fuck them.
I love you.
Jeff: I love you too.

But, the genre's capacity to exploit this rebellion by ramping up the spectacle is relentless and the show goes into a video game style "Sudden Death Overtime."

The audience in the film is encouraged to get virtually interactive and join the pursuit of a fleeing Dawn and Jeff, parodying interaction as nothing more than further production manipulation. Informing the audience of when the two finalists were last seen and what they were wearing, the voiceover encourages pursuit of the pair as if it were a kind of audience civic duty, echoing the interactivity of crime-appeal shows like *America's Most Wanted*: "With the help of audience members like you, our agents can trace the paths of these fugitives as they make their way through the city." There is a montage of viewer call-ins—with subtitled transcriptions over a visual of rolling tapes in the convention of televised 911 call-ins: "I think I spotted Dawn at the cash machine, at the corner of White and Main, trying to get some money but it wouldn't take her card." There are shots from security cameras that match the provided information, such as Dawn at the automated teller machine, and multiple frames of in-store or speed cameras that mimic the time, date, and recording appearance of such video surveillance frames. Comically, much of the detail of this interactivity is inanely irrelevant: "They came into my store just after 11. Jeff held me at gunpoint and Dawn took two dozen jars of baby food, a half a dozen veggie burritos and a box of power bars." The partnership of audience and producers is portrayed as a massive production effort to service the audience's desire for a pseudoreality in which it is both an observer and participant—complicit and exploited. The boundaries between the real and the fake collapse: "Due to a technical error, the footage you are about to see was destroyed. But our producers have spared no expense in reconstructing the scene as if it really happened." When everything is contrived, even a reenactment can be as "real" as anything else: "as if it really happened"—not as it did, but "as if," suggesting something more than non-fictional but less than fiction. The film

> explicitly implicates its own audience in its critiques of reality hybrids, rather than displacing negative assumptions about spectatorship onto an assumed niche of "other" television viewers.[181]

More than duped, the audience is corralled and at risk. Dawn and Jeff take a film audience of fans of the show hostage (to the fans' delight), and Dawn threatens to shoot the hostages if the show's producers do not return her baby to her and allow them to leave the show. The delusional fans applaud her bravado, ignoring the threat to their own lives, which Dawn uses to sardonically disparage them: "That means you, arseholes!" The audience is comically unaware of their own movement from the safe haven of viewership to the dangerous, if staged one, of participant in the show.

Contestants volunteer to put themselves on a visual pedestal that makes the participant the centre of the watcher's virtually directed gaze—an attention span that gives them their fleeting 15 minutes of fame: In Dawn's case it costs her life and Jeff tries to commit suicide. The show's pseudomemorialization ("Dawn Legarto, Jeffrey Norman, they were soulmates, warriors, misfits and heroes but we always remember them as Contenders") is supplanted immediately by the hyped promises of "*Series 8*" and the "new reigning Contender." Jeff wakes in a hospital bed, after yet another failed suicide attempt, announcing his disgust with both that failure and his failure to get off the show in an expletive: "Shit!" Jeff is left with the fact that there is no way out of exploitation. The film also targets the viewer of reality television, whose strongest engagement is not with the contestants but with the act of watching itself. The audience in the film, displaying ignorance of their inclusion as targets in Dawn's death threat, are caught in a virtual loop along with Jeff. Sardonically, the film paints viewer voyeurism as an existential trap that is, appallingly, self-sprung.

Audience Reception and Textual Interdiscursivity

The question remains: does audience complicity in indulging in the pleasures of entertainment as if it were a slice of authenticity equate with total cultural self-deception? *Series 7* reflects a postmodern ideological desire to quantify the degree of manipulation of actuality that fuels fan and critical debates.[182] However, once the audience is posited as a participant in reality TV action, even if duped as in the auditorium where they are held hostage in the film, the textual frames around production are acknowledged as subject to shifting. Hilarious as it is, *Series 7* does not offer much respect for reality TV audiences or acknowledge any of Andrejevic's researched savviness. As Craig Hight points out, there has been a theoretical history in the documentary genre about the "manner in which documentary *should* be engaging with social and political practice," with commentators "forced to rely on their *speculations* on how viewers interpret and respond to such forms."[183] As Deborah Jermyn points out, ideological assumptions behind aesthetic preferences are not always acknowledged in the current debate over the value of reality TV programming. She points out the common alarmist condemnation of reality TV that "apparently crystallizes all that is corrupt and debasing about contemporary television."[184] Critical unease with the hybridity and genre amalgamation of such formats, seemingly because they are *popular* commodities, is

> arguably characterized by a paternalistic and conservative impulse that, within the terms of the mass-society tradition, constructs the audience as vulnerable and malleable.[185]

An opposing political bias can be discerned in the view that reality TV embodies an antielitist, democratic cultural aesthetic. This critical preoccupation with the balance between the "stultifying binaries of such a pattern,"[186] between entertainment and the production of knowledge, is trying to resolve the narrative tension between empirical practice and the imaginary.

Ultimately such debates are a theoretical diversion rendered obsolete by hybridity where degrees of "faking it" are already acceptable creative methodology. This hybridity is aptly described by Kevin Glynn as a "slippery entity" and a "mixed bag" that "entails a variety of intertwined discursive formations that occupy a mobile space where journalism and popular culture intersect" in tabloid TV. He describes *America's Most Wanted* as "after the fashion of eclectic postmodern hybridity, part telethon, part newscast, part documentary, part cop show, and part family drama."[187] The problematic nature of analysis in the context of that interdiscursivity, "the stubborn problems of textual classification"[188] as Glynn puts it, means that specific media values and approaches to topics are more interesting in their individual details than they are for the ways in which they exemplify any given genre. In that sense, viewing them through the critical filter of fiction or nonfiction, or even as simply entertainment, is of little value or critical utility particularly if one includes analysis of audience reception. Michael Renov's anecdote describing the screening of a documentary that was an amalgam of fictional and nonfictional scenes to a group of students is illustrative.[189] He found descriptions of the students affective responses to the documentary experiences recorded no qualitative difference in response to fictional and nonfictional segments. The nonfiction/fiction divide was not a useful prism, at least for this group of students, to describe they way they extrapolated a meaningful sense of what real life was all about from texts.[190]

Reenactments in the text shown by Renov to his students have long been a tool of documentary forms that are considered separate from straight fictionalization. The responses of Renov's students reveal that there is extensive leeway given by audiences to nonfiction formats to creatively examine its topics in ways that will encourage serious consideration by the target audience of the issues raised. However,

> since these terms are currently under "reconstruction" and negotiation, our definitions of the relationship between television and realism, "fact" and "fiction," and "factual" and "entertainment" shows must also adapt.[191]

Using the term "doco-soaps" as her preferred term in her analysis of the Australian version of the reality TV show *Big Brother*, Toni Johnson-Woods points out that it is the problematic scripting of narrative through editing choices that adds the fakery to the "non-scripted footage of non-professionals" to create "cohesive storylines" that are controversial and entertaining: "The shots might be 'real' but they might not be related"[192] in time or space but suggestively placed for effect/affect. Editing actuality may throw a shadow over the validity of what is represented as authentic in reality TV. However, it is also true to say that it is not possible to eliminate it, or trust what is viewed, without its use as a tool from which audience members create their own, highly individualized perceptions of authenticity.

Editing Versus Authenticity

Aesthetic debate about the mediation of documentary actuality is not based on an agreed definition of natural ocularity[193] against which to oppose edited ocularity viewed through a camera. Johnson-Wood's reference to editing exemplifies a contemporary angst about editing reality as a form of corruption of authenticity seen with the naked eye. While editing is acknowledged as ordering authentic meaning in a text before the audience, in turn, selectively interprets that meaning, there remains a nostalgic discomfort with the tension that exists between authenticity and degrees of manipulation. Walter Murch, a veteran film editor, writing in his book *In the Blink of an Eye,* has a cinema practitioner's view of the abrupt act of cutting, "which represents a total and instantaneous displacement of one field of vision with another, a displacement that sometimes also entails a jump forward or backward in time as well as space."[194] Viewer trust in the documentary case is made convincing by the seamlessness of that displacement. Cutting assigns a necessary salience across time and space on which audience trust, the interpretation of meaning, and orientation toward perceived authenticity depends.[195]

Critical questions about documentary ethics often centre on the ethics of particular cases of editing. Audience expectations of a text can be disturbed by an element of sleight of hand in editing craft. While the cut may be skilful on screen, extratextual knowledge leads to receptive discomfort about that same skilfulness. The recent resurgence of the documentary on cinema screens in mockumentary[196] forms, in the work of practitioners such as Michael Moore, illustrate the genre's reliance for the effect of its aesthetic on shifts in viewer expectations of methodology rather than on the representation of the reality of the cinematic object. The act of being part of an audience for nonfiction is based on a voyeuristic desire for an enhanced knowledge not otherwise available that is not, strictly speaking, a desire to view objective reality. Jane M. Gaines, in her discussion of the documentary genre's "fascination with resemblances,"[197] points out that there is a contradiction at the heart of a voyeurism seeking knowledge through a camera. Early documentaries were not beyond supplementing reality for audiences whom it was assumed possessed a genuine desire for knowledge and a wish to view visible evidence of the foreign, the exotic, the picturesque, the freakish, and the hitherto unknown or hidden. The desire to be entertained has always been an element in audience attraction to documenting reality:

> Of every commercial documentary it must be said that there is a "Ripley's Believe It or Not" quality, a quality of "stranger than," and it is this particular quality that invites investigation and knowledge, even a questioning about the imagined world/real world distinction. And this brings me to a point that must be made about the wholesale political dismissal of reality-based forms

premised on their inability to achieve analytic distance from the cinematic subject as well as from their own aesthetic devices.[198]

Johnson-Woods cites one critic as far back as 1926 defining the term documentary as "creative treatment of reality,"[199] presumably in ways that were not then defined as pure storytelling. In addition, acceptance of the voiceover, satirized for its excesses in *Series 7*, denotes the audience expectation of a documentary convention[200] that is a believable guide against which to orientate personal assessments of plausibility and judgments of authenticity. Renov defines this as being dictated to by "the Voice of God" which "bespeaks a position of absolute knowledge"[201] of the subject as its documentary stance. As a result: "The validity of distinctions between types of realism is as much a cultural understanding between audience and producers as about accurate description."[202]

Bowling for Columbine and Editing the Polemical

Critical concerns about authoring ethics are an inevitable product of textual hybridity and fluxing audience expectations. Typical of the concerns about documentary fakery, that polemic and creative editing can give rise to, is the extensive debate about the journalistic integrity of Michael Moore's documentaries (which Moore himself has engaged in outside his documentary films). Dave Kopel is typical of Moore's critics in his view that

> *Bowling for Columbine* revels in the tabloid-style, raw exploitation of emotion—in promotion of unjustified fear, in falsehoods and quarter truths, in oversimplification of the problems of race, and in mean-spirited pandering to the audience's bigotry about people of different social backgrounds.[203]

For some viewers, *Bowling for Columbine* raised questions about the nature of documentary "truth" because Michael Moore did not edit to sequence events as they actually happened but to fit the methodological needs of an acknowledged activist stance—using the shooting at Columbine High School in Littleton, Colorado, as an incident to frame a polemic against institutionalized violence in American society. Moore's voiceover role off-camera, and his actions as a participant on-camera, are artfully constructed to mock the targets he pursues. He polemicizes about the need for stricter gun control in the United States and to attack political aggressiveness in American foreign policy. Moore's confrontational and blatantly directorial approach to his subject neither confirms nor denies authenticity but subsumes it under a political polemic that, as a *first* priority, aims to entertain. Moore's subjectivity is front and center in the film and the wit and panache of that subjectivity contrasts markedly with the far less subjective approach to a violent incident of a documentary like, for example, Errol Morris's *The Thin Blue Line*.[204] *The Thin Blue Line* investigates the shooting of a policeman and the subsequent wrongful conviction of Randall Adams for the crime by offering interviews with participants who speak with no voiceover while looking directly into "an unmoving, unblinking camera"[205]—leaving the audience to question whether the representation of reality can be trusted as maximally authentic when accounts differ. *Bowling for Columbine*, however, does not encourage the audience to make up its own mind or to question. It offers a miscellany of unabashedly staged interviews to make a case, including the documentary-maker as a part of that staged investigative and humorous performance.

As a result, Moore edits for performative effect rather than linear accuracy. David T. Hardy, clinically critiquing the editing of events in the film that satirically target the actor Charlton Heston—portrayed as callously appearing as the spokesperson at a National Rifle Association (NRA) rally in Denver, Colorado, soon after the Columbine incident—notes how Moore uses editing to imply sequencing when there is none.[206] The film cuts from distressed students outside Columbine to Heston at the NRA rally, holding up a gun triumphantly: "I have only five words for you: 'from my cold, dead hands.'" The implication is that the insensitivity of that gesture came from its being made right after the events at Columbine. In fact, the scene is taken from a speech made a year later in another state. As Hardy shows, when Moore then begins to edit Heston's actual Denver speech as if it were the same document, it is obviously done to drastically change the tone and make it far more aggressive. With Moore, the cuts are less about transition between events than about making large polemical leaps over time and space to develop the semantic logic of his political argument. The fact that the degree of that leap can only be discerned by watching frame by frame, as critics of Moore like Hardy do, is illustrative of the role played by rapid cutting in Moore's diversion of audience attention from the details as he offers his bird's eye semantic view of gun violence in America. Similarly, geographical proximity is, for Moore, enough to link events with complex causation when polemic can make use of it. He segues from an interview with James Nichols, the brother of one of the convicted Oklahoma bombers, by saying that across the bay from his farm, Eric Harris, one of the Columbine shooters, lived part of his childhood on an airforce base in Oscoda. Adding that Harris's father flew planes during the Gulf War: Moore opines, "twenty per cent of the bombs dropped in that war were from planes that took off from Oscoda." Personal actions thus become the responsibility of larger, vaguely defined, monolithic military/industrial forces because only a bay separates one form of violence from another. Guilt by geographic association works as a polemical segue rather than a logical one.

Similar to the satirical stance of *Series 7*, much of the passion with which Moore is criticized reveals a lingering nostalgic modern passion for truth-telling and fair play objectivity that is in a fraught relationship with postmodern nonfictional representation. The postmodern fans' accommodation with the artifice of reality TV, noted by Andrejevic, exists in the same cultural place on the continuum of authenticity with critical reception that has trouble including the sleight-of-hand with which Moore edits. The focus on Moore's editing, while it may raise some fundamental and legitimate issues about practitioner ethics in documentary making, is also a reflection of some reception discomfort with the hybridity of Moore's provocative approach. The Cannes Film Festival jury had to create a new category to judge Moore's work and on the Internet Movie Database (IMDb) *Bowling for Columbine* is categorized as comedy, drama, *and* documentary. In an Academy Award acceptance speech Michael Moore asserts it is reality that is "fictitious." "We're here because we like non-fiction. We like non-fiction and we live in fictitious times," epigrammatically positing the idea that it is the spin of postmodern life that is fictional and the nonfictional deconstruction of that which provides clarity. He would doubtless agree with Edward Spence that:

> The paradox is that our preference for truth is pushing marketing, advertising and public relations manipulators of information to present us with fiction or lies as truth.[207]

Moore's statement suggestively posits that it is only possible to deconstruct the spin of a fictitious reality with its counterpart, nonfictional spin. It is not a case for ideological fair play but for the polemical ends justifying the textual means. To borrow Patricia R. Zimmermann's comment made in relation to filmic unpacking of repressed ideological meanings, there is a need for "editing to expose the seams in the seamless representations"[208] of opposing rhetoric or, as Moore describes it, of our "fictitious times."

Bowling for Columbine makes a witty case for this fictive nonfiction polemic if audience expectations are adjusted to view it as entertainment with a license to modify authenticity for entertainment's sake and the sake of the polemic. He wants to entertain first and even political persuasion comes second to that: "I think the primary job of the filmmaker is to entertain the audience . . . I don't want them to get there and have to listen to some polemic that they can get by reading a book or going to a political rally."[209] People rarely speak for themselves without Moore setting them up to make a point or get a laugh. When Moore cuts to himself opening an account in a Midwestern bank that is a licensed firearm dealer, with 500 guns in a vault, and is given the free gun offered to new customers, he utters a typically deadpan punch line to a scene that was cleverly edited to lampoon the process and end on a sardonic note: "Don't you think it is a little dangerous handing out guns in a bank?"[210] Who as a viewer, after all, would give up that hilarious satirical punch line for the sake of an even-handed and lengthier description of the bank's checking processes? In a script that throws laugh-out-loud animation, with gleeful panache, in amongst interviews with a pastiche of an odd range of people to comment—inclusive of the expert, the nutty, the marginal, the totally irrelevant, the entertaining and the risible—factual accuracy and nonperformative verisimilitude are the least of Moore's interests.

Roger Ebert calls Moore "the jolly populist rabble-rouser" whose confrontational set-ups are "brilliant theater,"[211] a description that matches what we see on screen with far more accuracy than the term "documentary-maker" as it is traditionally used. Moore's voiceover is a means to setting the theatrical scene:

It was the morning of April 20th, 1999 and it was pretty much like any other morning in America. The farmer did his chores, the milkman made his deliveries, the President bombed another country whose name we couldn't pronounce . . . and out in a little town in Colorado two boys went bowling at six in the morning. Yes, it was a typical day in the United States of America.

The bombing is a reference to a raid in the Kosovo war and its placement in a voiceover about the Columbine shooters, Eric Harris and Dylan Klebold, going bowling is gratuitous and unrelated in factual terms. However, it is central to Moore's creative satirical purpose and argument—that in American society gun violence and the American military-industrial complex are all the same problem. The mention of the bowling is, typically, factually untrue—Harris and Klebold did not show up for their bowling class that morning—but, for Moore, its factuality is irrelevant. Along with the other examples of people going about their daily business, it is there to make a comic case for the unexceptionality of violence and militarism in the fabric of American culture—that Americans go bowling and bomb other countries with equal routine. The film is not interested in linear logic substantiated by fact but in yoking together the macro and the micro view of violence in America to devastating satirical and polemical effect.

Nor, despite the title of the film, is the mockumentary interested in profiling the students who perpetrated the massacre at the high school. Harris and Klebold are absent subjects, and have no identity in the film beyond their membership in a white, suburban, middle-class group. The film has little interest in them beyond their role as a launching point for the polemics of Moore's argument. The documentary is framed by the events in Littleton, Colorado, rather than set there, despite the fact that Moore actually spends time in the town. Harris and Klebold are phantoms, only seen in the chilling, shadowy highlighted circle of the grey surveillance tapes of the attack at the school. If you compare this with Harris and Klebold's own words on the tapes they made, reflecting their desire for vengeance in response to teasing and denigration by their high school peers,[212] the lack of any real sense of who they are or why they did it in Moore's documentary appears stark.[213] If we compare Moore's approach to a *Time* article by Terry McCarthy on Andy Williams, a 15-year-old who killed two classmates and wounded 13 two years after Columbine in Santee, California, the lack of interest on Moore's part in the complexity of who Harris and Klebold were is even clearer. Terry McCarthy writes of Williams:

> His schoolmates bullied him. His mother rarely saw him. His father neglected him. Even his friends taunted him—and may well have goaded him into his shooting rampage.[214]

McCarthy attempts to make sense of the event by looking at Williams' family background, a bullying peer group, his drug abuse, his isolation, and his access to his father's gun. Perhaps the most insightful point is the reference to the notoriety Williams hoped to achieve, evident in his boasting to friends about planning his massacre, in a culture "where Columbine had become a legend."[215] While the easy availability of the gun to the teenage shooter is a part of the story, the account does not begin and end with that as it probes issues of bullying, adolescent resiliency, and the links between the cultures of families, schools, and the broader American society. Even when Moore takes two of the Columbine victims with bullets still in their bodies to confront hapless public relations employees at K-Mart over their sale of bullets to the Columbine shooters, Moore's inclusion of the victims reveals little of who they are beyond their performative and polemical use in the confrontation with K-Mart over its corporate policies.

Bowling for Columbine is not a documentary that encourages sociopsychological interest in why Harris and Klebold pulled the trigger because Moore has more simply framed questions:

> When the shooting was over Eric Harris and Dylan Klebold had killed 12 students and one teacher. Dozens of others were wounded by the over 900 rounds of ammo that were fired. It is believed that the guns used were all legally purchased at stores and gun shows and many of the bullets were bought at the Littleton K-Mart just down the street . . . In the end, they turned the guns on themselves.

The shooting happened and Moore focuses on: where are America's guns, where are they sold, and who has them? He does pose more complicated questions such as "Are we homicidal by nature?" for which he has no answers. He also has rhetorical questions that are there to get laughs such as "Should you have the right to have weapons grade plutonium?" asked of James Nichols. When it seems he might probe more deeply he veers off or chooses the tangential over documentary substance. Rather than interviewing students at Columbine about what it was like to go to school in Littleton, he interviews Matt Stone, one of the creators of the animated show *South Park*, who grew up there. Stone talks about his own feelings of being different and his desperation to get out of small town education but the personal anecdote, interesting as it might be for an insight into the sources of his own creativity, turns into a diatribe against educational conformity that warns students "you are going to die poor and lonely" and veers off the documentary subject. This adolescent sense of a doomed future inculcated by a system is not specifically linked to either Harris's or Klebold's experience. Moore admits his own lack of interest in that sort of specificity when discussing a shooting at Buell elementary school in Flint, Michigan: "No-one knew why the little boy wanted to shoot the little girl." He answers in generalities when trying to fathom Harris and Klebold's actions:

> I guess we'll never know why they did it but one thing adults should never forget; it still sucks being a teenager. And it really sucks going to school. And after Columbine, it really sucked being a student in America.

Against a montage of suspensions, metal detectors, fake guns, and overreactions to minor student behaviors, Moore uses the impressionistic generalities of the macro, seductively and persuasively edited, to reinforce Stone's experience of alienation. As a viewer, it is easy to forget that the documentary has made large leaps away from the individuality of Harris and Klebold's experience of high school.

It is the satirist's eye for the ridiculous in human and political behavior, driving skilful editing choices, that locks audience perception into a convincing polemic that "A country that's this out of control with fear shouldn't have all those guns and ammo lying about." Much of the satirical entertainment value and humor that propels Moore's argument comes from his own performance in the movie as an innocuous investigator setting up his corporate, celebrity, and individual targets who are oblivious to the role he casts them in—a role that depends on them appearing stereotypical and stupid. Dressed as a crusading, disheveled, working class Columbo in a baseball cap, Moore asks leading, deadpan questions of a mélange of people (some, as in the case of Canadian students truanting school, are not particularly relevant interviewees). There are times when the performance dominates to the point of pantomime and Moore becomes the only subject.[216] His sentimentalized placement of a picture of the little girl who was the victim of the Buell elementary shooting outside Charlton Heston's home, as he calls out to Heston's retreating back to look at the picture of the dead girl, is one example. Moore performs a mournful crusading, public shaming of Heston for a camera that focuses on Moore, as almost a parody of himself, laying the picture on the ground. He is unremitting in his satirization of interviewees who do not know they are the butt of the joke and he is badly off-target in the final scene of the film as he interviews Heston, whom Moore accosts in his own home. Moore succeeds in humiliating a clearly disoriented Heston but the humor and the attack backfires. The kind of shaky, elderly disorientation shown by Heston in the film's climax, in the context of Moore's pantomimed use of the picture, leaves the viewer feeling more sorry for Heston than willing to condemn him—which Moore was clearly not aiming for as an audience response.

This lack of satirical aim, a wobbliness of tone, threatens the panache holding the polemic together. It is this movement out of satire—as authenticity in the subject asserts itself against the grain of the overall satirical tone—that hints at a lack of creative control on Moore's part. There is an awkwardness of movement between satire and emotional resonance that stems from a failure to maintain a sense of convincing stereotyping. In the case of Heston, it can be unsettling to watch as Moore himself delivers the barbs. The viewer is easily lured into laughing but can be left feeling soiled as a participant in such a cheap shot. Oscoda, Michigan is described unchallenged as a place that "has a bad habit of raising psychos," in an interview with two students who went to the same school as Eric Harris, prior to his moving to Littleton. When Brent, one of the students, says he was kicked out of school for pulling a gun, Moore gets him to admit, in a rather nasty and disturbing bit of speculation, that he too could have been another Eric Harris. The problem is Brent does not come across as a "psycho" but more as an obliging interviewee, inarticulate and easily led. Moore showcases an interview with members of the Michigan militia, chillingly associating that culture with Timothy McVeigh and Terry Nichols, the Oklahoma bombers, and satirically with Militia Babe calendars, conspiracy gun nuts, and paranoia. Over shots of them training he deadpans: "I'm sure you guys are the kind of people that people like to have as their neighbor. If somebody's in need you're there to help them." However, an unacknowledged sense of them being well-intentioned, if misguided, emerges when members of the militia mention concerns about their families: "If you're not going to protect your family who is?"

The humor appears even more fatuous when, after Moore ridicules the sales pitch of a home security consultant by pantomiming looking around as if a rapist might still be in the area, the consultant breaks down:

Consultant:	Columbine did a couple of things. One is, it changed how we talk. That's the first thing.
Michael Moore:	How's that?
Consultant:	Well, for instance, if I say Columbine, everybody knows what it means. I don't have to explain to you that Columbine . . . (breaks down)
Michael Moore:	What's wrong?
Consultant:	Sometimes Columbine bothers me . . . I'll be fine . . . There's something overwhelming about that kind of viciousness, that kind of predatory action, that kind of indiscriminate killing.

Abruptly, Moore then cuts to a shot of Lockheed Martin, styled as the worlds largest weapons manufacturer, jumping to political commentary and the corporate target with no placement or recognition of the security consultant's moving attempt to deal with what happened in the town he lived in. Focused as he is on satirizing security paranoia, it feels like Moore got something he was not looking for when the consultant broke down or did not know how to acknowledge it in his polemic. The decision to leave it in the documentary appears an odd creative choice given that it jars with, and undermines, the easy satirical tone with which the scene started and undercuts the satiric stance of the film as a whole. It plays refreshingly like the surfacing of authentic emotion in a film that prefers satiric bite to make its points. Moore's barbs earlier in the scene do not seem so funny in retrospect. Pauline Kael, in a review of Moore's *Roger and Me*, points out that audience discomfort with some of the comedy relates to its coming at the expense of inoffensive and ordinary working class people.[217] Moore's own presentation of himself as coming from the working-class, gun-crazy culture of Flint, Michigan, "a cleverly constructed 'man of the people' persona,"[218] is a gesture to deflect any outsider patronization of those he interviews: "Yep, this was the kind of place I was from." However, it does not deflect a disturbing sense that many of his barbs are class-based and directed against people who are not educated enough to see them coming. When Moore oversteps the mark it feels like cynical exploitation: "Nothing convinces us so much of its authenticity as the giggles at another's expense."[219] The viewer is left feeling that laughing at these people says something unpleasant about one's own self-satisfied superiority. Moore's satirical sting backfires on the viewer.

Amazingly, even his successful pillorying of Lockheed Martin as the world's largest weapons maker and corporate mass destruction machine—transferring its "Pentagon payload" undercover of "night while the children of Columbine sleep"— is undermined by his own investigative performance. Evan McCollum, a public relations spokesperson, comes across as just doing his job and sympathetically thoughtful when he reminds Moore that 500 of their workers live in Littleton, many of whom had children who went to Columbine. Despite the disclaimer that he does not understand why Columbine happened, he persuasively states that because his company felt it was about the adolescent shooters being angry due to issues in their lives, Lockheed Martin had donated $100,000 dollars to anger-management classes for schools in Jefferson county—to help students to learn alternative ways to deal with their anger. Moore is so busy targeting Lockheed, he appears unaware of the utility of that gesture. Instead he absurdly,[220] but with breathtaking satiric chutzpah, counters:

So you don't think our kids say to themselves, "Well, gee, you know, Dad goes off to the factory every day, you know. He built missiles. Ah, these are weapons of mass destruction. What's the difference between that mass destruction and the mass destruction at Columbine High School?

Unaware he is about to be made to look an idiot, McCollum confidently asserts an untenable difference: "We don't get irritated with somebody and just 'cause we're mad at 'em drop a bomb, or shoot 'em, or fire a missile at 'em." He gives Moore a clever editing segue into a superbly damning indictment of arrogant American foreign policy fiascos from 1953 up to the September 11 attacks on the WTC where they did precisely that (in a montage to the soundtrack of the song *It's a Wonderful World*). The montage ends on the tragic irony of "Osama Bin Laden uses his expert CIA training to murder 3000 people." Lockheed's anger management idea sounds sensible, Moore's question sounds ridiculous, though Moore's keen eye for satire leaves behind the flaws.

The segment with McCollum is illustrative of Moore's strengths and weakness as a polemicist. Moore cuts effectively to alert the audience to the satirical and ironic point he is about to make. However, his own investigative performance on screen is an often-blunt instrument that does not always serve his polemical or entertainment purposes well. The satirical tone, at times, sits oddly with lapses back into more staid traditional documentary modes, as in a subdued interview with Arthur Busch, the county prosecutor in Flint, Michigan. Busch offers a nonsatirical, thoughtful analysis of the way the public is entertained by the "crime of the day," on the way race is misused for scaremongering about crime, and how alienation in white suburbia is linked to crime in his community. Despite the fact that Moore includes an hysterically funny animation of the history of white racist, nonsensical fears leading to Americans being armed to the teeth, it is the prosecutor's words, tinged with a concerned, world-weary experience that leave a more lingering impression as having tapped into something authentic about public fear and gun purchase. In the context of the interview, the animation appears superficial.

Peter Hartcher, commenting on *Fahrenheit 9/11*, describes Moore's documentary method as a form of "grey propaganda" diatribe:

> He starts with accurate information that he then wraps in innuendo and whispers of conspiracy to extend a limited molehill of fact into a mountain of suspicion. With a shrewd use of humour, sarcasm and stunt, he builds a powerful effect ... Moore is not interested in the documentary form—he is waging a campaign.[221]

For Hartcher, Moore's place in the political discourse through *Fahrenheit 9/11* is as a promoter of public discussion of issues to moviegoers. The same could be said of the place of *Bowling for Columbine* in the discourse on gun control and violence. There is value in a satirical argument above and beyond its level of journalistic accuracy, logic, factual connections, and lapses in documentary rigor. Moore entertainingly raises issues about violence in American society for discussion in the mass public arena. If playing fast and loose with editing is taken beyond the ethical limits of creativity into fakery, alleging personal and institutional idiocy is still a provocative way of stirring up needed political and cultural debate. A U.K. documentary-maker (who acknowledges the use of similar techniques to Moore), Jon Ronson, describes Moore as "Chomsky with gags." He feels Moore is at his most compelling when he is "a brilliant collagist of both kitsch archive and liberal polemics" adding, however, that the "faux-naïf thing" can be annoying.[222] Of more concern to the viewer is Moore's periodic lack of directorial control over the hybridity he is in the process of creating. Here and there amongst the gags, the set-ups, and the questionable editing cuts is a more serious and moving documentary trying to get out from under the provocative and entertaining satirical glibness.

Unsettled audience and critical concerns about editing sleight of hand in *Bowling for Columbine* reflect the fact that it is an example from a documentary genre that is more than ever in a fluxing relationship with authenticity. It is not possible to resolve those concerns, that tension between text and authenticity, out of the context of audience reception. Vivian Sobchack, in her discussion of Jean-Pierre Meunier's phenomenology of perception points out that "a 'documentary' is not a thing, but a subjective relationship to a cinematic object."[223] It is the spectator who will subjectively decide how to engage with the cinematic experience irrespective of its fictional or nonfictional approach in soliciting viewer interest because

> a fiction can be experienced as a home movie or documentary, a documentary as a home movie or fiction, a home movie as a documentary or fiction. Existential knowledge and forms of attention structure cinematic identification with—and of—the cinematic object.[224]

Viewing nonfiction, as much as the fictional, still relies on audience affective response for the decision on what feels or seems "real." It is not simply about what the camera shows. "The core of the matter is not the picture, but the human being who looks at this tiny bit of data and says, "Yes, that's Aunt Mary,"[225] or, no, it is not the Aunt Mary I know. These are "volitional acts of perception: active, reflective, and judgmental."[226] If a nonfictional account is engaged with by an audience as a representation of authentic reality, such a response is not totally dependant on opinionated manipulation but, rather, on a processing partnership with authorial manipulation:

> In a documentary of behaviour, I often include in an early scene a shot of the documentary crew at work. It serves as a reminder to the audience that what they are seeing occurred in front of a camera, and that they should keep that in mind in evaluating the behaviour they see.[227]

Hampe stresses that the visual evidence is what is recorded on film while the documentary-maker is present and it is the editing of that which makes the documentary statement: "It's the documentary you show, not the footage you shot, that counts."[228] Distinguishing it from news he argues that, for the documentary-maker, it is the visual evidence that supports the argument that needs to be there: "The only real test is whether the images can stand on their own and *argue the case themselves*" (my italics).[229] He is a practitioner who sees himself as a participant in a process that follows an idea through to the audience and accumulates the behavioral visual evidence to make a point. The verisimilitude of the image comes from the appearance of truth in support of an authorial point of view. For Hampe, documenting is not the same as recording but the presentation of what the documentarian believes the experience to be. The same can be said of the other side of the partnership. What is represented is also what the viewer believes it to be.

Hampe's practitioner point of view raises the possibility of a space that is neither simply authentic nor false but argumentative and inclusive of both: a textual space that is creatively manipulated to develop the trust on which viewer belief is dependent, and which can partake of the possibilities of both fiction and nonfiction to polemicize. Thus, it can be virtually "true" but interpreted as false or poorly argued; or virtually "false" yet resonate as believable and convincingly argued. Useful in this context is Renov's concept of a conditional self constructed by an act of confessional in front of a camera. As Renov comments on Claude Lanzmann's *Shoah*, from a psychoanalytic point of view, the camera is "incitant to confession." It is "speech *for the camera*, for an apparatus capable of preserving, amplifying, and circulating . . . testimony" in the service of personal and public ritual.[230] Thus the self engaged in the confession is not necessarily the totality of the self outside the screen, but may be authentic to the documentary purpose or the moment of confession. Perhaps, even in moments of reality TV.[231]

However, Renov's argument for the utopian achievements of first person video confessionals, "in which the media facilitate understanding across the gaps of human difference rather than simply capitalizing on those differences in a rush to spectacle" does not entirely discard what he views as the media-specific limitations to its text-specific authenticity.[232] In the case of *Bowling for Columbine*, Moore's editing beats actual events into polemical submission with a satiric hammer that is entertaining but leaves the viewer willing to look a little more carefully with the disquieting sense that to live in "fictitious times" requires receptive vigilance on the part of the viewer toward all texts, inclusive of Moore's own polemic. Viewing Moore's work leaves you with a troubling sense of unease about the license that authorship of polemic seems to take when manipulating fact. Straddling fact and fiction through polemic is a grey area of authorial responsibility whether one starts out, as Moore does, on the documentary side or whether one leaps into fiction based on a true story, which will be discussed further in the next chapter. The problem with Moore's editorial sleight of hand is that it is a slippery slope and opens the door to a kind of "ends justifies the means" approach to polemic and to filmmaking in general. Insightfully using the term "faction" to describe the history of Hollywood storytelling based on historical facts about which there is some form of consensus as to factual validity (such as the fact that Heston gave two separate speeches and not one), Bruce Crowther highlights the kind of vigilance that is required when critiquing both representation and audience reception. As he notes when discussing audience reception of racism in D. W. Griffith's epic on the American Civil War and Reconstruction, *Birth of a Nation*:

> For the majority, the film was taken as gospel. It was seen as true not because it delivered the facts but because it showed the people what they wanted to believe and confirmed the nation's mistaken understanding of its own past.[233]

The allure of the voiceover of conviction in the polemical argument can be as dangerously seductive to the author as it is to the viewer or reader.

Norma Khouri and the Hoax as Reader Seduction

In the face of commodification, Renov's lingering doubts undoubtedly reflect a public and critical debate that has "resulted in simulation-anxiety and a felt need to reassert the existence of the 'real' as an accessible domain of experience."[234] The satire in *Series 7* and criticism of Moore's editing, for example, would seem to argue such a case. However, fan enthusiasm for such fetishization of reality would also argue that audiences have a more inclusive acceptance of the mixing of the fake and the authentic and are less anxious about where the boundaries are that separate them. However, tolerance and enjoyment of the attractions of the well-constructed hoax, as the quote heading this chapter puts it, certainly runs the risk of audiences finding themselves seduced in ways they regret. The aesthetic of activist polemic, allied with the subversive impulse at the core of the rhetoric against violence—including the violence done to authenticity as fact, truth, reality, or the less contentiously defined, point of view—can itself be subverted by authorial self-indulgence. The polemicist seeking to utilize cultural and political prejudices to expand on an initially legitimate case against violence, for example, runs the risk of destroying any authenticity in the narrative. A case in point is the public debate in 2004 over Norma Khouri's hoaxing of her Australian and international readers. The controversy is a contemporary illustration of the cultural belief in an indexical authenticity that is at odds with the acceptance of fakery. Her fraudulently nonfiction book, *Forbidden Love: A Harrowing True Story of Love and Revenge in Jordan*, was published as a factual memoir of her Moslem friend Dalia's murder at the hands of her family for falling in love with a non-Moslem man, Michael. Khouri narrates as a purported witness to the events, while offering their story as an example of the ideological, political, and cultural support of honor killing in Jordan and the wider Middle East. It led to bestseller author status and critical acclaim in Australia and overseas for Khouri in appreciation of her literary and personal activism as she toured the literary festival circuit and media outlets to promote her book and its cause.[235]

In 2004, Malcolm Knox, an investigative reporter for *The Sydney Morning Herald*, disclosed that her book was not an authentic, personal revelation but a hoax (just prior to the publication by Random House of a sequel): "Her tragic story stole readers' hearts . . . but Norma Khouri is a fake, and so is *Forbidden Love*."[236] Her book and cause had struck an affective political response in the Australian literary and reading public. As a result, a postmodern habitude with media manipulation did not, in the case of her book, preclude a publicly displayed sense of betrayal felt by her publisher, readers, friends, and critics. Unlike the "savvy" fans in Andrejevic's study, they were not *in* on the hoax. A similar controversy in the United States over the memoirs of a drug addict, James Frey's *A Million Little Pieces*, has led to similar excoriation for the author. This book initially received the support of Oprah Winfrey, who had chosen it for her Book Club.[237] This endorsement was subsequently withdrawn during an interview with the author on her television show, where the audience booed him. In defending the publishers, Doubleday, against Frey's claim that the publishers manipulated the factuality of his text,[238] the editor-in-chief of the book, Nan Talese, reveals the shifting sands on which the publishing definition of the merging of fact and fiction in memoir when editing takes place:

A memoir is different from an autobiography. A memoir is an author's remembrance of a certain period in his life. Now, the responsibility, as far as I am concerned is: does it strike me as valid? I mean, I'm sent things all the time and I think they're not real. I don't think they're authentic. I don't think they're good. I don't believe them. In this instance, I absolutely believed what I read.[239]

Validity and authenticity for Talese, as an editor, is as much about believability as an outcome of writing as it is about factuality. From that point of view, facts alone are not enough to create authenticity for the reader.

While Moore's polemic can be intermittently unsubtle, Khouri's desire to polemicize against honor killing illustrates the polemicist against violence descending into totalization. Most notably, her book portrays all Arab women as having no identity beyond victimhood. Arab women living in Islamic cultures are all portrayed as trapped, passive, and pathetically manipulative:

Although we didn't see it at the time, we were already using one of the few powers Jordanian women have: to bend their intelligence and imagination to plotting and planning to outwit men to get what they wanted.[240]

Arab mothers are all portrayed as complicit in their daughters' subjugation:

> Our mothers, like *all mothers of daughters*, did their job by training us to live
> in an unsympathetic, protected, male dominated world. *I'm certain no woman
> raised in Jordan* escaped her childhood and young adulthood without hearing
> things like: "A woman's honour, once ruined, can never be repaired" (My
> italics).[241]

There are no women in Khouri's book taking pride in any aspect of Arab culture
and they are, invariably, portrayed as incapable of assertiveness:

> Her small, emerald-green eyes were also marked by time. Whatever fires they
> had contained had burned out years ago, leaving them gloomy and dim.[242]

Added to that description of Khouri's mother's hopelessness is her emotional
unavailability to her children ("She maintained an emotional distance as a form of
self-preservation"[243]), which is linked to yearning for a different way of life ("There
were days I would catch her sitting alone . . . as if picturing herself in another life"[244]).
Legitimate, if predictable, targets of discrimination, such as housework—"Dalia
normally had to help her mother tidy the bedrooms and do the laundry as the men
ate their food"[245]—are also the symptoms for what Khouri perceives as a physical,
emotional, and spiritual illness that no woman in the book seems to be able to
emerge from with any nondowntrodden sense of self intact except, partially, Dalia
and Khouri. Khouri's hero, Michael, Dalia's lover, describes his own mother in that
motif of the downtrodden Arab woman:

> She isn't physically ill, or at least no one had diagnosed her illness. I think
> my father's tyranny has worn her down over the years. He's a very stern and
> controlling man. He spent most of his life in the armed forces and treats my
> mother like one of his recruits, always yelling at her and cutting her down. The
> whole thing makes me so angry. I wish I could get her away from him. Oh let's
> talk about something else; this is too depressing. Obviously, I don't come from
> a model family, but then who does.[246]

The description of Michael's father as cruel, controlling, and abusive, on its own
legitimately targets the chauvinism of one man. However, Khouri's unremitting
belief that there is no Arab family in Jordan untouched by such cruelty cumula-
tively becomes a picture of that culture as having no semblance of family life because
of Arab male chauvinism. She unrelentingly portrays Arab fathers, mothers, and
siblings alike as incapable of maintaining basic familial and emotional bonds with
one another.

With the exception of Michael the book, without qualification, vilifies the Arab male. Dalia's brother, who is assigned to guard the two young women in their unisex hairdressing business is characterized as a jailer: "not only our watchdog, he was our fathers' hired, loyal informant."[247] The only character distinction amongst her brothers as a group being one of degrees of cruelty. Rafiz is "one of the most cruel and argumentative young men I've ever known"[248] and her brother Nasar "was an older and, if possible, nastier version of Rafiq."[249] Michael, the doomed lover and exception to Arab chauvinism whom Dalia falls in love with, describes his family as a litany of oppressive marriages that only his sister, Jehan, has escaped because of her "continuing her studies so my father doesn't force her into an arranged marriage, as he did my other sisters."[250] One sister has a " husband whose OK . . . it's just that he wasn't her choice and she's not in love with him,"[251] and who will not let her work, though she has a nursing degree. Another sister, Miriam, at 23 is prevented from becoming an English professor and made to marry a 46-year-old man. Khouri jokingly suggests to Michael that he could set her up with one of his brothers but they, too, are dictatorial:

> Oh you don't want to get involved with them. Jerius is younger than me . . . He has two young sons, and sometimes I really think that he's trying to raise them to be the next Arab Hitlers . . . It's a pity, really, because his wife Samia is so gentle, quiet, and kind. She never smiles, though.[252]

Even more disturbingly, the individual "Arab Hitlers" forming the collective of Arab men in the book, in Khouri's eyes, typify all Arab men—as in this description of a brother of Michael's who becomes the template for the indictment of an entire culture:

> He's twenty-five, and the picture of male beauty—but that's where his perfection ends. I hate to say it, but he's very shallow, vain, and arrogant—everything you wouldn't want to spend the rest of your life with. He's a typical young Arab man, financially successful and expects everyone to treat him as if he's a god. I think he might actually try to force his wife to give up her religion and worship him.[253]

Khouri's father is described as capable of standing by while she is killed if she were to require it:

> My father, though more threatening in size, would probably be the least physically explosive of all my family members . . . he would be the driving force behind my brothers' violence.[254]

No Arab man in the whole country is capable of any other form of conduct as Khouri denigrates an entire male population in one fell swoop to claim "All the feelings I'd controlled so that I could be strong for us both against an enemy whose allies were every Arab man in Jordan, surfaced."[255] Her disgust as character, narrator, and author towards the Arab male is physical: "The thought of being married to an Arab man turned my stomach."[256] Norma's four brothers also become the emblem for "All Arab men":

> All Arab men are taught that it is their responsibility to discipline the women
> in their lives, and that the best way to do so is through corporal punishment.
> My brothers were no exception . . . I didn't doubt for a second that they would
> react violently over more serious matters, such as relationships.[257]

At no time is the book able to step outside this global framework in its characterization of Arab men as cruel or Arab women as downtrodden, spiritless, and defeated.

Racial stereotyping is maintained easily in the context of the equally stereotypical Middle Eastern image of the hero and heroine in the book, the doomed lovers Michael and Dalia. Reader desensitization to the generalization of the latter supports reader acceptance of the political and cultural accuracy of the former. Michael has "[b]road shoulders, thick, short, dark brown hair, black eyes—an image was coming."[258] The unintended irony of that "image was coming" is also an apt description of the generalized darkly beautiful and exotic Dalia who is straight out of stereotypes of the romanticized Other. As Kate Legge notes, "Cut loose from its claim to authenticity, *Forbidden Love* is Mills and Boon in a chador."[259]

> *Ya gazallae* is slang for especially attractive women—those with the melting
> eyes of a baby deer, like Bambi. Dalia definitely fitted into that category. She
> had waist-length, thick, wavy tresses, perfect light olive skin, and full lips.
> Most of all, she had these mesmerizing dark brown eyes. Nature had put her
> only roundness in the proper places.[260]

The cartoon image of "Bambi" is used as a stereotype for doe-eyed and there is little individual detail in the description of the heroine beyond the "wavy-tressed" pointer to an Arabian Nights Orientalism standing for Middle Eastern ethnicity. Racial profiling of beauty is the counterpoint to the racial profiling of threat and violence.

Apart from his Mills and Boon good looks, Michael is portrayed as distinguished from all other Arab men in the book exclusively by his Western experiences and education. He is described as schooled in London, able to speak European languages, and as having traveled in Europe. Khouri evangelically equates Western experiences with freedom and all that is culturally good:

> He's told me about all the different things he's seen and he says that he'd love to show them to me. Apparently we'd be free in those countries and wouldn't have to sneak around to see each other. I would be able to do what I want. Doesn't that sound like heaven?[261]

It is Michael's westernized masculinity that galvanizes both Dalia and Khouri to action: "I could feel our dreams, our stifled rebelliousness, being fanned into fire by his optimism and strength."[262] This idealized preference for Western over Middle Eastern education, and thus Western cultural values, easily segues into an often-hysterical tirade against the Islamic religion. Khouri's main discomfort with Islam, outside of her perception of its cruelty and chauvinism, is its all encompassing ordering of a believer's life which she excoriates as a "treacherous religious land-scape" because of "all of these regulations and customs"[263] and of "the laws that dictate the shape of every moment of every day of the ordinary lives of people like Dalia and me."[264] Khouri's distaste for non-Western culture is palpable and independent of any assessment of what might be positive or negative in the ways it might seek to operate for believers as a guide to life.

It is the act of regulation itself, for which she allows no possibility of freely accepting as an act of faith, which is a manifesto for political domination, even when it applies to men:

> Both sexes are bound by the thousands of rules that carpet Jordan and the Middle East with a dense tapestry of overlapping and interwoven layers of Muslim, Arab, Christian and Jewish codes and traditions, all of it dominated by the pervasive power of the Koran, Islam's holy book and manifesto.[265]

Her distaste for Middle Eastern "codes and traditions" leads her to single out the Koran as a source of violence and oppression to be feared:

> Violence is embodied in our laws, and in our history. It applies to warriors in battle, to perceived enemies of Islam, to Moslems who try to escape the faith, and, above all, it applies to women.[266]

Her political polemic shifts with unsettling ease from her target of honour killings to an indictment of Islam as, at its core, a violent religion and to sweeping, unsubstantiated, generalizations about the Middle Eastern culture from which it springs:

> We can lay the violence that has been part of the Islamic culture for nearly fourteen hundred years at the feet of another Mohammed. From the time

Mohammed's followers took Mecca by force, the story of Islam has been filled with wars and bloody battles. I've never found it surprising that a religion founded by vicious warriors, and scarred by centuries of bloodshed, contains such endorsements of violence, and then wraps it in the dignity of 'honour'— and the law—without qualm. It is safe to say, I believe, that Islam is a totalitarian regime operating under the guise of a religion. The Koran is its manifesto, claimed by Islam to provide guidance for all that is needed for a person's spiritual and physical well-being. It tells Muslims when and how to have sex and when and how to refrain from it, what to possess and what to give away, when to sleep and when to wake, when to speak up and when to remain silent, what and how to eat, to dress, and how to seek knowledge. It shows Muslims how to deal with the world around them; outlines the responsibilities of a person to himself, to his parents, siblings, offspring, spouses, neighbours, society, and nation; details what habits to cultivate and what to avoid. In short, Islam contains laws and restrictions covering every aspect of life, controlling you from birth to death. And, if born Muslim, there is no escape.[267]

To Khouri, Islam, religion and culture, regulation and law, even "guidance" for "spiritual and physical well-being" is totalitarian violence. Being born Muslim is represented as imprisonment and subjugation to vicious violence. The book unremittingly portrays Bedouin traditions, Jordan society, Arab culture, and Islam as unredeemably violent and morally bereft and portrays that culture as rooted in the timeless ancient desert secrets of Bedouin history:

For buried deep within the history of Jordan was a secret way of life, with its source in the nomadic Bedouins, the desert dwellers. Though they make up less than one per cent of the Jordanian population, they and their views dominate the country.[268]

When reading the above quote from the book's beginning, after the tirade of cultural abuse that follows, one is startlingly aware of how seductively that "secret" insinuates and arouses reader unease and suspicion, and lays the groundwork for the excoriation of an entire culture and ethnic group that follows in the book.

Gillian Whitlock offers by way of explanation that Australian readers were enamored of generic views of human rights oppression of women in unfamiliar countries—couched in the testimonial rhetoric of victimhood and designed to appeal to Western readers—and, as a result, were unquestioning in their reception of the book.[269] Disturbingly, a readership enamored of the book's passionate clarion call against an unquestionably horrific practice did not detect the author's blatant reliance on racism to shore up her political stance. Even with the revelation of the hoax Khouri perpetrated, the racism of the book continued to go unnoticed. While critiquing the dominant beliefs of Arab culture (or what she portrayed them to be), she wrote in tandem with the unacknowledged prejudices of her readers and reviewers. Such readers failed to recognize what the popularity of a stridently anti-Islamic and anti-Arab book revealed about an Australian literary culture that, in its enthusiasm to support a protest against the practice of honor killing, was willing to overlook the book's questionable views of Middle Eastern culture and ethnicity.[270]

There is no doubt that the general failure to question the book's explicit racism at the time of its bestseller popularity, or during the revelation of the hoax, had everything to do with its publication post September 11. It is with a confidence in the prejudices of her readers that Khouri has no problem exploiting that specter as a part of her cultural indictment:

> It is only now, looking back six years from the beginning of our dangerous adventure—years of experiencing freedom, traveling across oceans, continents and culture—that I can see that our actions would be incomprehensible to women of any liberated culture. As incomprehensible as the violent acts against non-Muslims, non-Arabs, that, since 11 September, have made the Western world suddenly hungry to understand this alien place.[271]

To be Arab is to be "alien," threateningly Other and to be feared. Khouri's admirable desire to polemicize against the honor killing of women in the Middle East and against the political, religious, legal, and cultural institutionalization and acceptance of it is not problematic simply because it is a hoax. Even as a hoax, and thus fiction, it could have had valid points to make if any publisher was willing to repackage it as such. What is far more disturbing is that it was accepted as a legitimate view of Islam and Arab culture despite its being a blatant rant against the ethnicity of being Moslem and Arab. As Ihab Shalbak points out, "Norma Khouri exploited prejudice about Arabs for an audience ready to believe her," using Western clichés about Orientalism and "confirming the audience's preconceptions, rather than enlightening them about the real suffering of Arab women."[272] Australian readers were less hoaxed by the fraudulent representation of Khouri's story as factual than they were by the stirrings of a latent cultural racism and fear of difference that allowed the book to be read unthinkingly.

Documenting lived experiences of violence invariably goes with a desire to polemicize in a text against its causes. In this context, the diversions of narrative argument can create a slippery relationship between lived experience and authenticity in text. It is not just definitions of reality that are in question, so are definitions of forms of mediation and fakery. Susan Sontag's statement about images of war: "The understanding of war among people who have not experienced war is now chiefly a product of the impact of . . . images"[273] is not true for other forms of violence. It is rare for anyone to get through life without witnessing or experiencing violence in some form, whether it is a parental slap, bullying at work, road rage, or a fight on the playground, at the pub, or on the street. As a result, experiential knowledge is a companion to discursive fear and anger about violence that drives narrative. That anger and fear opens the door to faking it, to manipulating text in ethically unsettling ways, for polemic's sake. At the same time, convincing polemic that draws on collective lived experience of violence makes fakery itself feel fissured, so that one cannot entirely jettison the tantalizing sense that something authentic about lived experience is being said, even at the heart of the fake. As Nichols notes, "The challenge is to untrack narrative without destroying it."[274] Analysis of such hybrid texts needs to evoke that strange, complex, and precarious interaction between the authentic and the fake which nonfiction polemical texts about violence embody. The role of fakery in the mediation of experience when polemicizing about violence is more complex than the simple quantification of a degree of fakery as the point of analysis. The function of "faking" aspects of actuality in nonfiction narratives about violence is, rather, related to audience enjoyment of some forms of manipulation, to shifting audience expectations of documentary genres and to the pressures placed on text by a polemical stance against the consequences of violence.[275]

Such cultural capitulation to the representational manipulation of authenticity in a text requires new definitions about the boundaries between nonfictional and fictional violence. All three texts considered in this chapter reveal a postmodern culture equally at home with, and unnerved by, the manipulation of authentic experience in text. Analysis reveals the necessity of placing them on a continuum of authenticity as violent texts on a case-by-case basis, rather than through genre or any other blanket categorization. Claims to representational "reality" require the viewer to be skeptical because it may be true, as Dawn says to her audience in *Series 7* that "we have a hostage situation here." Virtually speaking, remaining "savvy" about the scripted aspects of documentary forms frees the audience to indulge itself in being entertained. As Dawn also suggests to her audience captives: "If everybody just sits down and chills out, nobody's gonna get hurt." The trick is not to "chill out" so much that, as in the case of *Forbidden Love*, we end up not reading the text that is there. In the end, it may be that greater violence is done to the perception of authenticity by what we bring to perception, by the viewfinder of our own prejudices, than by the text we have before us. Inevitably, the documentation of "reality" is a grey area on the continuum. Perhaps, being often unsure about the exact boundary between authenticity and fakery is, finally, of less interest than what the texts, on their own terms, have to say.

In *Capturing the Friedmans*, a documentary that uses home videos to explore its subject—the family's disintegration under a father's and son's arrest and trial for child sexual abuse—the youngest son Jesse, who was wrongly convicted, poignantly describes how, even at the heart of the most reprehensible violent act, there is more than one kind of "real":

> I still feel like I knew my father very well. I don't think that just because there were things in his life that were private and secret and shameful that that means that the father who I knew and the things I knew about him were in any way not real.[276]

To respond to text is to live with a degree of uncertainty about authenticity and about the interaction of text with its subject: "Like when your parents take a picture of you, do you remember being there or do you remember just the photograph being on the wall?" As that line from *Capturing the Friedmans* suggests, the viewer's relationship with a text, even one that represents one's own lived experience, is fundamentally personal and made suspect by memory. A text that polemicizes about lived experience, violent or otherwise, simply increases that fundamental uncertainty and, eschewing responsibility, leaves the decisions about authenticity and fakery up to the reader or viewer. As Norma Khouri's book has proved, sometimes readers and audiences can be fooled.

3

"It Is a True Story but It Might Not Have Happened":[277] Voyeurism and Fiction in the True Crime Narrative

You should understand that I would not think of writing your *story. It would be* my *story. Just as* The Onion Field *was* my *story and* In Cold Blood *was Capote's story.*

(*Joseph Wambaugh* [278])

"I did it!" insists a frustrated Lawrie Nam. "But no one will believe me." [279]

While audiences have a love/hate relationship with ambiguous authenticity, that relationship is still subject to a degree of categorical signposting about actuality, even if it is perfunctory or illusory in its effect. Public annoyance with Khouri's fraudulent narrative was the result of the publisher's miscategorizing the book as nonfiction and readers finding that the claim that it was a true story proved to be an unreliable form of signposting for her readers. When distinguishing between nonfiction and fiction, as Noël Carroll puts it, viewers and readers rely on categories that are "indexed" and have expectations accordingly.[280] The impact on narrative of the claim that a text is "based on a true story" will be examined in this chapter through popular culture's fascination with the True Crime genre, the popular longevity of which proves that "truth" about murder is profitable and forms a central part of what has been called "the popular discourse of the dangerous individual."[281]

True Crime narrative sits at a transitional point on the continuum of textual authenticity where the extratextual actuality of violence becomes a mélange of nonfiction and fiction about murder. The claim that a text is "based on a true story," even when not a hoax, remains difficult to deconstruct for its links with an authentic actuality undiluted by fiction:

Claims to authenticity remain strong grounds of contestation, suggesting that authenticity is a desired attribute. Crime programs "based on a *true* story," films "based on a *real* case" or "our correspondent reports *now from the scene*" compete for an illusion of veracity which is by implication denied to other "stories."[282]

The source of that contention stems from what David A. Black has termed the forensics of audience reception of a text. He describes such reception as an "obsession with plausibility." An obsession that is evident in audience concerns with whether something, even in a fictional text, "would have happened," in "assertions that a character would not have done that"[283] and in "protests against lapses in continuity and psychological motivation; and more narrowly targeted complaints about a film's historical or biographical inaccuracy."[284] The effect created by "basing" narrative on a true event undoubtedly leaves what is "true" loosely defined, encompassing the nonfictional merging into fictional representations using actual events as a kind of plot launching point. The textual act of "basing" implies that the narrative connective ties to actual events are selectively chosen. True Crime narratives are generally inspired by headlines, which reflect press and popular obsession with the violent events they describe and the show trials that accompany them. True Crime texts reveal as much about an audience enamored with the promise of insight into something archetypally "true" about evil as a part of the human condition as they do about the individual nature of what causes someone to commit the violent crimes that are the genre's subject. It is a promise that is inevitably compromised by the textual commodification of murder in which perpetrators, the justice system and, occasionally, even the victim's relatives all participate.

In their entertaining exposé of the fraught relationship between fact and fantasy in Hollywood, *Based on a True Story: Fact and Fantasy in 100 Movies*, Jonathan Vankin and John Whalen chronicle the "informal lexicon" and "the flexible yardstick" by which producers of the true story genre (and presumably audiences) can "gauge its fidelity to reality."[285] The three categories of "based on a true story," "based on real events," and "inspired by actual events" form a decreasingly less stringent scale of adaptation until the last as Vankin and Whalen wittily assert, "is not so much an assertion as it is a disclaimer."[286] The controversy over the director Stephen Spielberg's *Munich*[287]—which asserts in its introduction that it is "inspired by real events" that occurred after the Palestinian Black September terrorist group massacred 11 Israeli athletes at the Munich Olympics in 1972—highlights aspects of audience rejection that can result from such loosely defined categorization. The film's portrayal of the Mossad operation to assassinate the terrorists who carried out the attack has received extensive criticism from the Israeli intelligence community for factual inaccuracies. The film was described as fantasy, fiction, "history Hollywood style," and "more Indiana Jones than any semblance of reality."[288] The use of the word "inspired" (even bearing in mind that what that means exactly is debatable) clearly signals a creative decision to use the actual for other narrative purposes than veracity. The fact that the script was based on a book whose factuality was also questioned when it was first published further complicates the chain of indexicality extending from the actual events to screen representation.[289] Behind such a negative reception lies the resentment of historical distortion evident in Spielberg's paradoxical designation of his film as "historical fiction."[290] Criticisms in a similar tone have been made of the True Crime genre by practitioners who see their work as aligned more with investigative journalism than with the tabloid side of the genre. As David Schmid reveals in his history of the genre, *Natural Born Celebrities: Serial Killers in American Culture*, that debate, while being an extension of the authorial desire for literary respectability, led to an emphasis on research and the social or criminological value of the genre's investigative conclusions and attempts to downplay elements of sensationalism.[291]

Sensationalism

The True Crime genre is characterized by a long history of sensationalism and a frantic commercial opportunism ready to feed popular interest in murder. More often than not, it is that urge to sensationalize, which Schmid notes is essentially Gothic, that is seen to be the genre's downfall. Rebecca Gowers in *The Swamp of Death: A True Tale of Victorian Lies and Murder*,[292] gives a lively historical account of an 1890 backwoods murder of a young Englishman, Frederick Benwell, in Woodstock, Canada—which mesmerized popular interest in that country and England. She describes the public gratification found in the high excitement and entertainment provided by press coverage of the murder and the investigation and the performance of the trial of Reginald Birchall and his execution. Such popular indulgence in news and pulp narratives about murder has long been typical of the genre's feeding of an obsessive public interest. Live coverage of the O. J. Simpson trial and Court TV[293] appear to be merely a recent incarnation of a far earlier commercialization in Victorian live media coverage—such as the telegraph and telephone connections used in the Birchall case in Gowers' book.[294] In response to this public fascination, she discusses how a True Crime writer of the day, John Arthur Fraser, wrote his heavily fictionalized, pulp version of the events prior to the trial even beginning, with two possible endings at hand. He was hoping for the far more dramatically satisfying guilty verdict, which would avert a "narrative crisis,"[295] if his preferred plot outcome of a guilty verdict did not eventuate. Narrative closure in a story about sensationalized evil depends on a public desire for retribution, and for Fraser, that meant a guilty verdict and an execution.

In post-Victorian popular culture there is still a broad tolerance for dramatizing the facts of a crime in recreated scenes and character conversations to drive the plot of True Crime narrative and there is the same competitive drive amongst publishers for topicality. Press and television coverage in Australia of the nine-week trial and conviction of Bradley John Murdoch in 2005–06 for the murder of British backpacker Peter Falconio in the Northern Territory, for example, was accompanied by the "rush to cash in" by no less than five authors completing their last chapters on the case as the verdict was announced so that the books could be on sale within days of sentencing.[296] Titles of the books such as Richard Shears *Bloodstain: The Vanishing of Peter Falconio*, Roger Maynard's *Where's Pete?: Unravelling the Falconio Mystery*, and Sue Williams' *And Then the Darkness*, all proclaim both the fascination with bloody detail offered by any murder story and a promise of the explication of a mystery which accompanies what is still unknown about motive and the act itself. In the Falconio murder, much of this mystery surrounds the fact that his body has not been found.[297] As with any good fictional murder mystery, the popularity of the True Crime genre is powered on the investigative level by the attractions of solving the crime, particularly when there may be unanswered forensic questions. The recent resurfacing of public interest in one of Australia's longest running unsolved murder mysteries, The Bogle-Chandler deaths in 1963, is a case in point. Revelations of a possible forensic solution to these deaths on current affairs television on *Four Corners*[298] led to a flurry of press coverage the following day. In a colorful turn of phrase, the television critic Ruth Richie captures the allure of such a long-running unsolved scenario when she describes the viewer being "sucked into the ultimate cold case vortex."[299] In the opening line to his article on the revelations, the reporter Malcolm Brown invokes the idea of the public imagination being in the thrall of mystery when murders go unsolved when he asks, "Could the Bogle-Chandler mystery, which has haunted the public imagination since New Year's Eve 1963, come down to a question of rotten eggs?"[300] Unsolved murder is seen as a source of viewer imaginative angst.

The Birchall trial in Gowers' book was held in a Town Hall that doubled as a rural theatre (an appropriate choice of venue given much of the circus atmosphere that accompanied the trial). Press coverage embroidered the facts and provided "a clear example of the sinister influence of fiction on the way the case struck its original audience."[301] Gowers' account captures the messy origins of popular interest in the True Crime genre where the audience wants more than just the bare evidentiary or factual bones of the crime:

> Right through the nineteenth century there was a market for books hastily produced in this way, to exploit recent, sickening murders; and Fraser's efforts in this instance was to be typical; a mishmash of facts, summaries of real documents, copied out of press reports, all carried on a surging tide of invention.[302]

As she notes in her comments on the memoirs of the primary detective in the case, the bleeding of fiction into True Crime was not just the purview of sensationalist newspaper reporting or hacks. There was a pressure to equal the allure of the fictional supersleuth, even a sense of rivalry with fictional detectives felt by those who wrote about their real detective work. Gowers describes the memoirs of Detective Murray, the investigator in the Birchall case as marked by the autobiographical self-gratification of Murray's ego.

> If Murray harboured doubts about the Birchall case, it is clear that the colour he added to his account was partly a response to the pressure exerted on all real detectives at this time by the icy mental strength and infeasible scientific abilities of their fictional counterparts. Murray was not shy in the memoir of admitting to the rough and ready violence, hard drinking and law bending that went with his work, but in his account of the Birchall case he also added in the suspense, gratuitous gore and cleverness of fiction. Genuine detectives, writing from the 1840s onwards, had produced in the main, a remorselessly crude literature, which described everything from the beating up of suspects and their forced confessions, through to grisly sentences based on trumped-up charges. Men with experience of the job wrote in this low-brow, gritty manner because nineteenth-century detection was almost always a dirty business, and they were describing how their work was actually done. By the end of the century, however, these men faced pressure from an awkward set of rivals, the bands of imaginary and idealized detectives who wafted in ever-increasing numbers through the pages of popular literature. An introductory tribute in Murray's memoir, claiming that his career was "a record of events outrivaling the detective tales of fiction," touched on a relationship with fabricated stories that was far less honourable than this confident assertion implied.[303]

However, fictionalizing actual investigations, coloring what happened to make seamless the progress from crime to conviction in a true crime narrative, is as much about reassuring the audience that knowledge about the "mystery" of murder as an act is discoverable as it is about factual investigation.

The pressure to be fictional shadows actuality. As Wendy Lesser notes: "Fictional murder seems more credible because more can be known about it" even though, to seem subtly convincing, it must retain a sense of "unknowability" because "the distance between our own lives and the act of murder leaves a space where mystery creeps in."[304] As Sara L. Knox adds, any account of murder, inclusive of trials, struggles with the ambiguity, and factual unreliability surrounding murder's occurrence: "Like all tales of death, the narrative of murder is freighted with a kind of awed bafflement at something visceral, yet inscrutable."[305] Today's forensic investigators working in the shadow of the contemporary *CSI* (Crime Scene Investigation) television franchise[306] created by Anthony Zuiker can feel the same pressure to be fictionally efficient as Murray did. Contemporary fictional counterparts brilliantly and inevitably solve their cases by the time the show ends when, in reality, it can take much more time to get similar results and many crimes go unsolved.[307] As Mark Tedeschi, New South Wales most senior Crown Prosecutor has dryly noted in relation to public expectations of DNA evidence created by fictional television shows: "Juries just expect that some scientific unit will come and do magic for them."[308] Fiction ends up shaping the expectations of the actuality it is based on.

If popular preoccupation with the textual makeover of factual violence suggests readers, audiences, and producers deem something is added to narrative by an appearance of fidelity to an initial event, then the addition may not simply be about the simple transference of facts to storytelling. The real attraction of the True Crime genre is not just about the offer of veracity but about the promise to open the window on the forbidden areas of violence and death, particularly murder, in the context of aesthetic satisfaction of audience voyeurism. Audience attraction is as much to the genre's aesthetic characteristics as it is to the actuality it promises. Describing the growth of the "forensic aesthetic" on television shows in the 1990s in his book on forensic photography, *City of Shadows: Sydney Police Photographs 1912–1948*, Peter Doyle calls it "a public response to the shamanic insights into the criminal's soul" in which "the magical power of forensic analysis turned the crime scene into a symbolic battleground."[309] The Gothic sensationalism in the True Crime genre is a part of that narrative need to aesthetically order and make sense of the act of murder through text. Blurbs designed to sell the books trumpet that fidelity to actuality is less about facts than the revelation to the reader of a hidden threat: "After years of exhaustive research he can finally reveal the extraordinary truth behind the murder inquiry that left Peter Sutcliffe free to kill again and again."[310] It is also about the belief that the revelation of that knowledge is a warning of social value: "Whatever the personal stories that emerge from this line-up of twisted individuals, *Evil Serial Killers* is a compelling testament, and warning of the potential of human behavior for true horror and pure evil."[311] Blurbs stridently pro-claims a sense of evil lurking beneath inadequate social constraints,[312] such as that for *Touched by the Devil: Inside the Mind of the Australian Psychopath*:

> Psychopaths. They intrigue and repulse, fascinate and frighten. They are all around us, yet are somehow hidden from view. They live apparently normal lives, for the most part doing normal things.[313]

Often, in sympathy with the victims, the narratives promise a contrasting story of hope in the face of seemingly unfathomable evil suddenly unleashed: "a story of courage in the face of tragedy, and strength in the face of mind-numbingly sense-less murder."[314]

Such selling points exist in the context of the more disquieting aspects of com-modification characterized by Schmid as a murder industry positing the serial killer as gothic celebrity. Schmid has an apt description of the True Crime writer's view of the serial killer as characterized by "the presumption of monstrosity" under "the mask of sanity" in a narrative "search for the origins of deviance,"[315] which never resolves the contending fascination and revulsion at the heart of the genre. That mix of fascination and revulsion often involves authors coating the forensics of murder in a lurid fictionality in which "the interior states of the serial killer himself seem nothing but the clichés du jour that make up a pop-psychology."[316] On the continuum of authenticity representing violence such stories are located at a point of transitional flux where elements of the Gothic and forensic plausibility intermingle, requiring both fiction and at least the believability of the re-creation of something factual to feed their popularity and create their aesthetic meaning—a sense of threat and disorder lurking beneath a fragile, endangered social fabric.[317] As Doyle notes, the success of the fictional and real-life crime scene investigators "allows the general public to experience a vicarious sense of control and victory over chaos."[318] The degree to which an aura of believability depends on aspects of the factual or the fictional differs from text to text but, on some level, all texts in the True Crime genre flirt with a fictional aesthetic in recreating the crime and its milieu for an unquestionably thrill-seeking audience enjoying a successfully commercialized, safely mediated (and possibly cathartic) shudder delivered via text.

Audience Voyeurism and Forensic Actuality

Voyeurism at the heart of the True Crime audience and reader experience is, perhaps, an inevitable characteristic of the detached public reception of murder, which is not shared by those directly involved, such as victims' families. Explanations in the True Crime narrative focus on arrest and trial and rely heavily on the detail found by professional forensic investigators and trial transcripts for their claims to the truth. However, if, as one screenwriter has put it, "You need to get down to the morgue"[319] to write true crime fiction convincingly, it does not mean audiences want that actuality unfiltered by the aesthetic choices of narrative. It is possible that forensic actuality might not even be recognized as such in a virtual context. The director of *Seven*, David Fincher, said he was surprised that people were stunned by the violence in that film because he had seen pictures of the real thing:

> At the LAPD, they have files of photographs that they pull out and show you. A guy shot in the head and his brains unravelled like shoe strings. If you took the pictures and put them in a movie, no one would believe you.[320]

While there is a strong voyeuristic audience fascination and desire to approach close to forensic detail which textual re-creations rely on, such re-creation, however lurid, remains protected from aspects of the actual experience.

Such mediation is unavailable to those who have to come closer to a crime scene in actuality:

> Gibbs has seen his fair share of real-life horror scenes, worse than anything a TV scriptwriter could imagine. His team worked in the Broad Arrow Café after the Port Arthur massacre in 1996. "There were 20 deceased persons, all very badly disfigured, "he recalls. "That was horrible. Those things get to you.[321]

In her autobiographical book, *Crime Scene: True Stories from the Life of a Forensic Investigator*, narrating her time as a forensic investigator with the New South Wales police force in Australia, Esther McKay startlingly reveals the voyeurism even some professionals in law enforcement feel that parallels the public interest in murder, death, and crime. McKay's book, with its spare, matter-of-fact tone stands out from much of the more tabloid tone of the genre as she describes her frustrating efforts as a junior constable to maintain the integrity of a possible crime scene under a bridge involving the bodies of two children in the face of the careless curiosity of some of her more senior colleagues. They are curious onlookers and a more detached audience than she feels herself to be:

> All right. All right. We just want to have a look. When can we see the bodies?
> You can't, so I suggest you get back to your station.
> 'We'll wait,' he retorted.
> 'No you won't,' I said.[322]

Her immersion at the time in the physical and emotional reality of the forensics of the crime scene and the exigencies of her gruesome job contrasts with the curiosity of policemen who were not directly involved in coming close to and touching the decomposing bodies. McKay, professional but struggling for detachment, conveys the immediacy of analyzing, recording, and collecting exhibits from a large and complex crime scene requiring the recovery of decomposing bodies from a "stinking hellhole,"[323] the putrid and watery grave filled with rotting body fluids that cover the rescuers in a "filthy grey waterfall":[324]

> Immediately, I was struck by a sickly odour that invaded my nostrils and made me wince. It was an unusually putrid smell, and not one I had encountered before. This was a new version of death, attacking my senses in an overwhelming way. I could hear a constant echoing of ba-boom, ba-boom as vehicles passed over the bridge's expansion joints; it was deafening. The smell combined with the booming sensation of the cars whooshing overhead gave the

eerie impression that the bridge had a heartbeat. We were forced to yell over the noise.[325]

The smell of death, in particular, is something she carries with her long after leaving the crime scene.[326]

McKay's struggle with the devastating smell exists side by side with a professional eye for the forensic detail often focused on in forensic investigation television show plotting and camera close-ups: "The faint impression of a shoe was visible on its dusty surface."[327] However, her experience of entering the manhole imprinted by the shoe is not aesthetically rewarding in the way plot detail would be in a television forensic procedural text like *CSI*. She discovers the sickening scene of decomposing bodies as she swats away escaping blowflies coming directly from "gorging themselves on the bodies":

> "Get them off me!" I screamed as they flew into my mouth and nose. Shane swatted at them as they swarmed around my head before disappearing into the darkness, blindly trying to locate the way out beyond the light bouncing of the watery grave some thirty-five metres below. I refocused my attention. There they were, lying side by side in the torchlight, both bodies moving grotesquely with the infestation of maggots.[328]

An awareness of what is distasteful about the experience is graphically held in check by McKay's spare prose but its re-creation as text resonates with a sense of her own immediate horror and emotions hovering on the edge of breakdown. Yet, above the entrance to the crime scene, foot resting on the manhole with the footprint possibly left by a perpetrator, stands a superior of McKay's, "puffing away on a pipe, and completely oblivious to any crucial evidence he might have been destroying."[329] McKay rebukes his role as careless bystander but, as a writer of her experiences, she is offering her textual record to those of her readers who share her colleague's voyeurism and a degree of their unaffected, voyeuristic detachment. The reader knows it is possible to look with her beneath the manhole cover because of the protection from the smell offered by the safety of the mediated textual re-creation. As an audience, the reader is equally curious about the reactions of McKay who dares to come closer than text allows: "I felt I was losing it."[330] Affecting as her descriptions are, the reader is in no fear of such loss of composure.

The arrival of the media leads her to explode with anger at their growing contingent as they are unauthorized onlookers contaminating the crime scene: "It was an absolute circus."[331] McKay echoes Gowers' description of the Victorian passion for murder in the Burchall case. Even at its most horrible, a possible crime scene is newsworthy and entertainment—even though it reeks of death at the source the smell cannot pierce the screen and the page. At the crime scene the gap opens up between McKay's detached colleagues, the media contingent (and by implication the voyeuristic reader), and McKay, who becomes coated with the actuality of the event:

> My skin was saturated with rotting, maggot-infested fluid. It was a hideous feeling.[332]

To be there recovering a body so rotted the head falls off as it is lifted into a body bag is to be physically vulnerable and revolted:

> Later, Lance told me that he had an overpowering urge to vomit; he hoped the hands didn't come off because he feared he would be sick into his face mask and choke.[333]

For one of the emergency workers, language breaks down under the attempt to convey the effect of being that close to the event:

> He didn't speak but there was no need, words could not convey how he felt. The most pressing thing on his mind was to get out on the road and under the fire hose; he needed to erase the smell that was torturing him.[334]

For participants at an actual crime scene there are more pressing needs than forming a verbal response that can be recorded in text as McKay's job forces her to experience reality as a "real-life horror show" and "nightmarish."[335] When the bodies are finally brought out of the manhole, physical actuality drives away the media audience: "Any curiosity about the scene had faded long ago and the smell of the two bodies had cleared the area in an instant."[336] It is crime at close quarters that dissipates audience curiosity while scientific curiosity and dedication powered by sheer professional willpower, in the role of McKay pursuing her investigation, remains.

McKay's account records that what she saw that day could not be erased later from her mind: "I was still there."[337] Unlike her unaffected colleagues and readers who can peek and move on, McKay remains haunted by the actuality of what she experiences. Later, during the autopsy conducted on the boys' bodies, she is, finally, emotionally and psychologically overwhelmed:

> I was consumed by this hideous situation. *How the hell did I end up here?* I willed myself to get it together and pull myself out of this hole. I realised I couldn't. Something had snapped. I wanted to rip my hair from my head. I clenched my fringe in my hands and pulled until I felt pain. Then I looked at my hands, shocked to see them trembling uncontrollably. My heart was pounding hard in my chest. What was *wrong* with me? Why couldn't I carry

on? I sat there trembling, horrified and despairing. I wanted to scream. I was weak. I was a failure.[338]

For McKay it was a long road back to psychological health after she is granted a medical discharge from the NSW police force for post-traumatic stress syndrome. Despite that trauma, even she felt it was momentarily possible to create photographic distance from actuality that can be aesthetically and scientifically gratifying:

> As I mounted the enlargement I thought how sad it was that I'd taken such a good photograph of something so tragic and, unlike the morgue photographs, which I couldn't face, I viewed this distant picture as a clinical piece of evidence.[339]

Even amidst all the devastating trauma of her work, McKay finds that she can, momentarily, bring aesthetic order to the unbearable. McKay is engaged in the process of forensic investigation with her camera that Doyle describes as aiming to "turn space into evidence."[340] However, her story is a testament to the fallacy of the assumption, expressed unsympathetically by a police medical officer to her that "Anything you've seen at a crime scene is no different to what you see on television!"[341] Her aesthetic appreciation of her own crime scene photographs and her textualization of her experiences in her book many years later could only come when distance existed between her and the actuality of decomposing death. It is a distance from the scene of investigation into whether a crime had been committed that is created by changing space and the passing of time. Given the harrowing nature of her experiences, her readers, safely insulated from the actuality that traumatized her, nevertheless, receive a sense of the experience's emotional authenticity through the steady, unflinching gaze with which McKay constructs a aesthetic textual frame around her experiences.

Joel Black rightly argues that murder is a cultural phenomenon when it is used artistically and that for audiences its aesthetic rendition can never equate with the vicious actuality of murder experienced by the victim and their families: "the rest of us view it at a distance, often as rapt onlookers who regard its "reality" as a peak aesthetic experience,"[342] seeking its reassuring aesthetic rendering to counter the fact that murder unsettles public belief in social order. He asserts the value of critiquing such representations with an aesthetic approach when an actual murder becomes "quasi-fictional"[343] through artistic representation. Black uses the term anaesthetization to describe the effect of mediated textual distance in audience engagement with such violence but this may not be simply equated with the degree of fictionalization. Difficult though it is to determine the extent of vicarious self-indulgence and thrill-seeking in audience reception and the desire to be entertained by violence, it is still possible for textual mediation to lead to audience emotional and moral investment, or even activism, that is more than the passive curiosity of the onlooker. Estelle Blackburn's *Broken Lives*, an account of the crimes of serial killer Edgar Cooke (the last man to hang in Western Australia who committed 22 murders from 1958–63), offers a clear counter-argument to the totality of audience passivity. Her book was instrumental in having the conviction of two men who were wrongfully sentenced for some of Cooke's crimes quashed. Her research and writing galvanized public support for that process as well as chronicling it.[344]

While it is commonplace in discussions of True Crime narratives to denote popular interest in murder as prurient, the fact that such narratives are as much about the prosecution by Law in response to the social threat of violence is often underestimated. Criminals, lawyers, police, courts, and the social milieu in which the crime takes place and is prosecuted are also the subject. Like crime, the Law "is no longer a concept limited to the law reports; it is a consciousness that permeates . . . culture."[345] Unsurprisingly, the processes of prosecution are a matter of public interest and such interest is built into the legal system itself in an established connection between the prosecution of criminal acts and the public investment in issues of social order. While Paul Gewirtz views the relationship between the public and the legal system as "ambivalent," he also notes that the public is an "indispensable audience and participant":

> First, although the public is not the direct subject of the trial, the public is a direct object or target of the trial, for a central purpose of punishing particular individuals for breaking laws is to deter criminal behaviour by others. Put another way, the public is a primary audience for the trial, although it has traditionally learned about the trial through the heavy filter of media accounts.[346]

Invited public scrutiny through the physical presence of the public in the courtroom space, the embodiment of community condemnation in sentencing, the role of the jury as community representatives, and of public confidence in the legal system, as Gewirtz points out, all form the cultural interest in crime and justice. Audience engagement with True Crime narratives as entertainment extends this scrutiny. Actual trials and True Crime narratives about them serve the same desire for belief in the strength of public order:

> The point here is not simply that the result of a trial can satisfy the retributive urges of the general public, although it surely can do that. The form of the trial—its structure and formality—is itself part of that coming to terms. The trial structures social disorder and thus makes it less disturbing and even enjoyable. It is the sustained process of imposing legal order on criminal violence that reaffirms that life's disorder can be controlled. One of the

cultural appeals of a television series like *Perry Mason*, a series that all but defined law for a generation of Americans, was the patterned closure of each program. The truth was always outed, the true criminal revealed; and the vindicated innocence of Perry Mason's client stood for the vindicated order that the legal process predictably imposed. The appeal of the classic detective story is similar, given its reiterated form: a puzzle of violence presented and ultimately solved (and solved through orderly reasoning). Real life trials obviously do not have the neatness of the trials represented on *Perry Mason*, but they have some of its patterned quality—and, above all, they usually reach closure.[347]

That a public audience for both trials and True Crime stories might find legal and narrative closure equally satisfying is due to the audience pressure brought to bear on both. Alan M. Dershowitz, at one point a consultant to O. J. Simpson's defense team in that most notorious of media trial narratives, warns fact finders and jurors "that life is not a Chekhovian narrative"[348]—where the gun mentioned in the first act must inevitably be discharged in a later act and there are no random events. The True Crime genre struggles with that Chekhovian dramatic imperative driven by its voyeuristic audience's need for explanations and closure that is narrative reassurance that violence will be contained by society in the end.

The acceptance of the fact that investigative journalism in the True Crime narrative is adulterated by fiction has in some instances been embraced as a selling point. The back cover blurb to Susan Mitchell's *All Things Bright and Beautiful: Murder in the City of Light* promotes the genre of True Crime as a hybrid of fact and fiction: "Using a compelling blend of investigative journalism, interview, fact, and fiction, Susan Mitchell reveals Adelaide's very different worlds, from wealthy and hedonistic, to the wretched and the deadly."[349] It is that blend that accounts for the allure of the genre, allowing fiction to fill in what investigation cannot, and avoiding what would be, from the audience's point of view, narrative letdown instead of a compelling story. Recalling Truman Capote's seminal designation of True Crime writing, embodied in his *In Cold Blood*—as nonfiction novelization—Susan Weiner, on the other hand, asks whether the contradictions inherent in such an approach, where reporting as an investigative journalist vies with the novelistic imagination, might not lead to fiction and fact being the same, or canceling each other out:

> Since by definition all events have occurred, the writer cannot possibly know what happened or what someone thought or said. Therefore, despite the extensive use of quoted conversations and cross-examinations, the reader has no idea of the source, accuracy, or completeness of those statements.[350]

The implication of such a view is that journalistic True Crime should just be called fiction and be done with it. However, the True Crime historian Jonathan

Goodman claims that it is precisely through the vantage point of recollection, or distance from the events of the crime, that the possibilities for narrative, if not actual truth, lie. Goodman argues that narrative truth is all that is possible in cases where events have occurred in a past beyond immediate recollection. Narrative is thus freed by time "to be thought of as a kind of fiction" with the writer "a novelist telling a truth."[351] As an author in the genre, Goodman clearly sees the facts of the case as essentially narrative fodder for a larger and "truer" story that can only be had by fictionalization. That such narrative truth may not be factual authenticity, or the truth assessed by those interviewed, or the truth of the trial verdict, for example, is clearly the implication of such a writerly, though somewhat vaguely defined, point of view.[352]

Contemporary writers in the True Crime genre certainly share with the novelist a strong interest in a broad definition of *setting* as an explanatory impetus to narrative, for example, with the scene of the crime understood to be not just the site of the murder but the broader milieu of the victim's and the criminal's life, often extending to links with the culture and society in which the crime occurred. Gowers' desire to explicate the Birchall case is brilliantly served by an intriguing re-creation of the Victorian society in which it unfolds. Similarly, a writer like Alston Chase announces in his title *Harvard and the Unabomber* that who or what made the subject of his biography become a serial killer can only be answered by placing him in an historical and cultural context of 1950's America and the philosophical alienation permeating his tertiary education:

> The Unabomber story, therefore, is not just about Kaczynski but also concerns the times in which he lived, and ultimately the evils to which the intellect is heir.[353]

Moving through Ted Kaczynski's high school and Harvard student years and his tenure as a professor of mathematics, Alston describes an educational culture of philosophical isolation shaped by the Cold War for an answer to why Kaczynski became a murderer. Yet, lucid as his argument is, the echo of the sensational fatalism and revelatory tone of traditional True Crime writing tinges his prose: "it's a story about intelligence and violence and the dark heart of modern evil that lurks, not at the fringes of civilization but at its very center."[354] Behind this tone, so prevalent in the Victorian literature that Gowers discusses, is the desire to create an explanatory and textual order on an archetypal level out of the moral mystery and chaos that violence brings. It is this textual purpose that opens the door to the fictional uses of "true" crimes to satisfy audience curiosity about the nature of what is often perceived as something mysterious about human evil, rather than simply explicating human dysfunction.

Illusory Forensic Authenticity in *Law & Order*

The description of the flooding of Esther McKay's senses described earlier goes some way towards piercing reader complacency encouraged by an aesthetically composed comfort zone as a vantage point for contemplating murder. Yet, independent of her writing skill, her description is ultimately forensically authenticated by reader acceptance of her narrative authority as witness because, as a crime scene investigator with the NSW police force, she was actually there. In contrast, television police and trial procedurals like the popular television franchise *Law & Order*,[355] which bases many of its episodes on actual high profile crime stories and cases covered extensively in the media—"ripped from the headlines"[356]—creates a True Crime narrative that utilizes illusory effects to create *believability*[357] as a form of aesthetic authenticity rather than forensic veracity. Typical audience enjoyment of the *Law & Order* franchise "can be attributed to straightforward storytelling, timely reactions to real-life news, and the writers' clever layering of plot line twists and turns" and an often "simple, elegant clarity" in the episode's narrative and ethical resolutions.[358] That elegance marks it as the designer template for crime procedural television.

Philip J. Lane notes there are television crime drama procedurals that have drawn a sense of professional authenticity by portraying the existential condition and absurdity of the pursuit of justice in the life of criminal investigators, such as *Hill Street Blues, Homicide: Life on the Streets*, and *NYPD Blue*.[359] If nothing else, skeptical audiences in a public often outraged by crime are likely to accept as authentic to some degree crime narratives which air "the culture's dirty laundry and mythic slack"[360] by holding fast to cynicism about the flaws and deal cutting in the justice system and by picturing crime as a staple of life on a city's "mean streets." That existential attitude is echoed in *Law & Order* by the cynical, world-weary wisecracks of characters like the conflicted, personally guilt-ridden, old-timer Detective Lennie Briscoe in the original *Law & Order*, and in the disgust of Detective Elliot Stabler for the perpetrators of the sexual crimes he investigates in the more emotional spin-off *Law & Order: Special Victims Unit* (SVU), which often results in Stabler's violent outbursts towards them.[361] However, the franchise is held back from being truly cynical by an overall neatness of ethical and legal debate, as lawyers in the District Attorney's office do "the moral math"[362] and clarify the legal parameters of "the moral mystery"[363] if the detectives solve the "whodunit." As Dawn Keetley notes in her discussion of the show's "six sides of a single issue"[364] approach, the neatness of the show's legal debate is focused on "the moral outlook that motivates the prosecutors" and thus "works to forge a bond between a sceptical American audience"[365] and the characters that represent the justice system trying to enforce a societal desire for accountability. This satisfying sense of televisual formula remains even when the plot does not, on occasion, finally resolve the issue with a legal conviction of the guilty.[366] When the prosecutors do not win the show ends and there is closure to the issue in viewing time, at least, as the credits roll and the audience moves on to other choices of entertainment or turns off the television. What the viewer is left with is the sense that the truth of the crime is contested ground in an adversarial justice system.

Despite the perceived gap between actuality and TV fiction, even a member of the homicide squad at the NSW State Crime Command, Detective Acting Inspector Joe Cassar, watches the fictionalization of crime procedurals for the aesthetic pleasures of fictional ordering, even when, in actuality, it would be ridiculous:

To be honest, I love watching the *CSI* shows. I just love the way Horatio (Caine) in *CSI: Miami* is always putting on sunglasses inside and in dark car parks. Nobody would do that, it would impair your vision and you'd miss evidence. We tape off a crime scene and only two investigators are allowed in—this preserves evidence. In *CSI*, they have an army of people walking all over the crime scene, then Horatio comes in, puts on his sunglasses and somehow finds a vital piece of evidence that all the others have missed.[367]

The sunglasses are for "cool" effect but, even for this forensic practitioner, they add a touch of glamour to his profession that he finds seductive. Such shows are counting on a characterization that attracts real-life investigators:

Cops like me playing cops . . . they dig it. They ID with me, because all of the cops in the streets, they think they're tough, they think they're hardcore. So I play that kinda cop, you know, the one that just wants to grab the perp and break his neck.[368]

The actor Ice-T's use of "they think" in his description of his character on *Law & Order: SVU* implies that authenticity in his role is less about portraying real-life police than about fulfilling the self-made fictions that actual police create around their role.

More than characterization, the aesthetic authenticity of the crime scene that the fictional *Law & Order* franchise aims for, straddles a gap across actuality and illusion with forensic, prosthetic, and production craftsmanship that is not so much lifelike as illusory believability. In his introduction to a fascinating photographic analysis of the cinematographic look of "the mothership" of the franchise, Dick Wolf, the creator and executive producer of *Law & Order*, describes the aesthetic appearance of the show as one of colour desaturation, which is used to give a documentary feel to fictional illusion. For Wolf, "humans live and die in color, but, when we think of crime and punishment, we want a justice system that is sharp, unsparing, and unsentimental about evil as well as clear and crisp about righting it—that is, a world of black and white."[369] Wolf's aesthetic belief is that the gritty cinematographic reduction of colour conveys authenticity and clarity of moral vision to an audience that wants to see fictional order created out of the chaos of morally complex situations present in the "colour" of factual crimes:

> In layman's terms, this means that in the final stage of post-production, most of the color is pulled out of the picture, leaving a "cooler" color temperature. Thus, it feels somewhat more like a documentary, subtly blending illusion and reality. It might be described as trompe l'oeil or, to cineastes, as cinema verité.[370]

This pseudodocumentary aesthetic Wolf terms "the gray area of real existence"[371] which the aesthetic of the show retains, despite the network's rejection of shooting entirely in black and white. The greyness posits a visual frame for narrative that is neither fact nor fiction but somewhere defined by both.

Peter J. Hutchings has noted that the law and policing depend on a forensic knowledge of the world that in an aesthetic context can have an unstable indexicality.[372] In Law & Order the forensic sits within the televisual illusion and is manipulated for aesthetic effect. Executive producer Jeffrey Hayes asserts the priority given to visual believability in the show: "In a show that is all about consequences, the crime scene is the most immediate consequence and must be believable for the episode to work."[373] One of the show's directors, Constantine Makris, adds that central to believability is the fact that televisual illusion is set within actual locations in New York which, for New Yorkers at least, means that distinguishing the actual from the illusory is not always easy:

> The Law & Order crew is expert at creating illusions at locations. My favourite location illusion was for the crime scene in the episode "Charm City" (Part One), where we created a fake subway station entrance, bricks and all. The delight expressed by so many passersby who thought they had a new subway stop was just extraordinary.[374]

While the subway stop is physically constructed as a set, and is fake, it nevertheless incorporates enough physicality to convince New Yorkers passing by that the illusion is actuality, not because they are viewing it on their television screens but because it sits on the sidewalk in the context of actuality. As Robert Thayer, a production designer on the show, points out, New York is "the seventh character" in the series:

> When I read the script, the very first thing I have to decide about any scene is "Would it happen here?". . . For exterior crime scenes, however, we let New York city play its part. We may change signs and the like and we certainly light at night, but we always let the texture of the city shine.[375]

The placement of the crime scenes in the nooks and crannies of the city revealing a familiarity with "every geometric angle of New York City"[376] encourages an affirmative answer to the question "Would it happen here?" allowing illusion to feed off actuality. As William Klayer, a chief lighting technician on *Law & Order* notes, shooting on location guarantees the proximity of the actual to the illusory:

> On one occasion, I sent a crew to pre-light a riverfront crime scene. They had to wait. The police were pulling a real body out of the Hudson.[377]

In this context, television production and a milling city life merge. Property Master, Ron Stone, recalls that sharing the physical location with actual events creates an overlap:

> I am constantly creating illusions because, in fact, on film, reality does not always feel real. Yet, in New York City, where just about anything can happen, I've had many moments in my job where illusion and reality meet. Among these moments was one that occurred in a West village building. While propping a *Law & Order* crime scene, suddenly, real police officers came running in. Apparently, there had actually been a crime committed on another floor. Unprepared, an officer sheepishly asked: "Would it be possible to borrow some crime scene tape?"[378]

Assistant director, Stuart Feldman, describes how crowd control becomes a part of television narrative when shooting the crime scene and using crime scene tape as a prop to keep New Yorkers, who are curious onlookers to the production, at bay: "If the public does stop to stare, it only enhances the air of authenticity."[379] The participation of extratextual onlookers roped off behind yellow crime scene tape merges into the illusion while they stand in the street leading their non-*Law & Order* lives. The crime scene tape borrowed from the film crew by the police attending an actual crime scene nearby while the television crew uses it as a set prop suggests how fluid that merging can be. It is the contextualization of the fiction in the actuality of location that allows it.

Onlooker willingness to be an audience to the production of illusion creates an openness to mistaking the illusion for the actual, evidenced in the confusion about the seemingly "real" subway station. Similarly, a make-up supervisor on the show, Sharon Ilsen, underscores how forensic detail created prosthetically is essential to what is believable about the physicality of the violence done to the actor playing the victim in the crime scene:

> As rewrites of the script occurred, I continuously checked my pathology books, had discussions with the producer and art director, and accessed a trusted site on the Web to make certain that every detail was correct. On location, I spent

most of my time working on the leg wound of the victim. I had to try to imagine what a wound would look like if one were thrown from a car, as the dead
body supposedly had been. Although the director had an idea of what would
"read" on camera, I needed to get every detail right.[380]

What "reads" as authenticity on camera, while subtly different from what appears
real to the naked eye, is still linked to accurate forensic detail. However, illusion, of
necessity, restrains that factuality. Producers on the series *Six Feet Under*, requiring
a variety of prosthetic dead and injured bodies designed to look real in order to give
viewers "the you-are-there sense" on television have also described the need for the
fake "to be super-lifelike or it's going to blow the quality of the scene,"[381] while needing to restrain forensics with art when it was "too much": "They wanted it to look
more like a Picasso painting . . . rather than be literally, 'This is a crushed skull.'"[382]
As the director of photography on *Law & Order*, John Beymer, notes, effects aiming
for forensic detail cannot be allowed to overwhelm narrative illusion: "the trick
is to light the victim subtly, so that the body (or the wound) will not visually
overpower the scene."[383] As we know from McKay's account earlier, "overwhelm" is
precisely what forensic actuality does to anyone close enough to it. For the priority
of illusion, piggybacking on the forensic actuality remains subservient to storytelling through illusion.

Jessica Burstein, the still photographer responsible for the black and white
photographs in Wolf's book, feels the sobering effect of the difference between the
creation of illusion and "real crime scenes":

Looking back through my early *Law & Order* crime scene stills, they now
appear to me as virtual shots in the dark. This was before I began to do
research, including studying crime scene photographs, having discussions
with the police, and, most sobering of all, visiting real crime scenes. But, no
matter how much research I have done and how much I have learned, the
work is a constant challenge because of the reality of the situation—that I am
shooting illusions. As someone who was drawn to photography as a means of
revealing truths, it is strange, indeed, to have spent so much time doing precisely the opposite.[384]

Nevertheless, out of the context of knowledge about the fictional source of her own
black and white stills of crime scenes from the television series, she takes pleasure
from the fact that they have been mistaken for records of actual events by professionals working in the police:

When taken out of context of *Law & Order*, the crime scene photographs
have generated reactions ranging from perverse fascination to genuine horror.

The most astonishing reaction came from four seasoned New York City homicide detectives who, when shown some photographs without explanation, began to argue with each other about who of them had been at which crime scene. Although I was surprised by their response, it would be disingenuous of me to claim that I was not pleased by it.[385]

There is real delight for the illusionist, as she admits, in the creative success of the illusion—independent of its illusionistic success as a part of its narrative use in the *Law & Order* story it served. However, the completeness of the illusion is only sustainable because the photographs are taken out of their fictional context and put back into the actual experience of forensic investigation as the homicide detectives experience it (the photographs are presented to the homicide detectives with no information about their source). Context is all.

The Author's Story Versus the Murderer's

If there were one story of a serial killer that typifies the transitional chaos from event to text in the True Crime narrative it would be that of Aileen Wournos. Nick Broomfield has documented the vulture-like rush to commodification that followed her arrest in *Aileen Wournos: The Selling of a Serial Killer*[386] (though not, as Paige Schilt notes, with a complete awareness of how his own documentary contributes to that commodification and its cultural and class stereotypes about her as white trash and a prostitute[387]). It is a process that Wournos herself tried to cash in on when she sold the rights to her story for a television movie. *Time* aptly described that marketing of herself as "killing her way to fame."[388] Lawyers, police, and people she knew all brokered the sale of the rights to their parts in her story in multiple and different versions. Vankin and Whalen, when discussing what they term the "fudging"[389] of the facts in the movie *Monster*,[390] the most well-known version of her story, wonder why the claim that a narrative is based on a true story is made if the facts are not adhered to. Such a view doggedly misses the point that fictionalizing actuality takes the facts to find *a* story the mystery of a murder suggests, not *the* story.

Like many other critics, Vankin and Whalen acknowledge that the Academy Award winning performance by Charlize Theron in the lead role is striking in its physical resemblance to the real-life Wournos: "Theron transformed herself into Wournos by burying her ethereal beauty under twenty extra pounds, a prosthetic overbite, and lots of freckle make-up."[391] General critical response to the film saw her as the physical reincarnation of Wournos: "Sporting extra weight and a puffy freckled face, Theron is a ringer for the executed serial killer."[392] There was a sense of receptive awe at the illusionistic conjuring act involved in the physical similarity of Theron's appearance to Wournos's. Such receptive amazement is riddled with stereotypical perceptions that equate the portrayal of deviance with bad skin and authentic acting with the shedding of celebrity beauty. However, it is the use of make-up or physical appearance to account for a narrative relationship in the film with what is "true" about Wournos's inner life story and her murderous acts that is of interest. The assumption of this approach is that, as an actor, physically incarnating Aileen is authentic narrative: "I was constantly trying to be Aileen: I was trying to walk like Aileen, to carry myself like Aileen." Theron's presence as an actor performing Aileen invoked authenticity on the set even when the camera was not rolling: "When I *wasn't* Aileen—when I didn't have the contact lenses in or the teeth in—they were treating me weird."[393] This physicality was perceived as so authentic that, when the film was shooting at The Last Resort, a bar frequented by the real Aileen Wournos, her former acquaintances found the resemblance disturbing: "This is really freaking us out, how much she looks like Aileen and how much she's carrying herself like Aileen."[394] As well, Theron assumes a one-to-one connection between the inclusion of biographical events and authenticity:

> It was only when we started reading some of (Aileen's) letters from death row that I started realizing how much research Patty (Jenkins) had really done as a writer, because actual moments in her life that she never talked about, that she only wrote about and talked to (Aileen's long-time friend) Dawn Botkins about, were actually in the script.[395]

Prosthetics, make-up, and biographical detail are seen to restrain the leeway given to fictional storytelling with the actuality of who Aileen Wournos physically was.

However, despite Vanken and Whalen's challenge and the striving for physical resemblance evident in the film, the more interesting question is what does the film offer as storytelling when it moves from its True Crime starting point located in the actuality of events. Theron herself felt that authenticity of portrayal required more than prosthetics:

> I didn't want it to become about the make-up or about a caricature . . . So the first day that we did all of it and I looked in the mirror, I was like . . . this feels very authentic to me and very real.[396]

The cosmetic transformation from a beautiful model/actress into "a woman who's not these things"[397] (overweight, with bad hair and teeth) was, for Theron and the director Patti Jenkins, crucially linked to a sense of emotional authenticity conveyed through acting:

> Both Theron and Jenkins were determined to humanize Aileen, a complicated, tortured, volatile roadside sex worker who was executed by the state of

Florida in October 2002. Both knew that Theron's physical transformation—the convincing makeup to weather her skin, the dentures and contact lenses, the 30 pound weight gain—would be powerless without Theron's ability to feel what Wournos felt. And that meant getting both the homicidal rage and the heartbreaking lesbian love just right.[398]

Theron extended her immersion in the role to "living more or less as Aileen during the filming," inclusive of "Aileen's way of walking and that amazing head toss that just captures her personality."[399] The physical traits she copied from viewing tapes of Aileen were mannerisms conveying personality and emotional truth, not simply resemblance: "What happened was, the more I dived into her life, the more I realized that everything she did physically came from an emotional place." For Theron, Wournos's physical bravado ("This is a woman who was 5 foot 3 . . . who looks like she's 6 foot 4"[400]) was the external sign of a homeless woman who has to take care of herself while living rough and working as a prostitute. Of interest to the actress was how telling the story with that kind of physical and emotional authenticity could answer the central question posed by the True Crime narrative: "How do people become killers?" Theron defines it as crossing a line; "Patty and I talked a lot about what it takes for somebody just like me and you to cross that line and actually become a bad person—to become a killer."[401] However accurate the resemblance to the real Wournos, the make-up and the adoption of the traits described by Theron remains a *characterization*, an approximation, and an interpretation of who the actual Wournos was. Where the line dividing fact from fiction can be found for a viewer of the film is probably irrelevant to the story's impact. What is undoubtedly added by that aura of True Crime, painstakingly cultivated in Theron's portrayal and the biographical detail of the screenplay, is a murder aesthetic that frames and ultimately reassures the audience that the contemplation of violence, of the criminal mind, can be contained and ordered—something the designation "serial killer" itself presumes in its suggestion that murder has its recognizable patterns.

Once Theron's make-up is in place, along with the mannerisms and biographical details, the film can use the factual as a springboard to its own speculative story about who Wournos was and why she killed. Jenkins actually met her subject, conducted extensive research, and has made claims to the authenticity of her story based on her access to Wournos.[402] In line with other true crime authors who have developed a relationship with their subject, this is a claim to authenticity based on geographical and interactive proximity from which much is still a matter of inference. Thus, Jenkins made the choice to view the events through Wournos's love for Tyria Moore, her girlfriend: "there's reasons why these kinds of couples stay together . . . and that was the kind of movie I wanted to make."[403] She created a touching story of Wournos as victim/killer, which is an artistic choice that ultimately requires a degree of fictionalization to tell and sustain its believability for the viewer. Wournos's life is the template that fiction appropriates to create its own retelling.

The degree to which the viewer invests the story with a sense of authenticity is one thing, the use the film makes of fact and fiction to create its meaning is another. A viewer who knows little or nothing of the real Aileen Wournos is likely to take the film for what it is. In essence, the claim to veracity is only where the film starts. It is the film's sympathetic portrayal of Wournos's unsympathetic character that, ultimately, reveals more about the use of her criminality to tell the film's story than about the factuality of Wournos's own. The emotional believability of the film's narrative partakes of the context of Theron's physical incarnation of Wournos's actual appearance but does not seek to be confined by the implication that the accuracy of physical resemblance requires equal veracity in all other aspects of the film.

If illusion and actuality depend so much on context, when True Crime narratives are so often the outcome of an author's search for a truth about a murder, then the writer's own characterization and point of view often dominates and colors the final, judgmental "truth." In those examples of True Crime that are written as journalistic investigation, the authorial stance *is* the context. Mick O'Donnell acknowledges his own vacillating journey as investigator and storyteller when writing about the murder of the Australian nurse, Yvonne Gilford, in Saudi Arabia:

> And so, over many months, in pursuing the truth about the death of Yvonne Gilford, I wandered between these two poles, from belief in guilt to belief in innocence—and back again. This is the story of my own pendulum of belief and where it finally came to rest.[404]

As the quote by Wambaugh at the head of this chapter recognizes, it is as much the author's story as it is the murderer's. In her book on the unflattering roles of *The Journalist and the Murderer* in a nonfiction narrative of a murder, Janet Malcolm holds the view that "the writer ultimately tires of the subject's self-serving story, and substitutes a story of his own."[405] She uses the metaphor of the love affair to describe how both the journalist and subject can be seduced by the pleasures and excitements of the process.

Malcolm discusses a case in which a murderer sued a journalist for portraying him untruthfully and for misleading him as the interviewee, by assuring him that he believed in his innocence when he did not and for portraying him as guilty. The journalistic subject is distinguished from the fictional literary character, in Malcolm's view, by their self-fictionalizing natures and is chosen for that reason. In True Crime

> the journalist must limit his protagonists to a small group of people, of a certain rare, exhibitionistic, self-fabulizing nature, who have already done the work on themselves that the novelist does on his imaginary characters—who, in short, present themselves as ready-made literary figures.[406]

Such subjects are "the "naturals" of nonfiction who . . . do a lot of the writer's work for him through their own special self-invention."[407] Perceived by the True Crime journalist/author as "the tabloid-ready subject,"[408] nevertheless, a murderer gives access to a journalist for self-serving reasons. Robin Bowles' book *Dead Centre*, with its exclusive access to Peter Falconio's murderer, John Murdoch, has been aptly reviewed as the author's "racy account"[409] informed by the murderer's lies. Malcolm characterizes such a journalist (echoing Truman Capote) a "non-fiction novelist"[410] who reports on an auto-novelization that is already underway when he arrives on the scene.

For Malcolm, there are dangers for the subject, whatever his agenda, when subjecting himself to the author's purposes because the transformation requires some form of getting "under the skin of the writer."[411] In that sense, the author is never a neutral voice and, with his own narrative agenda and presence, inevitably becomes a participant in the story, a character in the text, and subject to any fictionalization undertaken. It is suggested in *Capote*,[412] the biopic retelling of Truman Capote's experience in writing his novel *In Cold Blood*, that there were ruthless, sleazy, and egotistical motives at the core of Capote's narrative requirement for a conviction and hanging to produce the aesthetic of his nonfiction novel. In the film, Capote cries over the phone to his friend and assistant in what feels like self-dramatizing, pseudogrief after the hanging of the two killers, Perry Smith and Dick Hickock who are the subjects of his book. His research assistant, the novelist Harper Lee, is clear-eyed about his exploitation of his subjects, which undermines the sincerity of his comment to her that he will never get over seeing them hanged. "There isn't anything I could have done to save them," he says, to which she replies, "Maybe not," but "The fact is, you didn't want to." His calculating aesthetic motives as an author cannot be so simply untangled from any aspect of his personal relationship with his subject and those motives exist in the twilight zone of moral, factual, and fictional ambiguity.

Audience and reader perspective is shaped by the author's intrusion into the text. The reader of Gower's book is jolted into a reconsideration of all that has gone before in her narrative of the Birchall case when she reveals in a postscript that she is the great grand-daughter of one of the participants in the original case and that he left extensive primary resources that she used in her research:

> I would like to make special mention of the kindness with which . . . my Pelly relatives, some of them writers themselves, have helped me to take up a story that is a peculiar inheritance of theirs no less than mine.[413]

The reader is left to speculate about what might have been added to, or detracted from, reader interpretation if the personal authorial investment in the narrative through her kinship with the protagonist relative had been acknowledged upfront.

Paradoxically, that inherited affiliation with its access to primary resources may have both added (through access to resources) *and* detracted (due to bias) from factuality. If she had acknowledged her family affiliation in the beginning, it is possible for the reader to have read it as a different book altogether. The fact that her great-grandfather comes across sympathetically in the narrative becomes suspect, in retrospect, particularly given the fact that many of the records of interactions with the murderer that she recreates come from his point of view. In essence, Gowers was unacknowledged as a character in the story with a vested interest.

Taking Sides in *Joe Cinque's Consolation*

In contrast, when writing on the murder of Joe Cinque at the hands of his disturbed Australian National University law undergraduate girlfriend Anu Singh, Helen Garner, in her True Crime investigative book, *Joe Cinque's Consolation: A True Story of Death, Grief and the Law,* liberally peppers her own autobiographical presence throughout the story. In her account of Singh's murder of her boyfriend with heroin and Rohypnol and the subsequent trial and sentencing in Canberra, Australia, in the 1990s,[414] Garner makes no attempt to hide her partisan sympathetic narrator stance in relation to the victim and his family. As she observes the trial, she writes on issues of memory and proof, the drama and props of the trials and their outcomes, the flaws and triumphs of the adversarial legal system, and the grief of the victim's family. She puzzles over the unempathic roles played by the mutual friends of both the victim and killer (the strangely disconnected group of young people who failed to prevent Anu Singh from killing Joe Cinque, despite indirectly and directly knowing of its possibility). These topics are all typical True Crime concerns. She shares the urge at the Gothic heart of the genre to elevate the story to the level of didactic archetype, particularly in her portrait of Maria Cinque, the victim's mother: "there rose, from the depths of her a tremendous, unassailable archetype: the mother."[415] She finds the self-fictionalizing nature at the heart of murder that Grossman describes as the source of the True Crime story describing "the ceaseless drama Singh scripted and starred in, to make her collapsing life bearable"[416] and the way in which the killer dominates the story of the trial and its prior events as "Once again, Anu Singh took up all the available air."[417] She recognizes the audience's, as well as her own, attraction to the larger drama into which Singh, by her murder of Joe Cinque, pulled the legal system, Garner, and, by implication, the reader of Garner's book—all sucked into the drama inherent in murder and trial: "Court watchers seek drama. It is easier to understand than the law's intricacies."[418]

While giving voice to a range of opinions about Singh's actions, it is her own voice and opinions to which the book gives emotional authority in the face of Cinque's murder. Her narrative is one of warmth towards the victim and dislike for the killer. That dislike is immediate and permanent, provoked when she first looks through the cuttings file on the case in a newspaper office and has not yet decided whether to write on it:

> Anu Singh raised my girl-hackles in a bristle. Joe Cinque provoked a blur of warmth . . . These were my instinctive responses, and over the ensuing years, as I picked a path through this terrible story, they remained remarkably stable.[419]

She has a responsive partiality to other characters in the story as well, such as for the "thick-skinned" likeability of reporters who cover Supreme Court trials:

> The squalor and misery they are exposed to every day can make them seem thick-skinned, even coarse: I like them. They are always good company, full of "facts" and keen to gossip and speculate.[420]

As an author she uses her emotions as a singular conduit to narrative meaning. She breezily makes assumptions from her own experiences—"Any woman who has left home for university could fill in the gaps here, I thought"[421]—and seeks insight into Singh's behavior from details of her own personal history: "I wondered if my parents had guessed what was the matter with *me*, in 1964, when I took the train home to Geelong after I had had an abortion."[422] Refreshingly, she acknowledges her own voyeurism: "The blunt truth would have been, 'Right now, in spite of my notebook, I'm still only perving.'"[423] Observation and participation intermingle as the trial energizes her as a participant in its ritual dramas:

> I found I missed the trial: the daily intensity of the drama as it unfolded, the rituals of leaping to one's feet and bowing, the silent companionship of the other watchers, the long tracts of intent listening. I could hardly wait for Monday.[424]

Access to the story remains firmly through the filter of Garner's participatory reactions that she imagines are shared by others: "The shiver that ran across my skin seemed also to lower the temperature in Justice Crispin's veins."[425]

In essence, Garner's personal responses as an audience member and voyeur puts a passionate sense of human implication back into the narrative for the reader as a counterpoint to a legal context that aims to keep passion and "the relentless incursion of the tumult of ordinary life" separate from "the structured process of legal proof and judgment."[426] While Garner displays a fascination with murder that she shares with all True Crime writers ("A story lies in wait for a writer. It flashes out silent signals.")[427] she is watching the trial of Singh in Canberra for very personal reasons:

> I understand now that I went to Canberra because the break-up of my marriage had left me humiliated and angry. I wanted to look at women who were accused of murder. I wanted to gaze at them and hear their voices, to see the shape of their bodies and how they moved and gestured, to watch the expressions on their faces. I needed to find out if anything made them different from me: whether I could trust myself to keep the lid on the vengeful, punitive force that was in me, as it is in everyone—the wildness that one keeps in its cage, releasing it only in dreams and fantasy.[428]

The author in Garner needs to make sense of events out of the chaos of the conflicting stories accounting for the murder, such as the transcript of the committal proceedings in a "sprawling, undignified state"[429] and the actual trial transcripts that offer a narrative "mess."[430] Garner also chronicles her own narrative journey marked by its own thrashing about and confusion. However, she wants the meaning primarily for herself and only offers it to the reader as a secondary purpose.[431] Her own entry into the story as a character is even present in the question called up by murder itself and which all True Crime narratives try to answer—what kind of person could murder?

> Where *was* she in the tale? Sitting there in court she was real enough: she had shape, she had colour, she took up space. But in the last day's of Joe Cinque's life she remained a phantom. One's imagination strained to picture her, as the story circled back and round and back again towards the unbearable moment of Joe Cinque's death. It was wearying, it was exhausting—and yet somehow, appalled and incredulous, one went on swallowing it down.[432]

The question itself begs authorial intervention for answers, meaning, and significance, even if it strains the imagination ("Of course I knew that there was no 'significance', that I was projecting it") and, even when the invention of significance is acknowledged, author and reader can share the frisson ("But it unnerved me").[433] With revealing narrative honesty, Garner recognizes the professional tendency to this form of seduction posed by authorial participatory observation:

> Now I found a similar fantasy in myself—that for Madhavi Rao to turn her head and meet my eye with a long "significant" look meant I must be special, not square or old or boring, but a cool mature journalist who with her little notebook could go among killers and their cohorts and be accepted by them— slumming without comprising my virtue.[434]

Her own observations seek to break through what she perceives as the distance from the crime created by the legal system's conceptualization of it, which she sees as "Olympian in its remoteness."[435] Her sympathy for the victim's parents does not allow her that distance and the split between morality and legality that such a distance creates nauseates her. Legal arguments about the duty of care that bystanders to the murder might have exercised are brought back by Garner to whether she would have acted: "Couldn't she—shouldn't she—wouldn't I—oh God, wouldn't I have done *something*?"[436]

Garner contemplates the possibility, in the face of the wretchedness of human behavior, the lack of ethical subtlety in the legal system and psychiatric disingenuousness that not all stories allow the witnessing of meaning, nor "the high sheen of 'wickedness'"[437] which is so intrinsic to reaching the True Crime archetypal understanding of a murderer's actions as simply evil: "I wanted to ask her about her soul."[438] What she can observe of Singh's disturbed and banal self-absorption devolves narrative into a kind of mesmerized revulsion. For Garner, gestures from the killer that will repair "the rent in the social fabric" and the "possibility of soul— gestures that we would all understand died here long ago."[439] Singh refused to be interviewed for the book and, while Garner feels she "left the question of her remorse wide open,"[440] she is not satisfied with Singh's legal defense that mental illness is a sufficient explanation. Even Singh admitted that as an explanation for the Cinque family: "there's no legitimate explanation to be made."[441] In Garner's book, however, it is precisely the role of the inclusion of herself as a character that fills in at least one possible meaning, the one that she experiences emotionally and philosophically as a response to the rent in the Cinque family life. Her own distress over the tragic senselessness of Cinque's death and the lack of any meaningful closure to be had through the trial for the victim's parents ("All that remained was sorrow, and loss"[442]) only comes to a point of emotional and narrative stillness at the end of the book. Garner sits with Joe Cinque's mother and watches a video of him in a suspended kind of memoriam where virtual memory resurrects a sense of the life that was cruelly destroyed: "We gazed in silence on her undefended son."[443] In the end, Garner has chosen to movingly tell the story she believed in. That story was not the always problematic one of "true crime" which is the murder's or the murderer's "truth" but the much more authentically tellable story, for Garner, of the victim. It is to the defense of Joe Cinque and his family that she bears witness as author and participant in the narrative.

David R. Dow who coins the phrase "truthful fictions" opposes the belief that fictionality is by definition a less-authentic view of actual legal and criminal issues. Dow argues that a Hollywood film such as *Dead Man Walking* (telling the story of a guilty man on Death Row) makes a more complex, and thus truthful, case about the death penalty than many nonfiction documentaries on the subject because they use fiction to reveal moral complexity in ways that documentaries such as *The Thin*

Blue Line (focusing on the straightforward option of an innocent man on Death Row) do not.[444] Similarly, in Garner's case, her subjective and speculative re-creation of the actions of the participants in the murder does not simplify the issues in the case but opens them up to narrative scrutiny. Kerryn Goldsworthy's comment on Garner's "foregrounding of subjectivity" and the "frankly personal" as characteristic of her narrative stance in *The First Stone* applies equally to *Joe Cinque's Consolation*. The latter novel operates by "showing how much of 'the whole story'—any whole story—can be left out or disregarded and lost in the linguistic formulas of public life."[445] Garner's subjective interest in the case attempts to put back some of that neglected story. *Joe Cinque's Consolation* is above all about the failure of the legal discourse to account for the real tragedy of his death and the unethical actions of bystanders who could have prevented it.

In the True Crime genre, if actuality does not always fit the exigencies of dramatic narrative so that authorial subjectivity and fiction must compensate, the narrative space created will inevitably be a murky one. It is not possible to locate authenticity outside of a willingness to commit, as an audience or reader, to decisions about the narrative's believability. Like many movies before it, the comedy crime film *Fargo* begins with an on-screen claim that it is a true story; that the events took place in a specific time and place (1987 in Minnesota); that at the request of the survivors the names were changed and that "Out of respect for the dead, the rest has been told exactly as it occurred."[446] Subsequent to the release of the film, the cowriters of the script, Joel and Ethan Coen, enjoyed the critical speculation as to whether or not this claim was true, while admitting with a tongue-in-cheek vagueness that there was a kind of "outline" of events taken from actuality (though not necessarily one particular case) but that all the characters were invented.[447] Despite that concession, William Macy, a leading actor in the film, has said that they told him that, being a movie, it was obviously fictional. When he protested that they could not do that, given the claim at the start of the film, they simply said, why not?: "They were the one's who looked at it and said let's poke a hole in this true story baloney."[448]

The critical interest in trying to determine the degree to which the claim was true and the Coen brothers' use of the claim as a storytelling device for comic effect—the word "exactly" being the giveaway—both on and off the screen,[449] suggests that there is a lure for an audience in the claim to authenticity being made for a story, even while there remains something specious about its degree of "truth." Frances McDormand, the lead actress in the film, describes the lure as a calculated one in the case of *Fargo*: "it was calculated to see, okay, if an audience thinks this is true, will they go with it longer, will they make more leaps of faith and, so to a certain extent, I think they were wondering whether they could get away with that."[450] In the case of *Fargo*, the designation that a text is "based on a true story," could be seen as lending a borrowed authenticity of a nonspecific kind that will encourage audience suspension of disbelief. Presumably when the serial killer, Gaoar Grimsrud, minces up a dead body in a wood chipper in *Fargo*, if the audience knows such an outlandishly horrific fictionalized mode for disposing of a murder victim has been used by murderers in actuality then the scene may gain an extra chilling frisson beyond its comic black humour. Since few members of the film's audience are likely to know that, and the scene is comically gruesome without such knowledge, then the connection with believable authenticity is likely to be fiction-based. Jody Enders' contention about medieval urban legends that "[t]here was something about the realities of the experience of representation that made for true experiences, if not necessarily true accounts"[451] is equally likely to be the artistic belief behind the Coen brothers' muddying of the waters about the factuality of *Fargo*'s narrative sources.

When fact and fiction merge in the frenzied commodification of serial killing in the True Crime genre, then textual authenticity has its own area of narrative twilight where fact and fiction dance around each other in a blur. In 2004, a United States Senator, Fred Thompson, joined the cast of *Law & Order* as the elected chief prosecutor replacing Diane Wiest, who held the role for the previous two seasons.[452] As a former actor and a lawyer who had served as a federal prosecutor and Watergate counsel, essentially he became the fictional counterpart of a role he had actually lived or he brought unique experiential authenticity to his role's fictionality or, perhaps, a little of both. The deliberate conditionality of that last sentence says it all. It is not surprising, in the context of such a merging of the actual and the fictional in that cast change, that a sense of confusion can infect any aspect of production and audience reception of True Crime narratives. In 2005 the Texas 1st Court of Appeals in the United States overturned the murder conviction of Andrea Yates, a mother who received a life sentence for drowning three of her five young children.[453] The conviction had drawn support from the testimony of a psychiatrist who was a witness for the prosecution, Dr Park Dietz, who was also a consultant on the television series *Law & Order*. He had stated in evidence that an episode of the show had dealt with a story about a woman who drowned her children in a bath and was found not guilty by reason of insanity.[454] The prosecution had argued that Yates might have seen the episode prior to the murder—she was a regular viewer of the show—and conceived the idea that, if she committed murder, she could escape punishment due to her diagnosed postnatal depression. It was a writer on the show, present during testimony, who uncovered an error in Dietz's evidence by getting confirmation from the *Law & Order* producers that they had never aired such an episode.

Never has there been a better example of the complexity of the interaction between textual and actual violence.[455] The prosecution's argument assumed that there is a direct motivational ill-effect of crime drama on viewers in real life—that it was possible for a crime show to play a motivational role in a criminal act. The legal system erroneously accepted as factual evidence that the fictional episode had occurred and that it may have had factual relevance if viewed by Yates, while the fictionalized occurrence of the episode was uncovered by a writer, one of the creators of fictional stories that take their inspiration from actual events. The end result was, because a story was not told—the absence of the occurrence of fiction as a fact—the actual verdict based on a story that never happened was overturned. Perhaps, Dr Dietz—as a consultant to the True-Crime fictional world of *Law & Order* also contributing to Yates's trial as legal text—not only found himself suffering a memory lapse but was also confused by the elasticity of the boundaries between lived experiences of the violent and the True Crime fictional media texts within which he operates as a consultant. Put simply, he got lost in transition.[456]

4

Show Business or Dirty Business?: The Theatrics of Mafia Narrative and Empathy for the Last Mob Boss Standing in *The Sopranos*[457]

What must big Joey think of these singing bosses and their new partners, the celebrity feds? Sitting in his Brooklyn cell, awaiting a trial that could send him to prison for life or put him to death, he may be wondering if he chose the wrong line of work in an America where a man who keeps secrets can be worth less than a man who spills them. His one rueful consolation may be that much of the public thinks the Mafia is less dirty business than show business, and that a few will be rooting for him to be the last Don standing.[458]

It is when violence is fictionalized that audience unease about its use often manifests itself because ethical beliefs about the use of violence held by an audience outside the text may find themselves subject to textual challenge. For audiences who become attached to a violent character in a story, for example, the use of violence becomes an issue of justification and moral debate as texts are shadowed by public excoriation of violence offscreen. Unlike the violence used in the texts discussed in the first three chapters, which reference actual events with varying degrees of indexical accuracy, fictionalized violence moving away from indexicality on the continuum of authenticity frees us to respond to violent characters more within the moral paradigms framed by the text, even when it clashes with ethical convictions about violence outside narrative parameters. Chapters 4 to 8 examine texts about violence which, to borrow Mark Seltzer's phrase, are visceral "shocks of contact" between violence and its fictional representation in order to see "in what sense are we to understand these processes of substitution—as alternatives to or as components of 'real life' violence."[459] Audience response to violence is less hampered by the concerns of indexical representation and becomes subject to the ways in which narrative convinces on its own terms that violence is not inevitably a reason to reject a transgressor, even if such conviction leaves an audience feeling disconcerted by feelings of empathy.

As the authorial attraction to True Crime revealed, generic narratives emerge from authors and screenwriters finding inspiration in murder or in the settings in which extraordinary violence occurs in the ordinary fabric of life. Thomas Leitch accurately argues that it is the comprehensive umbrella of the crime genre itself rather than any subgenre definition "that accounts for the enabling ambiguity at the heart of all crime genres and every film within them: the easy recognition of the genre's formulas coupled with a lingering uncertainty about their import."[460] Yet the examination of a subgenre can provide a focus for clarifying the ways in which fictional texts use images of violence with graphic singularity to convince audiences that they have something authentic to say about violence in human affairs, or simply about human affairs, and to account with more particularity for that ambiguity of import. As Raymond Chandler has pointed out in *The Simple Art of Murder*, narrative about murder has a "way of minding its own business, solving its own problems and answering its own questions."[461] Such textually contained parameters are often generically defined and no more so than in the gangster genre. In reply to a question posed about writing for *The Sopranos*—"Do you have to speak Mafia to write the show?"—David Chase, executive producer and creator of that brilliant television series about organized crime, said: "I guess what you have to be able to do is bust people's balls," that a writer had "to have a feel" for the ways in which antagonism and sarcasm permeate human relationships, even those expressing warmth.[462] Implied in the question and answer is the acknowledgement that the wise-guy aggression of Mafia-speak is a symbolic shorthand for violence and adversarial complexity in relationships. It is assumed that the viewer will recognize that linguistic and dramatic generic code as a conduit to a story about aspects of the human experience beyond the criminal. The relationship of that dramatic textual code to real-life Mafia-speak is not through indexicality, even if a plot finds inspiration in actual Mafia crimes, but in the theatrical space the actual and the generic portrayal share.

The Sopranos draws extensively on Mafia dramatic shorthand and iconicity while referencing other gangster texts drawn from an extensive public fascination with real-life and fictional gangsters. Popular culture's fascination with organized crime, in which fictional and actual gangsters share an archetypal theatricality on the same media stage, bespeaks a recognition that the drama of the real-life events in gangster lives of crime is inherently theatrical fodder, ripe for aesthetic recasting. As Carmela Soprano says of her Mafia boss husband Tony: "My husband can be very magnetic, bigger than life."[463] The dramatic glamour of their stories, with larger-than-life characters and classic scenarios of greed, revenge, betrayal, power, survival, and execution draws the public gaze and the creativity of storytellers. The Sopranos has taken those fascinating theatrics inherent in mob murders, strip-club cultures, the vendettas between crime families, and the struggle for survival in courtrooms and on the streets to fashion an aesthetic of gangster drama that retains that archetypal theatricality, and reflects on it, while exploring the moral ambivalences of suburban life.

Given that academic criticism of the show is still in its nascent stage, its unique place in that popular tradition still remains to be assessed. Academic criticism of the show has concerned itself with the way the series develops its critique of American capitalism, psychiatry, and family suburban life in the context of the Mob, in the person of Tony Soprano, going mainstream as the gangster becomes the "galvanizing anti-hero on Prozac"[464] with a midlife crisis. In addition, critique has responded to the show's intertextuality. Glen Creeber has noted the show's reflection on its own "televisionization" in a narrative that deconstructs itself.[465] David Pattie has insightfully mined the extensive gangster movie referentiality of the show "as a symbolic framework within which Tony, Paulie, Christopher, Silvio, and most of the other Mafia characters in *The Sopranos* attempt to find a meaning and justification for their lives."[466] However, insufficient recognition has been given to the unique way the show draws on the theatricality real-life events and characters have always offered the gangster genre. While it does update the genre and its social critique for contemporary audiences and uses its gangster media referentiality to explore characterization, *The Sopranos* more interestingly offers a multilayered critique of the ambivalent performativity of the actual, cultural, and textual gangsterverse with which it shares a stage.

The recent quote from *Time* magazine at the start of the chapter is a typical example of the contradictory theatrical mythologizing of the real-life gangster figure as an archetypal hero and an idealist at the heart of corruption. Even in defeat, with "Big Joey" sitting in a cell with his life in the balance, he is nostalgically portrayed as a lone figure battling a justice system subverted by celebrity in an America that does not value the code by which he lives. Racketeer though he is, and the focus of a celebrity-hungry media, the partnering of "the singing bosses" and the "celebrity feds" highlights the shared moral dubiousness and common theatricality of the public narrative in which transgressor and legal system participate. A creature of corruption, he still evokes the possibility that "it never wholly determines him."[467] He even seems to stand a little taller than the ostensible good guys who are merely "celebrity feds" because he kept to a code and was betrayed by "an America where a man who keeps secrets can be worth less than a man who spills them." This is the "romantic fatalism" of the "promethean, system defying individual hero"[468] that the early gangster films originated.

As Jack Shadoian intimates in the title of his book on the American gangster film, *Dreams and Dead Ends: The American Gangster Film*, it is not hard to identify with an archetype characterized by the pathos of dreams coming to a dead end.[469] Since the prosecution of the Mafia is as much show business as dirty business, as much a compelling story as about a threat to public order, the article recognizes that the public as the audience is going to respond equivocally on the story and mythological level and barrack for a larger than life "big Joey" to be the "last Don standing"—particularly in a society that is not, itself, morally clean enough to make the choice of identification unequivocal. No doubt, because he is in a cell, total audience identification is inhibited but the article acknowledges reader empathy for the lingering presence of an American archetype of failed aspiration in a tainted system. The problem is succinctly portrayed in *The Sopranos* in the workplace camaraderie that exists between the long-time Mafia informant Raymond Curto and his FBI handlers, in the chattily shared complaints Pussy and his FBI contact have about their similar workplace problems, and in the brutal exploitation of Adriana, Christopher's girlfriend, by the FBI that leads to her death. Adriana's handler's claim that "[n]owhere but at the FBI is the line clearer between the good guys and the bad guys"[470] does not reflect the true ambiguity of the situation. As real-life mobster James "Whitey" Bulger pithily put that sense of moral relativism in testimony to Federal officials "You're the good-good guys, and we're the bad-good guys."[471]

Gangsters On and Off the Screen

Despite the documented devastation of the real-life and death consequences of gangster behavior, the Mob's fictional history in popular culture, inspired by intra-familial Mafia warfare and crime family legal battles, is one of mythologized codes and archetypal characters that sit on that overlapping boundary posited by performance theory where "[s]ocial dramas affect aesthetic dramas, aesthetic dramas affect social dramas."[472] *The Sopranos* itself satirizes the theatrical goldmine provided by actual Mafia events when giving a syndicated columnist's book the title "*Mafia: America's Longest Running Soap Opera.*"[473] As Richard Maltby notes in his analysis of the golden-age of gangster films in the 1930s:

> Beginning with the funeral of Big Jim Colosimo in Chicago in May 1920, big gangster funerals became media events, while police raids and gangland wars supplied the melodrama on which the tabloids and sensational magazines thrived.[474]

The theatricality conveyed by real-life mobster stories as inspirations for the fictionalized versions was also used by mobsters who role-played versions of themselves in the press and media: "Al Capone achieved national prominence not because he was particularly successful in his chosen field of endeavor, but because he so assiduously courted media attention."[475] As Lloyd Hughes also notes, the gangsters of the 1920s fought their gun battles on the streets with a public audience and "for those who didn't happen to be on the right sidewalk to see it"[476] the newspapers mythologized it in the next edition.

Promotion of *The Sopranos* engages with its own fictional theatricality in relationship to real-life gangsterism. In a DVD feature for the second season of *The Sopranos*, the show is promoted as "The Real Deal" in its image of gangsterism, quoting crime reporters who have also heard the same claim from the mobsters they have interviewed. The "Real Deal" is not explicitly defined but seems to be posited as its ability to capture something of the personalities of real gangsters and how they operate, rather than claiming that the fictional is reality television. It is the performativity of the real gangsters' behavior in the context of what they do, that they are entertaining characters as well as killers that is emphasized. John Miller, one of those quoted, an ABC reporter who has covered the Colombo and Gambino crime families, describes them as paradoxical figures: "They would tell stories and make you laugh until tears were streaming down your face . . . months later you would hear a recording of the same guy saying kill this guy, whack that guy."[477] As storytellers themselves, the gangsters can play to their reporter audience with comic timing and the crime reporters respond to their subjects as entertaining characters. It is when they are unaware of their audience—offstage as it were, presumably on surveillance recordings—that the gangsters are less entertaining than chilling.

However, defining what there is of the "real deal" in a fictional gangster is less interesting than looking at the ways in which the performativity and theatricality of real and fictional characters share the same role-playing space in media incarnations offered to an audience. One of the central traits of theatricality, Samuel Weber argues, is the staging of scenes or events on the presumption that they will be observed by an audience, without necessarily being able to contain them totally within the frame of that aesthetic (or even physical) space.[478] Aware they were subjects of legal surveillance, often tools of that surveillance themselves ("He was a wiseguy wearing a wire"[479]) real-life gangsters have always been conscious of themselves as having an audience, if not always a desired one. Rising to media prominence in the film and press in American culture from the early 1900s, gangsters have often been the unwilling subjects of media attention. *The Sopranos* notes the problems this makes for Tony: "How come every piss I take is a fuckin' news story?"[480] Tony is comically unaware how his story is fodder for an insatiable public appetite for gangster narratives. The show itself satirizes the way in which the interactive antics of the Mafia and law enforcement contribute to media industry and spectacle when the conflict to be generated by the "Mafia class of '04" is described as making "a good year for crime reporters."[481]

Crime bosses have also been conscious of the ways they could exploit the media for public relations purposes and, in turn, that attention has created an aesthetic space in which "the media gangster was an invention, much less an accurate reflection of reality than a projection"[482] of the possibilities and excesses of the urban culture they sprang from and reflected.[483] As David E. Ruth describes, in his aptly named book *Inventing the Public Enemy*, the press and films chronicling and mythologizing the exploits of legendary figures like Al Capone were less interested in the factuality of the underworld than the "imagined gangster."[484] That fanciful image was created in fascinating narratives of the dramatic rise and fall of an individual. "The Capone legend offered Americans a subversive set of metaphors for rethinking their business society,"[485] often blurring the boundaries between criminality and respectability while chronicling the personal and economic success to be won and lost through violent masculinity. As Letizia Paoli notes in a comparison of the Sicilian and American mafias, "For many people the Italian/American mafia *is* and *behaves* as it is recounted in these romanticizing novels and films."[486] Nor is this romanticism uniquely American, as the press coverage of the funeral in Melbourne of the murdered Australian gangster, Mario Condello revealed—headlining him as a "Gangster who nursed a sick mother, found God and loved a laugh,"[487] rather than as a criminal.

Where the boundary separating actuality from romantic myth might be is not something an audience can easily determine. Even Dr Melfi, Tony Soprano's initially reluctant but ultimately empathic therapist, as a nonmobster herself, only has media images to use to speculate about what his role as Mob boss might be like outside their sessions: "Granted I get most of my information from movies and Bill Curtis."[488] Given the same could be said by any reader of Mafia stories in the press or viewer of them on television or film, popular fascination with the gangster is more about responding to performance and theatricality than to authentic representation. As Robert Warshaw acknowledged over 30 years ago: "What matters is that the experience of the gangster *as an experience of art* is universal to Americans."[489] It may be, as Fred Gardaphe asserts: "The truth is that the fiction of the gangster is stronger than the facts, and the facts of American history will never be as attractive as the myths that have been created around the gangster."[490] The gangster as archetypal hero is transformed by narrative into more than the sum of his violent criminality by the theatricality that brings him to prominence in the public eye and makes of him a morality tale for outlawed individuality.

John McCarty trenchantly captures the blend of the "reel" and "real" with his description of the 1975 film *Lepke*'s literal reliance on actual mobster cache and biography of Murder Inc.'s Louis Lepke Buchalter,[491] as a movie "that plays like a filmed rap sheet."[492] McCarty sees that interaction as two-way when he notes that the actor George Raft replied to the question of why factual gangsters "sounded so much like their movie counterparts" by saying "that it was because gangster movies (his in particular, he noted) taught gangsters how to talk":

Raft's explanation is more than just off-hand quip or self-aggrandizing patter; it is an astute observation. America's gangsters have always been fascinated with the movies about them and their exploits, and they have always been interested in the movie business because of the huge amount of money that can be made . . . The story of Bugsy Siegel has special significance to this chronicle of bullets over Hollywood because Bugsy's rise and fall is not just a rattling good gangster story with all the genre's trimmings—money, power, violence—but a glitzy showbiz tale as well. That Robinson, Cagney, Raft, and other movie gangsters based their characters' styles of dress, their manner- isms, and other behavioral tics on the famous gangster personalities of their time we know. But the movie screen is a mirror with two sides, and gangsters, like children, are not immune from the desire to want to walk, talk, and be like their icons flickering back at them from the big screen. This may be why so many mobsters—from the big-time dons of New York to the street hood- lums we see on the nightly news—seem often like caricatures of their movie counterparts, acting out roles in their own real-life gangster melodramas.[493]

While performance theory supports the interrelatability of the social and the aesthetic, the degree to which cross-fertilization occurs is, ultimately, of less inter- est than the fact that there is a theatrical core to gangsterism that Hollywood can exploit, something even the gangsters themselves seem to be aware of. It is possible to find "Mafia comfortable with the idea of a fictional representation of their activi- ties" well before the FBI surveillance tapes of Mafia fans of The Sopranos noted by Patti.[494] McCarty notes that Siegel was a childhood friend of Raft's from the Lower East Side of New York and that he even took a screen test to become an actor when he reestablished his association with Raft in Hollywood while there on syn- dicate gambling business.

The Sopranos and Performativity

People are often shown watching television in The Sopranos, and its texts are a back- ground to events in the story which raise questions about what is real, whether people are as they portray themselves, and about what form of authenticity is to be had from television and film narratives. The intersection of actual Mob events with narratives in fictional entertainment and public perceptions of the Mafia is high- lighted in The Sopranos in "46 Long," when Tony and his gang are listening to a CNN-style television panel giving expert analysis for its viewers of the "situation on the ground today" in the Mafia. As Joseph S. Walker has pointed out, "the scene depends upon the audience's knowledge, or at least awareness, of a long tradition of stories about organized crime in America."[495] It is the easy acceptance by the gang that they and their business are the subjects of media punditry that denotes the way the Mob soap opera is integrated into the fabric of American culture. However, when Tony asks Silvio to role-play Al Pacino's line in the third Godfather movie ("Just when I thought I was out, they pull me back in"), as an antidote to the topic of mob decline being discussed by the panel, the gang place themselves as more than consumers and subjects of gangster film history, they are performers of it. Paulie illustrates appreciation of this performativity when he comments on Silvio's delivery: "Fuckin' spittin image." When Silvio does the same line later in the episode while trying on a heisted Italian suit and preening in front of a mirror, he is admiring the way he role-plays the theatrical image. When he reprises the line again in "A Guy Walks into a Psychiatrist's Office," there is not just a sense that it is Silvio's role to be the repository of that film's lore for instant access as inspiration, comfort, and humor, as Pattie argues, but that the Mafia occupies the same theatrical stage as the movie and that Tony and his gang see themselves as actors sharing that stage. Thus it is possible for Silvio to parody *The Godfather*'s theatricality, while *being* a parody—exaggerated curl of lip, clipped speech, and all—of the gangster stereotype.

Silvio and the rest of Tony's gang are attached to the stereotypical, nostalgic romanticism of the gangster image the *Godfather* films create and the glamour its mythology drapes over their own corruption. The expert whose opinions are given credence by the interviewer over those of the government official is one of Tony's detested show business Mob informants: "Vincent Rizzo, former soldier in the Genovese family, government witness turned best-selling author." Ironically, Rizzo's Mob origins have been a stepping-stone in a career path via the witness protection program to celebrity media pundit. It is black humor at its best—an ex-criminal pundit offers pseudohistoricizing of Mafia mythology with organized crime meeting basic human appetites in the culture of which the audience of *The Sopranos* forms a part ("As long as the human being has certain appetites for gambling, pornography, whatever, someone's always gonna surface to serve these needs"). The ironic subtext is that one of the appetites the existence of the Mafia indirectly feeds is for gangster stories.

Tony has "had offers" to be fictionalized, and *The Sopranos* may have had Bugsy Siegel in mind when the show gave Christopher Moltisanti, Tony's nephew and protégé, the same Hollywood crossover yearnings.

Christopher: You know my cousin Gregory's girlfriend is what they call a development girl out in Hollywood. She said I could sell my life story, make fucking millions. I didn't do that. I stuck it out with you.

Tony: I'll fucking kill you. What you gonna do, go Henry Hill on me now? You know how many mobsters are selling screenplays and screwing everything up?

Christopher: She said I could maybe even play myself . . .

Tony: Forget Hollywood screenplays, forget those distractions, huh. What do you think I haven't had offers? You got work to do.[496]

Christopher's belief that he could play himself on screen articulates the theatricality that is available to storytelling when real-life gangsters live the violent rituals that are mined for screenplays in the gangster genre. Wryly, the show places itself as one of those fictionalizations that is a part of that process of "making fucking millions" out of the mob genre and, ironically, allows Tony, to claim the moral high ground because he eschews selling out to show business. Tony does not simply mean that the mobster Hollywood sellouts are screwing things up because they are revealing too much. He dismisses the creativity of screenplay writing as "distractions" from "work" and scorns them as of little value in the larger scheme of things. The fact that the more important "work" is gangsterism, of course, undercuts Tony's moral values. However, in its first episode, the series is reflecting on the nature of its own endeavor as entertainment and on the potential for entertainment that is at the heart of real-life gangsters living out the potential screenplay as they go about their "work."

Christopher merges that theatricality and his own existence when he laments the lack of a story "arc" in his life in "The Legend of Tennessee Moltisanti"[497] ("Says in these movie-writing books that every character has an arc, you understand?") that will give him respect, purpose, and celebrity. Christopher is obsessed with the glamour of the movies, reflecting a popular obsession that mirrors his own ("mob stories are always hot"). He wants to parlay his mob cache, if he can just get some, into fame and fortune: "I could make my mark." His pursuit of media celebrity, which leads him to equate it with actual status, seems as much an addiction as his coke snorting. However unlikely it is that Christopher will achieve Hollywood success, his use of scriptwriting terminology allows him to find the words for his own lack of purpose in a life that seems to him to have no narrative throughline. However, his failure to embody the charismatic wise-guy image of so many screen versions of the gangster is pointed out in "A Guy Walks into a Psychiatrist's Office"[498] where he is shown uncharismatically getting high while Edward G. Robinson in a tough guy role appears on the television in front of him. As a drug addict, Christopher does not fit the romanticized stereotype of the movies he watches.[499] Similarly, in "Big Girls Don't Cry,"[500] when his feelings violently overwhelm him as he performs a scene from *Rebel Without a Cause* for an acting class, he has trouble sticking to imagined scripts. The tears he produces for the scene turn out to be real and he exits the class unable to deconstruct the scene as pretence. In a follow-up acting session, Christopher's unresolved feelings about his own father lead him to beat up the actor playing a father opposite him in the scene—giving a literal meaning to living vicariously through fiction. When his girl friend Adriana suggests to him, "Acting is mostly feelings," she is a voice for the recognition of the mixture of reality and performativity in Christopher's life. Christopher's desire for his real life to hit the beats of a theatrical arc falters as his life overwhelms a theatricality he struggles to hold onto. A fish out of water in the movie world in "D-Girl,"[501] Christopher makes a reality-based, but pathos-filled choice when he decides to stay with Tony rather than pursue his Hollywood aspirations at the end of the episode. He picks up the only "arc" he has ever followed leading him to eventually inform on Adriana to Tony, cause the murder of the woman he loves, and continue his moral bondage to the evil Tony represents: "I gave that fuck pieces of my soul Adriana."[502]

However, when he kills Emile Kolar in Centanni's meat market in the pilot episode of *The Sopranos*,[503] his physical stance and the camera angling up at him as he pumps bullets into his victim's dead body emphasizes the fact that a theatrical pose has been struck. The pose conveys an iconic empowerment, as does the intercutting with shots of posters from the wall of iconic gangster actors such as Humphrey Bogart and Edward G. Robinson. While the pig heads on the left of the screen undercut the romanticism of Christopher's stance because they are "not a flattering audience,"[504] there is no question the glamour of the pose remains—with Christopher and the audience free to enjoy its theatricality and its violent romanticism:

> In their quest to make entertainment out of taboo behavior, they treat crime as both realistic and ritualistic, a shocking aberration and business as usual, a vehicle of social idealism and of social critique. But although the nature of the character who embodies the heroic role the genre proscribes can vary from one crime film to the next even in the same multiplex, the genre itself is best defined in terms of a single constitutive theme: the romance of criminal behaviour.[505]

As Leitch argues, this is not to say that the behavior is not condemned but that the audience is offered the contradiction between that condemnation and romanticism as entertainment. That possibility complicates audience reception and leaves the door open to the frustration of intended authorial interpretations. David Ray Papke has chronicled Francis Ford Coppola's frustrations with popular reception of Michael Corloene as more of a hero than as a metaphor for a negative critique of American society, even after his attempt in a sequel to reiterate the point:

> What did trouble Coppola was the way the stories and characters in the film apparently continued to appeal to viewers. Coppola wanted to indict, to speak critically and symbolically. However, American myths about family and upward mobility and the American taste for authoritarian action qua violence continued to trump a tale of lawlessness with an increasingly corporate face.[506]

Despite the glamour of the pose, Christopher is a killer in that scene and he is, of course, deluding himself by striking a pose that seeks to deny his own degradation. The empowered nature of his pose is not a product of his act, but of the attractiveness of its theatricality, something it shares with the impact of *The Godfather* narrative that Coppola deplored. However, in a nice touch of irony, the audience of *The Sopranos* is later reminded in "The Legend of Tennessee Moltisanti" that neither killing Kolar nor the glamour of its theatricality gets Christopher the respect he craves: "I killed that fuckin' Email Kolar and nothing, I don't even move up a notch." He tells Tony that "the fuckin' regularness of life is too fucking hard for me or something." The emptiness of the glamour he hopes he can use to fill the void can reach no further than a mention in the local New Jersey paper, *The Star Ledger*, which he excitedly buys multiple copies of at the end of the episode. As he converses with Tony about the fates of other people so depressed, hopeless, and empty that they commit suicide ("Imagine those fuckin' losers blowing their skulls all over the bathroom"), they are both clearly avoiding their own feelings of hopelessness and the connections those feelings have with the violent corruption and self-deception at the heart of the lives they lead.

Tony Performing Tony

The theatrics of role-playing is above all a symptom of self-delusion and deception in *The Sopranos*' narrative. As David Chase has noted: "everything that everybody says is untrue: complete falsehoods, self-justifications, rationalizations, outright lies, fantasies and miscommunications."[507] Identity confusion requires clarification in media reports: "Little Pussy Malanga, sometimes confused with fellow reputed mobster, Big Pussy Bonpensiero, just returned from Florida."[508] Characters make use of theatrical imagery that implies role-playing: "Don't you think it's totally unfair what Mum's doing and now like making this little movie scene out of it?" says Meadow, referring to her mother, Carmela[509] and they are called on the sincerity with which they do it: "Don't call me Godfather with that fuckin' cute smirk" (Tony rebuking Feech La Manna in "All Happy Families").[510] As well, the show mines television and film imagery for epithets to typecast people as when A. J., Tony's son, is described as "Fredo Corleone"[511] by his teacher Mr Fisk or when there is a gap between characters and roles they may play, as when Pussy is irritated by playing detective to retrieve A. J.'s science teacher's stolen car: "I'm fuckin' Rockford over here."[512]

At one time or another, Tony too, lies to almost everyone in his life, including his family, other members of the Mob, his therapist, and to himself. Audience reaction to this deception and his violent, murderous gangsterism is complicated by the sympathy for the devil that has been noted in critical reception of his character[513]— sympathy that is the product of an aesthetic that appropriated the culture of organized crime and the sordidness of its subject matter to set its own ethical parameters. Graphic violence is *de rigueur* in the gangster genre (where, as Sonny Corleone pithily illustrates, "You've gotta get up close like this and—bada bing— you blow their brains all over your nice Ivy League suit."[514]). However, as McCarty notes, quoting the film *Goodfellas* with which *The Sopranos* shares an ongoing intertextuality, audience identification with the kitchen sink setting of Mafia crime comes from the fact that it seemed like a nine-to-five job: "It got to be normal," observes the gangster Henry Hill's Jewish outsider wife in the film,[515] "It didn't seem like crime at all."[516]

Similarly, Tony is not only defined by his gangsterism. The use of the gangster to explore "the multiplicity of lives one might lead in modern society"[517] is inherent in the genre. Ruth has noted that Americans were always "intrigued by this chasm between domestic and professional identities"[518] that was exemplified in the contrast between Al Capone's life as a gangster and family man. In Coppola's *Godfather* films, the code by which Don Corleone lives as the family patriarch enables the gangster dramatically "to live life as a critique of mainstream America and its hypocrisies."[519] Leitch notes the "defining paradox"[520] of the gangster narrative, after all, is that as characters gangsters both emulate and transgress social and moral norms. In Tony's case "contemporary suburban life breeds both middle-class ennui and a complex tension with his mob world"[521] and "dramatizes the struggle of middle-class American family *as* mob life."[522] His contemporary frustrations ("It's just a lot of bullshit, bullshit, bullshit"[523]), his appetites, his anger, his helplessness, his acquaintance with loss—all forge audience solidarity with his predicament. As Leitch argues, this is not to say that gangster behavior is not condemned but that the audience is offered the contradiction between that condemnation and romanticism as theatrical entertainment.

While there are enough scenes of Tony acting brutally to counter the undoubted empathy the show encourages the audience to feel for him, it is his own performance of the sentimental, idealist mobster that underpins the audience's sense that Tony is a bit of a ham actor as much engaged in self-deception as deceiving others and in role-playing an idealized version of himself masking the criminal at the core. This is particularly so when his behavior references the sentimentality of *The Godfather* movie as his life strains to fit the theatrical parameters it offers him for making sense of personal experience. (He tries, for example, to emulate Vito Corleone and goes back to the mother country in "Commendatori,"[524] only to learn he is more of a tourist than a native son.)

Tony is, in his deceptiveness, a sentimental dramatist and a mask wearer. Tony can perceive the cloying sentimental overkill in playing *It's a Wonderful Life* incessantly at Christmas: "Jeezus, enough already" in "To Save Us All From Satan's Power." However, he is not above using that sentimentality for cynical public relations purposes in an episode where he role-plays community spirit and throws a Christmas party for the local children. In a plot moving back and forth between the gang's current search for someone to play Santa at the Christmas party and Pussy playing Santa in the past—while wired up by the FBI as a part of his betrayal prior to Tony ordering his murder—Tony realizes the ease with which he was deceived by Pussy's role-playing. Comically, at the same time, he wishes for better acting from a reluctant Bobby Baccalieri who is a substitute Santa at the party. In a plethora of theatrical terms, Tony gives acting critique ("He's a method actor"); Silvio recommends theatrical training for Bobby ("Next year he goes to Santa school"); Bobby fights miscasting ("I don't wanna do this, shyness is a curse"); Paulie directs ("It would kill him to say Ho, ho, ho?"); and Tony realizes there is something to be said for an honest, if badly acted performance: ("I don't miss Pussy's fake, fuckin' good cheer, tell ya the truth"). The Christmas party is staged sentimentality but Tony's desire for a compelling performance is not without reservations. Feeling a sense of loss over Pussy's execution, Tony sentimentally agrees with Silvio that Pussy was great in the role of Santa. However, he also recognizes that Pussy was a great actor as an FBI informant. As Pussy's friend and his murderer, Tony can distinguish between the two roles and regret Pussy's death with no guilt at having had him killed. When Paulie, still angry at Pussy's betrayal, rejects any sentimentalism: "In the end, fuck Santa Claus," Tony still sighs, looks sad and, paradoxically, the audience is left feeling as sentimental as Tony over Pussy's loss while reminded by the exaggerated comedy of it all that it *is* overly mawkish.

It is often his wife Carmela or Dr Melfi who call Tony on his pretence. However, when Tony refuses to hand over his cousin Tony for execution to appease Johnny Sack in the middle of a gang war with Little Carmine, he justifies it to his own gang with the idealistic rhetoric of "we are a family and even in this fucked up day and age this means something."[525] It is his Consigliore, Silvio, who remonstrates: "With all due respect, you were ready to hand 'em your cousin a week ago, so it's not about standin' with the guys, or upholdin' some rules, not really." Silvio has known Tony since he was a kid and with clear-sightedness born of pretty close observation sees through his boss role-playing *The Godfather* myth:

It's about you don't wanna eat shit from John. You don't wanna bow down. You told him to go fuck himself which, to be honest, wasn't exactly appropriate, considering.

As Silvio points out, even by Tony's own sentimentalized standards of Mob protocol, thumbing his nose at the New York boss was not "appropriate" and, in what must be the most hilarious understatement in six seasons of the show, makes a diagnosis of Tony equal to anything Dr Melfi has come up with: "I've known you since you were a kid Ton, frankly, you've got a problem with authority." With the comedy of that line, Silvio bursts the bubble of the romantic theatricality of Tony's gangster honor code as a self-justifying cover for having a tantrum at being told what to do. The fact that this insight is given by a character who is himself a gangster stereotype and the parodied repository of *The Godfather* lore in Tony's gang, brings full circle the complex way in which the text of the show utilizes and reflects on the theatrics and performativity of real and fictional gangster narratives.

In a culture where real and fictional gangsters engage with the media in inventing their public personas, narrative takes place in a theatrical space that all real and imagined gangsters share. It is not surprising then, that in the film *Gang Tapes*[526] (which tells the story of the descent of a teenage boy into "gang banging" in South Central Los Angeles through the hand held video camera the boy uses to record the lives of those around him) that the director of the film used actor and nonactor residents with a history of participation in that gangster culture to portray the characters in the film. One of the gang member actors, Six Reasons—who plays the doomed adolescent "gang banger" Erik—heard about the murder of his actual cousin through a call to his mobile while he was on set for filming. In that moment, the filmic stage and the space outside it intersected. He remarked that "Erik and Six, you know, there's not too many big differences, 'cause that's the kinda person I am, I have family, relatives that gang bang.'"[527] I would argue that this is not to say that there is a biographical indexicality between the actor and the character but that the fictional character and the actor share a story that occupies the same performance space. The film's video documentary motif, its use of "gang bangers" as actors and the actors living the subject of the narrative as they fictionalized it, underlines how the theatrics of actual violence and its fictionalization creates a narrative space in which they can merge. The audience can be left with an authentic sense of gang culture where, as Six says, "there's no soft and sugar-coated violence, don't nobody get killed softly." However, when Erik points a camera at himself in the mirror and sees himself as filmmaker telling his own narrative of his life reflected back, the audience is confronted with the possibility that to be actual is to live theatrically. It is only the fact that the audience does not see itself in the mirror as it looks at his reflection that reminds us that Six and the audience are not completely one and the same.

The ex-gangster and current gangsta-rapper 50 Cent, musing on his engagement with the film version of his gangster past by playing himself in *Get Rich or Die Tryin',*[528] displays an amusing sense of confusion about the nature of that theatrical space he entered when he chose to play a filmic version of himself, while actors played the film's interpretation of people he knew in actuality. In the interview the reporter notes that 50 Cent was disturbed by the fact that "on set the actors seemed to forget it was *his* life they were talking about":

> "It's kinda weird watching actors. 'Cause you know actors gotta find them-selves,' and find the characters and they'll make references to things like, 'It could be like this,' or 'He could say it like this,' and they forget that the per-son that they're actually talking about is someone that I actually (know), you know what I mean?" . . . And they'll discuss it, as if it's not real. I mean it is a film, but it just feels weird at some point.[529]

50 Cent is struggling here with the recognition that in the transition to film—even though he is playing himself—he, and people he knew played by actors naturally feeling free to explore their characters, are both real *and* imaginative constructs

in a theatrical space and the narrative will lose indexicality as a result. No doubt, it feels "weird" but, since the film has been seen as a "vanity project"[530] and does sanitize his experiences in heroic rapper glamour, his naiveté about the performance space he exists in as rapper, actor, and embodiment of his own biography may be somewhat disingenuous.

It is inside such a theatrical show business space that audience sympathy for Tony Soprano thrives, despite the dirty business he engages in. By the end of "All Due Respect," as Tony stumbles through the snow, running from the scene of the arrest of Johnny Sack and into the safety of home and hearth, with Carmela comically exclaiming over his wet feet, Tony and the audience can breathe a sigh of relief that he is not named in the same indictment with the New York boss. His entry into his home contrasts with the ending to the previous season which had him thrown out of the house by his wife. He has resurrected his family life and eluded Big Joey's fate. In true show business style, an expectant audience is left rooting for Tony to be the last Mob boss standing, hoping that he will be able to hold his family together until the end of his story, despite knowing that he deserves a far darker fate.[531]

5

"Solving Problems with Sharp Objects": Female Empowerment, Sex, and Violence in *Buffy, the Vampire Slayer* [532]

Isn't that just like a slayer. Solving all her problems by sticking things with sharp objects. [533]
(D'Hoffryn, demon, Buffy, the Vampire Slayer)

As previous chapters have illustrated, the further one moves along the continuum of violence from the representation of indexical actuality and the more fictional the images of violence become, the more responsive analysis needs to be to the complex variety of narrative and ideological uses to which violence is put in texts. [534] *The Sopranos* offers its audience a space where it is possible to be repelled by a character's violence and to safely identify with other aspects of his character while the violence is used to comment on contemporary American society. That ideological purpose and audience identification with a character points to the central use of violence in a fictional text as a metaphorical shortcut to tell stories about subjects other than violence. In that sense, the audience or reader does not need to be convinced by the authenticity of the violence but by the emotional authenticity of the exploration of what it means to be human for which the violence is the metaphorical launching point. When the setting for that violence is fantastical in some way, as in the horror genre, then the violence itself can be convincingly authentic more because it is emotionally charged as a vehicle for characterization than because it is graphic or indexical to actuality. As a writer in that genre, Miguel Tejada-Flores notes: "there is emotional and personal truth in the best horror." [535] In addition, the master of slash and hack violence, director Wes Craven, has offered the view that the attraction of the genre's excessive violence for him is the opportunity it gives, outside of the mainstream limits of good taste, to comment ideologically on a cultural underbelly "in a way that is necessary for a culture's health." [536] As Richard

Maltby notes, it has been decades since "[h]orror has escaped from its Gothic castle"[537] and the genre has an ideological interest in the violence that social and political repression engenders. An example of that use of violence in the horror genre is the cult television hit show *Buffy, the Vampire Slayer* (*Buffy*). Joss Whedon's premise, as executive producer and creator of the show, epitomizes that metaphorical and fantastical use of violence for ideological and dramatic emotional purposes. He has said that he "designed *Buffy* to be an icon, not just a TV show."[538] Based on its portrayal of a strong, violent, female Slayer protagonist in a genre where the female is usually the victim, the nature of that icon has been firmly linked with contemporary phrases like "girl power," "female empowerment," and "feminism." Whedon, in a panel discussion at the Academy of Television Arts and Sciences described the "very first mission statement of the show" as "the joy of female power, having it, using it, sharing it."[539] The show and its Slayer superhero is offered as a cultural and ideological statement about gender but its use of violence to convey emotional truths about its superhero raises questions about whether or not Buffy as a female hero truly "represents her gender, herself, and more,"[540] as Anne Millard Daugherty puts it, and in what way the show's horror genre violence plays a part in that ideological statement.[541]

Female empowerment in *Buffy* is typically described as linked to her ability in the "masculine" role to "kick butt" as the positive stereotype of the female aggressor.[542] Buffy appears empowered as a Slayer because the violence she uses works in the fight against evil and saving the world. Until Xander, one of the Scooby[543] sidekicks, saves the world through love rather than violence in "Grave"[544] or when Buffy saves it through sacrificing her life in "The Gift,"[545] it is the main tool in an apocalypse. Xander, petulantly when he feels underappreciated for his use of it, calls it "quality violence."[546] Given that the evil characters seem to be good at it too, with "all those fancy martial arts skills they inevitably seem to pick up,"[547] it is a "solid call" to use it:

Xander: You don't know how to kill this thing.

Buffy: I thought I might try violence.

Xander: Solid call.[548]

Buffy's violence is in response to attack from the demon side in the battle between good and evil and she does not get to choose another method in those circumstances. Buffy knows that there is an art to her violence and she is proud of that. It takes training[549] and it is about survival. She is not paid to kill but she has a calling to do it and, like any good employee, she is thorough in her job. This dedication is comically highlighted when she is politely apologetic at having to stake an elderly woman who has been sired by the vampire Spike (Buffy's vampire nemesis in love with her): "Sorry, ma'am, but it's my job."[550]

It has also been frequently noted that Buffy fights with words as well as blows, that language for her is a weapon.[551] Both villains and the Scooby heroes acknowledge the "banter portion of the fight"[552] as a ritualistic and essential part of the fight scenario. Lame repartee can signal inevitable defeat as much as a poorly placed kick or punch. Repartee, whether Buffy's or from the core Scooby group, is a vehicle for the female empowerment message, which Buffy herself recognizes when words are not a part of the fight: "If I was at full Slayer power, I'd be punning right about now."[553] As Karen Eileen Overbey and Lahney Preston-Matto point out, in placing Buffy in the traditionally male stance of the sardonic hero, the show participates through language in gender reversal, as it does when it gives male characters like Xander the more traditionally feminine self-mocking and self-deprecating lines. Allusively self-referential as always, the show uses a nonsense pun to signal that having robot Buffy, the Buffybot, as a stand-in Slayer when Buffy is temporarily dead at the beginning of season six, is not nearly as effective as having the real Slayer: "That'll put marzipan in your pie plate, bingo!"[554] As Spike says, the Buffybot will never be Buffy "exactly" because Buffy is more than a fighting machine. Her language is not just the sarcastic word trappings of battle but, essentially, a signifier for the hero she is. This joy in language is, for Buffy herself, a part of the thrill of the fight. When the punning is bad, the fun goes out of the fight for her:

> That's it? That's all I get? One lame-ass vamp, with no appreciation for my painstakingly thought out puns? I don't think the forces of darkness are even trying.[555]

Language in a fight is Buffy's power, not simply because it is a part of her arsenal, but because it is the way she announces who she is. Concomitantly, her enemies are never more threatening than when they have a sarcastic remark to contribute to the encounter: "I think we already know what Lady HacksAway wants."[556] The leader of the Vengeance demons, D'Hoffryn, devastatingly pinpoints the lack of subtlety in Buffy's violent approach to some of the problems she wants to solve in that comment (and in the one at the head of the chapter). Manipulation of language for Buffy, as it is within the text of the show overall, is liberating. If Buffy were less articulate she would appear more brutal. The effect of this wordplay in the context of Buffy's use of violence is one of putting the audience "fray-adjacent,"[557] where the audience is given perspective on the violence and on other aspects of the show's construction. The audience is given the distance to consider how the characters are using the violence, what the blow is *for*, and how violence as metaphor is constructed in the show.

Given Whedon's female empowerment premise, it is not possible to discuss the use of violence in the show without discussing the degree to which that ideology is convincingly sustained beyond "butt-kicking" the generic horror denizens of evil in the narrative—the vampires and demons. It is not surprising that Patricia Pender asserts: "If one of the principle motivations of popular cultural studies is to decode the political subtext of any given work, then the central concern for students of the *Buffy* phenomenon is the question, is *Buffy* feminist?"[558] Academic analysis has circled around the "transgression/containment" model, which "dictates that Buffy is 'good' if she transgresses dominant stereotypes, 'bad' if she is contained in cultural cliché."[559] Some assessments like Gina Wisker's posit an ideological divide ("*Buffy The Vampire Slayer* treads an entertaining, if uneasy, course between conservatism and contemporary feminist girl power."[560]) Others, limited by being written early in the show's run, prematurely adopt Whedon's desire to subvert the horror genre "female-as-victim" role as the beginning and end of the story. Jim Thompson, for example, asserts that the show is in a "males-cannot-measure-up" scenario, fitting the criteria of a radical feminist superiority discourse: "Even Cordelia, the archetypal high-school cheerleader 'bitch' has a strength of character which males in the series cannot match."[561] However, one does not have to go further than Xander (one of Buffy's inner circle Scooby sidekicks) saving the world at the end of season six, or Spike doing the same at the end of season seven, to realize that "strength of character" is not exclusively the province of females in the Buffyverse.[562] In both Spike's and Xander's case, the message seems to be that whoever is best placed at the time to save the world in an apocalypse is the one who should do it, gender being irrelevant.

There is no question that the show's exploration of female empowerment is linked to the concept of power in male/female relationships and this is inevitably linked to the use of violence. Season seven is essentially an exploration of what Buffy's power might mean in a leadership context, as she takes her role to the level of commanding an army in a war against the First Evil in which Buffy battles a sexism-spouting misogynist villain, the preacher Caleb. She also successfully fights off the first patriarchal Watchers'[563] attempt (in a time travel scenario) to force demon power into her, a form of mystical rape (as they had done to the first Slayer). Finally, Buffy's discovery of the Scythe in the stone, forged by ancient female Guardians who through history monitored the patriarchal Watchers to help protect the Slayers, enables Buffy to reject patriarchal precedent and to change Slayer lore. In the final battle, she gives up her Chosen status and shares her powers with potential female Slayers all over the world, rejecting the idea that her life has to be predestined by patriarchal precedents.[564]

Sharing Gender Roles

For all the didacticism of that triumph, as one writer succinctly puts it, butt-kicking "girl power alone is not enough to propel a narrative, otherwise . . . *Charmed* might not seem so inane."[565] While gender subversion using superheroic violence is the intent of Whedon's horror genre premise, the show is a narrative that was prepared to take risks in exploring it. There are moments of ambiguity and flux where the premise is stretched to give the audience resonant dramatic, emotional, and ideological possibilities beyond the show's female empowerment boundaries. It is violence that is the vehicle for that resonance. Sherryl Vint is right when she says *Buffy* "opens productive space for getting young women (and others) to see how meanings are constructed"[566] about gender. However, it is essential not to miss the show's dramatic negotiation with its own premise. Whedon encourages us to specificity in ideological terms: "We think very carefully about what we're trying to say emotionally, politically, and even philosophically while we're writing it," but he qualifies this:

> The process of breaking a story involves the writers and myself, so a lot of different influences, prejudices, and ideas get rolled up into it. So it really is, apart from being a big pop culture phenomenon, something that is deeply layered textually episode by episode. I do believe that there is plenty to study and there are plenty of things going on in it, as there are in me that I am completely unaware of.[567]

In juggling discourses about male and female power through its violent superhero, the show works to embed them in a dramatic context that encourages a range of gender possibilities making for a far less static "girl power" thesis. Whedon admits: "The basic idea, the empowerment of girls and the toughness of this life, was always there, but it grew beyond my best intentions."[568] Just as "generalizations about gender can all too easily erase the multiplicity of experiences of gender,"[569] a too easy acceptance of what "empowerment" or "girl power" might mean in the Buffy-verse may lead one to miss the value of the show's exploration of such labels for the female experience. The simple reversal of culturally demarcated gender differences—so that

> women have been permitted in representation to assume (step into) the position defined as masculine, as long as the man then steps into her position, so as to keep the whole structure intact[570]

—is not exactly what is offered in *Buffy* because the reversal of gender roles is never a simple transgressive flip.

Sharing gender roles, rather than reversal, is closer to what happens in Buffy and Spike's often-violent relationship, for example. As Rhonda Wilcox notes, Spike's name denotes his violent masculinity because "it is phallic, it is violent" but his character is also "a work in progress."[571] There is a partial gender role reversal in Spike's damsel-in-distress status leading up to Buffy's rescue of him from the

Ubervamp's torture and the First Evil's imprisoning of him in season seven. Buffy is "not much for the damselling"[572] but Spike often is. Nor is he always in control of the sexual action between them. One of the "main indictments of Hollywood film has been its passive positioning of the woman as sexual spectacle . . . and the active protagonist as bearer of the look," a product of "masculine desire."[573] Reversing this tendency, Spike is objectified for the female audience in scenes where he is shirtless or naked while little is seen of Buffy's body by comparison, even to the point where Buffy is, ironically, totally invisible in sex between them in "Gone"[574] and Spike is, despite strategic placement behind props, barely covered. Spike's masculine beauty, his desirability "becomes a function of certain practices of imaging—framing, light-ing, camera movement, angle,"[575] so that the male is an object of spectator sexual voyeurism. Buffy also loses "some traditionally feminine characteristics"[576] to Spike in the relationship, such as the desire to communicate. He wants to analyze their relationship ("So, we gonna chat this out, or what?")[577] and to talk about what is happening between them in an effort to get her to acknowledge it ("What is this thing we have?")[578]—a process she rejects.

However, there are fissures in this reversal.[579] While the female audience is encouraged to gaze, as Laura Mulvey defines that term,[580] at Spike's body with pleas-ure, there is no reciprocity with Buffy gazing lustfully and directly at Spike. She is not literally, the vehicle for the gaze, to use Mulvey's concept, despite the fact that Spike's body is there to be looked at. She desires him, but because it is in spite of herself we see little of her indulging the pleasure of contemplating the object of her desire. Though he has no inhibition in raking her body with his eyes, as he kneels in front of her and sings of his love in the Musical episode,[581] she turns away instead of reciprocating. While pining after Buffy with unrequited love, Spike still embodies the traditional male-as-seducer role. His physical touch or caresses arouse her despite herself in the Bronze nightclub balcony scene in "Dead Things,"[582] for exam-ple, where he draws her into a sexual encounter in a public space she initially wants to avoid. The show offers shifting gender roles, shared between the male and female characters. That sharing, inclusive of Buffy and Spike's partnership in saving the world in the series finale "Chosen" denotes a tentative attempt in *Buffy* to change the discourse of gender reversal to represent an option of empowerment that is more than a "pattern of oppositions":

What rather has to happen is that we move beyond long-held cultural and linguistic patterns of oppositions: male/female (as these terms currently sig-nify); dominant/submissive; active/passive; nature/civilization; order/chaos; matriarchal/patriarchal. If rigidly defined sex differences have been con-structed around fear of the other, we need to think about ways of transcending a polarity that has only brought us all pain.[583]

Buffy is tentatively attempting to transcend polarity through its exploration of the aspects of Buffy's empowerment that relate to her engagement with violence and violent sex.

Violence and Buffy's Emotions

The show makes specific use of violence, beyond its role in action sequences and in word play, to define Buffy's strengths and weaknesses. Violence is recognized as a part of Buffy's power but in Xander's embarrassment that Buffy has brought her slaying into the real world of his construction job ("No, No, not here. Not at my job. That's your job")[584] we are reminded that, while violence works in saving the world, it is messy and annoying in other contexts. Buffy herself does not like to think that violence is her main resource:

> **Buffy:**   I wasn't gonna use violence. I don't always use violence. Do I?
> **Xander:** The important thing is *you* believe that.[585]

She often knows that what works on the killing fields of the Hellmouth in Sunnydale in the fight against demonic evil may hinder her in building relationships and a life. The killing of a human by the dysfunctional Slayer, Faith,[586] and Buffy's mistaken belief that she was herself responsible for a human's death in "Dead Things" (due to the manipulation of the comic nerd-trio of villains Warren, Andrew, and Jonathan) are just two instances where the show supports Buffy's moral compass. The misuse of violence in the context of the loss of human life is something that Buffy does not feel she can explain to someone like Spike, who is a vampire without a soul trying to join her side of the heroic fight:

> **Spike:** And how many people are alive because of you? How many have you
>   saved? One dead girl doesn't tip the scale.
> **Buffy:** That's all it is to you, isn't it? Just another body!
> **Spike:** Buffy . . .
> **Buffy:** You can't understand why this is killing me, can you?
> **Spike:** Why don't you explain it?[587]

It is ironic that later in this episode Buffy beats an unresisting Spike, who loves her, within an inch of his undead life after she asserts the sanctity of *human* existence. Spike is not human but demon. However, as she loses control of her anger and unleashes the full fury of her Slayer violence on Spike the scene leaves the audience with the sense that "the best theme song" for the relationship would probably be "Sympathy for the Devil."[588] Buffy is brutal in her beating of Spike and, as his vamp face changes to his bloodied human one, the show condemns the misuse of her "girl power."

In that beating, violence is a vehicle for exploring Buffy's attempts to transfer a quick fix, provided by violent, superhero Slaying skills required to fight evil, to solving problems in her personal relationships. When the kill is not clean in Buffy it is a signifier of emotional meltdown:

Buffy: What? I kill vampires, that's my job.
Giles: Well, true, true, although you don't usually beat them into quite such a bloody pulp beforehand. Everything alright?[589]

Violence *is* emotion in *Buffy,* it reveals inner life, and the characters fight their own demons when they fight the monster of the week. "How do you make each unstoppable monster unique and threatening?" Whedon was asked:

We got into a problem with that. We kept saying, "This monster can't be killed." It's like, "Well, have you used violence?" It was never about the unstoppableness. It was never about the monster. It was about the emotion. The monster came from that. We didn't always make them unique. We tried as much as possible, but what was important was how they related to the characters and that's what made them unique.[590]

As Buffy takes out her self-loathing on Spike it is the nadir of her use of violence. It is about as far as it is possible to get in the show from that sense of her resilience in the struggle to cope with life that is the heart of Buffy's empowerment: "Strong is fighting! It's hard, and it's painful, and it's every day. It's what we have to do."[591] As she speaks those words to a suicidal vampire with a soul, Angel, Buffy is not talking about her action-hero Slaying role, which seems straightforward by comparison. In the struggle to find the will to live and deal with life as it is, for Angel to find the will to go on as Buffy is trying to encourage him to do, you need more than fancy fight moves and sardonic repartee.

Her sexual relationship with Spike, embodying the sexuality of violence and the violence of sexuality, supports and questions our sense of Buffy's empowerment and, ultimately, affects the overt feminist ideology of the show.[592] Xander, when he finds out Anya, his ex-girlfriend, slept with Spike, echoes what Buffy has been feeling about the fact that she is sleeping with a vampire who is everything she hates:

You let that evil, soulless thing touch you. You wanted me to feel something? Congratulations, it worked. I look at you—and I feel sick—'cause you had sex with that.[593]

Xander's words echo Buffy's worst fears about what her friends would think of her if her sexual liaison with a vampire, one of the demons she is supposed to be eradicating, had been known to them. However, his black and white judgment does not account for the complex "interplay between disgust and desire, bad and good, violence and love"[594] that Buffy's relationship with Spike embodies. Her self-loathing puts her "at the mercy of her life":

> Buffy . . . goes through horrible pain every year. But last year, she really lost herself. And I think the audience felt that lack. They felt the lack of the strength . . . of, you know, grabbing that sword when Angel's about to stab her and saying, "I've still got me." . . . And I understand why they need that . . . because I need it, too . . . that very positive message that we had at the very beginning of the show . . . Buffy empowered again, instead of seeing her at the mercy of her life.[595]

However, it is not possible to be entirely in agreement with Whedon's assessment of season six in that comment, particularly given the prefiguring of Buffy's future depression in her often cynical view of life as a Slayer doomed to die young:

Buffy: World is what it is. We fight. We die. Wishing doesn't change that.
Giles: I have to believe in a better world.
Buffy: Go ahead. I have to live in this one.[596]

Such cynicism in a young girl has always held the seeds for a descent into the depression-like state she develops after coming back from the dead in season six. While the show is saying that dying and being resurrected will do that sort of thing to you, it is also saying that being the Slayer does not make you an optimist.

She has come close to losing part of herself in earlier seasons. Her breakup with her human boyfriend Riley is about that fluidity of her heroic self when she is confronted, as she is in her relationship with Spike, with moral ambiguity. In the underbelly of the vampire world, where the weak vampire dregs ply a centuries-old trade of feeding for money on those who find the "hazards of the underworld" addictive in the episode "Into the Woods,"[597] Buffy confronts the bloodsucking equivalent of a crack house. Weaker vampires survive by providing a service to humans who want the thrill of being fed on without being vamped. Giles, Buffy's Watcher and mentor, calls this more ambiguous evil in comparison with other "less ambiguous" evil she has always fought. Buffy, angry at Riley for paying for the rush of being fed on by vampire "trulls," wants the Buffyverse to stay black and white, and she asserts that she knows what violence is used for: "Vampires are vampires. And my job description is pretty clear." Hurt by Riley's betrayal, she is in no mood to hear Giles's uncertainty about killing the demon purveyors of this addiction. For Giles, the willing complicity of the humans in their victimhood muddies the moral clarity of her role as defender of "people out there who deserve your help," who are not colluding with the vampires in their fate. For Giles the distinction is about "focus," about where her efforts in the fight against evil can be best spent. Fighting unambiguous evil makes decisions and actions, heroism and killing simpler. When Buffy finally goes with Giles and the Scoobies to clean out the vampire purveyors' nest and finds the building abandoned, the palpable disgust she has towards "these creeps" feels personal. Her attitude and language is that of someone who has found that the fight here is not about her destiny but about the intrusion of some of the worst aspects of the vampire culture into her personal life. Riley, the epitome of normal and safe to her, the man she trusted, has sought out the very thing she is trying to stamp out. Buffy is turning her anger at Riley on the vampires, much as she turns her self-loathing on Spike in the alley beating.

Riley later tries to explain to Buffy why he allowed himself to be fed on by the female vampire. The most interesting contrast of terms in this conversation is when Riley calls the vamps that bit him "girls" and Buffy quickly counters with the correction "Vampires. Killers." She cannot understand what Riley is trying to tell her because the moral terms in which she judges the human/vampire dichotomy do not allow her to understand Riley's attraction to it. They fail to communicate but the real source of the distance between them is the limitation of Buffy's moral compass. There is no place, at this point in her journey, for moral ambiguity or shades of grey. It shocks her that Riley can claim to understand what the vampires are feeling: "You aren't a passion to them, you are a snack! A willing, idiotic snack." However, Riley says what vampires feel is analogous to the passion he feels for her:

> I know exactly what they feel when they bite me, because I feel it every time we're together. It's like the whole world falls away. And all there is . . . is you.

For Buffy the possibility that analogies can be made between human passion and vampire bloodlust echoes her ignorance of the existence of the nests where human and vampires meet in an exchange of needs. Sunnydale, small town though it may be, still contains within its borders both experiences and knowledge of the world that both Buffy the young adult and Buffy the superhero do not have the ability to understand. So when she stakes the pathetic, skeletal female vampire running away from her, essentially because she was the one that drank from Riley, it is brought home to us that there are times when "Yikes! The quality of mercy is not Buffy."[598] While Buffy is proved right when she asserts that "my emotions give me power"— that anger can give the Slayer the "fire" she needs to win—she is missing their paradoxical impact when she continues on to say that "They're *total* (my italics) assets."[599] Her emotions can result in misdirected violence and she can lose herself in them and the pain they embody. Spike's assessment of what loving Buffy feels like ("I have come to redefine the words pain and suffering since I fell in love with you")[600] devastatingly pinpoints that fact. As Whedon says, emotional pain *is* Buffy's story: "Buffy in pain, story more interesting. Buffy not in pain, story not interesting."[601]

However, that pain is often multifaceted, signaling a life passionately lived even when it is debilitating. The violent, lustful, and desire-driven sexual encounter between Buffy and Spike in "Smashed"[602] portrays what drives their attraction to one another and how both violence and their sexuality define the way they both cope with life. As they trade blow for blow and insult for insult, we get two superheroes evenly matched in the fight and in a personal relationship where gender submission or dominance is sidelined as an issue, despite their playing dominance sexual games later in their relationship. This scene is not about the reversal of gender roles as traditional gender roles are almost completely irrelevant to this violent coupling. Looking for a fight in that scene, Spike feels renewed power in the knowledge he now has that his behavior chip (implanted by Riley's government run Initiative agency to stop him hurting humans) no longer works against Buffy after her resurrection. He can now physically attack her again and is not "toothless." Everything that is predatory, dangerous, sneeringly derisive, and gleefully violent about Spike is conveyed in the way he warns her "you oughta be careful" as he goads her into punching him:

> **Buffy:** Get out of my way.
> **Spike:** Or what?

Unafraid, Buffy erupts into attack and, staggering from a flurry of punches and kicks that drive him backwards down the alley Spike only laughs with pleasure. He punctuates his verbal counter attack with blows to Buffy's face and body that do not hurt her and immediately bounces back from blows, grinning. He is enjoying his newfound equality with her, as much as the fight itself, as the verbal barbs they both fling become as pointed as the accompanying blows.

There is aggression in the fight music and it underscores their interaction even when they stop trading blows to talk. The verbal, as well as the physical, sparring is as much about how they can emotionally hurt each other as it is about their superhero enmity:

> **Buffy:** You haven't even come close to hurting me.
> **Spike:** Afraid to give me the chance?

When Buffy grabs Spike and pushes him up against the wall, cutting off another taunt by launching herself at him in a passionate kiss, we have the unification of sex and violence in their coupling. However, the ethereal, female choral voice underscoring as Buffy moves rhythmically against Spike, with its elegiac minor chords against low registers in the strings, creates a sense of melancholy. This could just as easily be a theme for a parting as a joining. As they stare at each other, finally prone on the floor, the music resolves on an A minor chord that signals inevitability. Along with the metaphor of the house falling down, the music is intimating that this sexual union is not going to bring them fulfillment. However, there is another resonance to the fact that what falls down is an abandoned and decrepit building. The simplistic black and white moral framework that has separated these two former enemies in the past is being brought down as well. It signifies a moral shift, a further greying of both their moral views and the destruction of the male-female power dichotomy they started out as representing.

It bears pondering whether Buffy *is* empowered in her relationships with men, given that every time she has sex emotional pain and relationship failure results.[603] It needs to be asked whether the show is in danger of promoting the disempowering message that indulging in sexual pleasure inevitably leads to some form of penalty and that the expression of desire always threatens life, self-esteem, and one's sense of self. All of Buffy's relationships seem to fall into the conventional "love hurts" discourse, which is about the disappointment and mistreatment women may experience and the compromise required by women "to compensate for men's apathy, neediness, or misconduct."[604] Angel loses his soul and turns evil after sleeping with her, Riley leaves her, and Spike's lack of a soul rocks her moral universe too much for her to find joy in her abandonment to the sexual excitement he arouses in her. Diane Dekelb-Rittenhouse describes vampire allure as the "eroticisation of death and the possibility of an eternity spent in sensual abandon."[605] Writing prior to season six, she too easily includes Spike in the same category as Angel when speaking of this myth as a "counterfeit" for love. If the show is aware and plays with the myth ("A vampire in love with a Slayer! It's rather poetic! In a maudlin sort of way"[606]) it does so differently for both characters. However, Buffy succumbs to both lovers because of something in herself, as much as she does to something in the different natures of her lovers. *Buffy, the Vampire Slayer* is predicated on the paraphernalia of Dracula and vampire mythology, even though it toys with it in postmodern ways and plays with it from a "girl power" viewpoint. Vampirism as evil is as firmly the canon in the Buffyverse as it is in the horror genre in general. As Robin Wood comments on Bram Stoker's *Dracula*: "Dracula is the product of Victorian sexual repressiveness" and "we are still trying to exorcise him"[607] from cultural concepts of sexuality. The potency of the vampire figure is the allure of irresistible, nonprocreative, abnormal sexuality and sexual freedom, to use Wood's paradigm. Dracula's darkness is "familiar" to us: "the sense of terrible familiarity . . . the familiarity of a disowned self that insists upon recognition."[608] The difference with Spike is that the supposed evil is given a "voice, a discourse, a point of view"[609] which Stoker did not give Dracula. As well, Buffy is not in supernatural thrall to Spike. She chooses to come to him, to a previously denied part of who she is, creating in the show the possibilities of a shared sexual freedom.

Violence and the Erotics of Shame

In Buffy's identity implosion after she initiates a sexual liaison with Spike we have the erotics of shame and a fascinating illustration of the show's complex engagement with its own empowerment premise. Her lust for Spike propels her indulgence in sexual practices with him involving dominance games and rough sex. When he compliments her by calling her animalistic in her sexual passion and she objects, he offers clear proof that she is not as sexually conservative as she thinks: "You wanna see the bite marks love."[610] She perceives those practices as deviant behavior despite sleeping with him: "That's the power of your charms. Last night . . . was the most perverse . . . degrading experience of my life."[611] Spike is full of admiration for the passion unleashed by their building-destroying sex, telling her that getting off on "the little nasties we whispered" is more than her "style," it's her "calling." To her that night was a "freak show," to him "a bloody revelation." Spike's enthusiastic but inappropriate compliment, "I knew the only thing better than killing a slayer would be f . . . ," shows that the "rush" of violence and sex are linked for him, an insight that Buffy is fighting within herself. In that sense, he does know her emotionally as well as physically intimately, better than she knows herself when he tells her, "You can act as high and mighty as you like but I know where you live now, Slayer, I've tasted it."

Buffy talks little about her feelings for Spike and when she does she either denies feeling anything meaningful or wants to keep it undefined so that she does not have to face the reality of what she may feel. She cannot even bring herself to call what they have a "thing": "We don't have a . . . thing, we have . . . this. That's all."[612] During their one relaxed and conversationally intimate, postcoital moment she reluctantly admits in "Dead Things" to liking him "sometimes." The rarity of this verbal intimacy leads Spike to dryly ask her "Are we having a conversation?" The most Buffy will admit is "Maybe," but she opens up to express a wry awareness of her own inconsistent moral stance in the relationship. She accepts Spike's pointed description of her postcoital fleeing "virtue fluttering," even jokes about doing it, "as soon as my legs start working," and grudgingly compliments him on his lovemaking skills ("You got the job done yourself"). The moment of communion between them is lost when Spike, meaning to compliment what he sees as her abandonment to passion, lust, and skill in their S & M games ("you make it hurt in all the wrong places") calls her an "animal." As he says to Anya elsewhere, when they commiserate later over their mutual rejection by those they love, "She was so raw, never felt anything like it."[613] Buffy, understandably, rejects Spike's "animal" description but he is right about her being "raw" in her sexuality and in the emotional needs she tries to use sex to satisfy.

From an ideological point of view, the question is: is the show as confused as Buffy about what is oppressive or liberating in her sexual relationship with Spike? When Buffy asks Tara later in the episode, after the postcoital conversation above, "Why can't I stop? Why do I keep letting him in?" female victimhood and male oppression are implied by her question. However, Buffy is portrayed as succumbing out of desire when having sex with Spike in a public place in the Bronze balcony scene, in the same episode as both the conversations above with Spike and Tara. Initially rejecting Spike, Buffy asks him to stop his advances but is sexually aroused by him:

> You see ... you try to be with them ... but you always end up in the dark ... with me. What would they think of you ... if they found out ... all the things you've done? If they knew ... who you really were?

Spike is right in much of what he says to her. Buffy voluntarily leaves the light-hearted company of her friends in the Bronze, clearly not sharing their mood. She does not deny his claims that she takes pleasure in what is forbidden, dark, dangerous, and hidden in their public coupling on the balcony in the shadows. She does not take him up on his challenge to stop him and she is enticed by what brings her shame. This is not coercion on Spike's part, her desire simply wins out over her shame and is aroused by the circumstances that produce it. However, Spike is only partly right. While her desire tells us that Buffy does feel emotional affinity with "the dark" which Spike embodies, it is also her discomfort with what she is doing that tells us she "belongs" downstairs with her friends. As Rhonda Wilcox points out, there are limits to Buffy and Spike's knowledge of each other:

> Spike tells Buffy that he knows her, that she is like him—and he is right; he knows her dark side in both its strengths and weaknesses. But he does not know all of her; and even more significantly, he does not know all of himself, any more than she knows all of him or of herself.[614]

Buffy has links to both the dark and the light and cannot, at this point in her life, find a way of uniting them in her sense of who she is.

Ideologically, the show is hovering around a particular sexual discourse in Buffy's sexual interaction with men where the show wants to acknowledge women's

> entitlement to express their full sexualities and makes clear that they are entitled to do so without losing social respect, being victimized, or being held accountable for their own exploitation.[615]

Vivien Burr has pointed out the ideological subversion inherent in the ambiguity created by the sadomasochistic eroticism in vampire/human relationships in the storyline.[616] However, the show's interest in the emotional pain relationships bring to Buffy, and in the consequences of Buffy's choices in relationships with men, portrays her lack of self-knowledge rather than her sexuality, as the problem. It is not simply the dominance games or sexual violence that frightens Buffy in her relationship with Spike. We can rely on Spike's mention of their five-hour sexual marathons, when Buffy breaks up with him in *As You Were*,[617] as saying something about her confident enthusiasm for what they do! What terrifies Buffy when she realizes she did not "come back wrong," as Spike puts it after her resurrection, is that she *is* the girl who wants sex with Spike: "I may be dirt . . . but you're the one who likes to roll in it, Slayer."[618] Her identity crisis about her Slayer role is played out in her emotional crisis about her sexuality but they are not the same issue. In the former, she does not know why she is back, given that she achieved a sense of completeness in Heaven,[619] or why she feels cut off from the world around her. In her relationship with Spike, her identity is shaken by discovering that her deepest sexual feelings are more powerful, and less socially mainstream or conventional, than she knew. Sleeping with a vampire whose appetites match her own unleashes that confrontation with herself. When her identity crisis about her Slayer role plays into her emotional crisis about sleeping with Spike, Buffy confuses the two issues. She links her sense of degradation from her sexual practices to her disgust at Spike's moral identity as a vampire but they, too, are not the same thing. Her issue with their sexual practices is one thing, the morality of enjoying them with Spike is another.

In their physically and emotionally violent sexual liaison we are given

> the variability and murkiness of the boundaries, or "edges" and "fine lines"— between seduction and domination, pleasure and danger, responsibility and exploitation, agency and objectification, consent and coercion.[620]

Buffy wants Spike to be the gatekeeper for her behaviors. As the benign demon Clem tells Spike in "Seeing Red,"[621] Buffy is a nice girl but she has "issues," and one of them is about giving herself permission to enjoy the sexual practices she wants to indulge in with Spike. Tara tries to give her that permission when she tells Buffy the results of her investigation of the spell that brought her back—that Buffy did not come back wrong. She tells Buffy that it is morally acceptable to be with Spike whether she loves him or not. Buffy weeps and begs Tara not to forgive her: "This just can't be me, it isn't me. Why do I feel like this? Why do I let Spike do those things to me?"[622] With the "let" she admits some participation, with the "do" she assigns him blame. What she does not take responsibility for is the initiation of their sexual interaction on occasions like their first coupling or her commanding him on another occasion to "Tell me you love me . . . Tell me you want me."[623] This lack of a sense of responsibility is even more patent in her excuse to Xander when he finds out about the liaison, "It just happened."[624] A vampire without a soul being the source of her feeling unbelievably alive terrifies her:

He's everything I hate. He's everything that . . . I'm supposed to be against. But the only time that I ever feel anything is when . . . Don't tell anyone, please.

In her confession to Tara, fear and shame battle with sexual self-realization. The one bit of self-knowledge Buffy does have in that conversation is that, whatever the rights and wrongs of allowing herself to enjoy what she has with Spike, the one thing she cannot do is continue to exploit his love for her by using him sexually to feel better about her life. Since she cannot give herself permission to enjoy sex with him guilt free (giving the relationship a degree of exploitation-free mutuality) then she is right to break up with him. Buffy's internal conflict is a part of the horror genre's "engagement of repressed fears and desires and its re-enactment of the residual conflicts surrounding those feelings."[625]

Buffy is a victim of wanting to be a "good" girl sexually. She thinks it is appropriate to express her sexuality but only if she expresses it within certain parameters. The fact that her socially acceptable relationship with Riley did not fulfill her needs (or his) has not taught her much about the futility of denying what she feels.[626] In "Buffy Vs Dracula"[627] she leaves her postcoital bed with Riley to go and find the rush from slaying that was not gained from sex with him. It is not surprising that Buffy seeks out the same sense of danger in her love life that she finds empowering in her role as Slayer. Buffy finds aggression erotic but she is not the sexually sophisticated young woman at ease with her sexuality that is ideologically stereotyped in today's magazines for young women. She is trying to reconcile a range of social expectations about the kind of young woman she should be sexually. She is struggling to be empowered when she declares her ambivalence and fears to Tara and it does lead her to insight about herself and her use of Spike. However, in that conversation with Tara, she abrogates some of the responsibility for her choices, denies her role as a participant in the pleasure Spike gives her, then succumbs to the sense of herself as a victim. It is the permission that Tara gives Buffy to just enjoy herself, or to love Spike, that saves the show from succumbing to it too.

The show does not let its audience see if Buffy integrates that aggressive aspect of her sexuality into a relationship with a man. Spike goes off to get a soul, they build a relationship of intimate trust and have a metaphorical sexual union before Spike's death, but they never have actual sex again. Metaphorical sex, with their joined hands bursting into flame before Spike dies, when Buffy tells Spike she loves him in "Chosen" is meant to give the story that integration. The show to some extent neuters Spike sexually in season seven when he has regained a soul. It is probably due to James Marsters' ongoing portrayal of latent sexuality in his characterization of Spike, undermining that didactic plot line,[628] that the show does not end up with Spike as a character for conveying, as Wood refers to in the analysis of *Dracula* and Victorian repression, "the evil that Victorian society projected onto sexuality and by which our contemporary notions of sexuality are still contaminated."[629]

Female Empowerment and the "Almost" Rape

It is not possible to consider the issue of Buffy's role as an empowered woman without consideration of the pivotal scene where she is portrayed as the victim of an attempted rape by Spike. Given the controversy this scene in "Seeing Red"[630] has generated between fans and the writers,[631] and the sensitive place rape narratives have in feminist and postfeminist discourse, research, and activism, it is not possible to read this scene as a straightforward narrative of male sexual violence. James Marsters has said: "That scene, more than any other, was very carefully choreographed."[632] Considered as a media event, inclusive of dialogue, acting, cinematography, and editing, the scene is technically and emotionally intricate and it encourages a complex audience engagement with both characters, the perpetrator and the victim, that is not typical of generic representations of attempted rape. From the beginning, we are asked to view the scene from more than one perspective through the dialogue. On Spike's entry, our attention and his is drawn to the fact that Buffy is injured after an earlier fight with a vampire where she has fallen and hurt her back. It is clear Spike enters the bathroom on the basis of an established intimacy because she objects to him being there, not because he has invaded her privacy, but because she feels they have nothing to talk about given the fact that he has slept with Anya after their breakup. Spike saying, "we have to talk," to apologize for sleeping with Anya is an imperative, but she curtly rejects this and orders him to leave. He asserts that it is not all about her "as much as you'd like it to be." This remark reminds us of Buffy's ongoing refusal to talk about their relationship with him and we feel the truth of his comment. Spike is aware that his apology will make no difference to the way she feels but he needs her to know that he was not trying to hurt her. There is deep despair and pain in his protest against Buffy's accusation that he initially went to Anya to get a magic spell to use on her: "It wasn't for you! *I* wanted something—anything to make this feeling stop. I just wanted it to stop! You should have let him kill me."

There is a shift from his despair when Buffy says she could not have let Xander kill him. He clutches at the hope that she prevented it because she loves him and he moves with more confidence towards her, accusing her of lying to herself. When she expresses her exasperation at his failure to accept what she says ("How many times . . . !? I have feelings for you. I do. But it's not love. I could never *trust* you enough for it to be love"), the scene shifts again to Buffy's point of view. Spike is not hearing the resolve in Buffy's voice, nor does he understand her need to trust if she is to love. His scoffing dismissal of the word and the need ("Trust is for old marrieds, Buffy! Great love is wild and passionate and dangerous. It burns and consumes"), alluringly passionate as the image is, returns to the dynamic of the relationship since they first coupled of two people on different wavelengths. For Buffy, that passion is something that burns "[u]ntil there's nothing left. Love like that doesn't last." He believes that her love for him is there and, now that all her friends know about their sexual liaison, she can allow herself to freely express it. What he does not understand is that her inability to say what she feels stems as much from her uncertainty about what those feelings are. What she does feel is that she cannot trust him, at least not enough to love. This assertion rings true in the context of Buffy's history with men who have left her: her father (who stayed away after her parents' divorce), Parker (a boyfriend who dumped her after a one-night stand), Riley, and Angel (who left her for altruistic reasons but left nevertheless). Her trust issues are not just about Spike. What is not clear is exactly the degree of trust that Buffy is talking about, given we have seen her trust Spike on countless occasions to watch her back in battle, to support her emotionally and receive confidences she cannot tell her friends, to protect her sister Dawn, and in dominance sex games that have required her to let him handcuff her. The perspective shifts again as Spike moves towards her, trying to hold her and begging her to let herself "feel it" and "Let it go . . . Let yourself love me . . . Buffy, Buffy." He is so desperate that he is not listening to what she is saying. He does not even notice her hitting herself on the bath when she falls as they struggle, even though she calls out in pain as her body jarringly strikes the bath. He repeats "you love me" and is oblivious to everything but his need. His eyes close as he tries to kiss her on the side of the head, not aggressively on the mouth, an action that disturbingly keeps us focused on his love for her and on his pain, even as we recognize with growing horror that he is losing himself. He closes his eyes, lost in his yearning: "Let yourself go. Let yourself love me."

The discontinuities of emotion in this scene, as we move back and forth from he interaction between Spike's and Buffy's points of view in the dialogue, are reinforced by the camera moving back and forth between upper body shots of Buffy and Spike separately, to close-ups of the struggle itself, and to wide shots of the assault. These changing angles, as much as the dialogue and the action itself, shape the nature of the discourse as an attempted rape narrative. The camera angles are used to follow the flow of emotion in their separate points of view, and to create audience response to them. Spike moves in on her in a predatory manner as the struggle starts and the camera cuts from close ups of individual body parts, such has his invasive hand inside her robe, to wide-angle shots. The close ups give you the sense of the struggle and its invasive, hectic movement. She fights him off, he alternately pleads with, and assaults her. When the camera switches to a wide angle, such as when he is lying on top of her, trying to pin her to the floor and holding her hands at her side, the audience is encouraged to adopt a detached way of seeing the action, not from Buffy's or Spike's point of view but the act for what it is—attempted rape. When they fall next to the bath, and she is sitting on the floor, with him kneeling in front of her, we shift to him pleading with her and for that moment his emotion is foregrounded, even as she struggles. When she falls back and he is lying on top of her, the scene shifts emotionally again and the brutality of what he is doing, in that overwhelmingly white and sterile bathroom, is paramount. The camera angles up from Buffy's point of view, and Spike's face shifts to naked aggression, teeth clenched, before the screen fades to black. When the scene resumes, it is as if Spike is talking to himself: "I know you felt it . . . when I was inside you." He clings to the empty hope that sex will reconnect them and at that point, more than any other, we know the futility of that belief as Buffy pleads with him to stop: "Don't . . . please, please Spike, please don't do this, please don't do this." When he finally abandons himself completely to the assault, ripping her robe from her breast, we lose all sympathy for him as his intention to coerce her takes over: "You'll feel it again, Buffy . . . I'm gonna make you feel it."

In addition to the camera manipulation, the fact that the whole scene is played with no musical underscore emphasizes, along with the stark sterility of the bathroom setting, the graphic violence in Spike's behavior. The man who, while he never denied his own history of violence, was convinced that he would never hurt the woman he loves, does what was unthinkable to him—he attempts to rape her. Buffy alternates between expressions of physical pain and pleading and when Spike says he is going to make her feel it and rips her robe open at the point where our sympathy for him has dissolved, she kicks him off, "Ask me again why I can never love you." Buffy asserts that it is only because she stopped him that it went no further. However, Spike makes no attempt to continue the attack. When Spike struggles to stand after Buffy has kicked him off, using the bathroom sink to raise himself up, the transition to his realization of what he has just done is signaled by the return of the musical underscore. By the time he stands opposite Buffy clutching her robe shut, Spike knows, and is horrified at, what he has done and almost done.

The difficulties one might have with placing the emotional impact of the above scene in the category of traditional rape narratives stems primarily from the use of it to tell a story about a character other than the woman facing the attempted rape, and that, from a feminist point of view, is disconcerting. More than one writer has acknowledged that the decision was made to have Spike attempt to rape Buffy, to give him powerful motivation to do what no vampire or demon has done in the Buffyverse—to defy canon,[633] do the unprecedented, and voluntarily go and get a soul in horror at what he has done without one. As Marsters says on the use of the scene to motivate his character's subsequent quest for a soul: "How do you motivate him—how do you make him make a mistake that's so heart-rending that he'd be willing to do that?"[634] His use of the phrase "heart-rending" is apt and the scene as a rape narrative is deeply disconcerting because of our empathy, albeit discontinuously in the scene, with the perpetrator. Writer declarations[635] and the soul revelation scene in "Beneath You"[636] in the following season seven make Spike's motivation for going on his soul quest clear. However, the seeds of his decision to seek out a soul so that he will never hurt the woman he loves again are present in the bathroom scene in his horror at what he has done.

Given audience empathy for the character, and his popularity, there were writer concerns about allowing Spike to attempt to rape Buffy if they had any intention of continuing the love story. Jane Espenson, a writer on the show, admits:

> I love Spike. I was very worried about the attempted rape ... because that's not something you play around with. That's not something ... it's very hard to come back from. And you know, you can say Luke and Laura came back from it, but that was a different time. I think we have to be very careful that we are not saying anything about humans. When we say that Spike looked into his soul, at that moment, and saw the demon in him and that's what made him want to go get a soul.[637]

Spike-fan response in the online discourse about this scene often described this plot development as a form of "character rape," in the belief that a morally developing Spike would never do such a thing.[638] This belief was not untouched by James Marsters' expressed distress at having to play the scene: "It still haunts me. I am artistically proud to have done it, but it was the hardest day of my career":

> It was written very carefully. But I was more freaked out about the scene than I should have been, and I think that freaked Sarah out, and then I, as the character, reacted to her freaking out and that dynamic kind of fed on itself.

I think it ended up being much more aggressive and violent than intended. I think there was an attempt to keep it from being painful, but it played that way and so we have to deal with it.[639]

It is clear, however, that fan empathy for the character in the scene is encouraged within the narrative itself.

How we view the attempted rape scene also depends on the degree to which it is outside the horror genre and vampire fantasy metaphor. Spike is not in vamp face so it appears that it is not the demon but the man attempting to rape her, despite Espenson's assertion above that it is the demon. Buffy being victimized because she is injured works if you can suspend your sense of her as the Slayer and a superhero; it feels odd if you cannot suspend that disbelief. The superhero kick that sends him flying back into the wall does not merely stop him; it serves to bring him back to himself. It is the man who decides not to renew the attack. However, the scene straddles its exit from the metaphor uneasily. The mention of the spell Spike went to get reminds us that we are in the Buffyverse metaphor, as do the careful references to Buffy's injury which call up the fact that the slayer super healing powers should be at work as much as it does that she is hurt. However, since we have never seen Spike even come close to physically overwhelming her she seems to take a long time to kick him off. The shift from Buffy as Slayer to Buffy as victim seems odd when she finally does send him flying into the wall. As often as the camera angles at Spike from Buffy's point of view to show his aggression, and as much as she struggles and protests, the effect is to leave us puzzling as to why it takes her so long to kick him off, particularly as all it takes is one kick. Perhaps, there is something in Buffy's pleading with Spike ("Don't do this") that implies she is holding to her belief that he will stop of his own accord, echoing the trust she has had of him in the past. Perhaps, she is attempting to give him the space to make that decision. Perhaps, her own stunned disbelief that he is doing this prevents her immediately reacting with the strength she ultimately uses. A clearer sense of these emotional possibilities would have allayed quizzicality about the delay in Buffy stopping the assault.

How we view the assault in the context of female empowerment also depends on what is typical, or atypical, about that scene in the context of the history of the representation of rape that Sarah Projansky describes as "the pervasive and persuasive power of the cultural narratives about rape and the cultural imperatives to represent it in particular ways."[640] This assault of Spike's is central to his decision to redeem himself and to go and get a soul, and if we hold to Spike's point of view, the attempted rape makes sense in the metaphorical Buffyverse. If we hold to Buffy's story, to her strength as a Slayer who can be run through with a sword in the series finale and get up again and throw herself into the battle, her victimhood here feels odd. There is some question as to whether the scene works as a discourse on rape being about power, in the sense that feminism might use it. The lack of premeditated hostility on Spike's part also prevents the easy categorization of it as making a statement about violent male response to female strength and independence. Nor does it fit the image of rape-revenge genre[641] when we have following scenes showing Spike's anguished soul-searching in his crypt with the benign demon Clem (where he makes the decision to go and get the soul), or Buffy seeking Spike at his crypt to leave her sister Dawn in his care. She even inquires with concern of Clem as to when Spike will return when she finds out he has left Sunnydale. We are left with a representation of attempted coercion, unquestionably, but also of the deep emotional pain that allowed Spike to slide into it. As another writer on the show, Rebecca Rand-Kirshner has said:

> It's so desperate emotionally and so horrific physically. We could feel how his very innards were twisted into this perversion of what he wanted. But it was disturbing to think of it from his perspective as well.[642]

Since the scene is being used to tell Spike's story as well as Buffy's, the scene straddles across the narrative divide of trying to make a feminist statement about rape, through Buffy's momentary disempowerment, and furthering Spike's character development. We are given Buffy's experience of the trauma of attempted rape while we get Spike's experience of emotional trauma and moral implosion. In the end, we do not have to choose one perspective over the other, or between a male or female perspective, the drama is complex enough to leave us with both.

What Buffy has discovered in trying to make sense of her relationships with men and her sexuality is that her slayer powers have been of little use in making life choices or in protecting her from emotional pain. Xander's description of Parker's sexual attraction to Buffy ("That's because he got hit by the Buffinator. Now he's powerless") points that out in its word play with the action hero, Terminator image.[643] The irony is that Parker uses her, dumping Buffy after a one-night stand despite her "buffinator" power. It is comic that when Harmony, Spike's ditzy vampire girlfriend before Buffy, dumps him, she takes a shorter time than Buffy to understand the basic facts of empowerment: "I'm powerful, and I'm beautiful, and I don't need you to complete me."[644] Buffy's boyfriend relationships with Angel, Parker, Riley, and Spike finally bring her to that point in her cookie dough analogy, in the conversation with Angel, prior to the final battle that destroys Sunnydale in "Chosen." Despite the didacticism of that analogy,[645] Joss Whedon's vision of female empowerment, in the context of Buffy's use of violence, her sexual identity and search for a life and love, has been encapsulated in an exploration of primal human urges that takes dramatic risks which do not support a simplified, gendered reading of the text as about "girl power." So Harmony's traditional empowerment statement seems too simple. As Buffy faces her new life at the end of "Chosen," no longer bearing the burden of being the only Slayer, a smile of anticipation on her face, it is not possible to assume that all will now be plain sailing for her. Writer and executive producer on the show, Marti Noxon, asserted, "What we want to show is an independent heroine who is not defined by her relationships."[646] Aspects of the dramatic context of the show ultimately contradict that statement. The audience knows Buffy through her relationships with everyone around her and she herself recognizes they say a great deal about who she is, especially her relationship choices in men. She is defined by her relationships and by her choices within them. She is a representation of the flawed human being within the feminist icon. The show does celebrate the "joy" of female empowerment but its final resting place in feminist ideological television can afford to incorporate into that definition the show's exploration of what it means to be human, and male, as well as female; "the more" that Daugherty said she might represent. After all, Buffy is not up on that screen alone and it is not necessary to see that fact as an ideological problem.

It is possible to agree with Whedon's belief in his "legacy":

Honestly, I hope that the legacy of the show would be that there is a generation of girls who have the kind of hero a lot of them didn't get to have in their mythos and a lot of guys who are a lot more comfortable with the idea of a girl who has that much power.[647]

However, Whedon's notion of "guys who are comfortable" might have as much to do with what is happening to the male characters on the show as it does with the heroine. The finale is as much about the culmination of Spike's journey as it is about the beginning of the rest of Buffy's life, and the show ends with them saving the world in partnership. The audience is left to read what it will into Buffy's enigmatic final smile but, when Giles asks in bewilderment who is responsible for the crater that is now the destroyed Hellmouth, the last word Buffy says in the show is when she answers "Spike." The Buffyverse does not, though it sometimes is tempted to, offer a closed definition of Buffy as a feminist symbol. The celebration of female empowerment is tinctured with a range of emotional colors, which site the Buffyverse at the centre of a resilient struggle to know what that empowerment might consist of, as a girl growing up lives it in a complex and fragile world. Buffy's heroic journey is one of authentic but flawed self-discovery. Like all of us, she fashions herself as she goes, and that resonates for her contemporaries in the audience precisely because she is a work in progress, and the signs of the struggle to simply become are there for contemplation. While the audience might cringe a little, as Angel does, when Buffy uses the analogy of unbaked cookie dough to describe where she stands at series end, it is easy to forget that Buffy is only 22 at that point, and she is at the end of the series, not the end of her life's journey. As Whedon commented: "The show is still about life and life is not a thing that says 'The End' at the end."[648] The story encourages looking beyond current simple definitions of butt-kicking "girl power" and female empowerment as the purpose of the show's metaphorical use of violence. It is not the violence that is authentic in *Buffy*; rather it is the complex emotional characterization, in the context of an ideological exploration of gender roles, which emerges from the metaphorical use of violence that is authentic. The butt-kicking violence is only the tip of that metaphorical iceberg.

6

"Getting Kicks from Action Pix": [649] Righteous Violence and the Choreographed Body in F(l)ight

You can take any genre and say these horror bits, these action bits, these are the musical numbers—these are the moments where we are uplifted. The shoot-out in The Wild Bunch, *the Neo and Agent Smith fight in* The Matrix—*those are the big closing numbers. The way a musical can make us feel is unlike anything else, in song and particularly in dance. I think people fly through plate-glass windows when they get shot because movies don't have dance scenes any more. This is what we do instead.*

(*Joss Whedon*)[650]

What if the body of the text is a dancing body, a choreographed body?

(*Susan L. Foster*)[651]

The film *Beautiful Boxer* [652] tells the real-life story of Parinya Chaoenphaol (Toom), the Muay Thai transvestite kickboxing champion. As she struggles to become a contender and resolve her identity crisis prior to deciding to undergo a sex change operation, Toom expresses doubt that the life of a kickboxer will ever suit her when it seems to be only about violence. A female friend at the training camp, Pi Bua, takes her to see the early morning practice of the advanced boxers and the aesthetic beauty of the violent sport is shown to her as the boxers display the traditional moves in formation and filmic slow motion. She watches a kickboxing ballet performed against the lush green, misty morning of the Thai countryside. Recognizing the beauty of the scene, Toom asks why she has not been taught those moves and the friend answers that she is not yet good enough. Full of doubt she asks, "What if I'm never good enough?" Pi Bua replies, "Then Thai boxing will be nothing to you but violence." That scene brings to the fore the fact that the body in motion in martial arts can be as beautiful as it is violent.

This chapter on fight scenes in martial arts and action movies brings my discussion to images of violence that exist closer to the margins of the story and to the penultimate point on the continuum of authenticity. It involves the discussion of texts in which the aesthetic pleasures of choreographed violence are prominent and the story is reduced to the precipitating event for that pleasure. It also suggests an approach for discussing the action genre, in particular its use of violence, to contribute to the resolution of the critical dilemma pointed out by José Arroya: "As yet we have no adequate vocabulary to describe or evaluate such films (which are now the dominant mode of Hollywood filmmaking) so we tend to dismiss them as popcorn."[653] Arroya, noting the often-reiterated analogy between action films and Musicals,[654] correctly argues that meaning in such films comes from nonrepresentational signs. Fight scenes in many contemporary films are primarily a testament to the fact that not everything about the viewing experience of violence is about the violence. Violence can be a medium through which fantasy about the choreographed fighting body can thrill, amaze, and uplift the viewer by creating a sense of the body liberated from its physicality. Viewing the fight scenes as fight text with its own aesthetic purposes, independent of plot narrative, foregrounds the lack of representational authenticity in that violence and how the audience is hermetically sealed off from real-life implications of what they see on screen. If it is true that in choreographed movement or dance "[t]he body says what cannot be spoken,"[655] then the fight text, being a choreographed fantasy about the body—kinetic art—can be viewed as saying something about violence in action that social and political taboos avoid: that it can be aesthetically beautiful and fun to watch. The audience is free to be entertained and uplifted by the fight choreography and stunt or digital virtuosity the scenes display as cinema embodies "kinesthetic artistry."[656]

As Joss Whedon implies when he yokes together *The Wild Bunch* and *The Matrix* in the quote heading this chapter, all action movies share that sense of performative display that can be likened to show-stopping Musical numbers. The action director John Woo has noted that his action sequences are directly inspired by his love of musicals and that he tries to capture "the musical rhythm and the beauty of action and the beauty of body movement."[657] That performative display in contemporary action movies, increasingly draining violence of its visceral effects, has its historical cinematic roots in the choreographed detail of the hail of bullets ending the lives of the protagonists in *Bonnie and Clyde* (1967), in the aesthetic of slow motion stylized violence in the films like those of Sam Peckinpah in the 1960s and 70s,[658] and in the Hong Kong martial arts cinema of the 1970s and 80s. The cinematic impulse to stylize violence increasingly present in American films in the 1980's—such as the *Dirty Harry* franchise, which echoes the violence of the Italian director Sergio Leone's work in the spaghetti western genre—has gone on to produce an emphasis on violence and the invulnerable body as a special effect embodied in graceful cinematic display that is aesthetically pleasing and far from viscerally horrific.

Thus Arnold Schwarzenegger's indestructible robotic body in *The Terminator* franchise can be aptly described by *Time* as "its own stunning special effect"[659] and Bruce Willis as John McLane in the *Die Hard* films can cause urban mayhem in exploding buildings and breathtaking displays of bullet shattered glass to appreciative audiences. Along with higher body counts and increasing postmodern reflexivity—the villain in the first *Die Hard* film says McClane is "another American who saw too many movies as a child. Another orphan of a bankrupt culture who thinks he's John Wayne . . . Rambo . . . Marshall Dillon"[660]—the action film over the last three decades has become, as Larry Gross notes, variously located in analogies with theme parks, thrill rides, comic books, or anything that is big and loud.[661] Such analogies are capturing what Jason Jacobs describes as the disintegration of plot justification for violent scenes as they become ends in themselves.[662] However, it is the analogy with the Musical or, more particularly dance, that comes the closest to invoking the way contemporary action films in the last decade, particularly those that are based on martial arts derived fight scenes, offer aesthetic pleasures to the audience. As Woo has noted of his own films, "Action pretty much looks like a dance, and dance pretty much looks like action."[663] Fight scenes transform violence into a special-effect dreamscape based on inspirational images of the body *in f(l)ight*—images that uniquely depend on depriving violence of its visceral authenticity to create a sense of audience wonder.

J. David Brimmer, a fight coach working with actors to create stage fights in the theatre, describes teaching actors to fight by removing the discomfort about violence they may feel. He notes that his "job is to get actors who may be uncomfortable with violence to realise that what we're doing onstage is a dance":

> We're magicians of violence. It is sleight of hand. I'm not really hitting you in the face. I'm moving my fist parallel with your face; you're reacting by isolating the muscles of your face. There's also misdirection, I want you watching my hand moving, not the slap I do against my body to simulate the sound of the hit. And there's macro-gymnastics: If I'm picking someone up, usually they're jumping and I'm supporting them. It's very similar to a lift in ballet. Of course the intention is different.[664]

In action films, fight scenes create a state of being for the body that is *dance-like* rather than *life-like*. Using Sandra Kemp's suggestion that dance is "poeticized walking" and noting the action choreography/dance analogy, Leon Hunt proffers "that one might usefully see martial arts choreography as poeticized fighting."[665] A sense of fight choreography as graceful redirection is implied in Larry Wachowski's comments on the fight scenes in his *Matrix* trilogy where gymnastic sleight of hand in wire-harness stunt work enables the fight text to ignore the laws of gravity to which the body is subject so that violent movement looks "very graceful and kind of surreal." For Wachowski, the effect of that aesthetic of the body in motion is beauty: "There are many incredible and beautiful images in violence."[666] The audience for martial arts and action movies is in the same place as Brimmer's actors when it comes to having its discomfort in the face of violence aesthetically redirected by choreographed sleight of hand and replaced by an enjoyment of the creative virtuosity involved in the fight as a dance production number. Films to be discussed in this chapter like *Crouching Tiger, Hidden Dragon* with its aerial ballet wire stunts, *Kill Bill Volume 1* and *Volume 2's* (*I* and *II*) anime inspired martial arts extravaganza, *The Matrix* trilogy's computer generated gravity-defying special effects, *Ong Bak's* amazing Muay Thai boxing gymnastics, and *Kung Fu Hustle's* comic martial arts high jinks all eschew the representation of the actuality of violence. They do so in favor of using the text of the fight to explore the possibilities of the body in motion—as if it were a dancing body ultimately liberated from physicality. This is not to say there is no story in these action films but that the fight scenes fulfill other aesthetic purposes that are not only story-based.

Supporting that aesthetic disassociation from actual violence is the moral case made for heroic violence in action films that would be unjustifiable off the screen. Violence when used by heroes in action movies is propelled by stories set in train by the archetypal precipitating events of crime, justice, and the righting of wrongs. Action heroes are strong characters driven by powerful motivations. Their motivations are often deeply personal or altruistic but are invariably aligned with the desire, also held by the audience, to see the villain of the piece get his just desserts and for the hero to find justice. Often formulated in explicitly defined warrior or superhero mythologies, or loosely backed by the hero being a law enforcement officer who uses extravagant violence beyond the sanction of the law, or couched in the terms of righteous vengeance at the hands of a deeply wronged protagonist or people, the premise of the films is that violence has its righteous uses in the right hands, whether or not such justice has the backing of the legal system. It is not surprising, that the film *Hero* (2002), starring the martial arts icon Jet Li, makes the connection between violence and the righteous cause explicit in the title. What would be vigilantism in actuality is assumed to be acceptable violence in heroic action. The central protagonists in the action films are essentially in agreement with the sentiments expressed by Batman to Superman, who is on the government justice system payroll in the graphic novel *Batman: The Dark Knight Returns*:

> You always say yes—to anyone with a badge—or a *flag* . . . You sold us out, Clark. You gave them—the *power*—that should have been *ours*. Just like your parents taught you to. My parents taught me a *different* lesson—lying on this street—shaking in deep shock—dying for no reason at all—they showed me that the world only makes sense when you *force* it to.[667]

As Aeon J. Skoble comments in referring to this speech of Batman's, "the crime fighting superhero does not let anything stand between him and the attainment of what he sees as real justice."[668] The attempt to bend actuality through force is the essence of this heroic impulse.

The frame of reference for both that form of heroism and the image of violence itself in action films is not actuality but the genres within which they sit and the special-effects technology with which they are often created. The Hong Kong martial arts films[669] have particularly invigorated Hollywood's interest in the kinetic possibilities of fight scenes and that has elevated the narrative of the fight to a text within a text. As the directors of *The Matrix* trilogy, Larry and Andy Wachowski, point out: "Hong Kong action directors actually bring narrative arcs into the fights, and tell a story within the fighting," as opposed to creating fights only through editing where "sequences are just designed for a visceral, flash-cut impact and the audience's brains are never really engaged."[670] While there is a story or plot agenda behind the use of violence, there is also a staging agenda, that, in common with the presentation and entertainment purposes of music and dance numbers in the Musical, puts the story on pause while the fight text explores the potential of the choreographed body. As Scott McMillin notes in his perceptive discussion of the integration of story and song and dance in the Musical:

> When a musical is working well, I feel the crackle of difference, not the smoothness of unity, even when the numbers dovetail with the book. It takes things different from one another to be thought of as integrated in the first place, and I find that the musical depends more on the differences that make the close fit interesting than on the suppression of difference in a seamless whole.[671]

It is that same sense of difference that separates the fight scene from the story in which it is embedded.

However, it has often been an oversimplified comparison of aesthetic constructs that limits the utility of the analogy of fight texts with the Musical. The basic import of the analogy has been to cite the pause for the staging of the fight as if it were a production number in a Musical and independent of narrative and, therefore, cinematic concerns. The film critic Kevin Maher comments on the inclusion of what he terms the obligatory "Big Disturbing Set-Piece of Violence" in contemporary violent films arguing that

> these movies more and more resemble old-style Hollywood musicals, where any semblance of narrative coherence usually collapses in the face of the Big Musical Number, one that exists primarily for its own spectacle. (Why else did Tarantino shoot the torture of Marvin the cop in *Reservoir Dogs* to music?)[672]

Maher's complaint is evidence of what Jane Mills has called "the false dialectic which poses spectacle in opposition to narrative" that she describes as a characteristic of screen criticism and theory.[673] While Maher is referencing what he terms the overuse of graphic violence in films like *Irréversible* (discussed in my introduction), and not the action genre in his remark, his comment highlights a confusion about conventions of violence (and Musicals for that matter) that is relevant to violence in the action genre where fight scenes are de rigueur. The analogy is not recognized as more complex than simply equating production numbers in different mediums.

While there are aesthetic needs as well as performance skills to display in the Musical song and dance routines that showcase talent and virtuosity, they are also there to say something affectively through the body and the voice about the energies and rhythms of their narratives. While musicals, like all art forms have their conventions that require the suspension of disbelief to enter the story, they are also conventions that uniquely serve the kind of story they are telling. The film critic A. O. Scott recognizes the aesthetic utility of that conventionality when he uses the same analogy with the Musical to describe the director Martin Scorsese's representations of violence with "its motivating forces, its effects, its fascinating rhythms":

> Martin Scorsese's first film, "*Who's That Knocking at My Door*" (1968), begins with a series of street fights, which seem to break out like tap-dance routines in a musical. His latest, "Gangs of New York," set in the same Lower Manhattan streets a century earlier, raises street mayhem to the level of opera. Most of the picture takes place in a pre-Civil War city governed by tribal codes, in which combat is an ancient ritual, Mr. Scorsese's subject is the way this archaic mode of violence is swept away.[674]

Maher is right to point out that spectacle can overwhelm narrative and risks the possibility of conventional predictability.[675] However, predictability is not necessarily a by-product of convention, musical or otherwise. Put another way, convention can exist side by side with an aesthetic pleasure derived from the conventions, and not from any expectation of substantial narrative consistency, if there is an affective narrative or aesthetic impact created by the convention. As Michelle Lekas notes in her discussion of opera and the cinema, the "status" of classical opera "is such that it need not even maintain a semblance of the "fantasy-real-world" even if it "risks excess."[676] Similarly, as Sandars notes, films using combat scenes "construct their meaning through an ongoing dialogue between the spoken narrative and the spectacle of a highly choreographed, physical display which, like dance in the Hollywood musical, is employed as a privileged state of discourse."[677] As Scott implies in his use of opera to delineate the effects of Scorsese's operatic use of mayhem, that excess is used in the film to convey the sweeping rhythms of tribal, ancient, and ritualized combat crucial to that film's narrative interest in mid nineteenth century gang culture.

Fightable Moments

Stephen Citron describes the spotting of a libretto, placing songs or dance numbers in a musical, as "places that will be musicalised"[678] in order to distil or amplify narrative. Rather than singable or danceable moments in a story, fight scenes in action movies are the *fightable* moments, with their own choreographed text. Rarely is a sense of the authentic danger of violence in actuality the affective narrative impact. The fight text in action movies takes the audience away from judging or responding to violence in film as if it had something to say about real violence. Instead the fight draws attention to what the action has to say about the film's own narrative and about the state of being of the choreographed body in motion *through* violence. In his discussion on the comparison between martial arts film and musicals, Leon Hunt, citing Greg Dancer, points out the fact that they share "what we might call 'plastic' and 'performative' traditions, one founded on artifice, authorial style and technological mastery, the other on pro-filmic virtuosity."[679] In Hunt's comparison, martial arts choreographers and Busby Berkely are aesthetic stylists for a plastic body. If, as the novelist Martin Amis offers, "the definition of fantasy is there's no real reason for what happens next—an inconsequentiality which is absolutely delightful but very, very difficult to sustain,"[680] then, within the framework of the plot justification for their occurrence, most fight scenes are not fantastical. The fantasy exists in the fight text itself, when choreography, stunt technology, or digital special effects serve their own aesthetic purposes as an addition to narrative, which can only be sustained for the duration of the fight. As such, one would want to qualify Sandars' statement above by saying that the fight text *can* blithely downplay its connection with the dialogue to concentrate on aesthetically startling displays, in order to create new visual vocabulary for the body and for the cinematic medium itself.

Using the analogy with the Musical makes available an aesthetic vocabulary that is uniquely appropriate to the state of the body in the fight text. However, trying to hold in analysis the kinetic effect of the fight scenes as bodies in motion, as choreographed dance, poses the same problems facing dance critics who "must of necessity freeze that motion temporarily in order to study it."[681] In discussing action films, this can cause critical language to struggle to define the exact impact of what is essentially the kinetic dynamics of athletic, aerial, and acrobatic movement, often aided by the fantastical visuality of special-effects or stunt technology. Analysis is driven to an almost blow-by-blow, or shot-by-shot account which runs the risk of feeling reductive (and somewhat stilted) when compared to the soaring visuality of the fight text as a whole. However, the choreographing of fight scenes can encourage such a pause for consideration in the conventional use of slow motion effects during fights and in the pausing of fight narrative to make way for preparatory martial art poses, dialogue, sound effects, or the next stage of the fight. *The Big Boss*,[682] starring the martial arts actor Bruce Lee, provides an historical example of the Hong Kong cinema origins of that pause. He plays the character Cheng Chao An,[683] a young man visiting relatives in Thailand and working in an ice factory that, unknown to him, is a front for a drug operation run by the gang boss of the film's title. There is a scene well into the film where he is finally driven to fight the drug dealer's henchmen. He has promised his mother that he will not use his martial arts skills and, in a series of prior scenes, has held back. When he finally strides into action and unleashes his skills, increasing his fury in the film as more of his friends are killed, his feelings of guilt mount at breaking his promise. However, when Cheng later finds the bodies of his friends including that of a child with a knife in his chest, masses of inauthentic pink blood, and the girl he loves kidnapped, the film reiterates the message that in warrior terms, the hero has no choice. A series of assaults take place against the drug boss's gang (which finally leads to the boss's death in one-to-one combat with Cheng) but, in this first fight, the film is ready to pause the story and allow the now-expectant audience to watch what happens.[684]

Being a Hong Kong action film, the audience is not going to receive a psychological analysis of Cheng's violation of his promise but the embodiment of it as a fight, precipitated by the inadvertent breaking of his amulet as he stands by watching the attack on his friends.[685] Along with the pause in narrative for the fight, the fight text also moves in a stop-start rhythm with a series of kicks, blows, and paused returns to a martial arts preparation stance or pose, retaining a sense of displayed choreography staged for the film audience. At one point Cheng, poised ready for attack, even asks dismissively: "Well, I'm waiting." The fight is far from a melee, as six attackers launch themselves in turn at him and, with a series of flying kicks at his opponents heads and a couple of punches, he also drops them one by one. Made before the use of wires and the marvels of digital effects available to contemporary action movies (editing for what now feels like a somewhat stilted flying effect was done in the film using leaps from a trampoline to simulate weightlessness), nevertheless, the body leaps and moves in between stillness and motion. Hunt, basing his analysis on Bordwell's description of Hong Kong action fights as "pause/burst/pause," quick action punctuated by a pose, notes that it forms a rhythmic patterning of fight action that requires graceful stasis as well as movement, the "wicked shapes" of still postures as well as the "wicked lies" of aerially assisted action.[686]

Despite the absence of special-effects technology that limited the aerial performativity in *The Big Boss*, in the final confrontation with the drug lord in which Cheng kills him the choreography is still characterized by aerial trampoline propelled leaps, spins, kicks, blows, pauses for circling and slow rises from the ground, throws, holds, and kicks for kick blocking. The fight is a kung fu pas-de-deux complete with the slow motion mutuality of a shared, midair leap in which Cheng gives the boss a kick to the head, only to have his opponent land on his feet and pose ready to continue the fight. The fight periodically pauses for the next display but, within the text between pauses, choreography and camera angles continually evoke the body in fluid athletic motion. Cheng grabs and fling-wraps a jacket around the knife arm extended towards him to disarm it. Leaps are accompanied by knife cuts that side swipe flesh as the leap is executed. The camera follows the two bodies as they roll locked together at the feet and violence as interaction is emphasized by varying point of view shots—looking down as Cheng fights to hold back a knife being forced down and zooming in after he kicks back a thrown knife into the gang boss's abdomen. As well, Cheng is shown in close up from below as, in a frenzy, he pounds the already-dead body of his opponent and, with a slow final two blows, falls spent on top of the dead boss.

Having held the audience suspended in the fight text with a martial arts display of kung fu athletics, it is only as the camera pulls back to survey the overall scene that the audience finally sees a sign of law enforcement as the police sirens sound and the cars pull up and Cheng is taken away.[687] While Cheng's taking the law into his own hands is a reprehensible civil act, the audience leaves convinced that the violence was definitely justified within the parameters of the narrative and the aesthetic pleasure it received. Bruce Lee called his style of kung fu Jeet Kune Dor, which Stephen Teo translates as "The Art of the Intercepting Fist"[688] and it is the artful athletic precision with which the body is controlled, along with minimal special effects, that restrains the fantasy element of this fight text. That being said, as Hunt points out in his discussion of the martial arts genre's concerns with the "archival authenticity"[689] of actual fighting styles and the fan debates about the "cinematic authenticity"[690] of martial arts fight scenes—in the context of the use of what is popularly designated as the technology of wire-fu—there is a paradox in debates about authenticity given the improbability of the heroes' invincibility against large numbers of foes in martial arts films.[691]

The Flying Body

While the limited special effects of *The Big Boss* may seem dated to contemporary audiences (though not the skill and precision of Lee's martial arts ability), its righteous heroic mythology would not. In a more recent martial arts film, *Crouching Tiger, Hidden Dragon*,[692] male or female, evil or heroic, rebellious or traditional, young and battle hungry or old and battle weary, all the characters live or die within the confines of the view of cinematic martial arts violence as ultimately heroic. More prominently than in *The Big Boss*, however, is the association of that heroism with an inner philosophical stillness embodied in its mythology and the lyricism of its balletic fight text. Ken-Fang Lee makes a convincing case for reading this film as a reinterpretation of *wu xia*[693] (defined as knight-warriors using martial arts on the side of good in historical settings). The film is a revision of *wu xia*'s patriarchal origins and a critique of a culturally nostalgic view of Chinese identity as a Chinese Diaspora dream that is historically illusory.[694] The experienced woman warrior Yu Shu Lien and her lover Li Mu Bai have repressed their mutual love for their calling. Jade Fox, an embittered female warrior, has lost her way due to ambition. The talented young female apprentice Jen wants to enter the warrior path the battle-weary Li and Yu are burdened with and within which they cannot find happiness. All their stories play out in the context of the possibilities of self-realization offered within that violent warrior context that is, nevertheless, viewed as elegiac. However, despite the film's recognition of its own nostalgia in the use of the warrior motif to make its critique, the hauntingly beautiful stylized choreography of its celebratory fight scenes—in swaying trees and across water and roof tops—the balletic choreography wrapped in images of the body *in f(l)ight*, maintains a view of violence as far from aesthetically futile, even in the context of elegy for a warrior past.

The fight text in the film associates the body with limitless aerial potential, embodying a sense of soaring self-realization in the aesthetic beauty and radiant pleasures of fight motion. The body's liberated state of being in this fight text is not predetermined by actuality but only limited by the inspiration driving the imaginative practices of the choreography and its expressive movement possibilities. In that sense it "embraces a circus aesthetic, mixing amusement, astonishment, and delight in far-fetched feats"[695] which Bordwell notes is a characteristic of the Hong Kong martial arts film. Stephen Dunne, in a review of Cirque du Soleil's *Varekai*, uses the terms "athletic extravagance"[696] and the "thrilling trajectory of performers soaring through space"[697] to describe its aerial acrobatics. He could just as easily be describing the fight text of *Crouching Tiger, Hidden Dragon*. *Varekai* is based on the myth of Icarus, itself an expression of the hubristic but, nevertheless, fundamental human desire to push the body to the impossible heights of flight and beyond the limitless upper edges of known space. It is an apt analogy for the aspirational fight texts under discussion. The audiences of Cirque du Soleil's aerial circus and *Crouching Tiger, Hidden Dragon* share the desire to see the body fly. While violence outside the screen involves the transgression of social norms, in the fight text it embodies, as Karmen Mackendrick says of dance, "the love and exploration of motion, arising as the desire for and exploration of movement."[698]

Pause for Applause

The analogy with the Musical and its dance numbers gives insight into the way performativity interacts with audience reception of violence in action movies to allow a pause for appreciation. Michael Bawtree in his discussion of musical theatre describes the manner in which speech gives way to song in that genre with the emotion of the moment in the narrative giving "the performers their starting note, until speech gives place to song." The end of the song pauses the narrative to allow for audience applause and, "before the applause dies away . . . action begins again, often accompanied by a return to speech."[699] In such musical settings, degrees of what Bawtree calls lifelikeness are modified by the acceptance by the audience of musical conventions. Similarly, the moments in which fights start and stop in film narratives, for the action genre audience, are the moments of acceptance of the pause in the story in order to appreciate the virtuosity of the fight text and its choreographed body. The audience is free to feel appreciation or to figuratively (and sometimes literally) "applaud" in response to the virtuosity of the body engaging in violent action, a response that relegates the reason for the fight to a temporary plot hiatus. Unlike the characters in the Musical who generally do not acknowledge that they have moved from speech to singing, characters in fight scenes recognize that they are fighting. It is the audience, who is there to view an action film *particularly* to see the fight scenes, which recognizes that the conventional suspension of narrative is there for their enjoyment of the fight as an aesthetic experience and an inspirational exploration of the cinematic body. Stefan Hammond and Mike Wilkins' comment on the colloquially named Chopsocky genre of Kung Fu films ("Plot? Characters? Nah, combat!")[700] is not only true of that often-satirized group of films. To some extent it is true of all fight scenes in contemporary films as their filmmakers consciously strive to outdo scenes in preceding films.[701] A fascination with detailed choreography and the technological tools that sustain fight text fantasy beyond plot purpose in narrative feeds audience expectations and cinema-going pleasure.

It is in recognition of that moment required for figurative applause warranted by spectator pleasure that the Muay Thai boxing film *Ong Bak*[702] contains instant replay of the amazing fight text gymnastics displayed by its lead actor, Tony Jaa (who did his own stunt work without wires), by often running the fight move or stunt two or three times in slow motion in addition to seeing it at the regular speed. *Ong Bak* presents itself as an ode to the fluidity of movement in classical Muay Thai boxing from the moment the audience watches the hero, Ting, training early in the film while his teacher/mentor calls out the names of the attack and blocking poses—names evoking Muay Thai tradition and Thai culture even in the somewhat stilted subtitles of English translation. Ting's mentor reiterates that he must maintain the purity of his martial arts calling and never fight for money. As is expected in Asian martial arts action movies this stricture is soon tested. The young peasant hero is sent to Bangkok to retrieve the head of Ong Bak (the Temple statue on which the prosperity of the village relies), which has been stolen before an upcoming festival by a member of an urban crime syndicate. In the course of the story Ting is forced to fight in a commercial fight club to retrieve money that was stolen from him.

However, the story is only the premise for the celebration of Muay Thai boxing tradition and the constantly breathtaking gymnastics that, while they remain within the realms of plausibility because the actor uses no stunt equipment, still push at the boundaries of acrobatic possibility because of the undoubted uniqueness of the lead actor Tony Jaa's amazing skills.

In a scene where Ting is chased through a market place by gang members, Jaa—as much athlete as actor—jumps through restricted spaces. (He folds his body in half through a small circle of barbed wire, squeezes between two stacks of boards on a moving cart, cartwheels between two sheets of plate glass, and slides with his body in a split position under a moving car.) He also leaps over obstacles (such as children blowing bubbles and consecutively placed stationary cars and market stalls) and scales high, smooth walls. In a beautiful slow motion montage he somersaults over a stallholder frying food and onto the stall to continue running on the bench top and sending a snowstorm of spraying flour into the air with his feet. Violence as dance is explicitly referenced at one point when he fights on a stall using his body like a break dancer in a series of flips, splits, and kicks swirling his legs like a rotor blade before dodging a stick and spinning off the table to his feet. After bouncing off a pile of tires and completing a triple somersault over the heads of his pursuers he climbs a high fence, only to find that his escape is cut off. To escape, he leaps and runs across the shoulders of five pursuers. Viewing from the actuality of its athletically challenged perspective, the audience shares the amazement of Ting's sidekick and the comic relief who comments as he fails to replicate Ting's leap in the same chase and tears his pants, "How does he do that?"

Multiple somersaults and body pirouettes are not the frantic moves of muggers in dark alleys and gang street fighting in actuality, nor of those who defend themselves in terror against such attacks. In Muay Thai technique moves and counterattacks, blocking, speedy parrying, and dodging occur in flurries of action that are never chaotic. The fight choreographer on the film, Panna Rittikrai, associated the authenticity of the film's representation of classic Muay Thai with deliberateness of movement:

> I paid particular attention to making the fight moves look real . . . All the attacking moves—punching, kicking, kneeing, elbowing—I had to make them look very deliberate.[703]

That formality of motion frames the violence in breathtaking but ordered performativity. The brutality of Muay Thai is not glossed over—it is, after all, defined by kicks, knees, elbows, and fists to the body. However, when collisions between opponents often occur in midleap or fall, and are then replayed in slow motion, suspending the violence and its acrobatic dance in filmic time and space, the formal presentation of violence as martial *art* is foregrounded more than its brutality.

Part of that formal aesthetic is the way in which the film uses objects in the fight text. While the film showcases traditional Muay Thai stick fighting, it also makes full use of everyday objects as weapons (plates, furniture, glass walls) with a dynamic prominence that incorporates them as characters into the fight.[704] In one scene, Ting fights both his opponent and a refrigerator that his opponent is slamming into him and it is as if he is fighting the fridge as a second opponent. In the finale fight that takes place in a large cave (and where the head of the statue of Ong Bak is finally retrieved), the blows are brutal but as the bodies spin around, cartwheel, dodge, parry, spring, and leap, the impression is not one of the desperate mayhem of unskilled fighting but of the body embodying the potential for flight. As the fight culminates, Ting leaps from a scaffold holding his feet to place his body in a kneeling position and plummets onto his opponent's chest through the floor to the ground below to land sitting on the dead body. The brutal beauty of it is repeated in slow motion several times so that, by the end, the viewer has almost forgotten that it *is* violent as viewer pleasure in the aesthetics of motion dominates reception.

The Invulnerable Body

For all that people die in action films, the primary discourse of the body in violent action is one of invulnerability. As the screenwriter Shane Black asserts, violence in narrative is dramatic propulsion: "It's hard to feel a concrete sense of danger if there's no violence."[705] However, when the action film's narrative arc pauses for the fight, the sense of danger created for the heroic character is ambiguous and countered by a sense of enjoyment for the audience that comes from viewing the choreographed body propelled to the limits of gravity or beyond to defy its own vulnerability *in style*. There is less a sense of heroes in danger than bodies in exhilarating athletic motion which celebrates the potential of the body to survive violent gymnastic challenges, even though it is subject to merciless pounding in extravagant martial arts pugilism or blasted by bullets. While the degree of brutality and fantasy varies from fight scene to fight scene and from film to film, the potential of the body for triumphing over its limitations is distilled. The images of the body in twirls, leaps, and falls in the fight text are, as a consequence, devoid of the primal fear of falling so central to the sensation of "gravity adventures"[706] in actuality outside of the suspended moment of the fight text.

It is with a spectacular free-falling fight scene that *The Matrix: Reloaded*[707] opens. The second film in *The Matrix* trilogy shows Trinity—the hero Neo's[708] romantic interest and partner in their Resistance struggle against the Machine world and its artificial intelligence Agents—clad completely in glossy black leather sleekly sculpting her body (inclusive of black helmet and the fetishized Matrix sunglasses), somersaulting out of a flying motorcycle. The motorcycle-as-bomb lands on her target building, which spectacularly explodes to fill the screen with a fireball behind her silhouetted body that has landed in a crouched angular martial arts pose. Her clothing is not only stereotypically "cool" but designed to enhance the focus on her choreographed body, which is less sensually female than sculpted into athletic androgyny[709] by its sleek lines. In the fight that follows, she somersaults up into the air and lands gracefully back down to continue fighting. That move is not there as necessary to the fight; it is there for the breathtaking spectacle of the body in motion.

The fight over her body disintegrates into the emerald green special effects dissolve characteristic of *The Matrix* trilogy special effects and segues into her somersaulting through the plate glass window of a skyscraper. Guns blazing, she enters a shattered glass freefall down the side of the building in slow motion, designated by the Wachowskis' as "bullet time."[710] Film time expands with the slowed down flashes of the bullets fired by her and a pursuing artificial intelligence agent firing back, following after her in what seems like a timeless fall. The pursuing agent finally fires a bullet, which is followed in a slow motion close-up to the chest of the falling, shocked Trinity as a hole opens up in her chest. Her body spectacularly flattens a car as the fall reenters, in a "whiplash effect,"[711] the movie's real-time motion. The film then switches to Trinity asleep in bed with Neo as he wakes and we discover the whole incident has been what Neo fears is a prescient dream. If Trinity is free from the vulnerability imposed on the body by gravity when in the Matrix, she nevertheless, as Neo fears, may still succumb to her own mortality within its confines. In the context of the film's human reality versus technology matrix dichotomy, the possibility remains that, unlike their virtual opponents, she cannot be endlessly recreated.[712]

However, *The Matrix* trilogy itself, in the fight text, provides the medium for dreaming of the body's invulnerability and thus its immortality. The above fight text is typical of the world of the spectacular computer generated imagery of existence in the Matrix that parallels the "real" world of humanity's Zion, which is a far more run down, if freer, place. It has been revealed in the first film of the trilogy, *The Matrix* (1999) that the appalling reality behind the virtual illusion of the Matrix is that it has been created to enslave and use humanity as fodder to fuel machines. As the humans resist it becomes a war. As the Counsellor, one of the leaders of Zion's government, says to Neo as they contemplate the engineering room that is the source of technological power on Zion in *The Matrix: Reloaded*: "The city survives because of these machines. They are keeping us alive while other machines are coming to kill us." However, as Aylish Wood notes, while technology is seen as a two-edged sword, the action that takes place in the virtual computer generated Matrix—allowing the human characters to access the virtual powers of game characters with limitless gravity-defying potential—foregrounds the special-effects technology that makes possible that virtual imagery.[713] While the Resistance is trying to free humanity from technology gone rampant the film dazzles us with it.

Jake Horsely, viewing *The Matrix* as a "pop parable about the enslavement of modern man to the machine," correctly describes the film as having a mythological and philosophical blend of thematic paranoia about technology: "It's an amazingly coherent blend of Philip K. Dick, H. P. Lovecraft, Jean Baudrillard, messianic prophecy, apocalyptic lore, martial arts mysticism, and technological paranoia."[714] Since this book began with Baudrillard's premise of the loss of indexical reality from the Real, it is timely to recognize that his premise works for aspects of the visual imagery in *The Matrix* trilogy, which uses it as a metaphor for the world of the film.[715]

However, the fight scenes alone argue against taking the film as a whole for a negative statement about technology when it clearly promotes the enjoyment of technologically generated aesthetic violence as entertaining, nor is it convincingly paranoid about technology when its use of it to create the film's world is so attractive. Far from placing its audience in a philosophical "tight place"[716] because it must face its own virtual seduction, as Horsley posits, the audience predicates its viewing pleasure on awareness of the difference between the virtual screen with its fantastic violence and the representation of actual violence. It is the fight text, above all, that depends on that recognition.[717] Horsely confuses the hero, Neo's/Anderson's experience with the audience's. Far from "exploding our sense of what is real,"[718] which is Neo's initial experience when he becomes aware of the world outside the Matrix, the audience settles into flights of special-effects fantasy, "the Wonderland of the film,"[719] as aesthetically pleasurable rather than discomforting. As Wood notes, this "splits the potential points of identification for the viewer."[720] While it is a shock to Anderson that he is enslaved to computer simulation, the audience looks forward to digital fight scenes that push the boundaries of what special-effects technology at the time of the trilogy's production makes possible. What Anderson experiences as dismay when he discovers he is living a virtual lie, the audience experiences as aesthetic delight in illusion and spectacle that it has voluntarily entered through the cinema door to enjoy.[721] Jane Feuer argues that self-reflexive musicals like *Singin' in the Rain* (1952) affirm an ideal of entertainment in its aesthetic.[722] *The Matrix* trilogy implies the same thing by foregrounding its special-effects displays as a utopian view of the potential of the technology of cinema.

The paradoxical affective impact of Neo's hero's journey is in the spoken narrative *and* in the aspiration expressed in the fight text that technology can make the body fly. The affective impact of the film relies on the special-effects challenges posed to the movie's creators to expand the aesthetic possibilities for the body *in f(l)ight*. The film is "a wonderland of tricks and stunts" and "it seems clear that the Wachowskis have discovered a gleeful utopia of their own."[723] As Angela Ndalianis argues in her book *Neo-Baroque Aesthetics and Contemporary Entertainment*, this creative stance participates in a neobaroque spectacle of the virtuosity of special-effects illusion that is present across a range of contemporary interacting media formats such as theme park rides, film, and video games. This virtuosity is calculated to create a sense of audience awe as it turns attention away from narrative to technological display. As she notes, the creators of the illusion are "impresarios of wonderment."[724] The audience is on a revelatory special-effects journey as well as on a narrative one about freeing the mind from technological imprisonment. It is not just a result of the excitement of the "pumping adrenaline-charged violence that characterizes the MTV movies,"[725] as Horsley describes the effect of the film's violence. At its most aesthetically exciting, the Matrix trilogy elates with its cinematic vocabulary for the body in motion. The effect is not pleasure in mayhem *per se* but in violence aesthetically ordered to create technology as a bodily experience.

An example of that cinematic vocabulary is when Neo battles an ever-increasing, improbable number of clones of Agent Smith, Neo's nemesis, in *The Matrix: Reloaded*. The singular effect of this fight text is its overarching sense of motion in an aesthetically balanced frame, signaled right at the start as Neo looks to the right and then the left before launching himself into the fray. Bodies move and punches are thrown in ostensible flurries but are patterned right then left, making the opponents almost mirror images of each other. No matter how big the horde of Smiths surrounding him, Neo is always the centre of the frame and the fight (like a spoke in a wheel) and when his body or fists flatten a number of Smiths they fall in order like dominoes. When the fight is shown from a bird's eye view the pattern of the bodies is geometric (such as a spiral), despite some minor variations on points of fight interest (such as one body flying towards a building or size variation due to perspective). With Neo's centrality in the visual pattern of bodies, such detail does not throw the visual design offside but gives it visual balance. The dominating aesthetic effect is one of technologically generated symmetry that is never under threat. When the clones move apart or attack they do so symmetrically. If the attackers surge or swarm towards him they do so from two sides. When the focus is on Neo's body, his upper body is the radius for the movement of his lower body when he kicks and when he uses the cloned Smiths as stepping stones he oscillates evenly from side to side. Even when he falls and the clones throw themselves on top of him, they do so from first one side then the other. When he throws them all off, heaving the bodies into the air, the bodies form a midair pattern that is fractal-like. As they fly up, the camera circles the spray of bodies as Neo stands in the centre turning with a body on his shoulders that causes the surrounding clones to collapse in an orderly sweep. When the fighting moves into a different plane or axis of rotation—as when Neo jumps up to kick and the fight stays there temporarily, when he flips and balances on one hand and kicks his opponents in a star-formation and when he is thrown back onto a bench and breaks it exactly in the middle—the effect is not battle mayhem but of martial arts display that is technologically controlled. When Neo leaps into the air and withdraws from the battle, the clones swarm in formation to the missing center of the frame and the choreographed violence ends.

Returning to Mackendrick's comments on dance we can find a description for the effect of this fight text: "it takes us beyond the limit of the very conditions for the possibility of movement," inclusive of space and time:

> "Beyond" these limits, and yet within them—having borne away the boundaries and changed the space of the game—dance creates not some unmoving, cosmic, transcendent unity but an extraordinary stillness-in-motion (and visa versa) immanent in the dance itself, shifting the limits of our senses of time and space.[726]

The Wachowskis' bullet time is, above all, the visuality of stillness in motion and motion in stillness, a "floating, time-delayed motion."[727] The cinematographer on the film, Bill Pope, discussing the cinematography of *The Matrix* franchise, has noted the directors' liking for overhead and long tracking moves.[728] Their use of the 360-degree shot, in particular, is an elaborate move that foregrounds camera technique in this multiple Smiths fight text, making motion almost decorative in a pan that says to the audience this is "cool" movie violence and "are you watching?" At one point, Neo uses a staff as a lynchpin as he spirals around the attackers in a circle, the camera following his feet in a 360-degree shot at the head height of his opponents which reminds the audience that it is watching an artfully constructed digital affray.[729] Further, it is a shot from an enhanced spectator perspective, not Neo's subjective one. There is no sense of what it might be like for Neo to spin in that spiral because the performativity of the fight text is more about the spectator's pleasure than the character's experience.

Later in *The Matrix: Reloaded* when Neo, after a fight with some attacking Agents, makes a spectacular leap from a sculpted kneeling pose into outer space, spinning to a moment of poise in the stratosphere, as his full-length black leather coat swirls around him like a cape before diving back to earth, the character Link remarks, "He's doin' his Superman thing"—an intertextual reference that signals there are no authentic boundaries to the potential of the body in the Matrix universe. In a scene following Morpheus's address to a crowd in a cave in Zion, in a celebration of a battle victory over the machines, the film shows oiled and sweating bodies in slow motion dance as muscled dancers intermittently jump up above the mass. The scene intercuts with Neo and Trinity naked in bed and making love. The audience is left with a sense of the physical pleasures the body derives from the sensuality and physicality of dance and the body. However, the dominant sense of the body in the film is not of its physicality but of its choreographed aesthetic liberation from that physicality. It is the technologically generated fight text in which the hero Neo displays his chosen status as "The One" that is described as a measure of his heroic humanity, which is, ironically, as much a product of technology as it is of his human and, ultimately, Christ-like willingness to die for his people. In the anteroom to the Oracle, the source for Neo of vital information, the guardian of the threshold and

Neo fight prior to his entry because, as the guardian says, he wanted to know if Neo was the One: "You do not truly know someone until you fight them."[730] However, for the audience, in the fight text the philosophical import of that remark is reduced to subtext as the fight itself becomes the cinematic equivalent of a theme park thrill ride for the body,[731] which celebrates cinematic technology and the offer it makes to let the body soar.

Killer Schlock

For the screenwriter and director Quentin Tarantino, himself a master of the use of violence for aesthetic effect in his films *Kill Bill I*[732] and *Kill Bill II*,[733] the ethical divide between the cinematic uses of fictional violence and real-life violence is clear:

> In real life, I have a moral stance towards violence, but in films, no. I feel completely justified in saying that I get a kick out of violence in movies while I abhor it in real life.[734]

That aesthetic kick in *Kill Bill I* and *II*, which he wrote and directed, depends on Tarantino's basic archetypal plot taking a secondary place to a delight in mythologies of pop-culture iconography and action schlock. Tarantino has acknowledged the minimalism of the story:

> Some people have said "There's not so much of a story." Well it's a revenge story, what more story do you need? Five people did something bad to this person and now they're just gonna make 'em pay. She's got the list with five names on it and she's goin' down it. There's not much more story.[735]

The film is the revenge of the Bride, a mother desperately and brutally acting out the pain of the loss of her child, whom she believes to have been murdered following a kidnapping in which the unborn child was taken from her womb, leaving her for dead and in a coma for four years. As a professional assassin code-named after a deadly snake, the Black Mamba, willing to murder on the instruction of her boss and lover Bill, falling pregnant to him leads her to make a failed attempt to flee her membership of the Deadly Viper Assassination Squad to find a new life, new friends, and a husband-to-be in El Paso, Texas. The murder of her fiancé and friends at the wedding rehearsal by Bill and four others and the loss of her daughter (whom she believes dead) leads her to set out on a journey for revenge (when she wakes from the coma to find the five members of the squad she knows to be responsible). She ultimately finds her daughter still alive, kills Bill, and escapes from her life as an assassin.

It is that narrative minimalism that allows Tarantino to spend cinematic time playing with filmic constructs of violence. It has been frequently noted that both *Kill Bill* films are riots of popular culture and cinematic intertextuality:

> *Kill Bill* pays tribute to all things "exploitation": samurai swordsmanship, Hong Kong wire fu," blaxploitation funk, Spaghetti Western standoffs, gang-land vendettas, sexy assassins and lots and lots of raspberry-red blood. (In true B-movie spirit, the plot is as cheekily monosyllabic as the title: an underworld boss named Bill double-crosses a hit woman known as the Bride, who then embarks on a mission to—well, you guessed it.)[736]

John Pavlus also describes it as a "kung fu blowout" and "chopsocky opus."[737] Horsely has rightly noted that that "[a]ll Tarantino's movies take place in a kind of vac-uum"[738] defined by that intertextuality, and both films suspend themselves in a cinematic hiatus that allows members of the audience to enjoy the stunt wire fight scenes and the splatter as connoisseurs of pop-culture genres. The word vacuum, however, hardly begins to capture the impact and cinematic complexity of Taranti-no's creative passion for popular and pulp culture cinematic violence. Both the *Kill Bill* films invoke the conventions of hundreds of action movie variations churned out in the production houses of Hong Kong martial arts cinema, particu-larly that of the Shaw brothers (to whom, in homage, Tarantino gives an opening credit reference at the beginning of the first film). As screenwriter and fight director, Craig D. Reid, who worked with the Shaw brothers in Hong Kong notes:

> The first lesson I learned in 1979, working as a choreographer with Shaw brothers and China Television, was that fight scenes must be entertaining. We relied on imagination rather than on any attempt to reproduce real-life fight situations.[739]

Both the *Kill Bill* films reflect the frenetic violence and gangster motifs that characterize many Hong Kong martial arts films—where corpses tend to end up in multiple pieces and with maximum splatter—demonstrating a "visceral, kinetic ferocity."[740]

Blood in *Kill Bill I* is red and projectile. It spurts, gushes, showers walls, clothing, and the bodies of anyone in the vicinity or is a slow motion fine red mist spraying into the air as life expires ceremoniously, even at the heart of visual mayhem. As professional fight coaches know, audiences have a confused sense of what real blood spurting from a wound looks like but the last thing Tarantino is trying to give the audience is any sense of real blood. He offers bloody gush with the extravagant colors and force of Japanese animé. He shifts his film into animation and out again to make clear that his violence does not have its origins in actuality but in other texts. The film does not use digital effects, either in the fight scenes or its blood. The blood has the fake look of the less sophisticated martial arts movies of the 70s or earlier as the film makes a fetish of schlock. The answer to Peter Conrad's question in his article on the iconography of carnage—"Is there any difference between the diurnal facts of our combustible world and the lurid inventions of splatter movies?"[741]—is in the affirmative.

Creating blood effects on stage and screen is always about that "effect" rather than authenticity. Audiences are in fact used to "effect" blood as being the benchmark for what is real on stage and screen, not actual blood. As one special-effects creator has noted:

> It's a lot of fun working out the logistics with the blood. Sometimes we need edible blood, that has to go into the mouth. Then we need detergent-based blood for the clothing. We often have to doctor it to get the right viscosity. Sometimes we need a tint of blue. Audiences have a very specific idea of what the blood looks like; they think it should have a dark, maroon look to it. I saw an actor injured in a show once; he got a sword cut across his forehead. Blood was pouring down his face. And I heard people in the audience say, "Oh, that's the fakest blood I've ever seen."[742]

Films like the *Kill Bill* volumes stylize graphic violence so that the audience can view it up close and with a delighted equanimity impossible in actuality. Tarantino makes plentiful directorial use of the Shaw Brothers style camera zoom to bring the audience close, not to actuality but to stylized schlock. The body is continually beaten up, bloodied, torn, ripped apart, blasted, and sliced and diced—in short, slaughtered with as much gore and stunt showmanship as possible and always with intertextual flair.

In the scene in *Kill Bill I*, where the Bride confronts the Crazy 88 Japanese Yakuza gang prior to her spaghetti western showdown with one of her hit list targets O-Ren Ishii (aka Cotton Mouth), the fight text is effectively a cinematic palette of color and shade changes. The black suited, masked gang members enter a predominantly red nightclub staged with warehouse size reminiscent of a Busby Berkeley musical, with a glassed-over water pool centre. Like chorus girls from the wings of the stage, a massive number of Yakuza gang members enter to the sound of percussive chorus line footsteps. The camera zooms in on the Bride's eyes registering that her opponents are entering from all sides and then pans up to a birds eye view to show the gang circled around her as she and the audience wait in anticipation for the fight to begin. With choreographed flair, the Bride swipes the air with her sword in a preparatory stance and the encircling gang step back in perfect chorus line unison as the camera gives a cleverly stylized shot of her opponents reflected in the gleaming steel of what we know to be a legendary sword (in the mythology of the film made by a peerless craftsman). The camera pans around, looks down from a birds eye view expectantly, and then the fight breaks out. As she decimates her opponents and the blood spatters she takes out an opponent's eye and the film switches to black and white, which while reminiscent of film noir, is more desaturated. In that desaturation the spraying blood, with spurting sounds that the audience can relish, renders even decapitation, a body cleaved from top to bottom, or sliced limbs fancifully distant as the film playfully increases the body count. The Bride's acrobatic balancing on the shoulders of a gang member while she continues to fight; her use of a sword stuck in a pole to catapult herself to a balcony above; her cartwheeling, somersaulting, and break-dancing body operating like a choreographed meat cleaver as she swings at floor level around the circle of her opponents cutting off feet; all incorporate contemporary wire-stunt fight moves in cinematized black and white that creates a space for the body in action that straddles cinema traditions and time. The film is a homage to those traditions and allows the cinematic body to be then and now, 2D and 3D, stylized and cinematically rounded, colored or outlined, posed and *in f(l)ight*. The display of cinematic artistry means that the fight text shares with *The Matrix* trilogy the desire to engage with the spectator as an aficionado of special effects and connoisseur of pop culture in a technological dreamscape.

David Bordwell has aptly reiterated that the cinema, while it can be representational, theatrical, and auditory, is also graphic art. In his history of cinematic staging and style he views the compositional resources available to a director as to be used to explore through camera stylization "the possibilities of depth in the frame."[743] For Tarantino, that exploration is about the visual possibilities of depth and movement entirely within the frame and across cinematic traditions so that the perspective of the spectator remains inside that frame. The viewer watches as the camera dances around inside it. The reflection in the sword, for example, is an arresting stylistic announcement of directorial display that transforms the lethality of the weapon into an attractive cinematic objet d'art and pauses the violence for an appreciation of directorial perspective on the translucent depth of *gleam*. The audience has seen shiny swords before but with that perspective the mythology of the sword is taken to a level beyond its ability to decapitate. For Tarantino the sheen of a sword is not an actual finite thing but a cinematic effect of light. The switch back to color during the fight—with a close up on the blink of the Bride's eye attached to the audio of a sword swipe as the lights go out and the fighters become silhouetted against a blue screen—shifts the fight text's perspective again and turns the violence into a shadow puppet play set on what feels like a cavernous sound stage instead of a puppet theatre. When the Bride defeats the entire gang and goes outside to a snowscape to fight and defeat O-Ren Ishii, her yellow blood soaked body against the snow and the white kimono of her opponent transforms their bodies into aspects of a composed graphic palette. The bright red blood on white becomes so brilliantly red it is pretty rather than horrifying. For all there is plenty of action within these scenes there is also action slowed down, or paused as the fight stops to contemplate cinematic effects or intertextual references as a commentary on the nature of violence as a cinematic experience.

The setting of the violence in Tarantino's cinematic version of Movieworld allows the audience to accept the Bride's violent and vengeful ruthlessness as morally superior to her equally ruthless and violent opponents. While the heroic protagonist, the Bride and her nemesis and ex-lover Bill are distinguishable from one another morally, they share similarities of code, behavior, and modes of killing. The Bride is a one-note hero, a mother out for revenge, up against one-note villains. The villains are distinguishable less by character or degrees of evil than by degrees of elegance of fighting skill, or the lack of it in a preference for straight brutality, and by adherence to a warrior code versus venal motivations. While the second film spends more time on character development and has a lower body count, there is only one scene in it where the narrative breaks through its intertextuality to allow the audience to believe in the emotional depth and misery such a loss as the Bride's would engender and to touch on some of the personal cost of the pursuit of violent revenge. The Bride, having rescued her still alive daughter from Bill, lies on the floor of a motel bathroom and weeps with a mixture of exhaustion, relief, and emotional rawness, while her daughter sits in the other room watching cartoons on television. However, even when allowing his stoic, killing machine hero to break down, Tarantino holds it affectively in check. Outside the bathroom door her daughter is entranced by the same animated universe which this film often graphically embodies.

Shai Biderman questions whether the message of the film is that "the unavenged life is not worth living?"[744] The answer is that the film is not interested in either the question or the answer. As B. Ruby Rich aptly notes: "It's so easy to be distracted in a Tarantino film"[745] by his intertextuality. The late appearance of the child in the story and the minimal attention given to convincing nurturing interactions between the Bride and the girl subordinates story to the time spent playing with film violence. The unisex nature of the fight scenes also contributes to the reduction of the sense of the motivation of the Bride as mother (or Bill as father or lover of the Bride, for that matter). While there are gender-based motivations that propel both characters to violent action, within the fight text there are no gender-based distinctions.[746] Jerry Palmer's classic book on the thriller genre notes that one of the essential distinctions to be made between heroes and villains when both use violence, if one is to ensure audience empathy for the hero, is that the hero must be driven to it and must not be cold-blooded about it.[747] In films like the *Kill Bill* volumes the former is true but the latter is not. While there is audience empathy for the Bride, her ferocity is no less ruthless than Bill's and audience confidence in her fighting ability removes the danger from her encounters necessary for a more intense form of audience identification. What ultimately distinguishes the Bride from her nemeses is that she is the better fighter. Issues of transgression are not the outcome of her fighting as an equal with men, or because her aggression contrasts with her nurturing as a mother. By the time of *Kill Bill I* and *II*'s release the Bride as an image of the female action hero or warrior is no longer disruptive as a feminist icon—the audience has seen females kick butt before. This is not to deny that viewing female action heroes "move in a physically assertive manner enforces imagined possibilities at the bodily level"[748] for the female audience but it is, for contemporary viewers one could argue, more of a unisex viewing response.

The Dance of the Parodied Body

When describing his training for his role in *Ong Bak*, Tony Jaa noted that he eschewed the use of stunt wires because he wanted to display, through his martial arts skills, that what he did was authentic:

> I wanted to show the public that you can attain real and authentic results . . . During the shoot, but also during the training, kicks and punches were genuine. Just like real fights, except that we took protective measures. For the feet and head, for instance. Those training sessions required great mastery. You have to be able to strike blows hard enough for them to look real, then gently pull back so as to not cause injury. Sometimes, on certain takes you have a mutual agreement with the stuntman to be hit for real in the face. We love it! Seriously, we don't mind getting hit when the end result is success. When the take is good it energises us.[749]

While it is intriguing that somewhere in the fight text one might be watching a "real," rather than a stunt blow landing, the cinematic frame of disassociation from actual violence is not likely to give the audience the chance to recognize it. Preexisting perceptions of actual violence are so subsumed by the parameters of the aesthetic of the fight text that anything approaching actual violence would look strange and unintegrated in an orderly account of violence where the body visually transcends the consequences of its physicality. Ultimately, choreography in the fight text uses violence as a launching pad for cinematic technology to aesthetically fantasize about the body's emancipation from its own gravity-bound mortality and for that, authenticity must be leeched from the dance.

It is when the martial arts/action genre takes a comic look at the absurdity of its conventions that the lack of authenticity is thrown into high relief. In *Kung Fu Hustle*,[750] where "Let's Dance" is an invitation to the hero to fight an evil opponent called the Beast, the fantasy of immortality is parodied in an exaggeration of heroic Zen mythology and special-effects techniques. Surviving improbable violence appears hilariously ridiculous. In the film, when a philandering husband is attacked by his wife he falls from a height with a satisfying splat. His wife drops a flowerpot on his head, which breaks exactly in half leaving the molded dirt and flower upstanding and blood seeping out. Needless to say, he survives. The wife is the Slum Queen of Pig Sty Alley, which is involved in a battle against a takeover by the urban upper crust Axe Gang. In a chase scene which provides the hilarity of *Crouching Tiger, Hidden Dragon* meets *Road Runner*, the hero runs from the Slum Queen with three knives sticking from his arms and shoulders while still capable of slow-motion leaping. The Slum Queen's legs rotate so fast that, like the Road Runner, they spin and churn up dust as they run along the road. The hero is flattened sideways as he ducks under an oncoming truck and, in a spectacular contrast with that sped-up hilarity there is a slow-motion sideways twist by the Queen as she goes over the truck. The camera cuts to her underwear and curlers flying off and she lands flat against a billboard, sliding slowly down it onto the ground. In a similar vein, there are three obligatory showdowns between the hero and his nemesis the Beast where bodies are frozen in an exaggeration of bullet time. In one encounter, when it appears the Beast has decapitated the hero, he looks down at a now empty hole in the floor and the audience sees the Slum Queen and her husband speeding through the air carrying the hero's body. The Beast, commenting on the outlandish unreality of the faster than the speed of light disappearance of his victim ("This doesn't make sense") comically speaks for the logic of the audience's actuality.

The use of digital animation effects for parody encapsulates what Mike Atkinson, in his discussion of the film *Who Framed Roger Rabbit*, which mixed live actors with cartoons, calls the "tooning" of 3D through "the dementia of 2D art."[751] This blend is equally the cinematic space occupied by "bullet time" where the fight text aspirations for the body exist. It is the performativity of cinematic style that is the attraction of the fight text in action films where "[c]onceptions of what looks good are derived as much from theatrical spectacle as combat traditions."[752] Andrew Hewitt in his book on ideology as performance in dance argues that dance is the study of time and motion and embodies the ideological possibility that all move-ments are not free but choreographed.[753] If the body is liberated in the fight text, nevertheless Hewitt's contention also remains true for its choreographed body. If cinematic technology visually frees the body it also propels it towards *Kung Fu Hustle*, bringing the kinesthetic dream about the body to a comic halt.

In the documentary film *Rize*[754] that chronicles the street dance phenomenon of Clowning and Krumping—which grew out of the racial riots in 1965 and 1992 Watts and South Central in Los Angeles as protest performance—African-American youth channel their feelings of racial oppression and aggression into an athletic and aggressive form of high-speed dance that is an alternative group activity of self-identification to "gang banging" for the practitioners. The film culminates in a competition between the Clowners and the Krumpers in a "battle zone," literally in an auditorium ring, where they aggressively vie for dance supremacy as the most authentic expression of ghetto identity. Despite the aggression of a dance form that can involve pushing and shoving and steps that are reminiscent of African warrior dance, one of the Clowners, Lil C, says: "Fighting is the last thing on our mind when we're dancin." For Lil C, dancing transforms aggression and violence even as it expresses it:

> The fact that you can get Krump, you can channel that anger, anything nega-tive that has happened in your life, you can channel that into your dancin'. You can release that in a positive way because you're releasin' it through art, the act of dance.

Dragon, a Krumper, calls it "ghetto ballet":

> This is our ghetto ballet, this is how we express ourselves, this is the only way we see fit of storytelling, this is the only way of making ourselves feel like we belong.

In *Rize*, dance retains the aggression it expresses while transforming it into a reflec-tion on ghetto life and identity and on its problems and violence. Clowning and Krumping encapsulate the ways in which the uses of violence in artistic forms always has the potential to become a vehicle for a subject other than itself. The ques-tion of authenticity in the representation of violence is always a matter of degree and, as *Kung Fu Hustle* illustrates above, violence can be ridiculous and comic and far from threatening.

In the third episode of season three of the Australian version of the reality televi-sion competition show *Dancing with the Stars*,[755] the Russian-born Australian and world boxing champion Kostya Tzu and his professional ballroom dancer partner made their entrance to compete with a round three sign upheld and Tzu disrobing from a fighter's robe before launching into their dance number. They danced to the tune of the lyric "Kostya Tzu, he loves to Tango" written, it was announced, by one of the Wiggles.[756] Fighter and dancer were portrayed in the routine as a reflection of each other in the space offered by commercial television, ballroom dancing, and a singing group with a toddler fan base. As Tzu tangoed with the competitive verve of the stocky pugilist and a better-than-average amateur ballroom dancer, one could not help thinking how completely the actuality of punching the body with a blow, the reality of boxing, had been drained of its bloody authenticity.[757] Tzu's performance sums up how "dance recodes the threat of violence"[758] in all the films under discussion. Thus, it is fitting to note, in conclusion, that Tzu's tango was lovely and the judges scored it highly, to the vigorous applause of an audience clearly delighted with the transformation of the boxer into a ballroom dancer.

7

"It's Just Detail":[759] Flaying the Sacred and Prosthetic, Pixilated and Animated Violence in the Hyperreal

Actors routinely "bleed" in medically remarkable ways, thanks to the make-up artist's skill. Bad guys are very bad, good guys very good: anything more complex interferes with the story line.

(Paula Fredriksen)[760]

I'm not bad, I'm just drawn that way.

(Jessica Rabbit)[761]

The sense of the body in graceful flight in action film fight sequences is not the only example of textual violence with loosened ties to the narrative in which it is embedded. The texts under consideration in this chapter are at the end of the continuum of authenticity where the viewer's astonished gaze is held on violence done to the body in images of its prosthetic, pixilated, or animated bloodied components. Far from the indexicality of the televised images of 9/11, is the representation of violence in films, video games, and cartoons that depend for their graphic effect on prosthetic make-up and CGI versions of violence in the hyperreal. Images of body components are stock-in-trade in fictional shows like the forensic investigation *CSI* franchise, *Bones*, and other forensic procedurals where depersonalized details of "corpses . . . are apparatus, bodies of evidence."[762] Leon Hunt describes such special effects as creating visuals of injuries in both games and films (and I would add television) that "fetishise physical damage."[763] However, a view of the body in fragments under the impact of violence is not confined to any one genre, media, or text. Violence is often done to the body in texts in ways that focus on its "supernumerary body parts,"[764] reducing the body to the sum of those parts. The audience shock or amazement which is often a result of special effect hyperrealized graphic violence has as much to do with that reductive fragmentation of the body as it does with any link with an actuality that may or may not be plausibly realized. Images involve a focus on increasingly perfected detail that is aided in films, animation, and video games by improvements in digital technology that amaze the viewer with their capacity to enhance a photorealistic representation of actuality. While I prefer the term "hyperrealistic" to "photorealistic" for reasons I will outline in this chapter, texts that focus on details of the body that are broken up into its special-effect components can often profoundly disturb the viewer with the specter of the body's vulnerability. Such details invoke the loss of a sense of the unity of the body that is culturally valued, even sacred. It is a unity that the body in graceful flight in action films embodies as the dream of its potential and liberation. On the other hand, when the body is blasted to its component bits in video games, destroying that culturally held sacred unity can become its own fantasy of liberation from cultural and social restraints.

In defense of the use of violence in his film *The Passion of the Christ*,[765] director Mel Gibson has commented, "To those who complain about the violence of my film I have two words: *Kill Bill*."[766] In the light of my earlier argument that the violence in action films like *Kill Bill* is an opportunity for viewers to delight in the grace of martial arts violence rather than be distressed by it, his analogy does not account for reported viewer unease in response to the graphic violence in his film.[767] For Jose Márquez, Gibson's film *is* an action movie, adhering as it does "to a tradition within the canon of filmmaking that is more phenomenal than symbolic" and not offering a narrative "journey" but a violent "event":

> Instead of offering its viewers a story, it gives them an experience: a slow, gut-wrenching mechanical ride through an old-fashioned house of horrors tucked away for centuries within the church.[768]

While I do not agree with Marquez that the film meets any definition of an action movie, it can be accepted as a truism that the images are disturbing and lingered on beyond the needs of moving the narrative forward.[769] While graphic representations of violence often disturb viewers, the clarity of definition about what "graphic" consists of in a film like Gibson's or in the much-excoriated violent video games,[770] for example, is less well defined as critics grapple with technological advances that improve photorealism in special effects. Undoubtedly, as John Shelton Lawrence and Robert Jewett note with regard to violence in video games, part of the use of violence in any genre is as "graphic hyperbole to raise the stakes and make us pay attention."[771] The results of that narrative approach can be a focus on violent imagery that is indulged in for the sake of the display involved in the technological rendering of the moment. As Peter Biskind notes, it is an indulgence that links aspects of films that make heavy use of special effects with video games and which owes a great deal to the special effects legacy of director George Lucas, Lucas Film, and the digital innovations of his company Industrial Light and Magic:

> *Star Wars* pioneered the cinema of moments, of images, of sensory stimuli increasingly divorced from story, which is why it translates so well into video games. Indeed, the movie leapt ahead—through hyperspace, if you will—to the '80s and '90s, the era of non-narrative music videos, and VCRs, which allowed users to view film in a non-narrative way, surfing the action beats with fast-forward.[772]

In a more philosophical vein, and far from viewing *The Passion of the Christ* as an action film, René Girard opines that it is possible to distinguish a mythological attitude to violence that tries to dissimulate it, to not look too closely for fear of contagion, from another more realistic attitude that is willing to contemplate its injustice and delusion. For Girard, the focus on the violence in Gibson's film reflects the steady gaze of the latter. Distinguishing it from earlier portrayals of the Passion with their "Hollywood saccharinity," Gerard sees the violence as "implacable realism."[773] Yet he offers little in his argument to define what he means by realism except to argue, in a circular fashion, that it seems to involve a willingness to portray, or look at, the graphic.

The question remains: look at what in particular? The nature of the representation of violence in a graphic film like *The Passion of the Christ* and its disturbing impact depends a great deal on the exaggerated bloody detail of scourged prosthetic skin on the body of the actor, Jim Caviezel, playing a theologically sacred icon. This impact lies primarily in the power of those details to disturb with their copiously detailed intensity rather than because it is indexical or realistically authentic. Its blood and gore is not so much "real," as Girard argues, but more graphic in ways that can be defined as exaggerated by the hyperreal. Violence denoted as graphic, such as that in *The Passion of the Christ*, is of interest in the context of what the links may be between such graphic images and actual violence and for what it reveals about a viewer's experience of hyperreal violence in all its forms. The audience for Gibson's film and for graphic violent video games (which are ubiquitous targets for public criticism for their violence) are responding less to aspects of verisimilitude and more to something disturbing about the hyperreal version of authenticity when it comes to violence. Mark Gillings has noted that the viewer can attribute authenticity to virtual representations in a process that downplays verisimilitude, "casting visual approximation as but one factor influencing the faithfulness of any representation."[774] The image of Christ's body in the prosthetics of flayed skin in Gibson's film does not disturb viewers because it is authentically actual but because it is virtually enhanced, which is something else altogether. It is responded to as disturbing for reasons other than its authenticity or realism. It is important, of course, to decide what is specifically meant by hyperreal when describing such graphic images.

Hyperrealism

Despite my concern about the use of definitions of postmodern simulacra and the hyperreal to define the images of 9/11 at the beginning of the continuum of authenticity, it is at the furthest end of the continuum that they are most useful when making distinctions between representations of violence. In seeking a definition for the much-bandied-about concept of "graphic" to describe violence in reference to media texts that use pixilated, prosthetic, and animated fictional forms the concept of hyperrealism comes into its own. It is timely to note that, as an art movement, Hyperrealism is an extension of Photorealism,[775] whose practitioners aimed to make paintings that heightened the visual experience of a secondary source, the photograph. Hyperrealism in turn exaggerated even further that photographic detail beyond the exactness of the camera's indexicality to over-emphasize its physical properties. The extreme, foregrounded luminous light of that detail heightened the materiality of its photographic representational reference. To quote the Tate museum curator Barbara Stafford, Hyperrealism is the painterly "revelation of the unexpected by magnification."[776] That sense of luminous and heightened detail characterized the entry into the hyperreal as much as the lack of indexicality that was precluded by the original use of photographs as a referent in Photorealism. In that sense, the hyperreal is no longer actuality but is its tangible transcendence.

Its cinematic equivalent, of which the copious blood in *The Passion of the Christ* is an example, is a focus on detail that feels so intense it is experienced as a state of "more" than accurate or disturbingly *overly*-accurate. When used in CG animation in what has been called an "algorithmic aesthetic"[777]—as in the ethereally lit effects in films like *The Polar Express* (2004) and the added sharp luminosity of physical detail embodied in the human characters in *Final Fantasy: The Spirit Within* (2001)—the hyperreal detail is so digitally perfect it feels like an animated version of corrected vision. The effect is to heighten the focus on what can be imperfect, blurred, unnoticed, impressionistically generalized, or even hidden-in-full-view on the surface of objects recognized as visually authentic outside the screen. It is a prosthetic or digital clarification that is an outcome of the questing technological desire to perfect the photorealistic detail of an image and the illusion of the real. It is a perfection of detail that leaves the viewer with a sense of hypervisuality, as if something is "off" because it is so revelatory in its sharpness and refined in its detail. It is the hyperreal version of a flawless physical tangibility that transcends the imperfections of the real. As Paula Parsi notes, "the absolute imperfection of living things is a renderer's nightmare"[778] in the quest to digitally capture the actual. There is a case to be made for points of merging between the desire for hyperrealistic, perfected detail, and the desire to embody that perfection in actuality. There is a link between the perfected lines and smooth, floaty, luminous surfaces of hyper-realistic graphic rendition, and the cultural value placed on the appearances of Hollywood celebrity actors and actresses in films and on the red carpet, the reed-thin physicality of models on the catwalk, the hard bodies aimed for in the physical fitness marketplace, the contemporary popularity of plastic surgery, and the "photoshopping" practices of magazine representations of the male and female form in articles and advertisements. In that sense, I would argue there is something impressionistically hyperrealistic about the veneered, orthodontically corrected, evenly spaced, ultra-white teeth of celebrity film actors that makes the teeth super-numerary to the rest of their appearance.

Hyperrealized enhancement of the actual on screen leads me to disagree with Paul Wells when he says:

> This scale of achievement with the new digital technologies has all but hidden the animation at its heart, preferring to heighten the sense of realism until the form does not "announce" itself as animation but insists upon its representational validity.[779]

Generally, that kind of detail is not seen when looking at the fast-moving, blurred world of mundane actuality. Awed, the viewer is still aware of the form of that detail in the hyperreal, of the "special" in the effects. As with fight scenes in action films, the viewer is being given the moment out of narrative to focus on and appreciate the amazing detail. Geoff King and Tanya Krzywinska highlight with reference to the appeal of graphic realism to players in video games that

> it also offers what can be termed a "spectacle" of realism: degrees of graphical realism that are flaunted and designed to be admired as striking or impressive images in their own right.[780]

While I would prefer the use of photorealism or hyperrealism to the use of realism in the above quote, it *is* the emphasis on spectacle that inevitably reminds the viewer that it is not the authentically actual but the narrative illusion of it that is being observed. It is the hyperreal that offers the suspension of narrative to the viewer to enjoy the entertainment diversion, often perversely disturbing when the images are violent. As Marie-Laure Ryan has pointed out, such an awareness of form while immersed in the fictional is a characteristic of art experiences in general and is not necessarily confined to the virtual in the CGI sense: "The same duplicity that diagnoses illusion allows one self to be immersed and the other to appreciate the vehicle of the experience."[781] However, in CG animation and prosthetic rendering particularly, the skill of the display inevitably breaks through immersion with a technical flourish.

Audience discomfort in the face of the prosthetically rendered violence in *The Passion of the Christ* is a state of reflection in which the viewer is also moving out of immersion towards critiquing the constructed format of what is recognized as the experience of illusion. The screenwriter Paul Schrader, lamenting the replacement of the existential hero by the ironic hero in contemporary film has described such irony as suspending violence in a kind of hyperreal "quotation marks":

> The existential dilemma is, "should I live?" And the ironic answer is, "does it matter?" Everything in the ironic world has quotation marks around it. You don't actually kill somebody; you "kill" them. It doesn't really matter if you put the baby in front of the runaway car because it's only a "baby" and it's only a "car."[782]

The idea of violence suspended in quotation marks captures exactly the sense of the hyperreal's distance from actual violence and the sense of it occupying a textual space where creators of text are free to intensify the shock to viewers by exaggerating aspects of actuality in a textual cocoon. In that sense, it is both safe and unsafe for a viewer to look because, while violence is not actual or indexical, it is *enhanced*. Confronting as it is, it is not blood seeping from flesh on the ground as life actually expires outside the screen but overblown to dominate the screen as aesthetic display. The detailed blood and gore of the prosthetic skin on an actor and the accompanying copious spilled special-effects blood used in *The Passion of the Christ* to represent the ferocity of the torture of Christ can be similarly seen as the hyperreal enhancement of detail less easy to see, or not seen or heard at all, in actual violence. Exaggerated violent detail, paradoxically, still reminds the viewer that it exists in text—despite the fact that he or she is also immersed in the suspension of disbelief required to accept aspects of constructed verisimilitude.

Violence Against the Sacred in the Hyperreal

Annette Hill, discussing the gender differences that emerged from her research into audience response to violence in film, noted that male participants chose to see violent movies as an "enjoyable ordeal":

> They may desire to look away, but by anticipating violence they can prepare to test their own boundaries of response, to test endurance levels . . . for some participants, to be desensitized to violent representations is not a negative reaction, indeed in many ways it is a desired reaction.[783]

The hyperreal nature of graphic violence is about having one's glance drawn to look at the exaggerated details of a violent visual event that one would instinctively want to look away from in real life. Paul Verhoeven (the director of the violent science-fiction fantasy *Starship Troopers*) has theorized on the exorcism of the fear of violence and the affective liberation offered to audiences by the destruction of life and objects held to be sacred:

> But why is violence funny? Why do we laugh when Arnie blows the mutha-fuckas away, or even when "Starship Troopers" innocents are mutilated by bugs? It has something to do with being at a safe distance, with knowing it is a fantasy: . . . A house, a car, a body, all these are sacred objects, and to see them manipulated, destroyed, when they're not yours, gives intense pleasure, almost a magic reaction.[784]

Verhoeven's extension of the definition of the sacred beyond the theological to other cultural objects that are revered and valued is insightful. *Starship Troopers*' (1997) focus on bodies being torn apart by giant alien insects in unremitting muti-lation itself reflects that desire to hammer at the vulnerability of the body, along with any illusions we may hold about its safety or its sacredness as a life form. Together, Hill and Verhoeven's statements pose the paradox of the viewing experi-ence of violence in the hyperreal as potentially being both an ordeal and a liberation. The difference between viewing the detailed graphic violence in *The Passion of the Christ* compared to *Kill Bill*, for example, is that the viewing experience of the former is more of an aesthetically constructed ordeal and the latter more of an aesthetic liberation.

Setting aside, for a moment, Verhoeven's notion of a range of artefacts being viewed as culturally sacred, the most obvious definition of the sacred in film has been a theological one. Like other art forms before Gibson's, film has had an interest in the theologically sacred and that interest has often led to controversy over theo-logical points of view. The release of *The Da Vinci Code* (2006) encountered similar religious controversy to Gibson's from those who questioned its theology, and led to public debates about the truth of sacred history. However, lukewarm reviews for the film worldwide[785] suggest that, independent of its subject matter, the film still stands or falls on its storytelling merits. In the case of *The Passion of the Christ*, that merit depends on the film's ability to create a sense of something sacred as well as depict the humanity of Christ in its violent story. Albert J. Bergesen and Andrew M. Greeley argue that an absence of realist constraints enabled by cine-matic storytelling frees the religious imagination to express spiritual and religious themes:

> They are not about representing losing faith in, say, the voice of God, but in representing the voice itself (*Field of Dreams*). They are not about thinking

about what might happen if God were to appear and talk directly to you, but about making that actually happen (*Oh, God!*) . . . To do this, to so attempt a direct representation of the religious imagination itself, requires finding a way to make real and observable that which is transcendent and unobservable, and to do that required violating the realist canon.[786]

The Passion of the Christ aims to give cinematic form to the theological belief in redemption through a representation of the sacred in the brutal suffering experienced by Christ's body. The film begins with the quote from *Isaiah* 53: "He was wounded for our transgressions, crushed for our iniquities; by His wounds we are healed." As David John Graham says in his discussion of Martin Scorsese's films as religious storytelling, "There is also an act of violence at the heart of the Christian faith,"[787] referring to the crucifixion as "sacred violence."[788] In line with that view of Christianity, the cross in Gibson's film is a symbol of unremitting torture. It is through the film's focus and bloody magnification of violence in the hyperreal that it tries to create a sense of the sacred in violated physicality. Gibson uses confronting violence to foreground Christ's suffering, not as a secular film raising religious issues, but to offer itself as similar to other religious Christian icons for the devout. As Margaret R. Miles describes it, the purpose of such iconic religious imagery is "to reveal the invisible world of spiritual reality."[789] For Gibson, the hyperreal copiousness of the prosthetic layering of the violence is a means of bearing witness to the invisible sacred.

Christ suffers his first blow after his arrest in the garden of Gethsemane and is taken in chains to Caiaphas, the High Priest, in the courtyard of the Jewish Temple. As the film deals with Judas's betrayal of Christ and Peter's denial of him, the audience sees him bound in chains and beaten by his guards on the way to the Temple courtyard. Blows rain down on him, he is knocked over a bridge to hang by the chains that bind him and then hauled roughly up again. By the time he reaches the temple he is bruised and bloodied. As Caiaphas interrogates him, he is struck and spat on by the priest for claiming to be the Son of God, and the Jewish crowd in the Temple follow suit in striking him and jeering. His body is further beaten and dragged by chains, often in slow motion. This is far from the use of slow motion violence discussed in the previous chapter, which was a means to create the body's capacity for graceful movement. Slow motion in Gibson's film becomes a means of prolonging contemplation of the violence being inflicted on the body and on the depth of its capacity to experience terrible pain and endure unspeakable suffering. For Gibson, blows to Christ's body are also an affirmation of his innocence. When interrogated by Caiaphas, Christ asks, "If I have spoken evil tell me what evil I have said. But if not, why do you hit me?" The film reiterates this sense of unfair conviction when the Jews bring Christ to Pontius Pilate, the Roman Governor, to be judged and executed according to Roman law. Pilate notes his bloodied condition and asks "Do you always punish your prisoners before they're judged?" The violence represents a statement by the film about the Jewish society that condemns Jesus as well as an essentially didactic statement about his suffering and his status as the innocent sacred incarnated in violated flesh.

As the violence continues, I would argue the viewer is left less with a sense of the spiritually sacred than with an overwhelming sense of the reduction of the body to its suffering and fragmented bloodied parts. After Herod refuses to judge him and Pilate fails to avoid doing so when the Jews choose the freedom of the murderer Barabbas over that of Christ, the film focuses on the execution of Pilate's sentencing of him to be scourged. The beating stops just short of death, shown in excruciating physical detail as the body degenerates into a whipping post, and is increasingly, in texture and outline, less recognizable as whole in its bodily humanity. In the following crucifixion scene, Christ's bloodied body scarred by earlier whipping and beating, crawls onto the cross to be nailed as the camera draws the viewer into more close-up contemplation of the process. In slow motion, the spike is pressed into the flesh of his left hand and the mallet comes down several times to the metallic ringing sound of the blows. A Roman guard, in an attempt to stretch Christ's arm for staking on his right side, pulls on a rope tied to his wrist, tearing and dislocating the shoulder with an excruciatingly emphasized click that is far louder than would be heard in actuality.[790] The whole scene up to the nailing of his feet consists of close-ups on the segmented bloodied parts of his body. Christ's hands, his beaten face with its bloodied teeth, his scored body from the chest up, his dripping or spurting blood, his legs, and feet as the latter are nailed—the body loses its unity in its suffering. When the cross is turned over to complete the nailing, and when it is raised at the process's end, the view of the body is more of its length. However, even then, the camera quickly returns to segmentation of the body as we see Christ at the ground level (from Mary Magdalene's viewpoint as she is sprawled in the dust) or from the onlookers' level as they raise their eyes to Christ's upper body. The spectacular detail of the prosthetic rendering of the bloodied teeth and brutally whipped skin further draws the focus from a sense of the body as a whole to the suffering of its brutalized parts.[791]

Amy Hollywood catalogues the use of static references in the film to traditions of religious art used as pictorial forms of meditation.[792] For such artistic and meditative sources, faith is associated with the depth and degree of Christ's physical suffering. Redemption through physical pain is not only the province of overtly religious films, of course, boxing films being the most obvious. Paul Schrader talking about the film he wrote for the director Martin Scorcese, *The Last Temptation of Christ*, refers to his own history of writing films like *Raging Bull* as the precursor to tackling the Christian "prototype."[793] His description of redemption in *Raging Bull* applies equally well to Gibson's version of the "prototype" as

redemption through physical pain, like the Stations of the Cross, one torment after another. Not redemption by having a view of salvation or grace, but just redemption by death and suffering, which is the darker side of the Christian message.[794]

Slow motion is thus used in the film to dissect the infliction of pain on a body disintegrating under flagellation and torture. That the violence of the event in the film is unremitting is the point. Short of leaving the theatre or closing one's eyes, the viewer has nowhere else to look. At one point, during the flagellation of Christ's body by the Romans in the public scourging, one of them stops to change implements. He picks up an instrument with nails capable of taking out clumps of flesh rather than just scoring the body. Prior to beginning he tests it on a table and the metal catches in the wood tearing out chips. Prefiguring the horror of what is about to happen to Christ's body in this way intensifies the audience's expectation. It causes the viewer to flinch at what has not yet happened as much as he/she will cringe when the body is further reduced to chunks of ripped flesh.

Significantly, it is the increasing reduction of Christ's dialogue that adds to the sense of the body's disintegration. Apart from a few lines, Christ's dialogue becomes inarticulate moans and guttural sounds after the scourging in the film's present (though not in flashbacks). By the time the film moves to the Stations of the Cross on the journey to Golgotha, the representation of the bloodied body is in danger of leaving little for the audience to identify with. Recognizing this problem, as Hollywood details, Gibson gives the film cuts from Christ's suffering to the reactions of those in the crowd, which are distraught, horrified, or jeering. The film relies on the empathic reactions of Christ's family and followers and on flashbacks prior to his arrest to revivify his personhood. Sentimental as it is, the inclusion of a flashback to Mary running to comfort Jesus as a toddler after a fall, and then forward to her doing the same as he stumbles with the cross, is one of those moments that reinstates that humanity.[795] In my view, it is one of the few truly empathic moments in the film that extends our sense of his humanity beyond the hyperrealized physicality of his flesh. It is a welcome gradation of story in what is otherwise a film built around the prosthetic rendering of violence done to the body. The more the body is flayed, the more the spectacle is in danger of overwhelming the narrative. I would argue that, in the film's reductive focus on bloodied body parts, it does overwhelm it.

In the discussion of the degree to which Gibson's film is based on the Gospels, the film's indebtedness to the fanciful description of the crucifixion details from the writing of the nineteenth-century stigmatic nun Anne Catherine Emmerich as a source (from *The Dolorous Passion of Our Lord Jesus Christ*) has been noted by critics and the director himself. For Paula Fredriksen, the reliance on the elaborated detail in Emmerich emphasizes "the extreme suffering of the good, the extreme villainy of the bad"[796] in the film. It accounts, in her view, for both the film's graphic violence and the good/bad moral dichotomy in its portrayal of the Jews. For Fredriksen, the film places itself in a religious tradition going back to medieval Christian practices and images of redemption as a "theology of pain"[797] found in "Passion plays, flagellant penitential practices" and the artistic imaging of "Christ as the torn and bleeding Man of Sorrows."[798] The film has much in common with the medieval mystical, visionary Christian tradition of meditation on Christ's death (that evoked the violence of his suffering while encouraging identification with the victim), and the suffering of Mary and Mary Magdalene. It was through that encouragement that, as Hollywood notes of medieval mediations on Christ's suffering, "Narratives such as the *Meditations on the Life of Christ* continually remind the reader that his or her salvation depends on compassionate mediation"[799] and try to place "the onlooker into the story"[800] with copious detail to effect that mediation. Recognizing the influence of that tradition on Gibson's focus on the detailed violence of the crucifixion certainly makes mute the critical discussion on where or how Gibson deviates from biblical sources:

> The truth of "the mysteries and events that occurred" depends less on their biblical or authoritative origins, although these are assumed, than on the violence of the images that heighten imagination and emotion, enabling the mediator momentarily to bring Christ, his mother, and his followers back to life.[801]

For Gibson, cinematic space filled with detail made possible by make-up and prosthetic special-effects technology, in particular, is a means to bringing his audience close to the crucifixion, writ large in the hyperreal in a way that he clearly feels cannot be reached by a more subdued, less copiously bloody, or less hyperrealistic representation.

The discussion of how far the theologically sacred seems authentic, as opposed to hyperreal, probably has more to do with the religious allegiances of the viewer than it does with the format of representation.[802] How to respond to attempts to portray the sacred in film is of particular import for Christian audiences.[803] Bryan P. Stone succinctly puts the creative challenge facing filmmakers as that of trying to reconcile the evangelistic and the historical, to harmonize four different gospel accounts and to reconcile respect and relevance in a story about the divine made flesh:

> If Christians across the centuries have consistently struggled to hold in tension the full humanity and full divinity of Jesus without letting one of these overshadow or negate the other, perhaps we can begin to appreciate how difficult it is to maintain this paradox on film.[804]

William Irwin calls films trying to portray Christ's death "crucifiction" to highlight the directorial interpretations and fictional choices that led to the decision in Gibson's film to portray the degree of torture endured by Christ:

> The mistreatment of the God-man is too much to take, with the indignities of being slapped, shackled, and spit upon. But even those who do not believe Jesus is God find the flogging, scourging, and fall-ridden way of the cross too much to bear. In a surreal scene one Roman soldier gives a lesson to another in "how it's done," oblivious to the suffering of the man whose flesh he impales with nine-inch nails. We just cringe.[805]

For Irwin, the visceral response is what compels moral reflection and the creation of an experience of the sublime.[806] Gibson's approach undoubtedly reflects the symbolic view of the crucifixion argued for by Craig Detweiler and Barry Taylor, who emphasize that the cross is a potent symbol of salvation when the bloodiness of the story is not avoided. Only then is the cross a realistic symbol of suffering:

> Yet the scandal, the absurdity, the messiness of the cross cannot be avoided ... A whitewashed cross, jumping ahead to the resurrection, won't do ... Christians must not take a shortcut to Easter Sunday. Blood, sweat and tears line the road to resurrection.[807]

Gibson's attempt to create a sense of the sacred made flesh by revivifying physical detail is an approach common to other films on religious themes. Henri Agel, describing Carl Dreyer's *The Passion of Joan of Arc* and its focus on the physical as a means to create a sense of the sacred, seems to me to parallel something of what Gibson is trying to do with his use of violence and which is made possible in the creative space offered by the cinematic hyperreal:[808]

> Thus Dreyer remains in love with the epidermic surface of things and beings. It is because Dreyer is concerned with this "physicality" of his characters (Joan of Arc), because "each pore of the skin is made familiar to us," that the transfiguration of a tormented human substance can become a Christ-substance.[809]

In Gibson's film it is every *bloody* "pore." In the final analysis, the highly visceral focus on brutality in *The Passion of the Christ* does not so much transfigure "human substance" as overwhelm it. Flaying that sacred body causes a sense of authentic bodily humanity to disintegrate and all but disappear in hyperreal blood. As a result, the sense of the sacred also struggles to surface, and in the end has to be taken on faith.

The Sacred and the Pixilated Dismemberment of the Body

To return to Verhoeven's designation of the body and commodities such as build-ings and cars as culturally sacred objects, it is possible to gain insight into the mythos of violent destruction in video games that focus on virtual worlds under threat, which can reference the theologically sacred or cast the player in a savior-like role. Lawrence and Jewett describe films that cloak violence in ambiguous polysemic references to Christianity and other religious faiths as "monomythic cre-dotainment."[810] In their chapter on monomythic video games, the cleverly titled *The Sound of One Hand Killing*,[811] they describe interaction with such games as "mythic socialization," which "allows the player to be a savior and to feel the tactical game pleasures of redeeming a situation from threat."[812] Lawrence and Jewett link the development of such a mythos with the god mode of the player role in games like the *Sim City* franchise with its "god-like planning responsibilities for the domains they govern."[813] Their description of gameplay in interactive violence as "gunslinging with a joystick"[814] captures the adrenalin rush that comes with player identification with a role in god mode, albeit with reduced invulnerability (since the player can be killed and forced to start again from his last saved game). The sce-narios of classic games like *Doom* and *Quake*[815] and the "every-man-a-hero theme"[816] of the *Duke Nukem* series, for example, gave the game player a "license to commit mayhem"[817]—despite missions being given some moral credentials based on a rescuing-the-world scenario and the defensive needs of survival.

Central to the motivation to play such games is the ludic pleasure of transgres-sive destruction. Gameplay as the outpouring of aggression and lawless fantasy for the sheer joy of being transgressive probably finds its peak in the franchise of *Grand Theft Auto*. In *Grand Theft Auto: San Andreas*,[818] player missions to increase the respect and chances of survival of the gangster character Carl Johnson (CJ) take place in a hostile urban underworld defined by crime, and gang wars over territory and drug deals.[819] Since the game begins with an unarmed CJ (who has returned home for his mother's funeral and to avenge her violent death) being dropped off in rival gang territory by corrupt police who falsely implicate him in a cop killing, the game is instantly defined by the struggle to survive in a world that does not allow the player to "play nice" and succeed. Gunning down people to reclaim turf and assert dominance, for the pleasures of melee combat and to protect your gang and family (along with the interactive aim of learning new skills to improve game success) are the motivations for action in the game. The weapons array available to the player is impressive, ranging from the lowly baseball bat through a range of guns and assault rifles to heat-seeking rocket launchers. The character's "ride," in escape and chase terms, is as important as any weapon. Vehicles can be transformed into weapons when used to run people down, with options ranging from bikes and SUVs, through combine harvesters and forklifts, to attack boats and superjets.

To succeed in the game you need to kill, provoke mayhem, and act violently at the level of urban warfare. If you need a ride, for example, you simply "jack" it. You can kill and destroy with abandon, not only for game advantage, payback, or rescue and not only towards those who are corrupt or enemies. It is possible to kill or maim characters who just happen to be bystanders, or a prostitute who you have just paid for sex to get back the money. While one can argue about the appropriateness of the game being played by certain age groups and/or personality types, if blood is spilled in *Grand Theft Auto: San Andreas* it still looks like the cartoon variety. The human body in the game, for all the photorealism of the graphics, is reduced to an object for destruction along with anything else that is there to be blasted. The player is freed from identifying much with game characters, apart from the limited identification with the character of CJ that is a result of the need to progress through the game by protecting him. That limited form of identification is far from a re-creation of a virtual surrogate second self—he is less a character than a means of staying in the game. The body in a game like *Grand Theft Auto: San Andreas* is denatured by its virtuality.

When Verhoeven refers to that pleasure of watching objects and bodies being blasted to smithereens he captures the sense of the body as the sum of its disintegrating, shattered parts that is the dominating image of it in violent videogames. So it is useful to remember, as Richard A. Bartle points out in his discussion of communities of players built around virtual worlds, that "[r]eality is another place"[820] from virtual reality. For Bartle, for whom games are only one aspect of possible virtual worlds, virtual spaces are primarily ones entered *from* the real: "Virtual worlds are *places*" with just enough aspects of authenticity to support a degree of immersion in the hyperreal:

> Virtual worlds are not simulations, because they do not simulate anything. They approximate aspects of reality—enough for the purposes of immersion—but that's all.[821]

As Bartle notes, while the virtual maintains aspects of the detail of the actual world, human flesh being combustible for example, it creates details that are ultimately accepted as a part of virtual reality and which may not be a part of the actual:

> The expectations that players have of virtual world physics don't *have* to map directly onto reality, if the context is right. The most conspicuous example is that of a genre boasting its own physics: cartoons. In cartoons, when you run off a cliff you don't fall until you realize you ran off a cliff. The laws of nature do apply, just not in the same way.[822]

As Dr Chris Chesher argues, games are invocational media rather than simulations: "it's better to say that VR systems invoke other worlds rather than simulate them."[823] That distinction is important if players are to *enjoy* the permission to be transgressive and shatter the body that a violent game like *Grand Theft Auto: San Andreas* gives them. One can safely assume that if players (barring the odd psychotic) believed they were shooting real people, the vast majority would not pull the trigger. The engagement with the violence remains a textually framed event that is "an activity having its own kind of rules, its own time and space, its own universe"[824] outside the less permissive actual.

In first person shooter games it is the virtual freedom to kill and destroy with abandon in contexts that normally require the due processes of law or battlefield command to act that is one of the attractions of playing:

> In the world of shooter games . . . [t]he firmly established traditions of this genre presume that your finger must always be on the trigger, that you must be ready to kill easily defined enemies, and that you will hesitate only for tactical reasons. It is a world that is completely militarized, but without a command structure or any accountability to political authority.[825]

Life is reduced to a target (both the player's character and the enemy may fit that category) and the player is encouraged to applaud aggression as a means of righting wrongs without the encumbrance of complex decisions about morality. In that vein, Adam Sessler aptly describes the satisfaction of playing the original game in the *Doom* franchise as "you shot a gun and something blew up in a cloud of pixilated blood, it was just perfect cause and effect."[826] His use of the word "perfect" illustrates how fantasy in virtuality creates that simplistic linearity as central to its illusion— untrammeled by the often-imperfect results of decision-making involving the use of violence in actuality. In all three versions of *Doom*, while the game develops increasingly sophisticated graphics with each version, the symmetry of that gameplay satisfaction remains the same.[827] The increasing sophistication of the graphic photorealism does not make the game more realistic in that context. The perfection of that linear connection is a product of the gameplay itself as the physical use of the joystick as trigger immediately erupts into gratifying violent display on the screen. While the body of the player sits safely in the real world, risks can be run and the odds defied in the hyperimmediacy of virtual action that gives instant and satisfying in-the-moment feedback as game accomplishment.[828]

It is in the movement of games to the big screen, such as in the *Lara Croft* franchise[829] and *Doom* which "eliminate the exclusively gun-sight view of the world,"[830] that the differences in perceptions of hyperreal violence in games and film are easy to distinguish. In the case of *Doom*, the differences between filmic violence and interactive video game violence can be seen in the transfer of the first person shooter perspective to the film version.[831] The film is set in the year 2026 on a research facility on Mars, where men from the Marine Rapid Response Tactical Squad are sent on a search-and-destroy mission to contain a genetic experiment that has gotten out of control. Within the confines of the research compound scientists are being attacked and turned into rabid flesh-eaters. At one point, as homage to the game, the film recreates the interface of the first person shooter sequence and the kill-anything-that-moves target practice action of the original game. It is a continuous action sequence with computer-generated effects, explosions and actors in prosthetic suits viewed over the barrel of a CG gun. The sequence begins with a Marine, seeing his reflection in a mirror and from then it switches to his point of view as the shooter, as towering monsters loom and attack out of the darkness.

However, unlike the player in computer games, the audience of the film is not the focus of attack and is not forced into a state of heightened tactical alertness in game mode. John Farhat, the visual effects supervisor for the film, describes the different aspect ratios[832] between the game as it was originally made for the squarer computer screens and then for the wide-screen film. He notes the squarer, higher screen of the computer allowed for more of a surprise factor for the player interacting with the action when playing the video game. As Farhat notes, the view of looking at the action over the barrel of a gun with the heightened awareness of limited peripheral vision was a part of the tension for the player in the game. Normal view is straight ahead with a certain relaxation, even a myopic vagueness about what is around, that the first person shooter takes away, creating an adrenaline rushing alertness to the periphery of vision as monsters suddenly appear from the side and pounce. The gun thus becomes dramatically, as well as visually, central as the player's means to game survival. The game creates threat for the player and requires adrenaline-inducing rapid response as interactive gameplay. As Henry Jenkins and Kurt Squire note, it is game conflict that involves the "immediate moment-by-moment participation in the struggles for spatial dominance."[833]

In the film, since the viewer is not the player and not in the game state of alertness, that sense of participatory game threat, the player performance, is absent and what the viewer is left with is the seesawing perspective over the constantly moving gun barrel as a special effect. Action is shown in whip panning camera movements, views around corners, through doors opening, and in slow movement from one point to another. It is a far less involving perspective, as the frantic camera movement is independent of story or cinematic effect. It is not so much that the hyperreal images of violence are measurably much different from the third version of the game, as it is the absence of interaction where player survival in the game is at stake. The kinetic limitation of the camera-as-gun-sight contains rather than expands the action on the film screen. Rather than being offered the cinematic possibilities camera work brings to narrative, the audience of the film is given the barrel of the gun moving in and out of view from the bottom of the screen. The camera work is left to create a visual replica of gameplay energy but fails to create cinematic and dramatic energy, no matter how much it jumps around.

While violence is a transgressive thrill, it is also a means to a performance end for the player. Ron Burnett notes that the "impulse to play video and computer games comes as much from the desire to play against the expectations of defeat as from the desire to collaborate with the game and understand its rules."[834] As he defines it, player narratives, created through the hypothetical possibilities in the maze of a game's fantasy, "are heavily influenced by action and reaction, by characters that 'do' things or have things done to them"[835] to overcome obstacles. Immersion in that performance of virtual play requires it to have some link with the performativity of reaction in actuality, though that sense of actuality can be created as much by interactions in game culture as it is by the game itself. In discussing the use of maps and images from the unfolding war in Iraq in April 2003 by gamers playing *Civilisation* online to discuss game tactics and military strategies, Burnett points out "the leakages from game to reality and from reality to game" that is a part of game culture:

> This is why the coding has to allocate so much of the direction of the games to alternative modes of action, reaction, and behaviour. Otherwise, it would be unlikely that the players would "believe" in the game to a large extent because the measurement for a game's effectiveness is often the degree to which it lines up with the real world. This fragmentary approach to fantasy is itself summed up by the fact that the American military used computer-based games to educate some of its troops before they went off to fight in Iraq . . . Part of the trickery and the magic is that the games must do things that by their very nature are antithetical to what would happen in the field and nevertheless "look" as if the impossible is possible.[836]

The role of graphic detail in the creation of that "belief" in the world of the game is not to recreate actuality but as with any art form, suspension of disbelief. In a first person shooter, given the limited time available for reflection before reacting, such suspension is as much a result of adrenaline producing gameplay action as it is of the quality of the graphical interface.

While it is an awareness of the hyperrealistic graphical "look" of the game space that maintains the sense of the difference between actual and gameplay violence, it also stems from the ludic immortality offered within the digital architecture of game spatiality. As King and Kryzwinska matter-of-factly note:

> The contexts of real and gameplay activities generally remain worlds apart, not the least in the obvious difference in what is potentially at stake in real and virtual instances of combat.[837]

Players do not usually confuse their "mode" of gameplaying with activities in actuality:

> Play in general is best understood as a *mode* rather than a distinct category of behaviour, suggesting a particular attitude towards an activity and how it is situated in relation to what is taken to be the real world.[838]

It is a promise of a place to play that is free of actuality at that most basic of levels that is common to all forms of play. Ndalianis describes the creative control of both programmer and player over game narrative scenarios with complex hypertext possibilities as "open spatiality":[839]

> Around each corridor, hallway, or doorway, a new space of exploration appears, and each space invites the player to colonize its form, to become familiar with its "rules," and to manipulate and master those rules for the sake of game advantage. Like gods, programmers create the spatial parameters of the games that players explore. Although these virtual worlds exist prior to the player's engagement with them, it could be argued that on the level of perception, virtual spaces and geographies do not exist until the player has mapped them.[840]

Whether as a first person shooter or as avatar, whether the player is in god mode or not, that open spatiality within a game supports an illusion of immortality that is itself a reminder that the player exists in the graphically fantastic. The violence experienced by the player as avatar defies the most basic consequences of violence in actuality—the permanence of injury or death: "Our avatars may die, but they can defy temporality by being resurrected, returning to the same place and time, and beginning their journey anew."[841] It is the essential promise of ludic performance that time and mortality will be transcended by fantasy.

The Simpsons and Flaying the Sacred in Satire

The pleasures gained from gameplay that transgresses social conventions about violence in pursuit of a feeling of liberation from social restraint have something in common with the entertainment gained from satire of those conventions. Verbally flaying the culturally sacred is the special province of satire, particularly when the topic is violence. The nature of satire is such that there are no sacred cows or, put another way, that whatever a society holds sacred is fair comic game. Steve Tompkins, a writer on the pop cultural animated television show *The Simpsons*,[842] described the satirical lack of reverence for all things on that show as "[t]he things that should be mocked are mocked, and the things that shouldn't be mocked are mocked."[843] (It has a transgressive impulse in common with *Grand Theft Auto's* gameplay in which things that should not be shot or beaten *are* shot and beaten.) Chris Turner's exhaustive analysis of the show describes its antiauthoritarian satire, its cultural insubordination, its impulsive antisocial characters and its profanity[844]—all of which have played a part in its pop-cultural ubiquity (testified to by its profitable merchandising, ratings popularity, and the cultural iconicity of characters like Homer and Bart who subvert accepted norms).[845] Bart, Homer, and the show itself embody what has been called "disrespectful discourse"[846] which, while not a mode of discourse that is unique to *The Simpsons*, has led to lines like Bart's "Eat my shorts," "Don't have a cow man" and "I'm Bart Simpson, who the hell are you?" entering the lexicon of contemporary speech with attitude. Turner insightfully uses the concept of riffing to describe the show's mode of ever-expanding satire from an initial premise as it comments on contemporary culture, family, and, self-reflexively, on its own place in the postmodern mediascape.[847] While one might disagree with the largesse of Turner's claims for the influence of the show,[848] one would have to agree that it's default tone is one of subversion of authority. Its popularity speaks to a desire to see objects held culturally, and sometimes theologically, sacred under satirical siege.

It is particularly in animation, where action is defined by cartoon physics, that the creation of the hyperreal relies on audience perceptions of actuality being in play in generic ways. Deborah Knight points out that each genre defines its own conditions of verisimilitude:[849]

> There is generic verisimilitude at work in any genre. This is what makes it reasonable for characters to break into song in musicals, action heroes to survive when outnumbered a dozen to one by bad guys with far superior fire power, and everyone to realize that, after Wile E. Coyote falls (again!) to the bottom of the canyon, in the next scene he will be unboxing a package from Acme Inc. to help him catch the Roadrunner.[850]

It is why cartoon physics are not directly about physics but about comic timing. Thus, in *Who Framed Roger Rabbit* (a film with animated characters interacting with live actors) there is a scene where the private detective Valiant, a live character, is handcuffed to the animated character, Roger Rabbit. While Valiant is trying to saw the handcuffs to break free Roger Rabbit slides out of them. When Valiant asks Roger why he did not tell him that he could easily slide out at any time from the handcuffs in a toon-like manner, Roger Rabbit replies: "No, not at any time. Only when it was funny."[851]

While *The Simpsons* uses cartoon physics with similar self-reflexivity, it has its own modification to them when it comes to violence:

> Homer frequently endures trauma of Wile E. Coyote proportions—he has bashed his head against pretty much every solid object in Springfield, for example, and has tumbled down most of its steepest slopes. Although there's a Wile-E.-ness in his ability to withstand such blows, Homer doesn't collapse into an accordion upon impact and slink away wheezing out musical notes as his body expands and contracts squeezeboxily. Instead he suffers bruises and oozes blood and breaks limbs, seeks medical attention, winds up in traction. He falls like a cartoon, but he lands like a real person.[852]

However, in common with the artistic modes of Photorealism and Hyperrealism, the setting of *The Simpsons* is ultimately a hyperreal copy of a copy, a copy of the "Everymanhometown" of traditional American television sitcoms: "The show's subject, then, is not even a soup can; it's a picture of a soup can."[853] In that sense, as H. Peter Reeves notes, it is "an eclectic mixture of geographic places" that leaves it "(dis)located"[854] in actuality but rooted in the details of postmodern sitcom hyper-realism. However, Turner defines its satire as dependent on the audience's recognition that while the satire is an exaggeration of authentic corruption, it refers to an actual fact that corruption exists in American culture. He describes the way the satiric edge of the show is built on small touches of such referential realism that become the basis for satire—such as Homer working as a low-level technician in a nuclear power plant allowing the show to probe environmental issues and pillory corporate culture. The recognition by the audience that authority is corrupt, for Turner, makes the world "ring true."[855] In that sense, Turner goes so far as to call *The Simpsons* satirical universe an animated version of reality TV.

It is primarily as that kind of social commentary that *The Simpsons* satirizes violence in American society. In the episode "The Cartridge Family,"[856] the subject is America's gun culture. The episode begins with a "traditional soccer riot" that becomes a citywide "orgy of destruction," leading the authorities in the form of Mayor Quimby to declare "mob rule" as Springfield is burned and looted. In classic Simpson's comic form, both sides of the gun debate and all views of violence are the target of satire. Lisa and her social conscience is contrasted with Bart as the voice of gleeful and ironically pragmatic anarchism:

Lisa: Somebody's gotta stop them.
Bart: Let's wait till they burn the school down.

The delight for the audience in that exchange is that one can in good conscience agree with Lisa (while recognizing that she is passively waiting for someone else to stop it) but empathizes with Bart's urge as well. The audience is given a virtual space where it can have a punt each way, morally speaking, without the need to feel guilty about the momentary identification with Bart's form of violent anarchy. When Homer seeks protection for his family in the crisis he finds his family values and loyalties tested by the cost and rejects paying five hundred dollars to a home security consultant:

Consultant: But surely you can't put a price on your family's lives.

Homer: (leaning casually against the door). I wouldn't have thought so either, but here we are.

The laugh raised by Homer's attitude comes from audience recognition that family loyalty *is* an annoying financial inconvenience. Despite initially placing money above family values, Homer's desire to protect his family and give Marge "peace of mind" leads him to buy a gun. The audience finds itself looking down the barrel of Homer's purchase from the Bloodbath and Beyond Gunshop. The barrel of the gun is shown in classic animation form with an expanded opening at the audience end of it as Homer frames the audience as the target of the gun-sight, closing one eye to aim:

Gun salesman: (as Homer plays around and points the gun at him). Whoa, careful there Annie Oakley.

Homer: I don't have to be careful, I got a gun.

Homer's line wittily captures the sense of power and liberation from restraint that gun possession promises, even while his reckless waving it around demonstrates he is far from having the skill or sense of responsibility required to manage those risks.

Homer waits for the five-day background check before he can buy the gun as the show delineates the parameters of the gun control debate in America. He is irritated by the legal restrictions ("How'm I suppose to wait five days without shooting something?"); the restrictions seem comically inadequate (the background check finds him to be potentially dangerous but only limits him to three handguns or less); Lisa counters Homer's claim to a constitutional right to bear arms ("The second amendment is just a remnant from revolutionary days, it has no meaning today"), and Homer takes Marge to an NRA meeting to be educated in the gun issue and change her stereotypical view of its members ("Homer you can't join up with these gun nuts"). In the end Marge leaves Homer because he will not get rid of the gun and his recklessness is too much even for his NRA buddies who remonstrate with him that "[g]uns are not toys." Despite being unable to fight an addiction to his gun, Homer is chastened: "This gun cost me everything, my wife, my kids" and he resolves to give it up: "I finally realized, what's the point of having a gun for protection when you've got no-one to protect." Mindful of his addiction, he asks Marge to get rid of the gun:

> I'm sorry I lied to you Marge but this gun had a hold on me. I felt this incredible surge of power like God must feel when he's holding a gun. So please get rid of it because I know I'll just lie to you again and again.

Even as it satirizes all sides of the issue, the show remains conscious of the attractions of violence as entertainment and indulges in them. During Homer's earlier recklessness, his gun goes off and causes a knife to fly across the room rotating and piercing a picture of Marge in spectacular stunt fashion. Even Lisa, who along with Marge is the antiside of the gun debate, voices her admiration for the special effect: "No offence Ma but that was pretty cool." At the end of the show, as Marge prepares to get rid of the gun, she catches sight of her reflection in the mirror holding it in an Emma Peel-like pose from *The Avengers* television show. Falling victim to the allure of "cool" it gives her and, equally unable to throw it away, she puts it in her purse and exits to a musical theme that recalls *The Avengers*. When Marge, who was willing to leave her husband to get the gun out of her house, is seduced by the fantasy of its transformative power, which has a long history in media imagery, the audience is forced to acknowledge that they share her seduction.

The Simpsons frequently satirizes the use of violence for entertainment purposes. The show reflects on its own use of cartoon violence as a part of that cultural consumption. In the first part of "Treehouse of Horror IX,"[857] titled "Hell Toupee," the episode begins with couch potato Homer complaining, "How come they only do crucifixions during sweeps"[858] while watching an execution reality show on the Fox network. In that one line, with typical Simpsonian irreverence, the show takes aim at religion, reality TV, and the corporate media conglomerate of which it is a part. (The Simpsons itself airs on the Fox network which gives an added twist to the satirical barb.) After receiving a hair transplant from death row inmate Snake, whose execution he has been watching, Homer's personality is taken over by that of the criminal. Snake periodically emerges and starts murdering the witnesses whose testimony led to his arrest and conviction. Snake-as-Homer kills the Kwiki Mart clerk Apu in his own squishy machine, Moe the bartender with a corkscrew (pulling out his heart), and tries to kill Bart. Having started with criminal violence and the media's obsession with it, the show does not neglect to point out that the state is also complicit in violence. Ever ready with a dry rejoinder (after Marge surmises that it might be Snake killing from "beyond the grave"), Lisa comments: "I told you capital punishment wasn't a deterrent."

Homer's parental behavior as the frustrated father of a rebellious Bart is embodied in the exaggerations permitted by cartoon violence. As in so many episodes, Homer is shown trying to strangle Bart in a literal version of the proverbial feelings of parental frustration towards a recalcitrant child. Homer-as-Snake tries to kill Bart with a mallet and Homer is forced to choose between a "lush" head of hair and his son's life when the toupee latches on to Bart's face. Homer begins punching his son in the face to save him but, when Bart calls him an idiot for hurting him, an angry Homer renews his attack on his son (and not the toupee), choking him, and threatening to kill him. When Police Chief Wiggum and his sidekicks arrive and use a massive hail of bullets to kill the offending toupee, it goes through a range of classic dying falls in an hysterically funny mime that satirizes the myriad ways actors die on screen. With the toupee finally dead, the police chief makes a lame joke about it's being a bad hair day. As everyone laughs in a reference to the cliché of traditional sitcom endings, Marge is momentarily made the voice of morality, remonstrating with them (and by implication the audience): "May I remind you that two people are dead." However, when she suddenly gets the bad hair day joke herself ("Wait, I just got it") and joins the laughter, the episode finishes on a typically Simpsonian point of balance that is both indulgence in violence as entertainment and a self-reflective satirical deconstruction of the social implications of that indulgence.

The show most regularly comments on violence in the media (and on cartoon violence) through the reappearance of Lisa and Bart's favorite television cartoon-within-a-cartoon, "The Itchy and Scratchy Show." In a second skit in "Treehouse of Horror IX," "The Terror of Tinytoon," Lisa and Bart get to experience the real-world implications of their consumption of such "ultra-violent eye candy"[859] as the show explores the ill-effects of violence debate and cartoon violence as a hyperreal format. As the host of his own television show Krusty the Clown announces the "violentest, disembowellingest, vomitinducingest Itchy and Scratchy Halloween special ever." It is a line that recognizes the "hyper" element in representation, the ultimate "est" that is the allure of transgressive violence in a range of media for audiences who consume it for its own sake. Marge switches off the TV saying that she would be a "lousy" mother if she allowed them to watch such a gruesome cartoon.[860] She leaves the house taking the remote batteries with her, only to have Bart replace it with plutonium. As Lisa and Bart fight over the glowing remote the enter button is inadvertently pushed and they find themselves zapped into the other side of the television screen as participants in the Itchy and Scratchy cartoon. Immediately, Itchy decapitates Scratchy and Lisa and Bart are splattered with blood to their own hilarity. As Itchy de-brains Scratchy and turns his head into a Halloween pumpkin complete with candle (the title of the cartoon-within-the-cartoon skit is "Candle in the Wound") the two laugh uproariously with enjoyment until Itchy and Scratchy turn the violence on them.

Scratchy: (putting his head back on his body.) Why are you laughing?
Itchy: They're laughing at your pain.
Scratchy: That's mean.
Itchy: Let's teach' em a lesson.

With the ethics of being entertained by suffering, even that of cartoon characters in question, the show reiterates public concerns about the borders between the virtual and the real and its interaction with viewing culpability. It acknowledges the undeniable fact that laughing at the pain of others is the core of comedy from slapstick to the satirically cruel. When Bart's head is pinned up against the wall as an axe strikes and just misses his head, still thinking he is safe in the audience and not a part of the action, he is initially pleased ("A cartoon axe, I love it."). He is suddenly horrified to discover the violence is "real" when he finds blood dripping down his forehead. He and Lisa scream at the realization that they are now the subjects of the violence that a few minutes ago they found so entertaining. Their eyes, in classic animation effect literally popping out of their heads, they run from a cannon firing a blast of assorted weapons and a chainsaw at them.

Homer comes home to find his kids on TV and highlights the role of violence in suspense in narrative when he ponders, "How are Bart and Lisa going to get out of this one?" He is comically an audience member rather than a father when his children are on the other side of the screen, distanced as he is from their predicament by the screen between them. When Lisa and Bart hail down a police car to escape, only to find that Itchy and Scratchy are the drivers ("We protect and sever"), Lisa's cry "We're done for Bart" is answered by Bart's resourceful, "Not if I know cartoons." He animates an eject button option on their seat and they are thrown high into the air and out of range as Bart saves them through his media literacy. They also enact the classic law of cartoon physics by only falling when Lisa makes Bart aware that they are in midair. When they end up back in Itchy and Scratchy's house, the former uses a hose to surround Bart with piranha fish who make a skeleton of his body from the waist down as he muses in terms that reflect authentic off-screen consequences to what is a cartoon act, "Oooh, that is gonna hurt tomorrow." They eventually beat against the screen for Homer to use the remote to get them out and, when he finally pushes exit and returns them to their living room, Lisa returns the flesh to Bart's skeletal body with the rewind button. As Itchy and Scratchy break through the screen into the "real" world of the Simpson characters, they are found to be only "real" world animal size and no threat and Homer places the "cute" Itchy on a wheel in a cage. Scratchy immediately falls in love with the Simpson's cat, only to have Marge grab him by the scruff of the neck, commenting with a smile on her face "That means you'll have to be neutered" in a throwaway reminder that humans do not only do violence to each other. The show ends with Scratchy covering his nether regions and screaming "Noooooooooooooo."

Having cartoon characters recognize their own status as animation, but only as characters in the cartoon-within-the-cartoon and not within the "real world" of their original animation, the show wittily dances around the space that is the hyper-real where, like light reflecting off the surfaces of crystal, representation is a hall of mirrors infinitely resonating with intertextuality.

Bart: Hey, Lisa, we are characters in a cartoon.
Lisa: How humiliating.

Having the A-grade student, cultured environmentalist Lisa humiliated by her cartoon status also adds a layer of the high-culture/low-culture debate to the mix of textual deconstruction. Behind the TV screen, when Bart and Lisa end up in a live action segment, as Homer inadvertently changes channels and they fall from midair to land in a pot of soup in a cooking demonstration in the Kathy and Regis daytime American chat show, the density of hyperreal intertextuality is posited as limited only by the number of times one can press the remote. The fact that Lisa and Bart's predicament as the self-aware subjects of cartoon violence is, for the audience, still not "real" (even as it relies on enough suspension of disbelief for the audience to laugh at the comic implications of their situation) is a fun state of media and satiric "play" for both the show's writers and the audience.

Unlike the cinematic palette of *The Passion of the Christ* or the hyperphotoreal-ism of videogames like *Grand Theft Auto: San Andreas*, *The Simpsons* is animated with a limited palette of colors, despite switching to CG animation in recent seasons. Thus, as it is ripped out in the "Hell Toupee" scenario, Moe's heart is a stylized flat dark red and the hole in Mo's chest is little more than a 2D blob. The hole, in its gaping flatness, as with Bart's skeleton, announces its own version of bodily dismemberment as a 2D aesthetic. Ever self-reflexive, the show in "Treehouse of Horror VI,"[861] has Homer experience being CG animated in 3D and then move in the "real world" in that form. Interestingly, it is not any newfound tangibility in that 3D detail that he finds most worthy of comment so much as the fact that, as a CG creation, he costs more to produce. That type of dry comment about com-modification, as noted in Turner's view above, is where referential authenticity lies in the show. In the context of a show whose graphic interface is far less sophisti-cated than CGI is capable of, it is a pointed reminder that authenticity in text is far from being merely a product of increasingly sophisticated photorealism and is a much more complex textual creation.

Animation, even at its most 2D, has always depended on the stylized use of physical detail to express character, comic timing, and emotion. As Angie Jones and Jamie Oliff observe:

[A] simple blink can make a scene funny and show what the character is thinking. Walt Disney always said, "The mind is the pilot," meaning that what-ever the character is thinking drives the action. So the details will reveal to us what the character is thinking. Details include hands, eyes, and facial. As animators, we have to pay close attention to the subtle motion we add to these small but very important parts.[862]

One only has to recall the emotive frustration of Wily E. Coyote to recognize that the believability of a character's emotional state with which an audience can empathize is not necessarily a product of realistic graphic detail but can be equally convincing as a product of stylized character rendered detail on the flat surfaces of 2D. As Jessica Rabbit says in the self-reflexive film quote at the head of this chapter, from *Who Framed Roger Rabbit*, "I'm not bad, I'm just drawn that way."[863] It is hyperreal detail that does not aim to create physical realism, but rather believable aspects of character. Jones and Oliff aptly note: "Animation is not about moving characters around. It is about creating characters that move people."[864] Jessica Rabbit is an illustrative example of the way in which animated stylization can heighten the physical while remaining far from realistic. With almost no nose, an impossibly narrow waist, a ballooning bosom, and overly arched heels in stilettos, she is both a caricature of sexuality and an evocation of sensuality. It is a sensuality that depends particularly on the drawing's focus, within the flatter aspects of the stylized graphic, on the sensuously flowing movement, and beautiful sparkle of her dress. Scott Wills, an animator on *Ren and Stimpy*, has noted that this design aspect of animation is not about realism but "reducing things to their essence."[865]

When the detail in CG animation or prosthetic violence is not about character but about capturing a sense of lifelikeness, as in the bloody detail of *The Passion of the Christ* and the photorealistic graphics of videogames like *Grand Theft Auto: San Andreas*, it is a product of a focus on increasingly complex visual and prosthetic textures that pause the viewers' gaze in amazement or shock and horror if the violence is graphic. Thus, while aiming for a disturbing effect, the Mayan sacrifice scenes in Mel Gibson's recent film *Apocalypto*,[866] as with the *Passion of the Christ*, are often less narratively gripping than the focus of prosthetic display. As villagers are sacrificed by having their hearts ripped out the audience is shown one victim, eyes wide open and still fantastically alive, gazing at his own heart held above him by the Mayan priest just before he succumbs, is beheaded, and his body and head thrown down the steps of the temple. With the body dismembered into prosthetically rendered components in this scene, Gibson signals his interest in the cinematic fantasy of the violence rather than its forensic representation when he portrays the improbable event of a man still being conscious as he views his own heart external to his body. Greater degrees of photorealistic and prosthetic textures are not *more* authentic but less so. On the contrary, such detail remains hyperconstructed.[867]

For the audiences who respond with "the aesthetic emotion of wonder" to CG photorealism, to quote Stephen Poole, the graphic splendor of such detail defines visual worlds filled with graphic liquidity of form: "If architecture is frozen music, then a video game is liquid architecture."[868] His description captures something of that feeling the viewer has that the CG effect is a kind of surreal sheen on verisimilitude. The animated feature *Monster House*[869] is illustrative of the way hyperrealism and extending photorealistic effects ultimately takes the audience out of the real rather than into it when the film opens by tracking a finely detailed leaf, as it is blown by the wind in a flurry of autumn leaves. Beneath the leaf is the more stylized (by comparison) toddler riding a tricycle moving through the swirl of leaves blown along the ground. The detail of that single leaf with its veined and burnished autumn orange coloring, holds the viewers' gaze as the action involving the less photorealistically animated character proceeds around it. *Monster House's* animation is often marked by that momentary focus on similar hyperrealized detail that is not necessarily intrinsic to the plot, such as close-ups of hyperrendered fingers ringing a doorbell or of a character's shoes crossing a floor. It is the moment in which the viewer cannot help but be aware of the subtlety of the animation and the digital luminosity of its detail, and feels suspended in the technological wonder of the hyperreal.

Perhaps the most convincing way of recognizing that hyperreal effect is to watch the leaf on screen in *Monster House* while holding a similar, actual crackling autumn leaf in one's hand.[870] The actual leaf announces its solidity by *not* having the animated leaf's hyperreal luminosity. The most violent character in that film is an animated haunted house but it is the leaf, in all the wonder of its aesthetic brilliance, as much as the fantasy of an object such as a house being animate, that signals to the audience that it has entered the illusion that is hyperreal space. Paradoxically, it is the murderous, hurt anger of the lost soul embodied in the haunted house that emotionally authenticates the story for the viewer. While the focus on the leaf enlivens the introduction it also lengthens it as both film and appreciative viewer bask in its hyperreal glow. Delightful as it is to watch in its windswept dance, the leaf is merely hyperreal glitter decorating a narrative that the viewer, as the toddler stops outside a threatening looking house, has almost forgotten is beginning underneath its breezy flight.

Conclusion

People say, my movie, it's really violent, but you know what? It's theatre. It's a magic trick. It's all done with corn syrup and fake blood. All my actors are still alive. What's worse, my movie or Dick Cheney? Nobody actually died in my movie. People actually die because of Dick Cheney and he doesn't allow you to see it.

(*Eli Roth, Writer/Director*)[871]

The journey along the continuum of textual violence has shown that the authenticity in the representation of violence in text, whether mimetic or not, exists in a fraught interactive relationship with the actual experience of violence outside the text. This interaction is particularly the case, when, as Roth reveals in his reference to Dick Cheney above, the political ramifications of actual violence are of ideological interest to producers of texts and their audiences. No matter how much audiences delight in violence as entertainment, the awareness of real-world violence impacts on its reception, even if only by its deflection. The trail left by the texts of violence across the continuum from the live news report of indexical violence through to texts that fictionalize violence illustrates that there is no broad generalization that can be made about the representation of violence outside individual texts or generic groups. Those researching such texts to theorize about the representation of violence in general, or as a part of the ill-effects debate, need to acknowledge this indisputable fact. The absence of indexicality allows audiences to be entertained by visual extravagances, entranced by the visual beauty of violence or appalled by the horror of the increasingly fantastical. While it is a continuum of representation between polar extremes, it is nevertheless a range of texts that is in a creative negotiation with how audiences and readers feel about the actual experience of violence. Whether texts use that prior knowledge to deflect the actuality of violence, so an audience can relax and be entertained or even laugh at the pain of others, or use the anxiety it engenders so an audience can be moved and disturbed by it, violence outside the text hovers around the textual frame.

Viewing texts of violence on a continuum shows that to over-generalize about violence in text is to muddy the receptive waters:

A violent movie that intensifies our experience of violence is very different from a movie in which acts of violence are perfunctory. I'm only guessing, and maybe this emotionlessness means little, but, if I can trust my instincts at all, there's something deeply wrong about anyone's taking for granted the dissociation that this carnage without emotion represents. Sitting in the theatre, you feel you're being drawn into a spreading nervous breakdown. It's as if pain and pleasure, belief and disbelief had all got smudged together, and the movies had become some schizzy form of put-on.[872]

While Pauline Kael's remarks are right in their reference to textual differences, her concerns about those polar opposites typify a long and ongoing popular and critical response to violence in text that struggles with the feelings of pleasure and discomfort that finding violence entertaining, or even watching it when it is not entertaining, has engendered. Such concerns have often been to the detriment of responding specifically to the detailed complexity of the texts themselves. It is an anxiety about the differences that I do not share. Her own sense of textual difference, defined simply as intensification or thoughtlessness, is itself undermined by the enormous range of texts within both groups, even supposing one was inclined to accept such a distinction. Viewing texts about violence on a continuum holds in play the contradictions inherent in the representation of the subject, without losing what each text uniquely tells us about the human condition or, at least, what we like to think it is. Such contradictions will necessarily lead to ambivalent reader and critical responses.

In setting out on a critical journey it is not necessary to resolve contradictions. A better sense of the cultural terrain occupied by texts about violence and their generic contexts is clearer if no attempt is made to resolve them, particularly by forcing them into a theoretical stance that they will not readily fit. It is not surprising that there is an inevitable critical longing for an ethic of reading, writing, and critique; a need to be "critically correct," when discussing the representation of violence because "[w]hat it means to be human, to be ethical, and to be narrative are very similar issues."[873] This triad may seem linked because actual and represented violence is often troubling. As viewer response to Tony Soprano has shown, the audience wants to invest its sympathies somewhere, even when the most sympathetic point of view is also a perpetrator of violence, a killer. However, the world outside the text will often not leave audiences or readers to themselves. Peter Josyph notes, when commenting on Cormac McCarthy's novel *Blood Meridian*:

Upon reflection, which the book does not encourage in this regard, indeed the kid is as bad as the rest of the gang: would we not think so if we counted our beloveds among the gang's many victims?[874]

Josyph's response to a fictional text, whether it is a fair comment on *Blood Meridian* or not, is sitting uncomfortably in the grey zone where fiction, nonfiction, and the world outside the text intermingle, where authorial choices are made that mediate violence for a reader. For readers of True Crime or appreciative viewers of mockumentaries like *Bowling for Columbine*, it can feel confusing if one wants to take a clear moral sense away from the text or be clear on what in the text can be taken as authentic. As Michel Kowalewski notes, "Violence in fiction can sometimes become 'tuneful tragedy' because the life in fiction is life as it is imaginable in words ... and words are capable of changing all they touch."[875] Readers like Josyph find themselves wondering if they are not being morally seduced by the aesthetics of the representation of violence when they should be making clearer moral judgments about violent content because violence has real world consequences. Undoubtedly, reader or viewer seduction which can be problematic, as in a text like Norma Khouri's *Forbidden Love*, is compounded by the tendency for the representation of violence to be linked to heroic images of resistance, even when they slide into a grubbier reflection of the heroic, as with Tony Soprano as the last man standing. The mix of violence in fiction, life, and the daily news with an audience's very human aspirational need for heroes they can relate to provoke moral debate.

An example of newspaper commentary on the Australian True Crime film *Chopper* (2000) highlights the clash between a film reviewer's ethical reading of the film's portrayal of the criminal protagonist (which is described as leaving the viewer with "a lingering feeling that it's telling us crime really does pay"[876]) and the view of a court reporter who was asked to assess the film's believability. It is the court reporter who decides that "it is an almost wholly believable portrayal of the behavior"[877] of a man who was in jail for 23 years. He singles out the lead actor's resemblance to the real-life subject, the fact that many extras used had been in prison, and that research was done with prison wardens, prison governors, and in conversations with the ex-prisoner, Chopper Read himself.[878] Two photographs accompany the article showing the actor, Eric Bana in the role of Chopper, and also his real-life counterpart Read, both in the same pose, pointing a gun to their own heads, grinning. None of this input guarantees authenticity, though it could be argued that it increases the chances that something of the "real" Chopper Read might be in the representation of him. The producer (and presumably the director who also spoke to Read), the film writer/critic, the court reporter, and the actor dressing up to "be" Read, were all concerned with the "truth" and the moral implications of what is represented of Read's violent and criminal life. However, the probability that it may not be possible to find the person that is reducible in representation to the factual or "real" Chopper is acknowledged by the producer of the film who said that when talking to Read, "He wanted to tell us about himself but we've never been able to determine what was true and what he wanted us to know that wasn't necessarily true."[879] The court reporter's part of the article also mentions that the film is based on Read's nine books, including an autobiography, so that "the film stays close to what could be the truth."[880] The uncertain possibility of representational, imaginative truth hangs on that rather precarious and conditional "could."

Foucault describes the disappearance of actual torture as a public spectacle in *Discipline and Punish: The Birth of the Prison*, but the public is still made anxious about its own craving for the spectacle of violence. Perhaps out of an urge to justify such interest, there remains the desire to disentangle grains of the authentic from representation in order to make moral, receptive, and ideological judgments, and determine who are the heroes and who are the villains. What is striking about the article is that it is a quote from Read himself, the perpetrator of violation, that is the most perceptive remark on the tension between representational authenticity and the actuality of a violently lived life: "Anything I say would be fiddling. I want to know what you think of me."[881] Read is right. While audiences are clearly interested in the facts and details of his life and will assume some level of authenticity resides in a film that fits the True Crime genre, they will also want to make a judgment about him and, by inference, about what it means to be criminally human. In Chopper Read's case, "what you think," ultimately, is to be pulled out of a mix of representations that includes the film, his books, newspaper articles such as the one under discussion, court transcripts, whatever comes out of his mouth, and, if they wish to talk, from the accounts of his victims or those who know them. The borders between those representations will merge if one takes the bird's eye view. The indisputable point is that audiences want to judge in their own readings, which may agree with or reject the stance of the text.

The desire to make judgments about authenticity in representations of violence is bound up with the desire to make judgments about violent life outside the text. As the scriptwriter Paul Schrader notes, "when you make a film and you can't really tell who the good guys and the bad guys are, people call it dark. But, in fact, it's just like life."[882] That "just" needs to be scrutinized on a text-by-text basis, of course, but Schrader has a point. He generally writes films "featuring tormented loners in morally ambiguous worlds"[883] defined by violence. Texts about violence often embrace that ambiguity, as in the emotional resonances of horror in Buffy's adolescent and 20-something journey, but are just as likely to hold onto the reassuringly clear distinctions between the good and the bad that leave room for violence to be used to tell stories about other things than itself, as in the dance of the kung fu action films. As Roger Ebert notes, commenting on a fictional interpretation of the Columbine High School violence in the film *Elephant*, if there is no pumped-up action the textual meanings of violence change yet again:

Van Sant's *Elephant* is a violent movie in the sense that many innocent people are shot dead. But it isn't violent in the way it presents those deaths. There is no pumped-up style, no lingering, no release, no climax. Just implacable, poker-faced, flat, uninflected death. Truffaut said it was hard to make an anti-war film because war was exciting even if you were against it. Van Sant has made an anti-violence film by draining violence of energy, purpose, glamour, reward and social context. It just happens.[884]

The possibilities for the textual representation of violence are only limited by the depths of the experience itself and the imaginative reach of those who seek to explore those depths in texts that are challenged by its complexity as a human experience.

Oliver Stone has expressed the problematic capability of cinema as a medium to represent truth and reality. Commenting on the representation of violence in the context of his own life and films with reference to his most nihilistic film, *Natural Born Killers*, he said:

The picture was made in a darker spot in my life. We were so far out there that it was scary. Our nature is a struggle between aggression and love. Obviously Vietnam clarified that for me, but I wasn't totally aware of it when I got back. I killed over there. I have still to deal with that. I have tried. It's become apparent to me that my films are violent. People would say that for years and I would deny it, I wouldn't face up to the violence in myself. I'm beginning to now. This film came from that spot.[885]

As a creator of texts about violence, expressing his doubts and uncertainties about the message of his film and the borders it shares with the experiences of his own life, Stone stands on that point where the aesthetic of the text draws on a life that has experienced violence. My discussion began at such a point, with Gail Bell's experiences in *Shot*. At a similar transition point where the personal experience of violence becomes text, Stone gives the representation of violence a larger context in the imaginative attempt to make meaning out of what is only one part of the larger "struggle between aggression and love." He recognizes it as only one part of a more-complex human condition.

However, the enormous range of the texts discussed in this book underlines the fact that the representation of violence remains central to the textual and imaginative view of our humanity. When a text drawing on actual experiences tries to gloss over violence, it is ultimately as troubling as the actuality of violence that is ignored. In the course of my research I attended a Sydney Festival performance of *Stickybricks*,[886] a community theatre production, calling on the experiences of the some of the residents of the troubled Northcott public housing estate in Surrey Hills, a 15 storey block in Sydney, Australia. Since its publicly touted opening by the Queen in 1963, the housing block's history has been defined by suicides from its ramparts, fear of violence, murder, a shooting incident that killed five people, resident mental health problems, and the rotting bodies of more than one isolated elderly resident being found dead in their flat weeks after dying. Studies of the community have recorded residents' fear in response to the violence and criminality that is a part of the community they live in.[887] *Stickybricks* utilized residents and professional actors to chronicle the experiences of residents since the opening of the estate. It was a laudable attempt to celebrate positive feelings of community that were previously ignored in narratives and publicity about the site and the residents' lives. It was a communal endeavor to bring the estate community together and remind them, and the broader public, of what they themselves bring of value in the lives they live.

As I sat watching the outdoor performance on a balmy summer night with an audience eating the food provided and clearly enjoying itself, I found myself agreeing with the program note comments from the director/writer Scott Rankin:

> *Stickybricks* is part architecture, part dinner, part awards ceremony, part soapbox, part mapping, part dance hall, part musical dream, all woven together to create a kind of utopian space in the centre of the estate, which captures the stories, sounds, flavours and histories of this ever changing community.[888]

Yet, however laudable the political and theatrical attempt to celebrate "award winning lives,"[889] in the context of an awareness of the violent history of the estate, the performance left me with a sense that an unpalatable actuality was being excluded from the narrative and that, hopeful as the text was, that hopefulness really was a fragile "dream." Sitting on the actual site, listening to the words and stories of the residents who were living the fear and violent reality that was not being represented, I found myself just about as far away from understanding what it was like to live in Northcott as it was possible to get. Like a tourist visiting some exotic site, I was being given an imaginative representation that was only partial, hiding as it did the violence, which it left far outside the frame of the text. Touching as the performance was, giving voice as it did to the resilient minutiae of residents' hopes, loneliness, and acceptance of each other, it was as if the dark corners of the experience of living in the building were hidden outside the spotlights on the stage. A recognition of the triumphant resilience of the lives of the residents really depended on its continued existence *in the face of* the experiences hidden in those unseen corners. I could not, of course, find a place for this play on the continuum of authenticity because it was not about violence, but it should have been.

Epilogue

I was sitting with five teenage female students in a high school reading-group watching the 1970s film version of *Jane Eyre*, as an illustration of the novel I am reading to them. We have been alternating bits of the film (and the BBC version with Timothy Dalton as Rochester) with the book. I have been using the film to overcome some of the difficulties the language of the book presents to the students. We come to the scene where Rochester's insane wife's brother is attacked by his sister. In the context of more contemporary representations of violence I have viewed, I think the '70s special effect blood and wound with its pink hue looks dated and fake. I am surprised at the reaction of the students who turn their heads or cover their eyes to a chorus of "Yuk!" I realize I have been desensitized by my research and by decades of viewing violence in the media as a consumer of film and television. The individuality of audience reception can never be discounted in the interpretation of text. In the end, even this book is only my view.

Watching the film *The Last Horror Movie*[890] for possible inclusion in for discussion in this book, I find myself responding as viewer first rather than academic. As a story about a serial killer I am finding it creepy and great horror. Then the academic kicks in and, as a hardened researcher into texts on violence who has seen it all, I tell myself it is an interesting conceit. It purports to be a film shot by a cameraman accomplice who is filming the murders of a serial killer, Max Perry, who is a wedding photographer by day and intent on recording himself killing outside of that façade. The conceit is that he has taped his film over a video called *The Last Horror Movie*, which is available for rent in stores. Clever, I think, I have just rented it; it is black humor and I appreciate that. At one point in the film, Perry kills a woman in front of her husband while the camera shows the husband's horrified reaction, and then it cuts away to the dead body of the wife while he kills the husband. The camera then returns to the killer who looks into the camera and asks the audience whether they were not a bit curious about how he killed the husband. Then the film shows the act again with a full view of him stabbing the husband in the stomach. Perry then asks: "Now, did you want to see that or not? And if not, then why are you still watching?" Clever, I think to myself, it raises issues of audience culpability. Then the killer gives the hitherto unseen cameraman the choice to try a killing but he does not want to participate, it would be too real. He says that when he was on the other side of the camera "It didn't feel real," with his knife in the hand trying to slit a victim's throat it is real and he cannot do it. Clever, I think to myself again, representation versus actuality.

Finally at the end of the film it is revealed that the killer is tying up someone who has rented the video, thinking they were borrowing a fiction, in preparation for killing him. It is revealed that his victims have been audience members who have rented the video and thought it was fiction. Unbelieving, not comprehending that the safety promised by violence on the screen that it is only entertainment has been violated, the final victim in the film asks, "This is a joke right?" Perry replies no and asks in return, "Tell me Neil, why exactly did you watch the film till the end . . . Did you think it was real?" The soon-to-be-victim, still not aware that it is definitely not a joke, admits that he did not. To Neil's growing horror, Perry insinuates, "Suppose it wasn't a joke. Do you think there'd be something wrong with you for having watched the film till the end?" Clever, I think again, appreciating the black humor in the camaraderie of the reassurance the killer gives to his victim/audience to help them confess their culpability, "Obviously there'd be something wrong with me for having made it, if that makes it any easier." When the punch line comes I find that as an audience member, the killer and the film implicates me:

> Let me clarify things. It was real. All of it. All of those people were really being killed. So there's definitely something wrong with me. What I want you to tell me is whether there's something wrong with you?

Something in me protests: "Hey, I have a reason for watching, I have scholarly justification." Anyway, it *is* just a movie. I just rented a DVD, so that undermines the whole overwriting the video conceit anyway. The film over, I get ready for bed. Then, feeling pretty stupid, I double check that my front door is locked and sleep with the hall light on. Good horror will do that to you.

In 2007 I was in New York and discovered there is a tour available for fans of *The Sopranos* that takes you to actual locations used in the show. As a tourist and fan in New York I contemplated taking the tour and getting a photo of myself outside any of the iconic settings. In the end, I decided 40 dollars, the cost of the tour, was too steep for my travel budget. I have been kicking myself ever since. I want a photo of myself with one foot in that physical yet still imaginary space. I need it to hang next to one of myself frozen in mid leap on the *Rocky* (1976) steps in Philadelphia, punching the air.[891]

At the beginning of *Kill Bill II*, halfway through her journey, the Bride informs the audience: "I've killed a helluva lot of people to get to this point." In a similar spirit of announcement I can say that I've watched a "helluva lot of fictional characters die on screen" to reach this epilogue. In the name of research, I have put myself through watching some violent texts that I would never choose to view otherwise. Eventually, I decided to confine my discussion to texts that would fall broadly into a definition of mainstream viewing choices but I only came to that point by watching outside that range. Here and there I could not watch and found myself saying enough is enough. I watched the film of *American Psycho* (2000), wished I had not, and could not bring myself to persevere with Brett Easton Ellis's book on which the film is based. I understood that it was a dark social commentary but the endless misogynistic violence repelled me. I got to the end of the film but wanted to leave the theatre every five minutes. It took months for some of those images to fade and I regret putting myself through it. I drew the line at reading the fiction of a serial killer, which he based on his crimes and which was used to convict him, while reading the preface written by someone who had read his fiction and was glad of that interpretive barrier.[892] I stood in front of a video store turning over in my hands a DVD that was a compilation of actual executions, ostensibly put together as an anti-capital punishment tract and then walked away from buying it to view for research purposes. So I discovered my threshold as a researcher and a consumer. Perhaps, being an audience member will always triumph over being an academic in the end, especially when it comes to texts representing violence.

Notes

1. Gail Bell, *Shot* (Sydney: Picador, Pan Macmillan, 2003), p. 95.

2. Susan Sontag, *Regarding the Pain of Others* (New York: Farrar Straus and Giroux, 2003), p. 13.

3. Quoted in Dominic Wells, "It's Life, Jim," *Time Out* December 17–31, 1997: 22. Verhoeven is the director of films such as *Starship Troopers* and *Total Recall*.

4. W. James Potter, *On Media Violence* (Thousand Oaks: Sage Publications Inc., 1999).

5. Quoted from an appropriately titled panel with the moderator Dan Petrie Jr., *Guns Don't Kill People Writers Do*, Video. Words into Pictures, Writers Foundation, Los Angeles, 1999. The quote is a transcript from a VHS tape. All transcriptions from audiovisual texts in my book are my own, except for those quoted in Chapter 5 for *Buffy the Vampire Slayer* where the source is cited.

6. Stathis Gourgouris, "Enlightenment and Paranomia," *Violence, Identity and Self-Determination*, eds. Hent de Vries and Samuel Weber (Stanford, California: Stanford University Press, 1997), p. 119.

7. It is the staggering amount of its incidence in text, as well as the perceived graphic nature of representation that fuels the ill-effects of violence debate. The most commonly quoted statistic: that American children and adolescents by the age of 18 will have viewed an estimated 200,000 acts of violence on television (without including video games and films) is to be found in The American Academy of Pediatrics, "Media Violence," *Journal of the American Academy of Pediatrics* 95.6 (1995). An overview based purely on the ubiquity of images of violence in television can be found in the three-year report of the National Television Violence Study in the United States. See The Centre for Communication and Social Policy, University of Southern California, Santa Barbara. *National Television Violence Study* (Studio City, CA: Sage Publications, 1996–97). A new study from the Parents Television Council argues that there has been a further increase in television violence in recent years; "the television season that began in the fall of 2005 was one of the most violent in recent history—averaging 4.41 instances of violence per hour during prime time—and increase of 75 per cent since the 1998 television season." (See Caroline Schulenburg, "Dying to Entertain: Violence on Prime Time Broadcast Television 1998–2006," Parents Television Council, *parentstv.org*. 2007. Available: http://www.parents.org/PTC?publications/reports/violencestudy/exsummary.asp January 28, 2007.

8. An illustrative chronicling of the history of regulation of violence in the cinema in the classic period of Hollywood films and of the inevitable attempts by filmmakers to stylistically subvert

regulation can be found in Stephen Prince, *Classical Film Violence: Designing and Regulating Brutality in Hollywood Cinema 1930–68* (New Brunswick, New Jersey: Rutgers University Press, 2003).

9. Probably the best summary of the research into the ill-effects of violence, and a thorough analysis of both sides of the debate, is in Jib Fowles, *The Case for Television Violence* (Thousand Oaks: London: New Delhi: Sage Publications Inc., 1999). A useful diversity of opinion can also be found in Martin Barker and Julian Petley, *Ill-Effects: The Media/Violence Debate*, 2nd edn. (London: Routledge, 2001). A typically polemical and populist version of the case *for* the ill-effects of violence can be found in Loren Coleman, *The Copycat Effect: How the Media and Popular Culture Trigger the Mayhem in Tomorrow's Headlines* (New York: Paraview Pocket Books, 2004). Contrasting with that view, and an indication of the range of opinions in the debate, is found in a recent paper reported in the *New York Times*, which argues that viewing violence actually reduces the likelihood of committing violent actions. See Peter S. Goodman, "Economists Say Movie Violence Might Temper the Real Thing, *New York Times*, January 7, 2008. One of the few examples of a discussion that links the ubiquity of the images to the content of a genre can be found in M. B. Oliver, "Portrayals of Crime, Race, and Aggression in 'Reality-Based' Police Shows: A Content Analysis," *Journal of Broadcasting and Electronic Media*, 38 (1994).

10. A discussion of research on social anxiety about the lived experience of violence created by media images of violence, particularly among women, can be found in John Tulloch, *Watching Television Audiences: Cultural Theories & Methods* (London: Arnold, 2000).

11. Robert McKee, *Story: Substance, Structure, Style, and the Principles of Screenwriting* (London: Methuen, 1999), p. 188.

12. Research has documented that even in war or for police in the line of duty, killing another human being is not easy. See Roy F. Baumeister, *Evil: Inside Human Violence and Cruelty* (New York: W. H. Freeman & Co., 1999). Textual mediation of a killing is the creation of a safe space to contemplate such an act, depending on how graphically the act is portrayed.

13. Michael Kowalewski, *Deadly Musings: Violence and Verbal Form in American Fiction* (Princeton, New Jersey: Princeton University Press, 1993), p. 7.

14. Certainly no definition along the lines of "Violence Explained," as hoped for in John W. Burton, *Violence Explained: The Sources of Conflict, Violence and Crime and Their Prevention* (Manchester: Manchester University Press, 1997). I would add the rider that degrees of interpretive certainty about the definition of violence can be arrived at within textual contexts and when definitions are viewed on the continuum offered by my book.

15. My decision to use "indexicality" was a product of the convincing argument made for its use as concept and term by Bill Nichols, *Blurred Boundaries: Questions of Meaning in Contemporary Culture* (Bloomington: Indiana University Press, 1994). In the following quote, citing his own source, Nichols states "(I mean indexical in terms of the trichotomy proposed by Charles Sanders Pierce. Iconic signs resemble their source [drawings, for example]; indexical signs bear a 'point-for-point correspondence' with their source [X-rays, photographs, fingerprints, for example], and symbols bear an arbitrary relation [words, Morse code, national flags].)" (p. 18). Further discussion referring to his use of the concept is in Chapter 1 of my book on the televirtuality of 9/11. As Martin Jay notes, Pierce considered an "index as a physical trace of a past event, as opposed to an arbitrary symbol or a mimetic icon." See Martin Jay, *Refractions of Violence* (New York: Routledge, 2003), p. 125.

16. The continuum posited has something in common with the methodology of applying mixed reality to entertainment used in the technology of film-based theme park rides which is seen as a

mixed reality continuum of fantasy and reality fused through technology. See Christopher Stapleton, Charles Hughes, Michael Moshall, Paulius Micikevicius, and Marty Altman, "Applying Mixed Reality Entertainment," December 2002, *Computer.org*. Available: http://www.computer.org/computer/homepage/1202/entertainment, June 22, 2004.

17. Francesco Casetti, *Inside the Gaze: The Fiction Film and Its Spectator*, trans. Nell Andrew and Charles O'Brien (Bloomington: Indiana University Press, 1998), p. 117.

18. Casetti, *Inside the Gaze: The Fiction Film and Its Spectator* p. 118.

19. Annette Hill, *Shocking Entertainment: Viewer Response to Violent Movies* (Luton, United Kingdom: University of Luton Press, 1997), p. 27.

20. Ibid., p. 113.

21. For an illustrative case study of the way some fans of the television show *Buffy the Vampire Slayer*, (the subject of Chapter 5) rejected the preferred canon of a text in favor of a subtext, inclusive of the debate about variant readings in which the shows writers and producers engaged; see Gwyn Symonds, "'Bollocks!': Spike Fans and Reception of *Buffy the Vampire* Slayer," March 2, 2003, *Refractory: A Journal of Entertainment Media*. Available: http://www.refractory.unimelb.edu.au//journalissues/vol2/gwynsymonds.htm, July 5, 2003.

22. Massimo Calabresi, Sam Dealey, and Stephan Faris, "The Tragedy of Sudan," *Time* October 4, 2004: 39.

23. Lambert Zuidervaart, *Artistic Truth: Aesthetics, Discourse, and Imaginative Disclosure* (Cambridge: Cambridge University Press, 2004), p. 1.

24. Zuidervaart, *Artistic Truth: Aesthetics, Discourse, and Imaginative Disclosure* p. 128.

25. Natasha Wallace, "Teenager Gets 24 Years for Merciless Rape," *Sydney Morning Herald* December 23–25, 2004: 5.

26. S. Caroline Taylor, *Court Licensed Abuse: Patriarchal Lore and the Legal Response to Intra-familial Sexual Abuse of Children*, New Literacies and Digital Epistemologies, eds. Colin Lankshear, Michele Knobel, Chris Bigum, and Michael Peters, vol. 11 (New York; Washington, D.C.; Baltimore: Peter Lang, 2004).

27. Donna Harkavy, "The Art of Bearing Witness," *The Culture of Violence*, ed. Helaine Posner (Amherst: University Gallery, University of Massachusetts Amherst, 2002), p. 19.

28. Todd Gitlin, *Media Unlimited: How the Torrent of Images and Sounds Overwhelms Our Lives* (New York: Henry Holt and Company, 2002), p. 23.

29. This text is discussed at greater length in Chapter 7.

30. Nick Giovanni, "To Be Black in America Is to Be Constantly at War," *Scars: American Poetry in the Face of Violence*, ed. Cynthia Dubin Edelberg (Tuscaloosa, Alabama: University of Alabama Press, 1995), p. 82.

31. *Irréversible*, dir. Gaspar Noé, prod. Christophe Rossignon, (France: 120 Films/Studio Canal, 2002).

32. Rodolphe Chabrier, "SFX Featurette": Extras: *Irréversible*, DVD Accent Film Entertainment, 2004.

33. Nicholas Schager, "Movie Review: *Irréversible*," 2003, *filmcritic.com*. Available: http://filmcritic.com/misc/emporium.nsf/84dbbfa4d710144986256c290016f76e/d792dfcead7fd85888256cc700167826?OpenDocument&Highlight=0,Irreversible, January 28, 2004.

34. Paul Schrader and Kevin Jackson, *Schrader on Schrader* (London: Faber and Faber, 2004), p. 116.

35. A photograph of the sculpture can be viewed in the catalogue for the exhibition under the artists name in Sue Williams, "Selections from the Exhibition," *The Culture of Violence*, ed. Helaine Posner (Amherst: University of Massachusetts Amherst, 2002), p. 82.

36. Harkavy, "The Art of Bearing Witness," p. 21.

37. Confusion in public policy and academic debate about violence has resulted from the failure to acknowledge that the boundary between texts and lived experience is porous and contextualized when inferring meaning. The ill-effects debate on violence in the media often engages with content definitions that rely on counting incidents of violence and mistakenly endeavors to use quantitative measures as a guide to what is a far more complex interpretive audience response. W. James Potter describes research and censorship methodology that includes counting the number of times an act occurs, codes for the type and duration of violent acts, as well as a basic recognition that narrative meaning depends on contexts for interpretation of meaning: "In general, the most popular contextual variables of violence have been (a) outcome of the violent act for the perpetrator (reward vs. punishment, or whether the act was successful), consequences of the act for the victim (harm and pain), and motivation (intent or reasons) of the aggressor. Also becoming popular are the variables of realism (setting in place or time), humor (tone), use of weapons, graphicness (gratuitousness), and justification." (See Potter, *On Media Violence*, p. 203.) Potter argues for more contextual sophistication in the measurement of audience reception.

38. Bell, *Shot*, p. 39.

39. Ibid., p. 101.

40. Ibid., 249–50.

41. Ibid., 39.

42. Ibid., 159–60.

43. Ibid., 24.

44. Ibid., 25.

45. Paul Virilio, *The Vision Machine*, trans. Julie Rose, Perspectives, eds. Colin MacCabe and Paul Willemen (Bloomington: Indiana University Press and BFI Publishing, 1996), p. 61.

46. Karl French, *Screen Violence* (London: Bloomsbury, 1996), p. 5.

47. Jake Horsley, *The Blood Poets: A Cinema of Savagery 1958–99*, vol. 1: *American Chaos: From Touch of Evil to The Terminator* (Lanham: Scarecrow Press Inc., 1999), p. xxxvi.

48. Ibid., xxxvii.

49. Sontag, *Regarding the Pain of Others* p. 23.

50. Ibid., 42.

51. This phrase is a variation of a promotional phrase I heard used by the reporter, Shepherd Smith, on the *Fox Report* on the Fox News Channel, July 23, 2004, when watching the channel in Sydney. He phrased it as "News at the Speed of Live."

52. When citing ABC broadcasts in this chapter, quotes are taken from the following archived tape: *ABC News Special Report*, rec September 11, 2001, 7:00 a.m., News and Public Affairs Collection, University of California Los Angeles Film and Television Archive, 2001. VHS Call No. 83656.

53. Jon Dovey, *Freakshow: First Person Media and Factual Television* (London: Pluto Press, 2000), p. 89.

54. *X-Men: The Last Stand*, dir. Brett Ratner, prod. Avi Arad, Lauren Shuler Donner, and Ralph Winter. (USA: Twentieth Century Fox, 2006).

55. Jean Baudrillard, *The Vital Illusion*, ed. Julia Witwer (New York: Columbia University Press, 2000).

56. The WTC images of the smoking towers are defined as iconic because of the impact they had at the time of the occurrence of the event and because they are frozen in public and private memory. As Jessica Helfand points out: "The images we remember are those that do indeed stop time." See Jessica Helfand, *Screen: Essays on Graphic Design, New Media, and Visual Culture* (New York: Princeton Architectural Press, 2001), p. 132.

57. Baudrillard, *The Vital Illusion* p. 63.

58. Ron Burnett, *How Images Think* (Cambridge, Massachusetts: MIT Press, 2004), p. 7.

59. Bill Schaffer, "Just Like a Movie: September 11 and the Terror of Moving Images," Archive 2001, *Senses of Cinema* 17. November–December. Available: http://www.sensesofcinema.com/contents/01/17/symposium/schaffer.html, September 9, 2004.

60. David Bordwell, *Figures Traced in Light: On Cinematic Staging* (Berkeley: University of California Press, 2005), p. 266.

61. George Weld, "Before," Journal 2001, *Like An Orb*. Available: http://www.likeanorb.com/wtc/before/index.php?Number=0, October 19, 2004. There is an extensive history of discussion on the referentiality of the photographic image in the context of its status as a memoriam of the past. While the second photograph of Weld's as it captures the first step in what will become the reduction of the WTC to its melancholy status of a trace of the past, that sense of having become the past is not present in real time transmission of the event itself as it is experienced by the viewer at the moment of instantaneous transmission. As I researched the topic and revisited its images I was, however, aware of the poignancy of that sense of pastness that all those images now have. However, the nature of that poignancy came from an awareness of the images I viewed as now artifacts that called up that event's indexical actuality and tragic reality. In a fascinating discussion of virtuality springing from ruminations on the speed of light, Martin Jay concludes that such images are not "in an atemporal cyberspace, but are parasitic on the prior experiences that make them meaningful to us today." See Jay, *Refractions of Violence*, p. 130.

62. George Weld, "9.11 (1)," Journal 2001, *Like An Orb*. Available: http://www.likeanorb.com/wtc/index.php?Number=1, January 26, 2006.

63. Nichols, *Blurred Boundaries: Questions of Meaning in Contemporary Culture* pp. 18–19. A more recent example than the King video is the news footage captured by a U.S. news crew embedded with a combat unit of a marine shooting an unarmed prisoner in a Falluja mosque while on patrol in Iraq. See Reuters, "A Marine Takes Aim and Shoots His Prisoner Dead," *Sydney Morning Herald* November 17, 2004: 1.

64. Michael Schudson, *The Sociology of News*, Contemporary Societies, ed. Jeffrey C. Alexander (New York: W. W. Norton & Company, 2003), p. 191.

65. David L. McArthur, Daniel Magana, Corinne Peek-Asa, and Jess F. Kraus, "Local Television News Coverage of Traumatic Deaths and Injuries," *The Western Journal of Medicine* 175.6 (2001).

66. Jean Seaton, *Carnage and the Media: The Making and Breaking of News About Violence* (London: Allen Lane, 2005).

67. John Frow, "The Uses of Terror and the Limits of Cultural Studies," *Media International Australia Incorporating Culture and Policy* 2003.109 (2003): 14.

68. Jean Baudrillard, *The Spirit of Terrorism and Other Essays*, trans. Chris Turner (London: New York: Verso, 2002), pp. 26–27.

69. Baudrillard, *The Spirit of Terrorism and Other Essays* p. 27.

70. Ibid., 29.

71. Paul Virilio, *Ground Zero*, trans. Chris Turner (London: New York: Verso, 2002).

72. Evans Chan, "War and Images: 9/11/0, Susan Sontag, Jean Baudrillard, and Paul Virilio," 2003, *Film International* September 5, 2003. Available: http://www.filmint.nu/netonly/eng/warandimages/htm, May 24, 2004.

73. The actuality of the event impacted on academic reception provoking, for one practitioner, a dissatisfaction with theoretical approaches to the event in the context of its "real" occurrence: "On the other hand, the "realness" factor of 9/11 has left me less interested in Baudrillard than I would have ever imagined" in B. Ruby Rich, "After the Fall: Cinema Studies Post-9/11," *Cinema Journal* 43.2 (2004): 112–13.

74. Baudrillard, *The Spirit of Terrorism and Other Essays* pp. 29–30.

75. Peter Hines, "Our Fifteen Minutes Are Up," *Inside Film* 40.30–32 (2001–02): 30.

76. Slavoj Zizek, *Welcome to the Desert of the Real* (London: Verso, 2002), p. 17.

77. J. Hoberman, "Made in Hollywood: How Movies Foretold the New Reality," *Village Voice* December 11, 2001: 109.

78. Ibid., 110.

79. Kenneth Jackson, "Kenneth Jackson Talks About 9/11." Part 2, Archive Interview December 11, 2001, *The Sonic Memorial Project*. Available: http://sonicmemorial.org/sonic/public/archive.jsp, September 28, 2004.

80. Ibid., Part 3.

81. Jaeho Cho, Michael P. Boyle, Heejo Keum, Mark D. Shevy, Douglas M. McLeod, Dhavan V. Shah, and Zhongdang Pan, "Media, Terrorism, and Emotionality: Emotional Differences in Media Content and Public Reactions to the September 11th Terrorist Attacks," *Journal of Broadcasting and Electronic Media* 47.3 (2003).

82. Schaffer, "Just Like a Movie: September 11 and the Terror of Moving Images."

83. Timothy Gray, M., "H'wood's Age of Innocence Is Over," *Variety* September 12, 2001: 8.

84. Ray Greene, "Counterpunch: 'Our' Violence Versus 'Theirs,'" *Los Angeles Times* September 24, 2001: F7.

85. Gregg Kilday, "No Escaping the Images," *The Hollywood Reporter* September 13, 2001: 1.

86. Steven J. Zani, "Traumatic Disaster and Titanic Recuperation," *Journal of Popular Film and Television* 31.3 (2003): 125.

87. Generally that optimism is further encouraged by romance subplots. A fuller discussion of aspects of the genre can be found in Maurice Yacowar, "The Bug in the Rug: Notes on the Disaster Genre," *Film Genre Reader III*, ed. Barry Keith Grant (Austin: Texas University Press, 2003).

88. Gary Arnold, "Cast in a New Light," *Insight On the News* 17.39 (2001): 27.

89. Unless otherwise stated, as in this case, when the recording viewed was a feed to Los Angeles and it is the local time that is noted, all times used for quotations are United States Eastern Standard time, which appeared on the recording of events viewed for this research.

90. When citing NBC broadcasts in this chapter, quotes are taken from the following archived tape *Today in L.A: NBC New Special Report*, rec September 11, 2001, 5:52 a.m., News and Public Affairs Collection, University of California Los Angeles Film and Television Archive, Los Angeles, 2001. VHS Call No. 83653.

91. It is interesting that some viewers who were in New York at the time of the 9/11 attacks have had mixed feelings about revisiting the trauma of the experience through fiction in films based on those events, such as *United 93* (2006)—the film of the hijacking and crash in Pennsylvania of United Airlines Flight 93—and Oliver Stone's *World Trade Centre* (2006). As one eyewitness to the actual events says in a decision to not see the films, "I would not see either film because I would be afraid of residual grief and distress." Quoted in Gary Maddox, "Time to Face the Pain, Not Blame," *Sydney Morning Herald* August 19–20, 2006. For such viewers, historical authenticity and memory impact on reception when a film strives to retain indexicality with events with which they are intimately familiar. In the case of a film like *United 93* (which viewers know from the outset is going to end with the desperate and failed attempt by the passengers to prevent the highjackers crashing the plane), there is also not going to be the heroic victory over the bad guys of the Hollywood disaster or action genres. Oliver Stone's film, released in the United States at the time of the London bombings had dwindling financial returns. (See Sharon Verghis, "Not Another Terrorist Movie," *Sydney Morning Herald* August 19–20, 2006.) In the latter film, as the reviewer Sandra Hall notes, Hollywood "glamour is a distraction" from what remains of indexical authenticity in the fictional and "genuine disaster is transformed into the making of just another action picture." Sandra Hall, "Tragedy as Tearjerker," *Sydney Morning Herald* September 30–August 20, 2006: 14.

92. It has to be said that the theoretical urge to see surrealistic justification for theories of postmodernism in contemporary media events occasionally leads to putting blinkers on commonsense. A more recent example than 9/11 can be found in the reporting about passengers of an American plane who were watching themselves on television, as their plane circled with faulty landing gear in a possible crash scenario. The commentator, A. M. Homes, describes the passengers' increased fear when the televisions on the plane were turned off as resulting from needing "to stop having the distance to watch it" and having "to actually live it." (Quoted in Madeleine Murray, "Cover Boys," *Sydney Morning Herald* December 29, 2005: 18.) It seems not to have dawned on Homes that the passengers had not stopped living what must have been a fearful experience because they were watching it on the screen. The passengers were likely more fearful when they lost the screen perspective on their predicament due to its loss as another source of information about their plight. They were then only left with what was coming from a crew trying to put the best spin on the situation to reassure them. The passengers were not lost in a virtual reality. They would have simply wanted to know as much as possible about their life threatening situation and about what was being done in the air and on the ground to help them.

93. When citing CNN broadcasts in this chapter, quotes are taken from the following archived tapes: *CNN Coverage of 9/11 (Paula Zahn Segments)*, rec September 11, 2001, The Museum of Television and Radio, Los Angeles, 2001. VHS Call No. 790–91. Times quoted from the tape are Eastern Standard Time.

94. James Brandon, "It Seemed Clear: They Were Going to Kill Me," *Sydney Morning Herald* August 16, 2004: 11.

95. Margaret Morse, "News as Performance: Image as Event," *The Television Studies Reader*, eds. Robert C. Allen and Annette Hill (London: Routledge, 2004), p. 224.

96. Joseph P. and Muncer Reser, Steven, "Sense-Making in the Wake of September 11: A Network Analysis of Lay Understandings," *British Journal of Psychology* 95 (2004).

97. The Sonic Memorial Project, Home Page 2002, National Public Radio, Available: www.sonic-memorial.org, October 3, 2004.

98. *11'09'01*: September 11: A Collective Film, dir. Alejandro González Iñárritu, prod. Alain Brigand (United Kingdom: Sequence 19 Productions: StudioCanal, 2002).

99. CBS, CNN, Fox News, and NBC only briefly showed footage of people jumping from the towers and the image, unlike others, was not repeated.

100. The technical phrase used on-air for repeating footage.

101. Steve Donohue notes network "wall-to-wall, commercial free coverage" and "repeated graphic footage of the airliners slamming into the twin towers." Quoted from Steve Donohue, "A Story Nets Could Not Overplay," *Multichannel News* September 17, 2001: 3. He notes that CNN had a live feed of the north tower burning two minutes after it was struck. Many of the images would have been the same across networks as Donohue and Gibbons note. (See Steve Donohue and Kent Gibbons, "Most Horrific Story of Our Time," *Multichannel News* 2001: 54.) They report that in the United States all news networks shared video feeds until midnight on the day of the attack. Not unexpectedly, ratings increased for all news networks such as CNN, Fox News Channel, and CNBC in response to the "live" coverage of the attacks. Entertainment channels such as Court TV, lifestyle channels, and the sport channel ESPN preempted their regular coverage to air live feeds from news sources. (See Linda Moss, "Entertainment Nets Turned to News," *Multichannel News* September 17, 2001: 4.) Major media corporations such as AOL Time-Warner Inc, Walt Disney Co., News Corp., and Viacom telecast from their news channels on their entertainment channels for nearly 48 hours. (See Jim Forkan, "Service Efforts Took Precedence," *Multichannel News* September 17, 2001: 4.) In Australia, the four major free-to-air networks in the first day or so of the event gave ongoing coverage to it, as did the local cable Sky News channel.

102. A selection of front pages illustrating this ubiquity can be found at "Today's Front Pages: The Story Behind the News." September 12, 2001, *Newseum.org.* Available: http://www.newseum.org/frontpages/index.htm, October 11, 2004. It could be argued that newspaper front pages with the smoking towers frozen in time and space have contributed as powerfully to the lodging of the images in collective memory as the television broadcasts.

103. A similar receptive effect can be discerned in the disparity between the public outrage at publication of the picture of the falling man, an iconic photo published of one of many jumpers from the towers as they were engulfed in flames, and the aesthetic judgments made of the photo itself. Taken by Richard Drew of Associated press, it shows a composed image of a man falling upside down aligned with the striped bars of the tower behind with no view of the destruction around the falling body. (See Paul Kalina, "An Image to Horrible to Bear," *Sydney Morning Herald* August 31, 2006.) In a documentary on the identity of the jumper, the reception of the picture, and the phenomenon of the suicidal jumpers (more than 100 people jumped or fell) the editor of the first paper to publish the photograph found the frozen calm and grace of the image in the context of the suicidal jump arresting. However, the arrested image was only one of a sequence of 12 that shows the man in struggling agony as he plummets towards his death seconds later. See *9/11: The Falling Man*, dir. Henry Singer, prod. Henry Singer (United Kingdom: Channel 4 Television Corporation, 2006). Public outcry over the confronting nature of the image led to the media ceasing to publish it. As with the still photography of the burning towers, the photograph was a part of the shock with which the public processed the indexical actuality of the events. At the same time, the power of its stillness abstracted

from the agony present in the movement of the fall itself made a symbolic, aesthetically constructed icon from an even more agonizing actuality. While a fuller discussion of the power of the still photography of the events of 9/11 is outside the interests of this chapter, it is crucial to be aware that there are different judgments to be made about the impact of the still versus the moving picture as visual imagery. Two crucial differences involve the changing narrative over time of the body of the text in the moving picture and the impact of the audio aspects. That being said, the decision of network television and the newspapers to cease rerunning any images of those jumping to their death in response to public outcry is undoubtedly an example of the inability of the public to view such images as if they were devoid of indexicality and the real. Such an aspect of audience reception is not confined to images of 9/11 and involves an ongoing public debate about the ethical issues involved when the camera intrudes into the realm of private human suffering. A recent case in point is that of the documentary maker, Eric Steel, who set up cameras on the Golden Gate Bridge in San Francisco from January to December 2004 to record 23 of the 24 suicides from the bridge that year. See *The Bridge*, dir. Eric Steel, prod. Eric Steel and Alison Palmer Bourke (UK/USA: First Stripe Productions, 2006). Public debate around the film inevitably centered on where the balance is between voyeurism and raising issues for public debate. The film crew felt they were human beings before filmmakers and notified bridge suicide prevention crews (which are in place because 1200 people have died since the opening of the bridge in 1937) if they thought someone was going to jump. (They saved six people, one of them several times.) The director clearly made the film because he felt it had something important to say about the complex phenomenon of suicide. However, what is relevant in the context of my argument in this chapter is that reception and ongoing debate about films such as *9/11: The Falling Man* and *The Bridge* is that indexicality affects audience reception profoundly, even if the lens of the camera can momentarily create a loss of the real before the real asserts itself. Indeed, one observer of a potential suicide on the bridge who was recorded in Steel's film using a camera to take pictures of a young girl climbing over the railings noted that, while it felt unreal as he initially viewed her through the lens, when it dawned on him what she was doing, he put down the camera and reached out and pulled her back to safety. Indexicality pierced through the camera lens.

104. Jerome Bourden, "Live Television Is Still Alive: On Television as an Unfulfilled Promise," *The Television Studies Reader*, eds. Robert C. Allen and Annette Hill (London: Routledge, 2004).

105. Morse, "News as Performance: Image as Event," p. 210.

106. Ibid., 214.

107. Anne Foster, "Anne Foster Recalls Bob Edwards' Calming Voice," Voicemail Search Archive 2002, *The Sonic Memorial Project*. Available: http://sonicmemorial.org/sonic/public/archive.jsp, October 3, 2004.

108. American Airlines Flight 11 crashed into the north tower (WTC 1) at 8:45 a.m. A timeline of events is available in Staff Report, "The Paths of Destruction," *Time* 158.12 (2001): 32.

109. A similar response from an American viewer can be found in Angus Kress Gillespie, "Professor Gillespie Remembers 9/11," Interview Search Archive 2002, *The Sonic Memorial Project*. Available: http://sonicmemorial.org/public/archive.jsp, October 3, 2004. I was watching the second plane hit in on CNN in Sydney, Australia and, while stunned by the event itself, could also not believe that the announcers were unaware of it happening while I, the viewer, could see it. The delay was only a few seconds but it was there, nevertheless. As a viewer used to the authoritative stance of presenters and anchors I found it to be a startling informational reversal.

110. Ratboy, "TV to Go," *Film West* Winter.46 (2001): 65.

111. American Airlines Flight 77 hit the Pentagon at 9:40 a.m.

112. Roger Simpson, "Journalism and Trauma: A Long Overdue Conjunction," *Nieman Reports* 58.2 (2004): 77–79.

113. The north tower (1 WTC) collapsed at 10:29 a.m.

114. Donohue and Gibbons, "Most Horrific Story of Our Time," p. 54.

115. Morse, "News as Performance: Image as Event," p. 217.

116. This was almost instantaneous confirmation of the crash.

117. Staff Report, "If You Want to Humble an Empire," *Time* 158.12 (2001): 33.

118. This sense of participation in the event while trying to act as a dispassionate record-taker was something that television presenters and reporters would have shared with print journalists. As a reporter for the *New York Times* admits: "It was in many ways far easier to tug at rubble or haul trash than to be at work uptown at the paper, where I would have had to interview grief directly and write, a process that would have required an understanding of what was happening that I did not possess." Quoted from C. J. Chivers, "September," *Esquire* 138.3 (2002): 145.

119. Staff Report, "If You Want to Humble an Empire," p. 32.

120. National Commission on Terrorist Attacks Upon the United States, *The 9/11 Commission Report: Final Report of the National Commission on Terrorist Attacks Upon the United States*, Authorized edn. (New York: W.W. Norton & Company, 2004).

121. William O' Rourke, "What We Saw: How September 11 Looked on TV," Archive Search 2001, *Commonweal Magazine* October 26, 2001/CXXVIII.18. Available: http://www.commonwealmagazine.org/article.php?id_article=352, January 24, 2006.

122. John Fiske, *Television Culture* (London: Routledge, 1987).

123. Andrew Goodwin, "TV News—Striking the Right Balance?" *Understanding Television*, eds. Andrew Goodwin and Garry Whannel (London: Routledge, 1990).

124. Denis McQuail, *Mass Communication Theory: An Introduction*, 2nd edn. (London: Sage, 1987).

125. Alexa Moses, "Beating About the Bush," *Sydney Morning Herald* July 2, 2004: 3.

126. Stuart Allan, "News from Nowhere: Televisual News Discourse," *Approaches to Media Discourse*, eds. Allan Bell and Peter Garrett (Oxford: Blackwell Publishers, 1998), p. 118. Allan's reading of encoding/decoding in news discourse is based on the seminal work of Stuart Hall to be found in Stuart Hall, "Encoding/Decoding," *Media Texts: Authors and Readers*, eds. David Graddol and Oliver Boyd-Barrett (Clevedon: Multilingual Matters and The Open University, 1994).

127. Cited in Morse, "News as Performance: Image as Event," p. 222.

128. Baudrillard, *The Vital Illusion* pp. 51–52.

129. Daniel Chandler, "Shaping and Being Shaped: Engaging with the Media," 1996, *CMC Magazine*. Available: http://www.december.com/cmc/mag/1996/chandler.html, June 17, 2004.

130. Virilio, *Ground Zero* pp. 37–38.

131. Colin Sparks, "The Global, the Local and the Public Sphere," *The Television Studies Reader*, eds. Robert C. Allen and Annette Hill (London: Routledge, 2004).

132. Virilio, *Ground Zero* p. 50.

133. Walter Murch, *In the Blink of an Eye: A Perspective on Film Editing*, 2nd edn. (Los Angeles: Silman-James Press, 2001), p. 144.

134. Louise Spence, "In Focus: Teaching 9/11," *Cinema Journal* 43.2 (2004): 90.

135. *11'09'01*: September 11: A Collective Film.

136. Gianpaolo Baiocchi, "Media Coverage of 9/11 in Brazil," *Television and New Media* 3.2 (2002).

137. Sontag, *Regarding the Pain of Others* pp. 109–11.

138. Ken Burns, "Television and the War on Terrorism: The Artistic Community Responds," Panel Discussion 2002, Transcript, *Museum of Television and Radio*. Available: http://www.mtr.org/seminars/satellite/terrorism/terrorism5.htm, May 19, 2004.

139. Bob Simon, Robert M. Batscha, Ari Fleischer, Colonel Jay M. Parker, Paul Friedman, Norman Pearlstine, and Rick Berke, *Television and the War on Terrorism: The War Abroad: The U.S. Perspective*, 2002, Panel Transcript, *Museum of Radio and Television*. Available: http://www.mtr.org/seminars/satellite/terrorism/terror2trans.htm, May 19, 2004.

140. Maria Elizabeth Grabe, Shuhua Zhou, and Brooke Barnett, "Explicating Sensationalism in Television News: Content and Bells and Whistles," *Journal of Broadcasting and Electronic Media* 45.4 (2001).

141. Nichols, *Blurred Boundaries: Questions of Meaning in Contemporary Culture* p. 19.

142. Ibid., 18.

143. A similar impact in the Australian context can be seen in the video evidence, widely shown in the media, of revenge attacks after the Cronulla beach riots in Sydney in 2006. The film was handed over by the police to the Islamic community leader, Keysar Trad, to distribute among Middle Eastern community members for perpetrator identification. (See Andrew Clennell, Ben Cubby, and Jonathan Pearlman, "Muslims Asked to Identify Attackers," *Sydney Morning Herald* January 27, 2006: 3.) It is the wider political implications that impinge on the impact of other controversial indexical images such as those of abuses by U.S. soldiers in Iraq at the prison of Abu Ghraib (see Johanna McGeary, "The Scandal's Growing Stain," *Time* May 17, 2004) and the more recent Iraqi television and bystander mobile phone images circulated on the internet and television of the execution of Saddam Hussein. (See New York Times and Agence France Press, "Execution Prompts Children's Hangings," *Sydney Morning Herald* January 6–7, 2007.) Such images resonate with the political and violent actuality outside the screen that they represent or become associated with.

144. Nichols, *Blurred Boundaries: Questions of Meaning in Contemporary Culture* p. 19.

145. Marian Wilkinson, "The Darkest Hours," *Sydney Morning Herald* July 24–25, 2004: 29.

146. Paul Harvey, *The Condition of Postmodernity: An Enquiry into the Origins of Cultural Change* (Oxford: Basil Blackwell, 1990), p. 201.

147. Scott Bukataman, *Matters of Gravity: Special Effects and Supermen in the 20th Century* (Durham: Duke University Press, 2003), p. 33.

148. Andrew Strathern and Pamela J. Stewart, "Introduction: Terror, the Imagination, and Cosmology," *Terror and Violence: Imagination and the Unimaginable*, eds. Andrew Strathern, Pamela J. Stewart, and Neil L. Whitehead (London: Pluto Press, 2006), p. 9.

149. Relatives accessing the media to publicize photographs of victims to help them in their search for missing relatives and extensive inclusion of eyewitness camcorder recording of events from members of the general public (which Morse terms "surveillance from below") was also a significant addition of nonprofessional access to the televised space that increased the range of voices in the news discourse and increased access to an authenticity that further modified the conventions of virtuality and its ideology. I would thus find myself in disagreement with Morse: "The advantage of surveillance from below is not in its greater reality or truth, but in its multiplicity—provided it is disseminated in a way that allows discourse to unfold." (See Morse, "News as Performance: Image as Event," p. 220.)

While not giving access to a totally objective reality, eyewitness camcorder reports undoubtedly increase perceived authenticity for the viewer. Incidents of victims using live television to publicize pictures of lost relatives in order to find them further challenges textual insulation from events outside the screen. It is also possible to see ideological shifts in the fact that media corporations set aside advertising revenue and ignored the increased costs of extensive reporting on 9/11 to expand coverage in what could be considered an act of journalistic responsibility.

150. Wells, "It's Life Jim," Paul Verhoeven' in an interview with Wells, p. 23.

151. Burnett, *How Images Think* p. 8.

152. Jane M. Gaines, "Introduction: 'the Real Returns,'" *Collecting Visible Evidence*, eds. Jane M. Gaines and Michael Renov, vol. 6, Visible Evidence (Minneapolis: University of Minnesota Press, 1999), p. 8.

153. Barry Hampe, *Making Documentary Films and Reality Videos: A Practical Guide to Planning, Filming, and Editing Documentaries of Real Events* (New York: Henry Hold and Company, 1997), p. 33.

154. Carl. R. Plantinga, *Rhetoric and Representation in Nonfiction Film*, Cambridge Studies in Film, eds. William Rothman and Dudley Andrew (Cambridge: Cambridge University Press, 1997), p. 2.

155. An illustrative example of how even indexical video footage can provoke a range of interpretations and debate over ambiguous meaning is to be found in the documentary *Raw Deal*. It incorporates actual footage of an alleged rape of Lisa Gier-King, an exotic dancer, who claimed she was raped at a party at a fraternity house. On viewing the footage the claim of rape was rejected by local law enforcement and she was charged with making a false accusation. However, the case became a feminist cause célèbre in Florida, in the United States, and the debate over whether it depicts rape or consensual sex is the subject of the documentary. The viewer, after hearing all sides and seeing confronting footage of the actual incident included in the documentary, is left with plenty of evidence to form an opinion. However, one is also left with a sense that there is enough ambiguity in the footage for the viewer to feel that there is a decision to be made about choosing a side in the debate, rather than deciding on a truth. Whether a viewer could be sure that the footage is clear evidence of one's reasons for having chosen a side is another matter altogether. See *Raw Deal: A Question of Consent*, dir. Billy Corben, prod. Alfred Spellman (USA: Imagine Entertainment, 2002).

156. *Series 7: The Contenders*, dir. Daniel Minehan, prod. Tom Brown and Michael Escott, (USA: USA Films, 2001).

157. *Bowling for Columbine*, dir. Michael Moore, prod. Wolfram Tichy (Canada/USA/Germany: United Artists, 2002).

158. Norma Khouri, *Forbidden Love: A Harrowing True Story of Love and Revenge in Jordan* (Sydney: Bantam Books, 2003).

159. For a discussion of the expressive complexity and categorical fluidity of the way nonfiction seeks to influence the viewer in a variety of documentary schemas to manipulate narrative, chronology, and relevance to create dramatic movement, see Plantinga, *Rhetoric and Representation in Nonfiction Film*.

160. Susan Murray, "I Think We Need a New Name for It: The Meeting of Documentary and Reality TV," *Reality TV: Remaking Television Culture*, eds. Susan Murray and Laurie Ouellette (New York: New York University Press, 2004).

161. Franklin E. Zimring, *American Youth Violence*, Studies in Crime and Public Policy, eds. Michael Tonry and Norval Morris (New York: Oxford University Press, 1998), p. 3.

162. Ibid., 160.

163. Ibid., 160.

164. Needless to say, this public tendency to generalize about crime or a group of possible perpetrators from particular high profile cases or statistics is not only an American phenomenon. The public panic caused by the James Bulgur case in Britain and the recent coverage in Sydney, Australia, of a teenage gang (inclusive of a fourteen-year-old girl) beating victims and murdering one of them, led to claims about increasing youth crime that were not borne out by research. (See Jonathan Pearlman, "Anything but Child's Play," *Sydney Morning Herald* February 3, 2006.) The same process has been examined in an Australian example of the role the media and public perceptions can play in criminalizing the Arab Other post-9/11 in Scott Poynting, Greg Noble, Paul Tabar, and Jock Collins, *Bin Laden in the Suburbs: Criminalising the Arab Other*, Sydney Institute of Criminology Series, eds. Chris Cunneen, Mark Findley, and Julie Stubbs (Sydney: Sydney Institute of Criminology, 2004). As a recent press feature on the prejudices feeding the politicization of crime as a Middle Eastern phenomenon in the western suburbs of Sydney aptly notes: "They call this a war zone, but the reality is a different story." (See Christopher Kremmer and Lisa Pryor, "Crime and Prejudice," *Sydney Morning Herald* August 5–6, 2006: 23.)

165. Peter Hogue, "Documentaries as Movies," *Film Comment* 32.4 (1996): 56.

166. Salman Rushdie, "Reality TV: A Dearth of Talent and the Death of Morality," *Guardian* June 9, 2001: 12. Research showing reality TV's similarities with psychological deprivation experiments and the occurrence of an offscreen suicide of a contestant, is a disturbing pointer to the format's potential for brutality in actuality. (See Sam Brenton and Reuben Cohen, *Shooting People: Adventures in Reality TV* (London: Verso, 2003.))

167. Craig Hight, "It Isn't Always Shakespeare, but It's Genuine: Cinema's Commentary on Documentary Hybrids," *Understanding Reality Television*, eds. Su Holmes and Deborah Jermyn (London: Routledge, 2004), p. 243.

168. For a comprehensive definition of this form as a genre see John Corner, "Performing the Real: Documentary Diversions," *Television and New Media* 3.3 (August) (2002).

169. Mary Beth Haralovich and Michael W. Trosset, "Expect the Unexpected: Narrative Pleasure and Uncertainty Due to Chance in Survivor," *Reality TV: Remaking Television Culture*, eds. Susan Murray and Laurie Ouellette (New York: New York University Press, 2004), p. 299.

170. Julie Baird, "Heroism Isn't a Hilton Ho and Tell," *Sydney Morning Herald* September 25–26, 2004: 37.

171. Dovey, *Freakshow: First Person Media and Factual Television* p. 4.

172. Mark Andrejevic, *Reality TV: The Work of Being Watched*, Critical Media Studies Institutions, Politics, and Culture, ed. Andrew Calabrese (Lanham: Rowman & Littlefield Publishers, Inc., 2004), p. 133.

173. Ibid., 132.

174. Ibid., 138.

175. Ibid., 207.

176. Ibid., 215.

177. Jeremiah Kipp, "Lock and Load: Daniel Minehan Broadcasts *Series 7*," Archives 2001, *film-critic.com*. Available: http://filmcritic.com/misc/emporium.nsf/84dbbfa4d710144986256c290016f76e/e8ef12d6a85001b588256a1200030bba?OpenDocument, July 9, 2004.

178. Andrejevic, *Reality TV: The Work of Being Watched* p. 209.

179. As I have noted elsewhere: "Put an actor on the stage and the identification of acting is more clearly perceived but "to feign, to simulate, to represent, to impersonate" (Kirby, p. 40) are fundamental intents of a range of human roles and behaviours." Quoted from Gwyn Symonds, "Not Taking It Personally": "Performing the Teacher's 'Role' and Responding to Challenging Behaviours," *Australasian Journal of Special Education* 27.1 (2003): 35.

180. Kipp, "Lock and Load: Daniel Minehan Broadcasts *Series 7*."

181. Craig Hight, "It Isn't Always Shakespeare, but It's Genuine: Cinema's Commentary on Documentary Hybrids," p. 248.

182. The following quote is typical of press interest in the degree of scripting in reality TV: "Through sources I cannot reveal but would definitely not go to jail to protect, I got hold of a 19-page, single spaced outline of an upcoming episode of "Queer Eye for the Straight Guy." Every moment is planned in advance, including a few specific lines for the straight guy to deliver, which Bravo says is not unusual for any reality show. It's something that people in Hollywood know and think is no big deal." See Joel Stein, "The New Quiz Show Scandal: Reality Television," *Los Angeles Times* December 5, 2004: M1.

183. Hight, "It Isn't Always Shakespeare, but It's Genuine: Cinema's Commentary on Documentary Hybrids," p. 233. For a descriptive, if somewhat colloquial outline of the love/hate debate over reality TV written by an Australian television reviewer see Kerry Murphy, *TV Land: Australia's Obsession with Reality Television* (Milton: John Wiley & Sons Australia, Ltd., 2006). She draws timely attention to the fact that audiences are not uniformly manipulated by reality TV when she chronicles the numerous instances in which some of the most questionable shows die in the ratings in the genre because audiences vote with their feet. As James W. Cook notes in his discussion of the "long-running manipulation myth" about one of the earliest promoters of culture as hoax, P. T. Barnum, the interaction between consumer and entertainment provider "was this dialectical, market-driven dance between restless promoter and fickle public that constituted the ongoing drama of the nineteenth-century culture industry." Quoted from James W. Cook, *P.T. Barnum Reader: Nothing Else Like It in the Universe* (Urbana: University of Illinois Press, 2005), p. 181. I would argue that not much has changed and that Cook's words are also an apt description of the relationship between the consumers and producers of reality TV.

184. Deborah Jermyn, "'This Is About Real People!': Video Technologies, Actuality and Affect in the Television Crime Appeal," *Understanding Reality Television*, eds. Su Holmes and Deborah Jermyn (London: Routledge, 2004), p. 71.

185. Su Holmes and Deborah Jermyn, "Introduction: Understanding Reality TV," *Understanding Reality Television*, eds. Su Holmes and Jermyn Deborah (London: Routledge, 2004), p. 10.

186. Dovey, *Freakshow: First Person Media and Factual Television* p. 4.

187. Kevin Glynn, *Tabloid Culture: Trash Taste, Popular Power and the Transformation of American Television* (Durham: Duke University Press, 2000), p. 2.

188. Ibid., 2.

189. Michael Renov, "Documentary Horizons: An Afterforward," *Collecting Visible Evidence*, eds. Jane M. Gaines and Michael Renov, vol. 6, Visible Evidence (Minneapolis: University of Minnesota Press, 1999).

190. Further discussion of this aspect of reception with a summary of significant research confirming its commonality as a mode of response to text can be found in Justin Lewis, "The Meaning of Real Life," *Reality TV: Remaking Television Culture*, eds. Susan Murray and Laurie Oullette (New York: New York University Press, 2004).

191. Holmes and Jermyn, "Introduction: Understanding Reality TV," p. 11.

192. Toni Johnson-Woods, *Big Bother: Why Did That Reality–TV Show Become Such a Phenomenon?* (Brisbane: University of Queensland Press, 2002), p. 55.

193. This absence of agreement is probably because there has never been one that did not have difficulty with some form of cinematic enhancement. The French scientist Etienne-Jules Marey, who in 1882 invented the first camera able to picture birds in motion through increasing the number of exposures had, as his stated aim, the capturing of movements the naked eye could not see—essentially, aiming to *enhance* natural ocularity by increased detail. At the end of his life in 1904, when commercial motion pictures as entertainment were already an outgrowth of research like his, he still felt that moving pictures "interesting as they are, are of little advantage to science, for they only show what we see better with our own eyes." Cited in Robert Sklar, *Movie-Made America: A Cultural History of American Movies*, Revised edn. (New York: Vintage Books: Random House Inc, 1994), p. 9.

194. Murch, *In the Blink of an Eye: A Perspective on Film Editing* p. 6.

195. Research on personal perceptions and saliency is a broad field but a basic text can be found in Byron Reeves and Clifford Nass, *The Media Equation: How People Treat Computers, Television, and New Media Like Real People and Places* (Stanford, California: CSLI Publications, 1996).

196. A descriptive history of the partially fictional documentary form and the term can be found in Gary D Rhodes, "Mockumentaries and the Production of Realist Horror," *Post Script* 21.13 (2002).

197. Gaines, "Introduction: 'the Real Returns,'" p. 8.

198. Ibid., 10.

199. Johnson-Woods, *Big Bother: Why Did That Reality–TV Show Become Such a Phenomenon?* p. 54.

200. There was a deviation from this trend with the influence of the French cinéma vérité movement of the 1960s with its emphasis on a minimalist fly-on-the-wall approach that has left a mark on techniques still thought of as less mediated—such as unedited, indirect address from recorded dialogue.

201. Michael Renov, *The Subject of Documentary*, Visible Evidence, eds. Michael Renov, Faye Ginsburg, and Jane Gaines, vol. 16 (Minneapolis: University of Minnesota Press, 2004), p. xxi.

202. Graeme Burton, *Talking Television: An Introduction to the Study of Television* (London: Arnold, 2000), p. 148.

203. Dave Kopel, "Bowling Truths: Michael Moore's Mocking," April 4, 2003, *National Review Online*. Available: http://www.nationalreview.com/kopel/kopel040403.asp, July 6, 2004. There are numerous Web sites that have extensively researched Moore's films and made available evidence of what they argue is Moore's lack of journalistic integrity in "tricky editing" of events, particularly their chronology, to falsify what happened in the service of what seen as "hypocritical spin." In short, they view his documentaries as lacking in integrity because he lies. Discussions of such issues about *Bowling for Columbine* with links to similar self-styled watchdog sites can be found at "Bowling for Truth," Main 2004, *RichWatch*. Available: http://www.bowlingfortruth.com/, July 6, 2004. Also at Ben Fritz, "Viewer Beware," Column Archives November 19, 2002, *Spinsanity*: Countering Rhetoric With Reason. Available: http://www.spinsanity.org/columns/20021119.html, July 6, 2004. Two site authors collaborated on a book vigorously slamming Moore on these issues of "deception" in Jason Clarke and

David T. Hardy, *Michael Moore Is a Big Fat Stupid White Man* (New York: ReganBooks, 2004). Moore's official Web site has engaged in partially refuting some of the claims and can be found at Michael Moore, "How to Deal with the Lies and the Lying Liars When They Lie About 'Bowling for Columbine,'" 2003, *Michael Moore.com*. Available: http://www.michaelmoore.com/words/wackoat-tacko/, November 24, 2004.

204. *The Thin Blue Line*, dir. Errol Morris, prod. Lindsay Law (USA: Miramax Films, 1988).

205. Richard K Sherwin, "Framed," *Legal Reelism: Movies as Legal Texts*, ed. John Denver (Urbana: University of Illinois Press, 1996), p. 75.

206. David T. Hardy, "Bowling for Columbine: Documentary or Fiction?" 2002, *hardylaw.net*. Available: http://www.hardylaw.net/Truth_About_Bowling.html, July 6, 2004.

207. Edward Spence, "Stranger Than Fiction: The Fabrication of Fact," *Sydney Morning Herald*, January 16, 2006: 9.

208. Patricia R. Zimmerman, *States of Emergency: Documentaries, Wars, Democracies*, Visible Evidence, eds. Michael Renov, Faye Ginsburg, and Jane Gaines, vol. 7 (Minneapolis: University of Minnesota Press, 2000), p. 169.

209. Jack Newfield, "An Interview with Michael Moore," 1998, *Tikkun*, November–December Available: http://www.findarticles.com/p/articles/mi_m1548/is_n6_v13/ai_21248742, July 6, 2004.

210. Amazingly, the scene was staged with the bank's cooperation and then edited to cut out the checks and processes, including a waiting period, before the guns are given to the customers. The point is that, even if information about the checks and balances were edited in, Moore's point would still be comic, if less pithy, given the fact that most audiences enjoy seeing banking monoliths pilloried, fairly or not.

211. Roger Ebert, "Bowling for Columbine," Movie Reviews 2002, *rogerebert.com*. Available: http://rogerebert.suntimes.com/apps/pbcs.dll/article?AID=/20021018/REVIEWS/210180303/1023, January 22, 2006.

212. Direct quotes taken from an article on the tapes in *Time* and cited in her bibliography can be found in Hilary Neroni, "The Men of Columbine: Violence and Masculinity in American Culture," *Journal for the Psychoanalysis of Culture & . . .* 5 (Fall).2 (2000).

213. I am aware of the dangers of criticizing Moore for not delivering a documentary he was not aiming for, as some feminists have done who are dissatisfied with his failure to "implicate masculinity or patriarchy as causes of violence." Quoted from Caroline Gage, "Bowling for Columbine: Michael Moore Off-Target," *Off Our Backs* January–February (2003): p. 53. However, the lack of a more detailed sense of who Harris and Klebold were, while it allows Moore's own panoramic arguments to stand, leaves the viewer with a lingering sense of human motivation being oversimplified.

214. Terry McCarthy, "Warning," *Time* March 19, 2001: 24.

215. Ibid., 26.

216. I would not go so far as one critic: "Everything—including accuracy and nuance—is subordinated to the presentation of his bullying, know-it-all self." (Richard Schickel, "The Alternate Realities of Hot Documentaries: Three Non-Fiction Films Are Attracting Lots of Attention This Summer—Maybe for the Wrong Reason," *Time* 2003: 67.)

217. Pauline Kael, *Movie Love: Complete Reviews 1988–91* (New York: Plume, 1991).

218. Peter Wilshire, "Presentation and Representation in Michael Moore's Bowling for Columbine," *Australian Screen Education* Summer.35 (2004): 92.

219. William Ian Miller, *Faking It* (Cambridge: Cambridge University Press, 2003), p. 229.

220. I am prepared to admit a certain professional singularity behind the analysis of this point as I am a special educator with extensive experience working with students with anger management problems and histories of violence which makes me aware of the gross oversimplification of Moore's comments here. Even allowing for the broadness of the satiric stroke, it seems to me the polemical point is unconvincing.

221. Peter Hartcher, "Speed of Lies Equals the Ease of Acceptance," *Sydney Morning Herald* July 23, 2004: 13.

222. Jon Ronson, "The Egos Have Landed." Features. *Sight and Sound* November (2002). British Film Institute. Available: http://www.bfi.org.uk/sightandsound/feature/37, June 13, 2004.

223. Vivian Sobchack, "Toward a Phenomenology of Nonfictional Film Experience," *Collecting Visible Evidence*, eds. Jane M. Gaines and Michael Renov, vol. 6, Visible Evidence (Minneapolis: University of Minnesota Press, 1999), p. 251.

224. Ibid., 246.

225. Hampe, *Making Documentary Films and Reality Videos: A Practical Guide to Planning, Filming, and Editing Documentaries of Real Events* p. 33.

226. James M. Moran, *There's No Place Like Home Video*, Visible Evidence, eds. Michael Renov, Faye Ginsburg, and Jane Gaines (Minneapolis: University of Minnesota Press, 2002), p. 175.

227. Hampe, *Making Documentary Films and Reality Videos: A Practical Guide to Planning, Filming, and Editing Documentaries of Real Events* p. 72.

228. Ibid., 53.

229. Ibid., 58.

230. Renov, *The Subject of Documentary* p. 127.

231. The recent controversy over racist remarks directed at an Indian contestant, a Bollywood star, and eventual winner of the 2007 UK *Celebrity Big Brother* clearly demonstrates that the contestant making the remarks (a previous *Big Brother* winner) possessed actual prejudices of questionable morality that she could not, even in front of the camera, pretend she did not have.

232. Renov, *The Subject of Documentary* p. 215.

233. Bruce Crowther, *Hollywood Faction: Reality and Myth in the Movies* (London: Columbus Books, 1984), p. 14.

234. Bradley D. Clissold, "*Candid Camera* and the Origins of Reality TV: Contextualising a Historical Precedent," *Understanding Reality Television*, eds. Su Holmes and Deborah Jermyn (London: Routledge, 2004), p. 49.

235. The attention given to Khouri's book was a part of the broader public interest in the political and social status of women in Islamic countries. Recent nonfiction books of note on that topic include: Mukhtar Mai's *In the Name of Honour*, Azar Nafisi's *Reading Lolita in Tehran*, Aayan Hirsi Ali's *Infidel* and *The Caged Virgin: A Muslim Woman's Cry for Reason*, and Jasvinder Sanghera's *Shame*. Burgeoning publication on the topic testifies to a public interest which Khouri's hoax undoubtedly exploited.

236. Malcolm Knox, "Her Life as a Fake: Bestseller's Lies Exposed," *Sydney Morning Herald* July 24, 2004: 1. Knox's article is a full account of his investigations of the fictional nature of Khouri's book and of the fictionalization of her public image. Revelations of financial fraud and the degree to which Khouri had lied about her personal life outside the framework of the story, to maintain a public persona supporting the nonfiction of her book, extended the hoax into her living an imaginary life that

left literati and friends feeling deceived but marveling at the convincing nature of her deception. (See Malcolm Knox and Caroline Overington, "An Imaginary Life," *Sydney Morning Herald* July 31–August 1, 2004: 25 and Malcolm Knox, "For Khouri's Ally, It Was a Friendship Stronger Than Fiction," *Sydney Morning Herald* August 1, 2004: 3.) In the light of the controversy and Khouri's inability to refute the allegations, the publisher, Random House, withdrew the book from sale. (See Malcolm Knox, "Khouri Lost for Words to Explain Book," *Sydney Morning Herald* August 1, 2004: 3 and Murray Waldren and Tony Koch, "Honour Kill Book's Shelf Life Runs Out," *Australian* August 1, 2004: 3.) *Forbidden Love* was published in the United States in February 2003 by Atria Books under the title *Honor Lost: Love and Death in Modern-Day Jordan*. It was withdrawn from sale in the United States in July 2004 following Australian revelations. The controversy continues to attract attention three years on with an Australian documentary released in 2007, entitled *Forbidden Lies*, which follows Khouri back to Jordan in an attempt to find out if she can substantiate her story. (See also Susan Wyndham, "Undercover: Forbidden but Not Forgotten," *Sydney Morning Herald* June 17–18, 2006: 30.) The film is a dazzling display of Khouri's ongoing obfuscation of the factual.

237. The discrepancies between claims made about his life in his memoir and the verifiable facts were revealed by the *Smoking Gun* Web site, which questioned details to do with his imprisonment, the nature of his crimes, and the details of his drug rehabilitation experiences. Frey defended his writing by saying that since the book was a memoir, rather than an autobiography, some embellishment or subjective retelling was permitted and that, in any case, it only referred to five percent of the book. Both Oprah's endorsement and the controversy shot the book up the bestseller lists in Australia and overseas. (See Gerard Wright, "Have I Got a Story for You," *Sydney Morning Herald* January 14–15, 2006: 23.)

238. Frey claimed that the editing manipulation of his original text in the publishing process by Doubleday altered the book in ways that were as much an indictment of the editing process as of his integrity as a writer saying: "I remember somebody at the publishing company told me that if the book's 85 per cent true, there's no problem." Quoted in Laura Barton, "The Man Who Rewrote His Life," *Sydney Morning Herald* October 7–8, 2006: 28.

239. Barton, "The Man Who Rewrote His Life," 29. While outside the scope of this chapter, there is a deeper investigation to be made into the definitional parameters of authenticity in the memoir or life writing genre. Peter Wilson, in commenting on the growing controversy over the factuality of Ishmael Beah's memoir of his time as a child soldier in Sierra Leone, *A Long Way Gone*, suggests recognition of the unreliability of memory might solve the problem for publishers and authors at least: "perhaps in a disclaimer at the start of the book." (Quoted in Peter Wilson, "Thanks for the Memories", Weekend *Australian* February 2–3, 2008: 23. The accuracy of the book was defended by its New York publisher Sarah Crichton Books and its Australian publisher Harper Collins.

240. Khouri, *Forbidden Love: A Harrowing True Story of Love and Revenge in Jordan* pp. 6–7.

241. Ibid., 19.

242. Ibid., 38.

243. Ibid., 175.

244. Ibid., 32.

245. Ibid., 42.

246. Ibid., 50.

247. Ibid., 15.

248. Ibid., 41.

249. Ibid., 42.

250. Ibid., 49.

251. Ibid., 49.

252. Ibid., 51.

253. Ibid., 51.

254. Ibid., 32.

255. Ibid., 143.

256. Ibid., 30.

257. Ibid., 31.

258. Ibid., 15.

259. Kate Legge, "Hoaxer So Hard to Read," *Australian* July 31–August 1, 2004: 2.

260. Khouri, *Forbidden Love: A Harrowing True Story of Love and Revenge in Jordan* p. 12.

261. Ibid., 92.

262. Ibid., 49.

263. Ibid., 56.

264. Ibid., 57.

265. Ibid., 57.

266. Ibid., 59.

267. Ibid., 60–61.

268. Ibid., 26.

269. Gillian Whitlock, "Tainted Testimony: The Khouri Affair," *Australian Literary Studies* 21.4 (2004).

270. I could only find two articles in the plethora of Australian press reports on the hoax, apart from Ihab Shalbak's quoted later in this chapter, which questioned Khouri's anti-Arab prejudice, independently of whether the book was fiction or not. One article was only published several months after the discovery of the hoax. (See Nada Jarrar, "Betrayal but a Small Part of the Larger Deception," *Sydney Morning Herald* November 24, 2004: 17.) Another, a review, apparently published before the hoax was revealed, by Eva Sallis describing it as a book that "sanctioned forbidden hatreds." (Quoted in Legge, "Hoaxer So Hard to Read," p. 2.) If there are others, they certainly did not impinge on the general debate in Australia about the book. Interestingly, as Legge reports, despite her misgivings about the book, even Sallis succumbed to the charisma of Khouri's personal presence and sent a letter of support to her campaign.

271. Khouri, *Forbidden Love: A Harrowing True Story of Love and Revenge in Jordan* p. 57.

272. Ihab Shalbak, "The False Identity That Helped Provide a Moral Case for War," *Sydney Morning Herald* August 3, 2004: 15.

273. Sontag, *Regarding the Pain of Others* p. 21.

274. Nichols, *Blurred Boundaries: Questions of Meaning in Contemporary Culture* p. 120.

275. Academic analysis of violence can also succumb to a polemical urgency that divests itself of textual substance, as in Christopher Sharrett, *Mythologies of Violence in Postmodern Media* (Detroit: Wayne State University Press, 1999). Sharrett too easily elides into an apocalyptic description of American society as the embodiment of the ideological ills of late capitalism. His polemical passion in the face of the commodification of violence immerses his description of sociocultural malaise in the language of Armageddon: "Postmodern America now demands revelry in sacrifice as panicked

validation of its already-dead self-concept . . . the representational culture that follows from all of this are indeed merely the product of a civilization that despises history and any reasonable understanding of material reality and human needs (p. 432). Sharrett's critical stance is overwhelmed by the tension inherent in the interplay between the representation of violence, entertainment, morality, ideology, interpretation, and the lived experience of violence.

276. *Capturing the Friedmans*, dir. Andrew Jarecki, prod. Andrew Jarecki and Richard Hankin. (USA: Magnolia Pictures, 2003).

277. The comment was made about the movie *Fargo*, by the actor Peter Stormere, who played the character of the serial killer Gaoar Grimsrud. See Jeffrey Schwartz, *Minnesota Nice: A Documentary*, rec 2005, Special Features: *Fargo* DVD Gold Edition, MGM Home Entertainment, 2003.

278. Quoted in Janet Malcolm, *The Journalist and the Murderer* (London: Papermac, 1998), p. 29.

279. Spoken by a father claiming he committed the murder his son was charged with, despite eyewitnesses to the contrary. Quoted in Kate McClymont, "I Shot the Lotto Winner's Standover Man. Honest." *Sydney Morning Herald* December 11–12, 2004: 1.

280. See Noël Carroll, "Non-Fiction Film and Postmodernist Skepticism," *Post-Theory: Reconstructing Film Studies*, eds. David Bordwell and Noel Carroll, Wisconsin Studies in Film (Madison, Wisconsin: The University of Wisconsin Press, 1996), p. 287. Interestingly, when commenting on the controversy over James Frey's *A Million Little Pieces* Oprah Winfrey pointed out her own reliance on that signposting when she endorsed the book: "I rely on the publishers to define the category that a book falls within and also the authenticity of the work." Quoted in Wright, "Have I Got a Story for You." 23.

281. Rosanne Kennedy, "The Dangerous Individual and the Social Body," *Thinking Through the Body of the Law*, eds. Peng Cheah, David Fraser, and Judith Grbich (Sydney: Allen & Unwin, 1996), p. 195.

282. Sheila Brown, *Crime and Law in Media Culture* (Buckingham: Open University Press, 2003), p. 71.

283. The centrality of that discussion to audience acceptance or rejection of a violent act committed by a character in a text was an issue for fans of the character Spike in *Buffy, the Vampire Slayer* whose sexual assault of Buffy is discussed in Chapter 5. Fans of the character were adamant he would not have assaulted her in that way and it led to writers on the show defending and explaining their reasons for their choice to write that plot development. For a case study of audience reception of that development see Symonds, "'Bollocks!': Spike Fans and Reception of Buffy the Vampire Slayer."

284. David A. Black, *Law in Film: Resonance and Representation* (Urbana: University of Illinois Press, 1999), pp. 143–44.

285. Jonathan Vankin and John Whalen, *Based on a True Story: Fact and Fantasy in 100 Movies* (Chicago: Chicago Review Press, 2005), p. xv.

286. Ibid., xvi.

287. *Munich*, dir. Steven Spielberg, prods. Barry Mendel, Kathleen Kennedy, Steven Spielberg, and Colin Wilson (USA: Dreamworks Distribution LLC and Universal Pictures, 2005).

288. Gordon Thomas, "We Know Where You Live," *Sydney Morning Herald* January 14–15, 2006: 25. See also a response from a former head of the Mossad at Ephraim HaLevy, "Spielberg's Facts and Fiction," January 15, 2006, *Times Online*. Available: http://www.timesonline.co.uk/article/0,923-2000576,00.html, January 21, 2006.

289. The book is *Vengeance: The True Story of an Israeli Counter-Terrorist Team* by George Jonas. It was purportedly written from contact with someone claiming to be a Mossad agent but whom the Israeli sources have denied ever worked for them.

290. Richard Schickel, "Spielberg Takes on Terror," *Time* December 12, 2005: 64. Film reviewers have raised issues of the interaction between indexical facts and fiction in response to the recent emergence of fictional films of the events of 9/11 such as *United 93*. (See Paul Byrnes, "Truth, Fiction and the Flight That Fell to Earth," *Sydney Morning Herald* August 10, 2006. Also Verghis, "Not Another Terrorist Movie.") The film closely follows what can be verified of the events on the plane and on the ground following the hijacking but created unknown dialogue and events through actor improvization based on interpretations of known facts and the characters of participants. It aimed for further authenticity by having some actual participants from the real life events play themselves.

291. David Schmid, *Natural Born Celebrities: Serial Killers in American Culture* (Chicago: The University of Chicago Press, 2005).

292. Rebecca Gowers, *The Swamp Death: A True Tale of Victorian Lies and Murder* (London: Hamish Hamilton, 2004).

293. The evolution of the Court TV cable channel in the United States has been from unadorned live transmission of trials "to a glitzy, mainstream-influenced, dramatic, sensational, and celebrity-based concept." See Chuck Kleinhans and Rick Morris, "Court TV: The Evolution of a Reality Format," *Reality TV: Remaking Television Culture*, eds. Susan Murray and Laurie Ouellette (New York: New York University Press, 2004), p. 173.

294. As noted by Gowers, in the trial of the accused, Reginald Birchall, an overflowing courtroom had suspended telephone transmitters above the judge's seat to provide live coverage for the households of local people of prominence and those who wanted to pay for the privilege of listening in rooms at the Woodstock Hotel. In addition, a telegraph company ran lines to press tables, with operators provided, so that court reporters could update national and international press by the minute.

295. Gowers, *The Swamp Death: A True Tale of Victorian Lies and Murder* p. 209.

296. The first book was on the shelves within 24 hours of the verdict. The almost simultaneous publication of four out of the five nonfiction books (the fifth was timed for much later in 2006) speaks to the publishing opportunism that assumes a fairly large public appetite for true crime, particularly in high profile cases. See Lindsay Murdoch and Liz Gooch, "Family Begs Outback Killer to Reveal Body," *Sydney Morning Herald* December 15, 2005: 7.

297. The release of the Australian movie *Wolf Creek*, based loosely on the backpacker murders committed by the serial killer Ivan Milat in rural New South Wales and on the Murdoch case was delayed in the Northern Territory where the case was in progress until after the verdict on Murdoch's guilt. Interestingly, in the context of the legal issues of the case, this delay presumes that whatever fictional liberties were taken with the events in the film, the connection with the factual is viable enough to prejudice public opinion while the trial is in progress. The film was released nationally in November 2005 but only in the Northern Territory in January 2006 following the trials completion there.

298. The show aired on the Australian public broadcast network, the ABC, in 2007.

299. Ruth Ritchie, "Truths Are Still Simple," *Sydney Morning Herald* September 9–10, 2006: 10.

300. Malcolm Brown, "The Gas Did It: Bogle-Chandler Theory Blames Toxic Cloud," *Sydney Morning Herald* September 8, 2006: 3.

301. Gowers, *The Swamp Death: A True Tale of Victorian Lies and Murder* p. 201.

302. Ibid., 205–06.

303. Ibid., 174–75.

304. Wendy Lesser, *Pictures at an Execution* (Cambridge: Harvard University Press, 1993), p. 22.

305. Sara L. Knox, *Murder: A Tale of Modern American Life* (Durham: Duke University Press, 1998), p. 202.

306. The American television franchise includes *CSI*, *CSI: Miami*, and *CSI: New York*.

307. Patrick S. Pemberton, "Watching the Detectives," *Australian*, September 25–26, 2004: R24–R25.

308. Robert Wainwright, "The Case for the Prosecution," *Sydney Morning Herald* September 9–10, 2006: 29. As the head of forensic pathology at a Sydney morgue dryly commented on how *CSI* investigators seem to be able to divine a plethora of information from a fatal stab wound to the chest: "In reality, I might be able to say he's definitely dead and it was probably the stab wound that killed him." Quoted in Michael Duffy, "Death in the Afternoon, Morning and Night." *Sydney Morning Herald.* September 29–30, 2007: 29.

309. Peter Doyle, *City of Shadows: Sydney Police Photographs 1912–48* (Sydney: Historic Houses Trust, 2005), p. 20.

310. Michael Bilton, *Wicked Beyond Belief: The Hunt for the Yorkshire Ripper* (London: Harper Collins, 2003). Back cover.

311. Charlotte Grieg, *Evil Serial Killers: In the Minds of Monsters* (London: Capella, 2006). Back cover.

312. Such thematic interests are not only the subject of True Crime narratives, of course. The fiction film, *A History of Violence* (2005), which tells the story of the unmasking of an ex-hitman for the Mob who is trying to escape his past by living an American small-town life with a family and friends who see him as the guy next door is a recent example. See *A History of Violence*, dir. David Cronenberg, prods. Chris Bender and J. C. Spink (USA: New Line Cinema, 2005).

313. John Clarke and Andy Shea, *Touched by the Devil: Inside the Mind of the Australian Psychopath* (Sydney, Australia: Simon & Schuster, 2001). Back cover.

314. Mike Bingham, *Suddenly One Sunday: The True Story of the Port Arthur Tragedy Based on Eyewitness Accounts* (Australia: Harper Collins, 1996). Back cover.

315. Schmid, *Natural Born Celebrities: Serial Killers in American Culture* p. 205.

316. Mark Seltzer, *Serial Killers: Death and Life in America's Wound Culture* (New York: Routledge, 1998), p. 169.

317. This genre effect undoubtedly taps into the fear of crime as a public concern, the subject of extensive criminological research, which is generally defined as an individually held "diffuse sense of danger about being physically harmed by *criminal* violence." Quoted from Elizabeth Stanko, "Naturalising Danger: Women, Fear and Personal Safety," *Dangerous Offenders: Punishment and Social Order*, eds. Mark Brown and John Pratt (London: Routledge, 2000), p. 152. The book containing Stanko's chapter is an excellent overview of the dangerous offender as a figure of public anxiety.

318. Doyle, *City of Shadows: Sydney Police Photographs 1912–48* p. 21.

319. Pemberton, "Watching the Detectives," R24.

320. Amy Taubin, "The Allure of Decay," *Action Spectacle Cinema: A Sight and Sound Reader*, ed. Jose Arroyo (London: BFI Publishing, 2000), pp. 154–55.

321. Chris Sheedy, "The Real CSI," *Sydney Morning Herald* September 8, 2004: 4.

322. Esther McKay, *Crime Scene: True Stories from the Life of a Forensic Investigator* (Melbourne: Viking, 2005), p. 208.

323. Ibid., 226.

324. Ibid., 231.

325. Ibid., 208–09.

326. An article on professional Crime Scene Cleaners describes the way memory, after exposure to actual death, becomes wired to an olfactory system that comes to know the gradations of the smell of death intimately. See Adam Higginbotham, "Blood on Their Hands," *Sydney Morning Herald* September 4, 2004: 30–35.

327. McKay, *Crime Scene: True Stories from the Life of a Forensic Investigator* p. 209.

328. Ibid., 210.

329. Ibid., 214.

330. Ibid., 215.

331. Ibid., 223.

332. Ibid., 232.

333. Ibid., 234.

334. Ibid., 235.

335. Ibid., 237.

336. Ibid., 238.

337. Ibid., 241.

338. Ibid., 249.

339. Ibid., 259.

340. Doyle, *City of Shadows: Sydney Police Photographs 1912–48* p. 15.

341. McKay, *Crime Scene: True Stories from the Life of a Forensic Investigator* p. 290.

342. Joel Black, *The Aesthetics of Murder: A Study in Romantic Literature and Contemporary Culture* (Baltimore: The John Hopkins University Press, 1991), p. 3.

343. Ibid., 10.

344. Estelle Blackburn, *Broken Lives* (Melbourne, Australia: Hardie Grant Books, 2002). Author activism as a consequence of a true crime narrative investigation still operates in a True Crime twilight zone where the legal accounts of appeals and evidence, media reports, and ongoing authorial textualization compete to convey narrative authenticity to the audience. A classic case in point are the documentaries directed by Joe Berlinger and Bruce Sinofsky, *Paradise Lost: The Child Murders at Robin Hood Hills/Paradise Lost 2: Revelations*, (USA: Warp Films, 2005). Along with the bonus features on this DVD release of the HBO films, they chronicle a seven-year involvement by the filmmakers in following the case of the accused Memphis Three and of the supporters who were convinced by the first documentary that they were wrongly convicted. The films themselves are a powerful narrative about competing participant agendas, inclusive of their own narrative one—the second film reflects on the impact of the first on subsequent courtroom processes and the growth of supporter activism.

345. John Denver, "Introduction," *Legal Reelism: Movies as Legal Texts*, ed. John Denver (Urbana: University of Illinois Press, 1996), p. xiii.

346. Paul Gewirtz, "Victims and Voyeurs: Two Narrative Problems at the Criminal Trial," *Law's Stories: Narrative and Rhetoric in the Law*, eds. Peter Brooks and Paul Gewirtz (New Haven: Yale University Press, 1996), p. 149.

347. Ibid., 151.

348. Alan M. Dershowitz, "Life Is Not a Dramatic Narrative," *Law's Stories: Narrative and Rhetoric in the Law*, eds. Peter Brooks and Paul Gewirtz (New Haven: Yale University Press, 1996), p. 105.

349. Susan Mitchell, *All Things Bright and Beautiful: Murder in the City of Light* (Australia: Macmillan, 2004).

350. Susan Weiner, "True Crime: Fact, Fiction and the Law," *Legal Studies Forum* 17.3 (1993): 280.

351. Jonathan Goodman, *Tracks to Murder*, True Crime Series, ed. Albert Borowitz (Kent: The Kent State University Press, 2005), p. xiv.

352. The difficulty (and, perhaps, the pointlessness) of looking for complete and incontrovertible factuality in the context of nonfiction being represented in fictional terms has been noted by the playwright David Edgar with the illustration of the three dramatizations on American television of Amy Fisher, known as the "Long Island Lolita," who tried to kill the wife of her lover, Joey Buttafuoco. "The story was dramatized by CBS from the point of view of the husband, by ABC from that of a campaigning journalist, and by NBC from the point of view of Fisher herself." Engagement with the factuality or fictionality of the event depends on point of view. (See David Edgar, "Rules of Engagement," Digital, October 22, 2005, *Guardian Unlimited*. Available: http://books.guardian.co.uk/review/story/0,12084,1596971,00.html, March 11, 2006.) Since her release the now-married Fisher, her exlover, and his now exwife, Mary Jo Buttafuoco, have continued to give media interviews to further muddy the waters of factuality on tabloid shows like *Entertainment Tonight* (ET).

353. Alston Chase, *Harvard and the Unabomber: The Education of an American Terrorist* (New York: W.W. Norton & Company, 2003), p. 33.

354. Ibid., 33.

355. The *Law & Order* mothership, as fans call the original show, has led to three spin-offs—*Law & Order: Special Victims Unit*, *Law & Order: Criminal Intent*, and *Law & Order: Trial by Jury*. The series popularity can be measured by the fact that it has aired on network television for 18 seasons at the time of writing, is on network and cable around the world and can, in any given Australian or American 24-hour period, be viewed at just about any time.

356. Given the franchise in its permutations has been on air for so long, chronicling the shows "ripped from the headlines" would be too extensive to list here but a few illustrative examples are "Subterranean Homeboy Blues," 1:2 (1990) which tells the story of the shooting of two African-Americans by a white woman in a subway taken from the Bernard Goetz case with its racial tensions and police corruption; "The Serpents Tooth," 1:19 (1991) based on the case of the Menendez brothers; "Conspiracy," 3:2 (1992) based on the assassination of Malcom X; "Doubles," 4. 21 (1994) based on the Tanya Harding attack on Nancy Kerrigan; "Hot Pursuit," 6.5 (1995) based on the Patty Hearst case; and "Age of Innocence," 16.4 (2005) based on the court battles over the removal of Terry Schiavo's feeding tube. A more recent example is "In Vino Veritas," 17.7 (2006) which is based on Mel Gibson's arrest for drunken driving and the controversy that erupted after his racist remarks to the arresting Jewish policeman. An excellent episode guide to seasons of the original show which gives details of the show's links to headline news can be found at *TV.com*, "Law & Order Episode Guide," Season Episodes 2006. Available: http://www.tv.com/law-and-order/show/180/episode_guide.html, January 22, 2006. Episode guides to other series of the franchise can be found at the same web site.

357. This concept has obvious roots in Aristotle's theory of mimesis, concerned as it is with verisimilitude and plausibility, in *The Poetics*.

358. Thomas A. Mascaro, "The Network Executive Did It: Law & Order Indicts Network Programming Practices for Ethical Lapses in Reality TV," *Journal of Popular Film and Television* 31.4(2004): p. 149.

359. Phillip J. Lane, "The Existential Condition of Television Crime Drama," *Journal of Popular Culture* 34.4 (2001).

360. John Leonard, *Smoke and Mirrors* (New York: The New Press, 1997), p. 114.

361. There is a sense of the city of New York as crime-ridden with a justice system fighting for control, particularly when the viewer watches all shows in the franchise with regularity. The panorama of crime is exhaustive, inclusive of serial killers, domestic disputes, robbery, corrupt city officials, sadomasochism, rape, cop killing, child killers, drug dealing, illegal organ dealing, money laundering, murder, mugging, child abuse, arson, illegal immigration, stalking, illegal weapons dealing, hit men, kidnapping, cult killing, fraud, terrorism, media negligence leading to death, and prostitution. In one episode, "Mayhem," 4.17 (1994), during a 24-hour period Lenny Briscoe and his partner Logan in the original *Law & Order* have caseloads that include five unrelated murders and a domestic quarrel which results in the maiming of the husband. This sense of a crime-ridden city overwhelming law enforcement was occasionally reinforced by crossover episodes with the darker and more existential show *Homicide: Life on the Streets* such as "Charm City," 6.13 (1996) and "Baby, It's You," 8.6 (1997). The inclusion of a sense of problematic morality in the characters involved in law enforcement and the political process linked to its functions reinforces the sense of imperfection in the system and in its ability to keep violent chaos in check without corruption and injustice. However, the elegance of plotting and of the legal and ethical discussions of topical issues, a sense of ordered debate, and the sense that the system mostly functions and the criminal is mostly caught, keeps a more existential mood at bay.

362. Leonard, *Smoke and Mirrors* p. 159.

363. Dick Wolf, *Law & Order: Crime Scenes* (New York: Barnes & Noble, 2003), p. 132.

364. Dawn Keetley, "Law & Order," *Prime Time Law: Fictional Television as Legal Narrative*, eds. Robert M. Jarvis and Paul R. Joseph (Durham, North Carolina: Carolina Academic Press, 1998), p. 35.

365. Ibid., 34.

366. While a list of issues debated dramatically in the show would be too extensive to include here, typical episode examples are slum landlords and rent laws in "Cradle To Grave," 2.18 (1992); homophobia in the police in "Manhood," 3.21 (1993); battered-woman syndrome in "Blue Bamboo," 5.3 (1994); the death penalty in "Savages," 6.3 (1995), and the right of a jury to protect a defendant from an unjust law in "Nullification," 8.5 (1997). A more contemporary debate dealing with public issues in thematic ways is the episode "Fear America," 17.4 (2006), which deals with a murder in the context of public fear of terrorism, racism, and the implications for Muslim identity in America after 9/11.

367. Sheedy, "The Real CSI."

368. Daniel Fienberg, *Thirst for Ice-T Quenched on New SVU*, March 1, 2004, Zap2it: TV News. Available: http://tv.zap2it.com/tveditorial/tve_main/1,1002,271%7C86678%7C1%7C,00.html, December 7, 2005.

369. Wolf, *Law & Order: Crime Scenes* p. 13.

370. Ibid., 13.

371. Ibid., 13.

372. Peter J. Hutchings, *The Criminal Spectre in Law, Literature and Aesthetics* (London: Routledge, 2001).

373. Ibid., 26.

374. Ibid., 29.

375. Ibid., 30.

376. Leonard, *Smoke and Mirrors* p. 159.

377. Ibid., 44.

378. Ibid., 43.

379. Ibid., 33.

380. Ibid., 39.

381. Lynn Elber, "Making the Dead," *Australian* September 4–5, 2004: R24.

382. Ibid., R25.

383. Wolf, *Law & Order: Crime Scenes* p. 40.

384. Ibid., 40.

385. Ibid., 40–42.

386. *Selling of a Serial Killer*, dir. Nick Broomfield, prod. Peter Moore, (USA: DEJ Productions, 1992).

387. Paige Schilt, "Media Whores and Perverse Media: Documentary Film Meets Tabloid TV in Nick Broomfield's *Aileen Wournos: The Selling of a Serial Killer,*" *Velvet Light Trap* 45.Spring (2000).

388. "Killing Her Way to Fame," *Time* February 18, 1991: 45.

389. Vankin and Whalen, *Based on a True Story: Fact and Fantasy in 100 Movies* p. 110.

390. *Monster*, dir. Patti Jenkins, prods. Mark Damon, Clark Peterson, Charlize Theron, and Brad Wyman, (USA: Media 8 Entertainment, 2003).

391. Vankin and Whalen, *Based on a True Story: Fact and Fantasy in 100 Movies* p. 110.

392. Fred Topel, *Charlize Theron Interview: Portraying Monster Aileen Wournos*, Action-Adventure Movies 2005, About Inc. Available: http://actionadventure.about.com/cs/weeklystories/a/aa121903. htm, January 13, 2005.

393. Bruce C. Steele, "The Making of a Monster," *Advocate* March 2, 2004: 38.

394. Ibid., 38.

395. Ibid., 34.

396. Charlize Theron's reply when asked what she thought when she first looked into the mirror in full make-up and contact lenses to look like Aileen Wournos, the female serial killer she played in the film *Monster*. In Steele, "The Making of a Monster," p. 41.

397. Ibid., 38.

398. Ibid., 34.

399. Ibid., 37.

400. Ibid., 38.

401. Ibid., 36.

402. Patty Jenkins has claimed that "everything's informed" by her access to Wournos, particularly through letters in which she opened up about herself. (See Jerome Gary, *Master Seminar: Patti Jenkins, Steve Perry and Guy Livneh*, rec January 28, 2004, Panel, Disc 1, Track 1. American Film Institute, Los Angeles, 2004.) Available at the Institute library in Los Angeles under catalogue number T-04-05.

403. Gary, *Master Seminar: Patti Jenkins, Steve Perry and Guy Livneh*. Track 2.

404. Mick O'Donnell, *Mercy: In Pursuit of the Truth About the Death of Yvonne Gilford* (Pymble: N.S.W.: Harper Collins, 1999), p. 4.

405. Malcolm, *The Journalist and the Murderer* p. 20.

406. Ibid., 71.

407. Ibid., 96.

408. Caryn James, "A Heart of Darkness Lurks Below," *Sydney Morning Herald* February 9, 2006: 16.

409. Phillip Cornford, "Intrigue and Frailty on a Desert Highway," *Sydney Morning Herald* March 4–5, 2006: 24.

410. Malcolm, *The Journalist and the Murderer* p. 73.

411. Ibid., 96.

412. *Capote*, dir. Bennett Miller, prod. Caroline Baron, Michael Ohoven, and William Vince (USA: Sony Pictures Classics, 2005).

413. Gowers, *The Swamp Death: A True Tale of Victorian Lies and Murder* p. 365.

414. Singh served four years of a ten-year sentence in jail on a conviction of manslaughter, inclusive of the time from her arrest in 1997, and was released in 2001.

415. Helen Garner, *Joe Cinque's Consolation: A True Story of Death, Grief and the Law* (Sydney: Picador, Pan Macmillan Australia, 2004), p. 131.

416. Ibid., 180.

417. Ibid., 257.

418. Ibid., 241.

419. Ibid., 18–19.

420. Ibid., 30.

421. Ibid., 27.

422. Ibid., 33.

423. Ibid., 39.

424. Ibid., 42.

425. Ibid., 244.

426. Gewirtz, "Victims and Voyeurs: Two Narrative Problems at the Criminal Trial," p. 135.

427. Garner, *Joe Cinque's Consolation: A True Story of Death, Grief and the Law*, p. 25.

428. Ibid., 25.

429. Ibid., 170.

430. Ibid., 141.

431. Garner has offered the personal nature of her motivation to write as the source of all her writing, not just of the book under discussion: "I'm working absolutely from the inside out." Quoted in Kate Grenville and Sue Woolfe, *Making Stories: How Ten Australian Novels Were Written.* (Sydney: Allen & Unwin, 2001), p. 71.

432. Garner, *Joe Cinque's Consolation: A True Story of Death, Grief and the Law* p. 222.

433. Ibid., 231.

434. Ibid., 236.

435. Ibid., 248.

436. Ibid., 253.

437. Ibid., 256.

438. Ibid., 289.

439. Ibid., 290.

440. Susan Wyndham, "On Death and Madness," *Sydney Morning Herald* August 9, 2004: 15.

441. Ibid., 15.

442. Garner, *Joe Cinque's Consolation: A True Story of Death, Grief and the Law* p. 317.

443. Ibid., 328.

444. David R. Dow, "Fictional Documentaries and Truthful Fictions: The Death Penalty in Recent American Film," *Constitutional Commentary*, 17.3 (2000).

445. Kerryn Goldsworthy, *Helen Garner*, Australian Writers, ed. Chris Wallace-Crabbe (Melbourne: Oxford University Press, 1996), p. 87.

446. *Fargo*, dir. Joel Coen, prod. Ethan Coen, (USA: Polygram Filmed Entertainment, 1996).

447. Charlie Rose, *Interview with the Coen Brothers*, Special Features: Fargo DVD, Gold Edition, MGM Home Entertainment, 2005.

448. Schwartz, *Minnesota Nice: A Documentary*.

449. William H. Macy, a lead actor in the film describes the humorous use to which the Coen brothers put the mystification they encouraged offscreen: "after the movie was out for a while, there was this great article in the Post saying that we just discovered it wasn't based on a true story. And Joel and Ethan wrote a letter to the paper saying we're doing an internal investigation to find out how something like this could have happened." Quoted in Schwartz, *Minnesota Nice: A Documentary*.

450. Schwartz, *Minnesota Nice: A Documentary*.

451. Jody Enders, *Death by Drama and Other Medieval Urban Legends* (Chicago: University of Chicago Press, 2002), p. xxiii.

452. Josh Grossberg, "Law & Order Gets a Senator," August 28, 2002, *Eonline*. News. Available: http://www.eonline.com/News/Items/0,1,10454,00.html?newsrellink, December 12, 2004. His recent decision to leave the show and run for political office for real in the Republican presidential candidate primaries in 2007–08 posits the link between the fictional and the actual as a revolving door! As one reporter who watched Thompson on screen the week he declared his candidacy noted: "In real life, Mr. Thompson wants Americans to believe he will bring those same leadership qualities to the highest office in the land: the US presidency." (Quoted in "Anne Davies, Actor Poised to Follow in Reagan's Footsteps." *Sydney Morning Herald*, June 1, 2007: 8)

453. She killed all five, ranging in age from six months to seven years, but was only tried for the murder of three.

454. Caroline Overington, "As Not Seen on TV: Non-Existent Crime Script Overturns Murder Sentence," *Sydney Morning Herald* January 8–9, 2004: 3.

455. The extensive coverage was a response to public horror at a mother being capable of such an act and centred on whether postnatal depression was a psychosis and whether it met the criteria for a legal defense of insanity.

456. When interviewed on the Fox network's *The Big Story*, which aired in Sydney on January 9, 2005, Dr Dietz said he had sent a letter to the prosecution following his testimony correcting his statement but had not followed up on it as he had not thought that the case depended in any significant way on the belief that a television show had led to the murder. He thought he *might* have been confused by an episode that had matricide plot similarities.

457. *The Sopranos*, exec. prod. David Chase, (HBO, 1999–). An earlier version of this chapter was published in Gwyn Symonds, "Show Business or Dirty Business: The Theatrics of Mafia Narrative and Empathy for the Last Mob Boss Standing in *the Sopranos*," *Reading the Sopranos: Hit TV from HBO*, ed. David Lavery, Reading Contemporary Television (London: I. B. Tauris, 2006).

458. Richard Corliss and Simon Crittle, "The Last Don," *Time* March 4, 2004: 50.

459. Seltzer, *Serial Killers: Death and Life in America's Wound Culture* (New York: Routledge, 1998) p. 159.

460. Thomas Leitch, *Crime Films*, Genres in American Cinema, ed. Barry Keith Grant (Cambridge: Cambridge University Press, 2002), p. 294.

461. Raymond Chandler, *The Simple Art of Murder*, Vintage Crime (New York: Vintage Books; Random House, 1988), p. 2.

462. David Chase, Susan Billington-Katz, Mitchell Burgess, Frank Renzulli, and Robin. Green, *Words into Pictures: Anatomy of a TV Drama: The Sopranos*, rec June 6, 1999, Panel Discussion, VHS The Writer's Guild Foundation, Los Angeles, 1999.

463. "All Happy Families," 5.4.

464. John McCarty, *Bullets over Hollywood: The American Gangster Picture from the Silents to "the Sopranos"* (Cambridge, MA.: Da Capo Press, 2004), p. 246.

465. Glen Creeber, "TV Ruined the Movies: Television, Tarantino and the Intimate World of the Sopranos," *This Thing of Ours: Investigating the Sopranos*, ed. David Lavery (New York: Columbia University Press, 2002).

466. David Pattie, "Mobbed Up: The Sopranos and the Modern Gangster Film," *This Thing of Ours: Investigating the Sopranos*, ed. David Lavery (New York: Columbia University Press, 2002), p. 137.

467. Edward Mitchell, "Apes and Essences: Some Sources of Significance in the American Gangster Film," *Film Genre Reader* III, ed. Barry Keith Grant (Austin: University of Texas Press, 2003), p. 223.

468. Leitch, *Crime Films* p. 300.

469. Jack Shadoian, *Dreams and Dead Ends: The American Gangster Film*, 2nd edn. (Oxford: Oxford University Press, 2003).

470. "Rat Pack," 5.2.

471. Jerry Capeci, *Wiseguys Say the Darndest Things: The Quotable Mafia* (USA: Alpha, Penguin Group (USA) Inc., 2004), p. 15.

472. Richard Schechner, *Performance Theory*, Revised edn. (London: Routledge Classics, 2003), p. 214.

473. "The Legend of Tennessee Moltisanti," 1.8.

474. Richard Maltby, "The Spectacle of Criminality," *Violence and American Cinema*, ed. J. David Slocum (New York: Routledge, 2001), p. 125.

475. Ibid., 125.

476. Lloyd Hughes, *The Rough Guide to Gangster Movies*, Rough Guides Reference, ed. Mark Ellingham (London: Rough Guides Ltd., 2005), p. 4.

477. John Miller, *The Real Deal*, Documentaries, Special Features, *The Sopranos: The Complete Second Season*, Disc 3, DVD HBO Home Video, 2000.

478. Samuel Weber, *Theatricality as Medium* (New York: Fordham University Press, 2004).

479. George Anastasia, *The Last Gangster: From Cop to Wiseguy to FBI Informant: Big Ron Previte and the Fall of the American Mob* (New York: Regan Books; Harper Collins, 2004), p. 304. This book is one of the countless biographies of crime lords or families available detailing Mob dealings and selling to a public whose interest remains unsated.

480. "Big Girls Don't Cry," 2.5.

481. "Two Tonys," 5.1.

482. David E. Ruth, *Inventing the Public Enemy: The Gangster in American Culture, 1918–34* (Chicago: The University of Chicago Press, 1996), p. 1.

483. This contemporary media urge to romanticize the gangster is not confined to urban contexts, of course, and has much in common with what has been called social banditry in peasant communities. See Anton Blik, *Honour and Violence* (Cambridge: Polity, 2001).

484. Ruth, *Inventing the Public Enemy: The Gangster in American Culture, 1918–34.* p. 6.

485. Ibid., 130.

486. Letizia Paoli, *Mafia Brotherhoods: Organized Crime, Italian Style.* (Oxford: Oxford University Press, 2003), p. 3.

487. Steven Waldon and Selma Milovanovic, "Gangster Who Nursed Sick Mother, Found God and Loved a Laugh," *Sydney Morning Herald* February 11–12, 2006.

488. "To Save Us All From Satan's Power," 3.10.

489. Robert Warshaw, *The Immediate Experience* (New York: Atheneum, 1974), p. 130.

490. Fred Gardaphe, "Fresh Garbage: The Gangster as Suburban Trickster," *A Sitdown with the Sopranos*, ed. Regina Barreca (New York: Palgrave, Macmillan, 2002), p. 98.

491. A contract killing organization run by Lepke for the gangsters Lucky Luciano and Meyer Lansky on New York's Lower East Side in the 1930s.

492. McCarty, *Bullets over Hollywood: The American Gangster Picture from the Silents to "the Sopranos,"* p. 214.

493. Ibid., 241–42.

494. Pattie, "Mobbed Up: The Sopranos and the Modern Gangster Film," p. 140.

495. Joseph S. Walker, "Cunnilingus and Psychiatry Have Brought Us to This: Livia and the Logic of Falsehoods in the First Season of the Sopranos," *This Thing of Ours: Investigating the Sopranos*, ed. David Lavery (New York: Columbia University Press, 2002), p. 112.

496. "The Sopranos," 1.1.

497. "The Legend of Tennessee Moltisanti," 1.8.

498. "A Guy Walks into a Psychiatrist's Office," 2.1.

499. The comparison with Robinson's gangster character Rico in *Little Caesar* (1931) is direct. Rico does not drink alcohol while on the rise as a bootlegging gangster and his fall is signaled by his taking up heavy drinking. Referential intertextuality of this kind, deepened by the shows use of actors that have themselves played in many of the texts referenced (see note on Lorraine Bracco below), creates a constantly expanding sense of theatricality within the televisual frame. Like refracting light off a crystal, referentiality in *The Sopranos* truly does make the viewer feel all the world is text.

500. "Big Girls Don't Cry," 2.5.

501. "D-Girl," 2.7.

502. "Long-term Parking," 5.12.

503. "The Sopranos," 1.1.

504. Maurice Yacowar, *The Sopranos on the Couch: Analyzing Television's Greatest Series*, Expanded edn. (New York: Continuum, 2003), p. 25.

505. Leitch, *Crime Films* p. 306.

506. David Ray Papke, "Myth and Meaning: Francis Ford Coppola and Popular Response to the Godfather Trilogy," *Legal Reelism: Movies as Legal Texts*, ed. John Denver (Urbana: University of Illinois Press, 1996), p. 14.

507. Virginia Heffernan, "Cut to the Chase," *Sydney Morning Herald* May 3, 2004: 5.

508. "The Sopranos," 1.1.

509. Ibid., 1.1.

510. "All Happy Families," 5.4.

511. "Sentimental Education," 5.6.

512. "46 Long," 1.2. It is a rather nice incidental intertextual reference for fans as David Chase was a writer and producer on the television show *The Rockford Files* created by Stephen J. Cannelli.

513. For three responses that epitomize discussion of the issue see chapters in the section titled Aesthetics: The Beauty of Crime inclusive of Noel Carroll, "Sympathy for the Devil," James Harold, "A Moral Never-Never Land: Identifying with Tony Soprano," and Mike Lippman, "Know Thyself, Asshole: Tony Soprano as an Aristotelian Tragic Hero" in Richard Greene and Peter Vernezze, "The Sopranos and Philosophy: I Kill Therefore I Am," *Popular Culture and Philosophy*, ed. William Irwin (Chicago, Illinois: Open Court, 2004). Such an audience response is not confined to only to this series, of course. In that context, transgressive acts are not necessarily an alienating factor in audience reception because, as Peter Liguori, the creator of *The Shield* noted about the flawed antihero of his own show, "moral ambiguity is highly involving for an audience." Quoted in Warren St. John, "What Men Want: Neanderthal TV," December 11, 2005, *nytimes.com*. Available: http://www. nytimes.com/2005/12/11/fashion/sundaystyles/11MEN.html?pagewanted=print, December 15, 2005. Audience identification with a transgressive character is a complex reception process. Anette Hill's study quoted earlier is probably the definitive work on this aspect of audience reception. Independent of what the audience brings to the receptive table and the story itself, the actor's performance needs to be acknowledged. James Gandolfini's contribution to his character's engaging portrayal is unquestionable. For a discussion of the part played by an actor's performance in creating audience empathy, even beyond the empathy created by the scripted words, see Gwyn Symonds, "Playing More Soul Than Is Written: James Marsters' Performance of Spike and the Ambiguity of Evil in Sunnydale," 2005, *Slayage: The Online International Journal of Buffy Studies* 16: March Available: http://www.slayageonline.com/ essays/slayage16/Symonds.htm, January 28, 2007.

514. *The Godfather*, dir. Francis Ford Coppola, prod. Albert S. Ruddy, (USA: Paramount Pictures, 1972).

515. Incidentally, a character played by the same actress who plays Dr Melfi in *The Sopranos*, Lorraine Bracco.

516. McCarty, *Bullets over Hollywood: The American Gangster Picture from the Silents to "the Sopranos,"* p. 219.

517. Ruth, *Inventing the Public Enemy: The Gangster in American Culture, 1918–34*. p. 140.

518. Ibid., 141.

519. Ingrid Walker Fields, "Family Values and Feudal Codes: The Social Politics of America's Twenty-First Century Gangster," *Journal of Popular Culture* 37.4 (2004): pp. 618–19. The critique of contemporary America in mob stories is always imbued with its Italian feudal origins, resonating with archetypal tribalism. The liberal reference to the Corleone name in *The Sopranos* not only invokes *The Godfather* films but the Sicilian town from which the film took the name. The town was particularly notable for being the birthplace of the brutal Sicilian Mafia boss Bernardo Provenzano, known as the Phantom of Corleone, due to his being on the run from Italian law enforcement from 1993 until his capture in 2006. See Stephen Corby, "De-Capo-Tated," *Sunday Telegraph* April 16, 2006: 2.

520. Leitch, *Crime Films* p. 103.

521. Fields, "Family Values and Feudal Codes: The Social Politics of America's Twenty-First Century Gangster," p. 615.

522. Ibid., 619.

523. "Cold Cuts," 5.10.

524. "Commendatori," 2.4.

525. In the season five finale "All Due Respect," 5.13.

526. *Gang Tapes*, dir. Adam Ripp, prod. Steve Wolfson and David Goodman, (USA: Lions Gate Films, 2002).

527. Six Reasons, *Gang Tapes*, Special Features: "The Making of Gang Tapes," DVD, Lions Gate Entertainment, 2004.

528. *Get Rich or Die Tryin'*, dir. Jim Sheridan, prods. Jimmy Levine, Paul Rosenberg, and Jim Sheridan. (USA: Paramount Pictures, 2005).

529. Elise Davidson, "For Rhymes against Humanity," *Sydney Morning Herald* January 13, 2006: 7.

530. Paul Byrnes, "Just Like a Rapper, This Doesn't Sing," *Sydney Morning Herald* January 19, 2006: 15.

531. That uncertainty about Tony's final fate is maintained in the last scene of the final episode of the series in season six. Tony sits in a restaurant with his family, the target of an imminent mob hit, as the screen fades to black with the audience not knowing the outcome.

532. *Buffy, the Vampire Slayer*, exec. prod. Joss Whedon (WB and UPN, 1997–2003).

533. "Selfless," 7.5. An episode from *Buffy, the Vampire Slayer*. Transcriptions of dialogue from the episodes are not my own but taken from that outstanding online resource assiduously compiled by the dedicated Victoria Spah, *Buffy Dialogue Database*, 2003. Available: http://vrya.net/bdb/quips/php, June 30, 2003. Transcripts.

534. This chapter is slightly revised from my earlier published article Gwyn Symonds, "'Solving Problems with Sharp Objects': Female Empowerment, Sex and Violence in *Buffy, the Vampire Slayer*," 2004, *Slayage: The Online International Journal of Buffy Studies*, April 11–12. Available: http:www.slayageonline.com/essays/slayage11_12/Symonds.htm, January 28, 2007.

535. Miguel Tejada-Flores, Wes Craven, Rusty Cardieff, Steven Gaydos, Debra Hill, and Neal Moritz, *Words into Pictures: I Know What You Screamed Last Summer*, Panel Discussion, VHS The Writer's Guild Foundation, Los Angeles, 1999. It is important to note that my discussion accepts Flores's qualification of "the best." The focus of this chapter is not on the uses of violence in less character driven examples of the horror genre known as slasher. However, Carol J. Clover wittily resurrects such films from the "cinematic underbrush" of theoretical discussion in her insightful analysis of the gender shift present in the role played by the final girl survivor in such films. (See Carol J. Clover, "Her Body, Himself: Gender in the Slasher Film," *Screening Violence*, ed. Stephen Prince (New Brunswick, New Jersey: Rutgers University Press, 2000), p. 125.) A longer discussion of that genre by the same author can be found in *Men, Women and Chainsaws: Gender in the Modern Horror Film* (Princeton, New Jersey: Princeton University Press, 1992). Brigid Cherry's research reveals that there is a significant female audience for the slasher horror genre which overlooks or interprets female stereotyping in ways that allows them to maintain viewing pleasure in the face of patriarchal readings in the films. See Brigid Cherry, "Refusing to Refuse to Look: Female Viewers of the Horror Film," *Horror, the Film Reader*, ed. Mark Janovich, In Focus: Routledge Film Readers (London: Routledge, 2002).

536. Tejada-Flores, Craven, Cardieff Gaydos, Hill and Moritz, *Words into Pictures: I Know What you Screamed Last Summer*.

537. Richard Maltby, *Hollywood Cinema*, 2nd edn. (Oxford: Blackwell, 2003), p. 354.

538. Joss Whedon, *Behind the Scenes of Buffy, the Vampire Slayer*, Panel Discussion, June 18, 2002, Academy of Television Arts and Sciences, Special Features, Season 6, Collectors Edition, Season 6, Disc 3, DVD Twentieth Century Fox Home Entertainment, 2003.

539. Ibid.

540. Anne Millard Daugherty, "Just a Girl: Buffy as Icon," *Reading the Vampire Slayer: An Unofficial Critical Companion to Buffy and Angel*, ed. Roz Kaveny (London: Tauris Parke Paperbacks, 2002), p. 153.

541. The show's interest in singling out gender as an issue for comment is a conscious attempt by Joss Whedon to distinguish his show from the more patriarchal aspects of the genre's past. An overview and an excellent history of the genre's interest in patriarchy, the family, apocalypse, alienation, and the critique of social institutions can be found in Mark Jancovich, *American Horror: From 1951 to the Present*, British Association for American Studies, Pamphlet 28 (Staffordshire: Keele University Press, 1994). Janovich makes the salient point that patriarchal or not, audiences can enjoy horror without accepting the genre's preferred readings. For analysis of generic horror cinema, family, and social repression see Vivian Sobchack, "Bringing It All Back Home: Family Economy and Generic Exchange," *American Horrors*, ed. Gregory A. Waller (Urbana: University of Illinois Press, 1987). Both *Buffy, the Vampire Slayer* and its offshoot series *Angel* maintain the genre's exploration of family, both traditional and alternative forms. For a discussion of that interest see Jes Battis, *Chosen Families in Buffy, the Vampire Slayer and Angel* (Jefferson, NC: McFarland, 2005). With specific reference to horror and family in *Angel* see Gwyn Symonds, "The Superhero Versus the Troubled Teen: Parenting Conner and the Fragility of Family in *Angel*," *Super/Heroes: From Hercules to Superman*, eds. Wendy Haslem, Angela Ndalianis, and Chris Mackie (Washington: New Academia Publishing, 2007).

542. Susan Hopkins, *Girl Heroes: The New Force in Popular Culture*, The Media Culture Series, ed. McKenzie Wark (Sydney: Pluto Press Australia, 2002).

543. The "Scoobies" designation is a reference to the friendship group in the Scooby Doo comic, animated, and film series. In *Buffy* the inner circle making up the group who fight evil are Buffy, Willow, and Xander who are mentored by their high school librarian and Watcher, Giles. At various points in the show there are fringe dwellers on the group such as Tara, Willow's lesbian lover; Anya, Xander's demon girlfriend; Cordelia, a catty high school rival; etc.

544. His friendship and love for the witch Willow, another of the Scoobies (who in grief at the death of her lesbian lover, Tara, has turned evil) persuades her to stop destroying the world. See "Grave," 6.22.

545. "The Gift." 5.22.

546. "The Zeppo," 3.13.

547. "Lessons," 7.1.

548. "Killed by Death," 2.18.

549. There is an illustrative slow motion training montage in the episode "Once More, with Feeling," 6.7.

550. "Sleeper," 7.8.

551. See Steve Wilson, "Laugh, Spawn of Hell, Laugh," *Reading the Vampire Slayer: An Unofficial Critical Companion to Buffy and Angel*, ed. Roz Kaveney (London: Tauris Park Paperbacks, 2002). Also Karen Eileen Overbey and Lahney Preston-Matto, "Staking in Tongues: Speech Act as Weapon in Buffy," *Fighting the Forces: What's at Stake in Buffy the Vampire Slayer*, eds. Rhonda V. Wilcox and David Lavery (Lanham: Rowan & Littlefield, 2002).

552. "Prophecy Girl," 1.12.

553. "Helpless," 3.12.

554. "Bargaining, Part 1," 6.1.

555. "Wild At Heart," 4.6.

556. "Selfless," 7.5.

557. "The Zeppo," 3.12.

558. Patricia Pender, "I'm Buffy and You're . . . History: The Postmodern Politics of Buffy," *Fighting the Forces: What's at Stake in Buffy the Vampire Slayer*, eds. Rhonda V. Wilcox and David Lavery (Lanham: Rowan & Littlefield, 2002), p. 36.

559. Ibid., 38.

560. Gina Wisker, "Vampires and Schoolgirls: Highschool Hijinks on the Hellmouth in Buffy the Vampire Slayer," 2001, *Slayage: The International Online Journal of Buffy Studies* 2. March 2001, Available: http://www.slayageonline.com/essays/slayagea2/wisker.htm, January 28, 2007.

561. Jim Thompson, "Just a Girl: Feminism, Postmodernism and *Buffy, the Vampire Slayer*," 2003, *Refractory: A Journal of Entertainment Media* 2. March 2003. Available: http:www.sfca.unimelb.edu. au/refractory/journalissues/vol2/jimthompson.htm, June 23, 2003.

562. "Buffyverse" is a term coined by fans and adopted by academic writers to denote the stage, setting, or totality of the show.

563. A Watcher is a guide assigned to a Slayer such as Buffy from the Watcher's Council based in Britain.

564. "Chosen," 7.22. While sharing her power allows Buffy to retire from having sole responsibility for saving the world as a Slayer, the sharing occurs in the series finale and the series does not have a convincing sense of feminist sisterhood. The effect is similar to the one Lillian S. Robinson describes in her discussion of *The Sensational She-Hulk*. "Unlike *Wonder Woman* in its feminist moments, *The Sensational She-Hulk* does not teach that sisterhood is powerful. It is *power* that is powerful, and power is most often modified with *super*." (Quoted from Lillian S. Robinson, *Wonder Women: Feminisms and Superheroes* (London: Routledge, 2004), p. 104.)

565. Vinay Menon, "The Eternal Buffy," May 17, 2003, *Toronto Star*. Available: http://www.thestar. com/NASApp/cs/ContentServer?pagename=thestar/Layout/Article_Type1&c=Article&cid=105225 1582169&call_pageid=968867495754&col=969483191630, May 18, 2003.

566. Sherryl Vint, "Killing Us Softly: A Feminist Search for the "Real" Buffy," 2001, *Slayage: The International Online Journal of Buffy Studies* 2. March 2001. Available: http://www.slayageonline.com/ essays/slayage5/vint.htmn, January 28, 2003. par. 24.

567. Joss Whedon, "10 Questions for Joss Whedon," Readers Opinions, 2003, *New York Times*, May 16, 2003. Available: http://www.nytimes.com/2003/05/16/readersopinions/16WHED.html?ex=10580 68800&en=f8e6a8f6097acef9&ei=5070, May 18, 2003.

568. Steve Murray and Phil Kloer, "Buffy's Deep Inner Meaning," May 17, 2003, *TheState.com*. Available: http://www.thestate.com/mid/thestate/5878387.htm, July 14, 2003.

569. Penelope Eckert and Sally McConnell-Ginet, *Language and Gender* (Cambridge: Cambridge University Press, 2003), p. 47.

570. E. Ann Kaplan, "Is the Gaze Male?" *Feminism and Film*, ed. E. Ann Kaplan, Oxford Readings in Feminism (Oxford: Oxford University Press, 2000), p. 129.

571. Rhonda V. Wilcox, *Why Buffy Matters: The Art of Buffy, the Vampire Slayer* (London: I. B. Tauris, 2006), p. 59.

572. "Chosen," 7.22.

573. Jackie Stacey, "Desperately Seeking Difference," *Feminism and Film*, ed. E. Ann Kaplan, Oxford Readings in Feminism (Oxford: Oxford University Press, 2000), p. 450.

574. "Gone," 6.11.

575. Mary Ann Doane, "Film and the Masquerade: Theorising the Female Spectator," *Feminism and Film*, ed. E. Ann Kaplan, Oxford Readings in Feminism (Oxford: Oxford University Press, 2000), p. 421.

576. Ibid., 129.

577. "Gone," 6.11.

578. "Dead Things," 6.13.

579. Gender reversal in the context of a romantic or sexual relationship with a violent woman is not confined to *Buffy*, of course. For further discussion of the complexity of the use of violent women in love and gender complementarity in the cinema see Hilary Neroni, *The Violent Woman: Femininity, Narrative, and Violence in Contemporary American Culture*, Suny Series in Feminist Criticism and Theory, ed. Michelle A. Masse (New York: State University of New York Press, 2005). There is also an extensive discussion of horror and the often limited generic opportunities that it provides for gender-bending its subject and alternating between the female and male gaze. See Linda Badley, *Film, Horror, and the Body Fantastic* (Westport, Connecticut: Greenwood Press, 1995).

580. L. Mulvey, "Visual Pleasure and Narrative Cinema," *Feminism and Film*, ed. E. Ann Kaplan, Oxford Readings in Feminism (Oxford: Oxford University Press, 2000). This reference is a reprint of Mulvey's 1975 journal article in *Screen* 16.3 (Autumn).

581. "Once More With Feeling," 6.7.

582. "Dead Things," 6.13.

583. Kaplan, "Is the Gaze Male?," p. 135.

584. "Life Serial," 6.5.

585. "Inca Mummy Girl," 2.4.

586. Faith is a rogue Slayer who completes her own journey from evil back to good on the show and in crossovers to the spin-off series *Angel*.

587. "Dead Things," 6.13.

588. Kate O'Hare, "'Buffy' Relationship Tips Into Domestic Violence," February 8, 2002, *Psi Fi*. Available: http://pub128.ezboard.com/fpsififrm55.showMessage?topicID=42.topic, July 9, 2003.

589. "Ted," 2.11.

590. Fred Topol, *Ending Buffy: Talking About the Buffy Series Finale*, Action Adventure Movies 2003, About.com. Available: http://actionadventure.about.com/cs/weeklystories/a/aa041903.htm#b, July 7, 2003.

591. "Amends," 3.10.

592. Of course, the erotics of violence are not necessarily a gender-based issue any more than love or lust are. The emotionally resonant *Brokeback Mountain* (2005) is a recent film that reflects the relationship intimacy of that paradox from a same gender perspective. It is the love story of two men who convey their feelings of love and lust through elements of violence that reflect both eroticism and the difficulties encountered in coming to terms with, and expressing, what they feel for each other.

593. "Entropy," 6.18.

594. Mary Hammond, "Monsters and Metaphors: *Buffy the Vampire Slayer* and the Old World," *Cult Television*, eds. Sara Gwenllian-Jones and Roberta E. Pearson (Minneapolis: University of Minnesota Press, 2004), p. 161.

595. Patrick Lee, "The Creators of Buffy Head into Season Seven with a Lighter Heart," 2002, *scifi.com*. Available: http://www.scifi.com/sfw/issue282/interview.html, July 7, 2003.

596. "The Wish," 3.9.

597. "Into the Woods," 5.10.

598. "I Only Have Eyes For You," 2.19.

599. "What's My Line? Part 2," 2.10.

600. "Never Leave Me," 7.9.

601. Film Force, "An Interview with Joss Whedon: The Creator of *Buffy, the Vampire Slayer* Discusses His Career," June 23, 2003, *IGN.com*. Available: http://filmforce.ign.com/articles/425/425492p1.html, June 28, 2003, par. 8.

602. "Smashed," 6.9.

603. In the horror genre having sex often leads to violent disaster for female characters and how far Buffy's emotional problems remain outside that patriarchal trope remains an open question. For an analysis arguing that the show's representation of sex and desire is ultimately repressive see Dawn Heinecken, *The Warrior Women: A Feminist Cultural Analysis of the New Female Body in Popular Media* (New York: Peter Lang, 2003).

604. Lyn Phillips, *Flirting with Danger: Young Women's Reflections on Sexuality and Domination* (New York: New York University Press, 2000), p. 69.

605. Diane Dekelb-Rittenhouse, "Sex and the Single Vampire: The Evolution of the Vampire Lothario and Its Representation in Buffy," *Fighting the Forces: What's at Stake in Buffy the Vampire Slayer*, eds. Rhonda V. Wilcox and David Lavery (Lanham: Rowan & Littlefield, 2002), p. 146.

606. "Out of Mind, Out of Sight (Invisible Girl)," 1.11.

607. Robin Wood, "Burying the Undead: The Use and Obsolescence of Count Dracula," *The Dread of Difference: Gender and the Horror Film*, ed. Barry Keith Grant (Austin: University of Texas Press, 1996), p. 365.

608. Ibid., 369.

609. Ibid., 368.

610. "Dead Things," 6.13.

611. "Wrecked," 6.10.

612. "Dead Things," 6.13.

613. "Entropy," 6.18.

614. Rhonda V. Wilcox, "'Every Night I Save You:' Buffy, Spike, Sex and Redemption," 2002, *Slayage: The International Online Journal of Buffy Studies* May 5, 2002. Available: http://www.slayageonline.com/essays/slayage5/wilcox.htm, January 28, 2007, par. 18.

615. Phillips, *Flirting with Danger: Young Women's Reflections on Sexuality and Domination* p. 78.

616. Vivian Burr, "Ambiguity and Sexuality in Buffy the Vampire Slayer: A Sartrean Analysis," *Sexualities* 6.3–4 (2003).

617. "As You Were," 6.15.

618. "Wrecked," 6.10.

619. Buffy reveals to the Scoobies, who used magic to bring her back from the dead and what they thought might be a hell dimension, that they ripped her out of what she thought was Heaven and a

sense of completeness. (See "Once More, with Feeling," 6.7.) It is the loss of that afterlife sense of peace which causes her depression-like state after her resurrection.

620. Phillips, *Flirting with Danger: Young Women's Reflections on Sexuality and Domination* p. 3.

621. "Seeing Red," 6.19.

622. "Dead Things," 6.13.

623. "As You Were," 6.15.

624. "Seeing Red," 6.19.

625. Clover, "Her Body, Himself: Gender in the Slasher Film," p. 130.

626. For further discussion of normality as an ideological space and the monstrous as a challenge to patriarchal repression in the horror genre generally see Robin Wood, "An Introduction to the American Horror Film," *Planks of Reason: Essays on the Horror Film*, ed. Barry Keith Grant (Metuchen, New Jersey: Scarecrow Press, 1984).

627. "Buffy Vs Dracula," 5.1.

628. For a more extensive discussion of the effect of this aspect of the portrayal of Spike by the actor see Symonds, "'Playing More Soul Than is Written': James Marsters' Performance of Spike and the Ambiguity of Evil in Sunnydale."

629. Wood, "Burying the Undead: The Use and Obsolescence of Count Dracula," p. 378.

630. "Seeing Red," 6.19.

631. Symonds, "'Bollocks!': Spike Fans and Reception of *Buffy the Vampire Slayer*."

632. Abbie Bernstein, "Blonde Ambition," *Buffy the Vampire Slayer, Official Magazine* 8 June/July 2003: 20.

633. The term canon is used by fans and academics who write on the show to describe mythical givens of the storyline. In Spike's case, the canon he is bound by is the show's premise that a vampire cannot, due to his evil nature, decide to seek to have his soul returned to him. The only other vampire with a soul in the Buffyverse, Angel, had his soul forced back into him through a gypsy curse.

634. Bernstein, "Blonde Ambition," p. 20.

635. Jane Espenson, "Interview Succubus Club," Hour One, May 22, 2002, *slayage.com* Transcript: rally@rallyvincent.com. Available: http://www.slayage.com/news/020522-je_int.html, July 7, 2003. Also at Espenson's Web site at http:www.janeespenson.com/media.php January 28, 2007.

636. "Beneath You," 6.2. In this episode, Spike tells Buffy that he now has a soul that he went to get so that he would never hurt her again.

637. Espenson, "Interview Succubus Club," Hour One.

638. Gwynneth Rhys, "Why Spike as Rapist Feels Like Character Rape to Me or, Seeing Red Over Seeing." Red, 2002, *Chez Gwyn*. Available: http://www.drizzle.com/~gwyneth/morestuff/spike.html, July 20, 2003.

639. Bernstein, "Blonde Ambition," p. 20.

640. Sarah Projansky, *Watching Rape: Film and Television in Post-Feminist Culture* (New York: New York University Press, 2001), p. 230.

641. Jacinda Read, *The New Avengers: Feminism, Femininity and the Rape-Revenge Cycle* (Manchester: Manchester University Press, 2000).

642. Rebecca Rand-Kirshner, *Life as the Big Bad:* A Season Six Overview, Buffy, the Vampire Slayer, Special Features, Disc 6, Collectors Edition, DVD Twentieth Century Fox Home Entertainment, 2003.

643. "Living Conditions," 4.2.

644. "Pangs," 4.8.

645. Buffy tells Angel that she is unbaked cookie dough and will only be ready for a relationship when she is baked.

646. Marni Noxon, "Interview in Watch with Wanda: Grill, Gossip and Gripe," March 29, 2002, *Eonline.com*. Available: http://www.eonline.com/Gossip/Wanda/Archive2002/020329b.html, July 14, 2003.

647. Steve Hockensmith, *Dialogue with 'Buffy' Creator Joss Whedon*, May 16, 2003, Hollywood Reporter. Available: http://story.news.yahoo.com/news?tmpl=story&u=/nm/20030520/en_nm/television_whedon_dc_1, May 16, 2003.

648. Menon, "The Eternal Buffy."

649. This title references that of an interview with the action director John Woo in Richard Setlove, "Woo: Getting Kicks from Action Pix," *Variety* November 18–24, 1996: 25.

650. Sian Stott, "Film-Makers on Film: Joss Whedon: Joss Whedon Talks to Siân Stott About Vincent Minnelli's Brigadoon (1954)," Arts Home, March 4, 2006, *film.telegraph*. Available: http://www.telegraph.co.uk/arts/main.jhtml?xml=/arts/2006/03/04/bffmof04.xml&menuId=564&sSheet=/arts/2006/03/04/ixfilmmain.html, March 5, 2006.

651. Susan L. Foster, "Textual Evidences: Organizing Dance's History," *Bodies of the Text*, eds. Ellen W. Goellner and Jacqueline Shea Murphy (New Brunswick, New Jersey: Rutgers University Press, 1995), p. 234.

652. *Beautiful Boxer*, dir. Ekachai Uekrongtham, prod. Ekachai Uekrongtham (Thailand: GMM Pictures, 2003). The film can found with subtitles on DVD in the well-known Eastern Eye Asian Cinema collection.

653. Jose Arroya, "Mission Sublime," *Action Spectacle Cinema*, ed. Jose Arroya (London: BFI Publishing, 2000), p. 22.

654. As Diane Sandars reveals in her discussion of the generic hybridization of the fight sequence embodying the aesthetics of techno and rave musical performance in 1990's sci-fi films such as *The Matrix*, the use of the analogy with the Musical to describe the use of fight scenes is not new. (See Diana Sandars, "From the Warehouse to the Multiplex: Techno and Rave Culture's Reconfiguration of Late 1990's Sci-Fi Spectacle as Musical Performance," July 29, 2005, *Screening the Past*, 18. Available: http://www.latrobe.edu.au/screeningthepast/firstrelease/fr_18/DSfr18a.html, April 13, 2006. It is generally held that Stuart Kaminsky was the first to make the comparison between the Musical and the martial arts film. See Stuart M. Kaminsky, "Kung Fu Film as Ghetto Myth," *Journal of Popular Film* 3.2 (1974). Also Stuart Kaminsky, *American Film Genres*, 2nd edn. (Chicago: Nelson-Hall, 1984). Leon Hunt even notes that the analogy is now almost a cliché. Despite Hunt's view, this chapter is based on the belief that there is more that needs to be said with greater specificity about the convergence of the two forms. For Hunt's analysis see Leon Hunt, *Kung Fu Cult Masters: From Bruce Lee to Crouching Tiger* (London: Wallflower Press, 2003).

655. Ellen W. Goellner, "Force and Form in Faulkner's *Light in August*," *Bodies of the Text: Dance as Theory, Literature as Dance*, eds. Ellen W. Goellner and Jacqueline Shea Murphy (New Brunswick, New Jersey: Rutgers University Press, 1995), p. 43.

656. David Bordwell, *Planet Hong Kong: Popular Cinema and the Art of Entertainment* (Cambridge, Massachusetts: Harvard University Press, 2000), p. 199.

657. Quoted in Robert K. Elder, *John Woo Interviews*, Conversations with Filmmakers, ed. Peter Brunette (Jackson: University Press of Mississippi, 2005), p. 176.

658. Stephen Prince, "The Aesthetic of Slow-Motion Violence in the Films of Sam Peckinpah," *Screening Violence*, ed. Stephen Prince (New Brunswick, New Jersey: Rutgers University Press, 2000).

659. Quoted in J. Hoberman, "Nietzsche's Boy," *Action Spectacle Cinema: A Sight and Sound Reader*, ed. Jose Arroyo (London: BFI Publishing, 2000), p. 30.

660. *Die Hard*, dir. John McTiernan, prod. Lawrence Gordon and Joel Silver, (USA: Twentieth Century Fox Film Corporation, 1988). There is a tradition of cinema self-reflexively deconstructing the spectator position posited by its own use of violence. Nowhere more graphically than in Stanley Kubrick's use of music and the musical as a counterpoint to his use of violence in *A Clockwork Orange*. The film puts its sadomasochistic violence in musical contexts that heighten its satirical effects. The association of the musical form directly with violence on screen was memorably done with an effect that is the opposite of the transformation of violence argued for in this chapter. The main character, Alex, along with his gang, engages in the violent beating of a married couple and the raping of the wife while dancing a parody of Gene Kelly's dance steps and the song "Singin' in the Rain" from the film of the same name. The use of the song serves to increase the visceral horror of the violence being perpetrated while stylistically staging it at arms length through its theatricality. The song, which still retains its catchy tunefulness in that context, leaves the audience experiencing a disjunction between a sense of being entertained and of unease in viewing violence made disturbing by contrast with the perversion of the song's meaning. For a more detailed discussion of the effects of this complex scene and the film's use of music see (passim) Margaret DeRosia, "An Erotics of Violence: Masculinity and (Homo)Sexuality in Stanley Kubrick's *A Clockwork Orange*," *Stanley Kubrick's A Clockwork Orange*, ed. Stuart Y. McDougal (Cambridge: Cambridge University Press, 2003).

661. Larry Gross, "Big and Loud," *Action Spectacle Cinema: A Sight and Sound Reader*, ed. Jose Arroyo (London: BFI Publishing, 2000).

662. Jason Jacobs, "Gunfire," *Action Spectacle Cinema: A Sight and Sound Reader*, ed. Jose Arroyo (London: BFI Publishing, 2000).

663. Elder, *John Woo Interviews* p. 176.

664. Catherine Foster, "Fight Coach Toils to Make Violent Scenes Bloody Good," *Boston Globe* August 5, 2005: D.6.

665. Hunt, *Kung Fu Cult Masters: From Bruce Lee to Crouching Tiger* p. 25.

666. Christopher Probst, "Welcome to the Machine," p. 1, April 1999, *American Cinematographer*. Available: http://www.theasc.com/magazine/apr99/matrix/pg1.htm, March 13, 2003, 2.

667. Frank Miller, *Batman: The Dark Knight Returns* (New York: DC Comics, 2002) Book 4, pp. 190–92.

668. J. Aeon Skoble, "Superhero Revisionism in *Watchmen* and *the Dark Knight Returns*," *Superheroes and Philosophy: Truth, Justice and the Socratic Way*, eds. Tom Morris and Matt Morris (Chicago, Illinois: Open Court, 2005), p. 32. The action heroes under discussion in this chapter tend to avoid the revisionism of contemporary graphic novels like *Watchmen* and *The Dark Knight Returns* which views the superhero as also a force for repression. Their actions proclaim the heroic clarity embodied in the traditional Superman ethos. For an outline of the classic traits of that ethos see Richard Reynolds, *Superheroes: A Modern Mythology* (London: B. T. Batsford Ltd., 1992). For further discussion of the self-appointed vigilante justice that revisionary versions of the superhero foreground, with the hero sharing some of the darker character traits of the villains they oppose see Geoff Klock, *How to Read Superhero Comics and Why* (New York: Continuum, 2002). The links that a cleansing use of violence has with the mythology of the American West and its Puritan origins is classically discussed

in Richard Slotkin, *Regeneration Through Violence: The Mythology of the American Frontier, 1600–1860* (Middletown, Connecticut: Wesleyan University Press, 1973).

669. An exemplary tour through that genre can be had in the pithy, wackily expressive Stefan Hammond and Mike Wilkins, *Sex and Zen & a Bullet in the Head: The Essential Guide to Hong Kong's Mind-Bending Films* (New York: Fireside: Simon & Schuster, 1996). More scholarly histories include Stephen Teo, *Hong Kong Cinema: The Extra Dimensions* (London: BFI Publishing, 1997) and Bordwell, *Planet Hong Kong: Popular Cinema and the Art of Entertainment.*

670. Probst, *Welcome to the Machine.* The Wachowski brothers may be trying to distinguish that kind of fight text from the style resurrected by the Rock in *Walking Tall* which the latter describes as not being like "today's cinematic world of all the explosions and the gun play, the knife play and every-thing else you can possibly imagine, and people floating through the air. There is none of that. It is just straight up, old fashioned, old school, hard-nosed, blue collar, four by four, piece of cedar, all day long, fresh-assed wupping." Quoted from The Rock, "Fight the Good Fight," *Walking Tall*, Special Features, DVD MGM Home Entertainment, 2005. A similar desire to return to less stylized fight as more authentic can be found in martial arts critique preferring "pull-no-punches action" over wire work. See Rick Baker and Toby Russell, *The Essential Guide to Hong Kong Movies* (London: Eastern Heroes, 1994), p. 47.

671. Scott McMillin, *The Musical as Drama: A Study of the Principles and Conventions Behind Musical Shows from Kern to Sondheim* (Princeton and Oxford: Princeton University Press, 2006), p. 2.

672. Kevin Maher, "What's Behind the Gore?" *Observer* January 12, 2003.

673. Jane Mills, *The Money Shot: Cinema, Sin and Censorship* (Sydney: Pluto Press Australia, 2001), p. 215.

674. A. O. Scott, "True Horror: When Movie Violence Is Random," *New York Times* March 23, 2003: 2.

675. For a sample discussion on the difference between innovative action and cliché focusing on the work of the action director John Woo see Manhola Dargis, "Do You Like John Woo?" *Action Spectacle Cinema: A Sight and Sound Reader*, ed. Jose Arroya (London: BFI Publishing, 2000).

676. Michelle Lekas, "Ultrasound: The Feminine in the Age of Mechanical Reproduction," *Music and Cinema*, eds. James Buhler, Caryl Flinn, and David Neumeyer (Hanover: Weslyan University Press, 2000), p. 280. Sandars has a discussion of the explicit link between opera and a fight in the sci-fi film *The Fifth Element* in the internet article cited above. The link between the theatricality of combat in Hong Kong martial arts films and that of the Peking Opera, whose troupes were a training ground for martial arts actors and choreographers such as Jackie Chan, is discussed in Bordwell, *Planet Hong Kong: Popular Cinema and the Art of Entertainment.*

677. Sandars, "From the Warehouse to the Multiplex: Techno and Rave Culture's Reconfiguration of Late 1990's Sci-Fi Spectacle as Musical Performance."

678. Stephen Citron, *The Musical: From the Inside Out* (London: Hodder & Stoughton, 1991), p. 175.

679. Hunt, *Kung Fu Cult Masters: From Bruce Lee to Crouching Tiger* p. 26.

680. Murray, "Cover Boys," 17–18.

681. Goellner, "Force and Form in Faulkner's *Light in August*," p. 184.

682. While the film was released in 1971 and earlier DVD releases are still available the best way of viewing the film would be in the recently digitally remastered and restored DVD transfer in the Hong Kong Legend series, *The Big Boss*, dir. Wei Lo, prod. Raymond Chow, *Hong Kong Legends*, remas-tered edn., (Hong Kong: Contender Entertainment Group, 2005).

683. The transliteration of the character's name is taken from the film's subtitles. A range of versions can be found in discussions of the film. See "Cheng Chui-On" in Teo, *Hong Kong Cinema: The Extra Dimensions*.

684. Part of the affective impact of moments like these in any Bruce Lee fight text, unavailable to Western audiences, is its nationalistic concerns as a defense of Chinese honor in a Thai context. For a discussion of this and the text's narcissism see Teo, *Hong Kong Cinema: The Extra Dimensions*.

685. As Richard Dyer in his review of the action film *Speed* breezily appreciates, action means providing the audience with an adrenaline rush that drives the pace of the film rather than characterization: "No naff attempts at psychologising the villain: he's a nutcase." See Richard Dyer, "Action!" *Action Spectacle Cinema: A Sight and Sound Reader*, ed. Jose Arroya (London: BFI Publishing, 2000), p. 17.

686. Hunt, *Kung Fu Cult Masters: From Bruce Lee to Crouching Tiger* p. 28. Hunt takes his use of the phrases "wicked shapes" and "wicked lies" from a fan vignette in Stefan Hammond's book *Hollywood East* that shows an audience distinguishing between stunt effects that are lame "lies" and effects that are clever or "wicked lies." "Shapes" refers to frozen fighting stances. An analogy can be fruitfully made between this aesthetic and the still motion captured in dance photography, exemplified by artists such as Lois Greenfield in her book *Breaking Bounds*. "Here, writ large for the audience, are those 'frozen moments' she is so fascinated by: a body snapped in mid-twist, a leap caught in one split second frame (1/2000th of a second, to be precise), and dramatically illuminated by strobe lights." Quoted from Sharon Verghis, "Collaboration Sets Off Motion Senses," *Sydney Morning Herald* August 10, 2004: 15.

687. The arrival of the police at the end of a film to make a point that the use of violence in this way is a crime was a Hong Kong martial arts film conceit when the film was made. Coming after the visceral acrobatics of the fight text it remains, as Cheng is led away, a cursory gesture to the public attitude to violence held outside the screen.

688. Teo, *Hong Kong Cinema: The Extra Dimensions* p. 110. As Teo points out, Chinese audiences of the film, with more knowledge of martial arts than Westerners, would have seen Lee's achievements as achievable with skill and training and more than a cinematic illusion.

689. Hunt, *Kung Fu Cult Masters: From Bruce Lee to Crouching Tiger* p. 29.

690. Ibid., 35.

691. Hunt has a full discussion of the martial arts genre's and the fans' concerns with fight authenticity, which Hunt separates into archival authenticity, cinematic authenticity (a desire for transparent mediation), and corporeal authenticity (the proven physical risk taken by the actor, often present in outtakes, as in the Jackie Chan films). See Hunt, *Kung Fu Cult Masters: From Bruce Lee to Crouching Tiger*. For the purposes of my interests in this chapter, the debate is not of central concern as the absence of authentic violence in the fight text is something I take as a given.

692. *Crouching Tiger, Hidden Dragon* (*Wo Hu Cang Long*), dir. Ang Lee, prod. Li-Kong Hsu, Bill Kwong, and Ang Lee (Taiwan, Hong Kong, China: Sony Pictures, 2000).

693. The basis for Chinese martial arts hero films since the 1920s before the less supernatural Kung Fu style had its impact on martial arts films in the 1960s. See Craig D. Reid, "Fighting Without Fighting: Film Action Fight Choreography," *Film Quarterly* 47.2. Winter (1993–94).

694. Ken-fang Lee, "Far Away, So Close: Cultural Translation in Ang Lee's Crouching Tiger, Hidden Dragon," *Inter-Asia Cultural Studies* 4.2 (2003).

695. Bordwell, *Planet Hong Kong: Popular Cinema and the Art of Entertainment* p. 220.

696. Stephen Dunne, "Flights of Fantasy," *Sydney Morning Herald* April 1–2, 2006: 2.

697. Dunne, "Flights of Fantasy," p. 3.

698. Karen Mackendrick, "Embodying Transgression," *Of the Presence of the Body: Essays on Dance and Performance Theory*, ed. Andre Lepecki (Middletown, Connecticut: Wesleyan University Press, 2004), p. 141.

699. Michael Bawtree, *The New Singing Theatre: A Charter for the Music Theatre Movement* (Bristol: The Bristol Press, 1990), p. 162.

700. The word "chopsocky" was coined to describe low-budget, B-grade Hong Kong martial arts films, often seen in the West with atrocious translations, with wildly improbable plots, and extensive mayhem. Much of the satire and denigration of the films, which has led to overlooking of some of the cult-audience appreciated moments in the genre, has resulted from poor dubbing and subtitling of the films, particularly with nonsensical phrases added to put the dialogue in sync with actor mouth movements. As Hammond and Wilkins note: "Poorly dubbed into English, a never changing stable of hammy voice-overs delivered in dialogue like 'Chan, you're too arrogant, see? So we're going to chop off your arms" (*The Crippled Avengers*)." Quoted from Stefan Hammond and Mike Wilkins, *Sex, and Zen & a Bullet in the Head* (New York: Fireside: Simon & Schuster, 1996), p. 204.

701. This attempt to constantly increase the spectacle of the fight is also true of car chase scenes in films.

702. All comments on this film relate to the uncut Thai version of the film which is available, along with the version released to western audiences (designated the French version) on Disc 1 of the DVD release. See Prachya Pinkaew, *Ong Bak*, Eastern Eye Asian Cinema, Sahamongkol Film International, Madman Entertainment Pty. Ltd. DVD, the AV Channel Pty. Ltd., Thailand, 2003. The DVD release is also valuable for its special features section on Disc 2 which gives a captivating insight into how the fights were choreographed, trained for, and shot.

703. Panna Rittikrai, *Cast and Crew Interviews*, *Ong Bak* Documentary and Interviews, Disc 2, DVD Eastern Eye Asian Cinema, 2003.

704. The characterization of objects in the dance narrative is a well-known convention of the Musical, the most classic examples being Fred Astaire's use of the coat stand in *Royal Wedding* (1951) or Gene Kelly's use of the umbrella in *Singin' in the Rain* (1952). Sandars ascribes the same status to bullets in fight scenes in *The Matrix* where Neo dodges them. See Sandars, "From the Warehouse to the Multiplex: Techno and Rave Culture's Reconfiguration of Late 1990's Sci-Fi Spectacle as Musical Performance."

705. Eric Bauer, "Sex, Violence and Spec-Scripts: Interview with Shane Black," *Creative Screenwriting* 3 (Winter).3 (1996): 33.

706. Gary Soden, *Falling* (New York: W. W. Norton & Company, 2003), p. 305. Soden uses the phrase to describe participatory gravity-defying experiences like thrill rides or bungee jumping or audience observation of entertainment like trapeze artists and wire walkers.

707. *The Matrix Reloaded*, dir. Andy Wachowski and Larry Wachowski, prod. Joel Silver and Andrew Mason (USA: Warner Bros. Pictures, 2003).

708. The hero in the film is initially introduced as John Anderson. Neo is a reversal of the One he becomes, the savior of humanity in the face of the Machines.

709. An effect that Sandars convincingly argues is a part of the film's unisex rave culture aesthetic. See Sandars, "From the Warehouse to the Multiplex: Techno and Rave Culture's Reconfiguration of Late 1990's Sci-Fi Spectacle as Musical Performance."

710. The Wachowski brothers called the slow/fast motion action of the images "bullet time." See Probst, *Welcome to the Machine*. Probably the most exact description of the effect is in Michele Pierson, *Special Effects: Still in Search of Wonder*, Film and Culture, ed. John Belton (New York: Columbia University Press, 2002), p. 163. "What came to be referred to as "Bullet-Time" or "Flow-Mo" was a technique for creating the illusion of movement around objects in the foreground. In defiance of the natural laws of cinematography, elements of the filming could be made to appear to be moving at different speeds ... *The Matrix* featured this technique in a number of key action sequences combining stunts with subtle 2D and 3D animation." The use of speed and motion in *The Matrix* as a reflection of social and cultural lifestyle and work realities where "Time must be expanded at the same time it is accelerated," is posited by Joseph Natoli, *Memory's Orbit: Film and Culture 1999–2000*, The Suny Series in Postmodern Culture, ed. Joseph Natoli (Albany: State University of New York Press, 2003), p. 34.

711. Aylish Wood, "The Collapse of Reality and Illusion in *the Matrix*," *Action and Adventure Cinema*, ed. Yvonne Tasker (London: Routledge, 2004), p. 124.

712. Though she is brought back from death once, he cannot save her a second time and she dies at the end of the trilogy.

713. Wood, "The Collapse of Reality and Illusion in *the Matrix*."

714. Jake Horsley, *The Blood Poets: A Cinema of Savagery 1958–99* vol. 2, Millennial Blues: From Apocalypse Now to The Matrix, p. 432.

715. Early in the first part of the trilogy, Neo is given a copy of *Simulacra and Simulation* and opens it at the chapter "On Nihilism."

716. Horsley, *The Blood Poets: A Cinema of Savagery 1958–99* vol. 2, p. 433.

717. The indulgence in special effects in *The Matrix: Revolutions* (2003), the final film in the trilogy, becomes repetitive. While the special effects violence remains spectacular in the fight in the rain between Agent Smith and Neo—leading to Smith's defeat and Neo's quasicrucifixion and self-sacrifice—its overuse kills the thrill. It is a fight of slow motion rain drops, spraying water, lightning flashes, shattering glass, and the protagonists bodies in collisions with blows of seismic affect as they grapple in the air, smash into buildings, or plummet to the ground in cataclysmic motion. The special effects orgy loses the sense of the liberated body, as well as any sense of drama, by the scene running too long.

718. Horsley, *The Blood Poets: A Cinema of Savagery 1958–99* vol. 2, p. 433.

719. Wood, "The Collapse of Reality and Illusion in *the Matrix*," p. 125.

720. Ibid., 126.

721. The trilogy has received extensive academic interest for its philosophical underpinnings, something the film encourages with its direct reference in the film to Jean Baudrillard's *Simulacra and Simulation*. A central source of discussion of the films philosophical interests is William Irwin, *The Matrix and Philosophy: Welcome to the Desert of the Real*, Popular Culture and Philosophy, vol. 3 (Chicago, Illinois: Open Court, 2002). Contrasting views in the debate on whether the distinction between the real world and the virtual world is clear in the film can be found in David Lavery, "From Cinescape to Cyberspace: Zionists and Agents, Realists and Gamers in *the Matrix* and *Existenz*," *Journal of Popular Film and Television* 28.4 (2001) (for the affirmative) and Wood, "The Collapse of Reality and Illusion in *the Matrix*" (for the negative). Yet, it is less the image of human bodies trapped in the Matrix that the audience remembers than the technological liberation of the body from the forces of gravity in a virtual dreamscape of kinetic fighting energy. The cinematic philosophical

treatise on the nature of the real and its virtual subversion is the least interesting part of the Matrix trilogy, it is the staging of the fantasy about the potentiality of the body that is the delight of the film experience. The interface between bodies and machines as a filmic subject in *The Matrix* is not new but is of particular interest to the science-fiction genre with its cyborg and artificial intelligence themes—which Forest Pyle argues is itself a tradition that extends back to Mary Shelley's *Franken-stein*. As Pyle notes with reference to *Blade Runner* and the *Terminator* franchises, there is a cultural and cinematic interest in the way "we make and, on occasion, unmake our conceptions of ourselves." (See Forest Pyle, "Making Cyborgs, Making Humans: Of Terminators and Blade Runners," *Film Theory Goes to the Movies*, eds. Jim Collins, Hilary Radner, and Ava Preacher Collins, AFI Film Readers (New York: Routledge, 1993), p. 228.)

722. Jane Feuer, "The Self-Reflexive Musical and the Myth of Entertainment," *Film Genre Reader III*, ed. Barry Keith Grant (Austin: University of Texas Press, 2003).

723. Phillip Strick, "The Matrix," *Action Spectacle Cinema: A Sight and Sound Reader*, ed. Jose Arroya (London: BFI Publishing, 2000), p. 261.

724. Angela Ndalianis, *Neo-Baroque Aesthetics and Contemporary Entertainment*, Media in Transition, ed. David Thorburn (Cambridge, Massachusetts: The MIT Press, 2004), p. 212.

725. Horsley, *The Blood Poets: A Cinema of Savagery 1958–99* vol. 2, p. 433.

726. Mackendrick, "Embodying Transgression," p. 141.

727. John Shelton Lawrence and Robert Jewett, *The Myth of the American Superhero* (Grand Rapids, Michigan: William B. Eardmans Publishing Company, 2002), p. 295.

728. Simon Gray, "Rebooting a Sci-Fi Spectacular," Index, June 19, 2003, *American Cinemato-grapher*. Available: http://www.theasc.com/magazine/june03/cover/index.html, March 13, 2004.

729. The fight with the staff appears the most computer generated in effect, as does some of the flying effects. It is in the landings when the camera pauses on close-ups of Neo and Agent Smith, and the actors' bodies that one has a greater sense of the body's gravity-bound solidity.

730. As John Zavodny notes, discussing the film *Fight Club*'s view of fighting of "unmediated animal aggression," as being a means to self-knowledge, this is essentially a Romantic view of personal authenticity and identity. See John Zavodny, "I Am Jack's Wasted Life: *Fight Club* and Personal Identity," *Movies and the Meaning of Life: Philosophers Take on Hollywood*, eds. Kimberly A. Blessing and Paul J. Tudico (Chicago, Illinois: Open Court, 2005). Self-realization through violence is a com-mon theme, particularly in decades of Hollywood boxing films.

731. The thrill of the fight text in this film, as with action films in general, is as much the product of the musical underscore and the Foley sound effects. Music energizes, dramatizes, and comments on the aesthetic of the fight text. Audio manipulation to enhance the percussive sound of the impact of a blow or bullet for audience entertainment creates a far different sound to the way they would be heard in actuality and contributes to the exhilaration of fight text fantasy.

732. *Kill Bill: Volume 1*, dir. Quentin Tarantino, prod. Lawrence Bender, (USA: Miramax Films, 2003).

733. *Kill Bill: Volume 2*.

734. Geoff Andrew, "Killing Joke," *Time Out* September 24–28, 1994: 24.

735. Quentin Tarantino, *The Making of Kill Bill Volume 2*, Special Features, Kill Bill Volume 2, DVD Buena Vista Home Entertainment .

736. John Pavlus, "A Bride Vows Revenge," October 2003, *American Cinematographer*. Available: http://www.theasc.com/magazine/oct03/cover/index.html, March 13, 2004, p. 1.

737. Ibid. 1.

738. Horsley, *The Blood Poets: A Cinema of Savagery 1958–99* vol. 2, pp. 230–31.

739. Reid, "Fighting without Fighting: Film Action Fight Choreography," p. 31.

740. Horsley, *The Blood Poets: A Cinema of Savagery 1958–99* vol. 2, p. 220.

741. Peter Conrad, "The Art of Pain," *Observer* April 4, 2004: 6.

742. Quoted from Foster, "Fight Coach Toils to Make Violent Scenes Bloody Good," D. 6.

743. Bordwell, *Figures Traced in Light: On Cinematic Staging* p. 239.

744. Shai Biderman, "The Roar and the Rampage: A Tale of Revenge in *Kill Bill Volumes 1 and 2*," *Movies and the Meaning of Life: Philosophers Take on Hollywood*, eds. Kimberly A. Blessing and Paul J. Tudico (Chicago, Illinois: Open Court, 2005), p. 201.

745. B. Ruby Rich, "Day of the Woman," Features, June 2004, *Sight and Sound*. Available: http://www.bfi.org.uk/cgi-bin/wac.cgi/http://www.bfi.org.uk/sightandsound/2004_06/killbill.php, June 17, 2004.

746. Discussion of whether there are gender-related preferences for action flicks that relate to the primacy given to the fight text is a question that has some relevance to the limits that might be put upon the amount of screen time given to the Bride as a rounded character outside of her role as martial arts hero. Whether such a perception about audiences for action flicks is a production consideration is discussed in Judy Muller, Shane Black, Manohola Dargis, Leslie Dixon, Buffy Shutt, Alex Siskin, and Courteny Valenti, *Words into Pictures: Chick Flick Versus Dick Flick*, Panel Discussion, VHS The Writer's Guild Foundation, Los Angeles, 1999. For a full discussion of the gender issues related to a range of female action heroes see Sherrie A. Inness, *Action Chicks: New Images of Tough Women in Popular Culture* (New York: Palgrave Macmillan, 2004).

747. Jerry Palmer, *Thrillers: Genesis and Structure of a Popular Genre* (London: Edward Arnold, 1978). An interesting commentary in support of Palmer's point of view, in the context of films such as *Pulp Fiction* can be found in George Petersen, "Building Character Through Violence: A One-Two Punch," *Creative Screenwriting* 3.1 (Summer) (1996).

748. Charlene Tung, "Embodying an Image: Gender, Race, and Sexuality in *La Femme Nikita*," *Action Chicks: New Images of Tough Women in Popular Culture*, ed. Sherrie A. Inness (New York: Palgrave Macmillan, 2004), p. 105.

749. Tony Jaa, *Cast and Crew Interviews*, Documentary and Interviews, *Ong Bak*, Disc 2, Eastern Eye Asian Cinema. Madman Entertainment Pty. Ltd. DVD, The AV Channel Pty. Ltd., 2003.

750. *Kung Fu Hustle*. 2005. Dir. Stephen Chow (USA: Columbia TriStar Films).

751. Mike Atkinson, "Delirious Inventions," *Action Spectacle Cinema*, ed. Jose Arroyo (London: BFI Publishing, 2000), p. 90.

752. Bordwell, *Planet Hong Kong: Popular Cinema and the Art of Entertainment* p. 202.

753. Andrew Hewitt, *Social Choreography: Ideology as Performance in Dance and Everyday Movement* (Durham: Duke University Press, 2005).

754. *Rize*, dir. David La Chapelle, prod. David La Chapelle (USA: Lions Gate Films, 2005).

755. It aired in Sydney on the Seven network in 2006 in the fourth series of the Australian version of the show.

756. The Wiggles are an Australian singing group that perform here and overseas to preschool audiences and their parents.

757. The theatrical touring arm of the Shaolin Temple monks of China are a similar example of that blended theatrical performativity characterized by music, dance, and martial arts. The entertainment success of this ancient spiritual warrior tradition and its commodification as dinner sets, table

runners, and cushion covers amongst other forms of decoration also transforms violence into décor. (See *Chinavoc.com*, "Shaolin Kung Fu", Home 2007. Available: http://www.chinavoc.com/kungfu/index.asp, Jan 20, 2007.) I would argue that action figures and pop-art designer toys based on anime (for examples see *Vinyl Abuse* at vinylabuse.com and *Kidrobot* at kidrobot.com), with their blend of violence and child and adult aspects—they are both adult collector items *and* toys after all—also transform their origins in representations of violent lethality into décor for the amusement of the hobbyist and the child.

758. Sandars, "From the Warehouse to the Multiplex: Techno and Rave Culture's Reconfiguration of Late 1990's Sci-Fi Spectacle as Musical Performance."

759. The comment is Mel Gibson's, referring to the violent details he took from the meditations of Anne Catherine Emmerich, one of the sources he used for his film *The Passion of the Christ*. Quoted from John Dominic Crossan, "Hymn to a Savage God," *Jesus and Mel Gibson's the Passion of the Christ: The Film, the Gospel's and the Claims of History*, eds. Kathleen E. Corley and Robert L. Webb (London: Continuum, 2004), p. 12.

760. Paula Fredriksen, "Gospel Truths," *On the Passion of the Christ: Exploring Issues Raised by the Controversial Movie*, ed. Paula Fredriksen (Berkeley, Los Angeles: University of California Press, 2006), p. 34.

761. Who *Framed Roger Rabbit*, dir. Roger Zemeckis, prod. Frank Marshall (USA: Buena Vista Pictures, 1988).

762. Badley, *Film, Horror, and the Body Fantastic* p. 22.

763. Leon Hunt, "'I Know Kung Fu!': The Martial Arts in the Age of Digital Reproduction," *Screenplay: Cinema/Videogames/Interfaces*, eds. Geoff King and Tanya Krzywinska (London: Wallflower Press, 2002), p. 203.

764. Alphonso Lingis, *Body Transformations: Evolutions and Atavisms in Culture* (New York: Routledge, 2005), p. 74. Lingis makes the comparison when using this phrase with the violence in horror films, the word "supernumerary" evokes their extravagant supply of wounded body parts.

765. *The Passion of the Christ*, dir. Mel Gibson, prods. Mel Gibson, Bruce Davey, and Stephen McEveety (USA: Icon Entertainment International, 2004).

766. Quoted in Amy Hollywood, "Kill Jesus," *Mel Gibson's Bible: Religion, Popular Culture, and the Passion of the Christ*, eds. Timothy K. Beale and Tod Linafelt, Afterlives of the Bible (Chicago: The University of Chicago Press, 2006), p. 159. Gibson has fallen into a common tendency of defining graphic violence by measuring quantity rather than distinguishing its representations by aesthetic differences or similarities.

767. The comparison with *Kill Bill* is certainly apt in ways that Gibson may not have intended. His film offers the same fan satisfactions to Christians as Tarantino's referentiality did to martial arts action fans. As José Márquez notes, "Gibson's hectic screenplay requires the audience to fill in the story's considerable gaps while acknowledging their familiarity with knowing esoteric nods." Quoted from Jose Marquez, "Lights! Camera! Action!" *Mel Gibson's Bible: Religion, Popular Culture, and the Passion of the Christ*, eds. Timothy K. Beale and Tod Linafelt, Afterlives of the Bible (Chicago: The University of Chicago Press, 2006), p. 178.

768. Marquez, "Lights! Camera! Action!" p. 179. Márquez sees the film as drawing on the same tendency that action films have to "resort to exclamation" (p. 180) rather than subtlety, and associates its bloody violence with mutilation in horror movie classics, while being devoid of the self-consciousness that takes such films beyond mere gore to an interest in broader themes. When Marquez

uses a phrase such as "house of horrors tucked away for centuries within the church" his analysis is beginning to slip over into an opinion about the church and doctrine itself. Given the passions aroused within the controversy the film provoked, it is necessary to be alert to this tendency when weighing up opinions expressed about the theology of the film.

769. The three most discussed issues relating to the film are its level of violence, whether it is anti-Semitic and its biblical accuracy. A Web site that exhaustively catalogues reviews of the film and the controversy it aroused, including its use of violence, can be found at *Rotten Tomatoes, The Passion of the Christ*, Reviews 2006. Available: http://www.rottentomatoes.com/m/passion_of_the_christ, September 5, 2006. The academic debate with a range of views is encapsulated in Paula Fredriksen, *On the Passion of the Christ: Exploring the Issues Raised by the Controversial Movie* (Berkeley: University of California Press, 2006). For a discussion with a focus on the film's historical roots and the controversy it provoked see Kathleen E. Corley and Robert L. Webb, *Jesus and Mel Gibson's the Passion of the Christ: The Film, the Gospels and the Claims of History* (London: Continuum, 2004). The anti-Semitism debate in relation to the film is also covered in chapters by Thomas E. Wartenberg, Paul Kurtz, J. Angelo Corlett, and Eric Bronson in part 2, "Is the Passion Anti-Semitic?" in Jorge J. E. Gracia, *Mel Gibson's Passion and Philosophy*, Popular Culture and Philosophy, ed. William Irwin, vol. 10 (Chicago, Illinois: Open Court, 2004). The controversy over this issue at the time of the film's release was reignited when Mel Gibson was arrested for drunk driving in 2006 and was recorded making belligerent anti-Semitic remarks to the Jewish arresting officer. See Gerard Wright, "A Drunk, Angry Bigot: Mel's Mouth Proves His Most Lethal Weapon," *Sydney Morning Herald* July 31, 2006. Press coverage in Australia and in the United States has particularly focused on Gibson's father's history of promoting holocaust denial and his voicing of anti-Semitic beliefs. See Gerard Wright, "You're Not a Jew, Are You?" *Sydney Morning Herald* August 5–6, 2006.

770. The ill-effects of violence debate has also involved video games, outlined in Chapter 4 of Geoff King and Tanya Krzywinska, *Tomb Raiders and Space Invaders: Videogame Forms and Contexts* (London: I. B. Tauris, 2006). Their discussion emphasizes the difference between violence as fantasy play and real-world violence. The most passionate advocate for the capacity of video games to shape real-world responses to violence is probably found in the work of Dave Grossman. See Dave Grossman, *On Killing* (Boston: Little Brown, 1995). See also Dave Grossman and Gloria DeGataetano, *Stop Teaching Our Kids to Kill: A Call to Action against TV, Movie and Video Game Violence* (New York: Crown, 1999).

771. This is *Computer Gaming World's* editorial director Johnny Wilson's description cited by Lawrence and Jewett. Lawrence and Jewett, *The Myth of the American Superhero* p. 203.

772. Biskind, *Easy Rider's Raging Bulls: How the Sex 'N' Drugs 'N' Rock 'N' Roll Generation Saved Hollywood*, p. 343.

773. Rene Girard, "On Mel Gibson's *The Passion of the Christ*," 2004, *Anthropoetics*, 10:1 (Spring/s\ Summer). Available: http://www.anthropoetics.ucla.edu/ap1001/RGGibson.htm, September 5, 2006.

774. Mark Gillings, "The Real, the Virtually Real, and the Hyperreal: The Role of VR in Archaeology," *Envisioning the Past: Archeology and the Image*, eds. Sam Smiles and Stephanie Moser, New Interventions in Art History (Oxford: Blackwell Publishing, 2005), p. 230.

775. For a scholarly overview of the Photorealism movement with catalogued examples see Louis K. Meisall and Linda Chase, *Photorealism at the Millenium*, vol. 3 (Harry N. Abrams Inc., 2002). I have found it useful to enter the discussion of hyperreal plausibility through an art movement definition as the terms *hyperreal* and *virtual* are often used as if there were agreement on what is meant by

them when, in actual fact, the specifics vary greatly across disciplines. In information technology terms, hyperreality is defined as "the commingling of physical reality with virtual reality and human intelligence with virtual intelligence." Quoted from John Tiffin, "Introduction," *Hyperreality: Paradigm for the Third Millenium*, eds. John Tiffin and Nobuyoshi Terashima (London: Routledge, 2001), p. 1. Clearly, whether it is the real time news images of 9/11 or the most advanced digitized imagery of the actual, debate continues over how far, by that definition, we are immersed in the matrix of the virtual.

776. Horst Bredekamp and Barbara Marie Stafford, "Hyperrealism: One Step Beyond," Interview, Magazine Archive, Visiting and Revisiting Art 6 (Spring) 2006, *Tate Online*. Available: http://www.tate. org.uk/tateetc/issue6/hyperrealism.htm, September 5, 2006.

777. Alice Crawford, "The Digital Turn: Animation in the Age of Information Technologies," *Prime Time Animation: Television Animation and American Culture*, eds. Carole A. Stabile and Mark Harrison (London: Routledge, 2003), p. 116.

778. Maureen Furniss, *Art in Motion: Animation Aesthetics* (London: John Libbey, 1998), p. 190. The challenge is to render the way human characters have individual walks and facial expressions or over the texture of hair and fur on both humans and animals in realistic ways. A recent heralded triumph was the animation of the fur on the penguin hero in the animated film *Happy Feet* (2006): "The main character . . . has about six million feathers, each with individual texture and colour." (Nicole Breskin, "Lighting up the Big Screen," *Jewish News* January 5, 2007: 8.) Marveling at the photorealism of the image is subsumed into wonder at the technological ingenuity of its achievement: "We had to develop processes for rendering fur and feathers, and then the moisture of them, and the way they reacted to light."(Remark from the managing director of Animal Logic, special effects animators for *Happy Feet*, in Miawling Lam, "Creating a Big Song and Dance," *Sunday Telegraph* January 14, 2007: 20.)

779. Paul Wells, *Animation: Genre and Authorship*, Short Cuts, ed. Maureen Furniss (London: Wallflower, 2002), p. 13.

780. King and Krzywinska, *Tomb Raiders and Space Invaders: Videogame Forms and Contexts* p. 153. King and Kryzwinska illustrate the way video games are a product of the interaction between the needs of graphic "realism" and the functional realism of gameplay and the way this has affected marketing and player reception of games that emphasize one or the other.

781. Marie-Laure Ryan, *Narrative as Virtual Reality: Immersion and Interactivity in Literature and Electronic Media*, Parallax: Revisions of Culture and Society, eds. Gerald Prince and Wendy Steiner Stephen G. Nichols (Baltimore: The Johns Hopkins University Press, 2001), p. 352.

782. Albert J. Bergesen and Andrew M. Greeley, *God in the Movies* (New Brunswick: Transaction Publishers, 2003), p. viii.

783. Hill, *Shocking Entertainment: Viewer Response to Violent Movies* p. 70.

784. Wells, "It's Life, Jim," p. 22.

785. Stephanie Bunbury, "The Sound of No Hands Clapping," *Sydney Morning Herald* April 18, 2006.

786. Bergesen and Greeley, *God in the Movies* pp. 166–67.

787. David John Graham, "Redeeming Violence in the Films of Martin Scorsese," *Explorations in Theology and Film: Movies and Meaning*, eds. Clive Marsh and Gaye Ortiz (Oxford: Blackwell Publishers, 1998), p. 88.

788. Graham, "Redeeming Violence in the Films of Martin Scorsese," p. 91.

789. Margaret R. Miles, *Seeing and Believing: Religion and Values in the Movies* (Boston: Beacon Press, 2002), p. 46.

790. Hyperreal enhancement is particularly the product of the postproduction of sound. On the screen, the audience can now hear bones being broken with audio enhancement and are not just reliant on an actor's reaction to tell it that the violence has painfully occurred. When Christ's shoulder is wrenched the viewer is not hearing it from a distance. The audience is helped to feel it is closer than right next to the body being racked. Even for that distance, the sound is enhanced.

791. As Chris Shilling notes, the role of prothesis in human embodiment is usually one of restoration through technological supplementation and is judged as successful by the restoration of function or appearance. See Chris Shilling, *The Body in Culture, Technology and Society*, Theory, Culture and Society, ed. Mike Featherstone (London: Sage Publications, 2005). The aesthetic role of successful prosthetics in images of violence such as the crucifixion scene can be seen as the opposite of the practicality of restoration. In that vein, Alphonso Lingis singles out the art of the horror film as an example of "adding prosthetic body parts in excess of what the natural body has." As any fan of the slash and hack type of horror film would agree, the most obvious example of this would be the copious amounts of blood used to signify wounding. (See Lingis, *Body Transformations: Evolutions and Atavisms in Culture* p. 74.)

792. Hollywood lists the set scenes used in the film's final moments as the deposition (taking Jesus down from the cross, the pieta (Mary cradling her dead son in her arms), and the *arma Christ* (a camera shot of objects symbolized as weapons against sin and Satan (the ropes and nails form the cross and the crown of thorns). See Hollywood, "Kill Jesus."

793. Schrader and Jackson, *Schrader on Schrader* p. 135.

794. Ibid., 133. Differently from Gibson's aim, Schrader notes that *Raging Bull* was about the inner struggle of a spiritual life and was not aiming to be a transcendental film "trying to create a holy feeling." (Schrader and Jackson, *Schrader on Schrader* p. 136.)

795. It is less the character's status as a sacred icon, or the suffering as such, that is moving. Rather, it is the maternal trying to express itself in protecting a child in the context of that overwhelming and implacable torture that arouses viewer sympathy.

796. Fredriksen, "Gospel Truths," p. 34.

797. Paula Fredriksen, "Preface," *On the Passion of the Christ: Exploring the Issues Raised by the Controversial Movie*, ed. Paula Fredriksen (Berkeley: University of California Press, 2006), p. xxii.

798. Fredriksen, "Preface," p. xii.

799. Hollywood, "Kill Jesus," p. 163.

800. Ibid.

801. Ibid.

802. The differences between films that raise religious issues and those that act religiously to further faith can be found in Miles, *Seeing and Believing: Religion and Values in the Movies* p. 46.

803. Theological responses to film in general amongst Christian critics reveals a range of theoretical approaches. Films can be a vehicle for spiritual lessons for the viewer, even when the narratives have no overtly Christian theme. (Catherine M Barsotti and Robert K. Johnston, *Finding God in the Movies: 33 Films of Reel Faith* (Grand Rapids, Michigan: Baker Books, 2004). A history of theological

approaches to film can be found in Robert K. Johnston, *Reel Spirituality: Theology and Film in Dialogue*, Engaging Culture, eds. William A. Dyrness and Robert K. Johnston (Grand Rapids, Michigan: Baker Academic, 2000). Theological film criticism sees cinema as continuing the classic religious concerns of precinematic art forms. However, the definitions of religion in film can be broad and incorporate theological, mythological, and ideological approaches exemplified in the collection of Joel W. Martin and Conrad E. Ostwalt Jr., *Screening the Sacred: Religion, Myth, and Ideology in Popular American Film* (Boulder, Colorado: Westview Press, 1995). Approaches extend to spiritually themed popular culture, inclusive of film, as in Craig Detweiler and Barry Taylor, *A Matrix of Meanings: Finding God in Pop Culture*, Engaging Culture, eds. William A. Dyrness and Robert K. Johnston (Grand Rapids, Michigan: Baker Academic, 2003). Specific case studies center on whether particular franchises have overt or covert religious or spiritual moral lessons, such as Mark I. Pinsky, *The Gospel According to the Simpsons: The Spiritual Life of the World's Most Animated Family* (Louisville: John Knox Press, 2001) and Mark I. Pinsky, *The Gospel According to Disney: Faith, Trust and Pixie Dust* (Louisville: John Knox Press, 2004). In essence, the definition of God and spirituality as subtext has become expansive. Thus we arrive at an esoteric, non-Christian collection which ranges from Robert Bresson's obvious symbolic Christian references in *Au Hasard Balthazar* to a less convincing argument for the inclusion of Harold Ramis's *Groundhog Day* in Mary Lee Bandy and Antonio Monda, *The Hidden God: Film and Faith* (New York: Museum of Modern Art, 2003).

804. Bryan P. Stone, *Faith and Film: Theological Themes at the Cinema* (St. Louis, Missouri: Chalice Press, 2000), p. 69. Stone outlines the history of that filmic struggle from biblical epics like *The Greatest Story Ever Told* (1965) that overemphasized Jesus's otherworldliness to the humanity emphasized in the provocative version of Jesus's life in Martin Scorsese's *The Last Temptation of Christ* (1988). He locates Pasolini's *The Gospel According to St. Mathew* (1996) as somewhere in between and finally concludes that all three films are "forced into a trade-off between his holiness and his humanity" (p. 79). A history of the heyday of Hollywood biblical spectaculars (prior to the 1960s) is given by Gerald E. Forshey, *American Religious and Biblical Spectaculars*, Media and Society, ed. J. Fred Mac Donald (Westport, Connecticut: Praeger, 1992). William Telford describes the genres of the Christ film as biopic, allegory, and satire—with the reverent classical images of Christ as patriarchal, adolescent, pacifist, subversive, or mystical and always white, rather than Semitic. He notes the 1960s as the beginning of less traditional representations of Jesus—inclusive of musical versions in the 1970s such as *Jesus Christ Superstar* and *Godspell* and the more accessibly human portrayals such as Scorsese's film mentioned above. (See William R. Telford, "Jesus Christ Movie Star: The Depiction of Jesus in the Cinema," *Explorations in Theology and Film: Movies and Meaning*, eds. Clive Marsh and Gaye Ortiz (Oxford: Blackwell Publishers, 1998). The concept of filmic "transfigurations" of Jesus (characters who have Christ-like characteristics without being an explicit biopic rendition of his story) has been a constant theme as in Neil P. Hurley, "Cinematic Transfigurations of Jesus," *Religion in Film*, eds. John May and Michael Bird (Knoxville: University of Tennessee Press, 1984). The genre is seen as discernible by Passion motifs that are not necessarily explicitly evangelistic, as in Peter Fraser, *Images of the Passion: The Sacramental Mode in Film* (Westport, Connecticut: Praeger, 1998).

805. William Irwin, "Gibson's Sublime *Passion*: In Defense of the Violence," *Mel Gibson's Passion and Philosophy: The Cross, the Questions, the Controversy*, ed. Jorge J. E. Gracia, vol. 10, Popular Culture and Philosophy (Chicago, Illinois: Open Court, 2004), p. 57.

806. There are implications of that emphasis on relentless violence for other aspects of Christian belief in Christ and redemption, noted by Charles Taliaferro, "The Focus of *the Passion* Puts the Person of Jesus Out of Focus," *Mel Gibson's Passion and Philosophy: The Cross, the Questions, the Controversy*, ed. Jorge J. E. Gracia, vol. 10, Popular Culture and Philosophy (Chicago, Illinois: Open Court, 2004).

807. Detweiler and Taylor, *A Matrix of Meanings: Finding God in Pop Culture* p. 314.

808. A quirky view posits the bloody makeover of Christ's body as similar to the destruction of personality behind the contemporary obsession with cosmetic surgery makeovers and their depersonalization of identity in favour of aesthetic models. See William G. Little, "Jesus's Extreme Makeover," *Mel Gibson's Bible: Religion, Popular Culture, and the Passion of the Christ*, eds. Timothy K. Beale and Tod Linafelt, Afterlives of the Bible (Chicago: The University of Chicago Press, 2006).

809. Quoted in Michael Bird, "Film as Hierophany," *Religion in Film*, eds. John May and Michael Bird (Knoxville: University of Tennessee Press, 1984), p. 15.

810. Lawrence and Jewett, *The Myth of the American Superhero* p. 295. The bullet time in *The Matrix* is described as a special effect that "gives faith an invincible armour" with the violent mythos of *Star Trek*, *Star Wars*, and Steven Seagal's "Smash-Face Buddhism" as examples of the genre (see p. 290). For an analysis that takes the Christian creed of that genre as a source of spiritual revelation in a case study of *The Matrix* see Chris Seay and Greg Garrett, *The Gospel Reloaded: Exploring Spirituality and Faith in the Matrix* (Colorado Springs: Pinon, 2003).

811. Ibid., 199.

812. Ibid., 200.

813. Ibid., 221. My focus in discussing video games in this chapter is on graphic interfaces and some characteristics of gameplay performativity. It needs to be acknowledged that I cannot do justice to the extensive range of interactive options, narratives, and digital special effect gradations available in contemporary video games, which could easily be a book in itself. My interest is in the graphics of violent imagery and my discussion is limited to a through-line of characteristics in a vast mediascape that is constantly undergoing technological change. Given that change is so rapid in contemporary gaming, academic comment dates quickly. Just about any book on video games gives at least a summary historical overview. For a survey of some broad trends in video games as a cultural phenomenon see Lucien King, *Game On: The History and Culture of Videogames* (London: Laurence King Publishing, 2002). In discussing central design changes, Ste Curran highlights the point that performance pleasure generated by a game, particularly if combat is involved, is not just a matter of how the interface looks but of the range of interactive options it provides the player. See Ste Curran, *Game Plan: Great Designs That Changed the Face of Computer Gaming* (Hove: RotoVision, 2004). There are also important distinctions to be made between the topology of animation in 2D compared to 3D or CG and the process of transfer from one to the other beyond the space I can give to it in my book. A description of the process from a practitioner's point of view is given in Angie Jones and Jamie Oliff, *Thinking Animation: Bridging the Gap Between 2D and CG* (Boston, MA: Thomson Course Technology, 2007). For a substantive insight into the design of virtual game playing worlds from both the designer and player points of view it is fundamental to start with Richard A. Bartle, *Designing Virtual Worlds* (Indianapolis: New Riders, 2004). While Bartle's focus is primarily MUDs (multiuser dungeons) or virtual worlds (text based and graphic) where players assume fictional identities in multiuser

games, many of the points he makes with regard to the relationship between immersion and interactivity apply to virtual behaviours and the interfaces of video games in general.

814. Ibid., 212.

815. Launched in 1993 by Id Software, the *Doom* franchise was an elaboration of the company's classic *Wolfenstein* and a forerunner of the enormous popularity of its follow-up *Quake*. *Doom* helped to popularize the first-person shooter game as a genre. For a history of the Id Software developments and these games and of the aesthetic of first-person shooters in general see Jo Bruce and Jason Rutter, "Spectacles of the Deathmatch: Character and Narrative in First-Person Shooters," *Screenplay: Cinema/Vidoegames/Interfaces*, eds. Geoff King and Tanya Kryzwinska (London: Wallflower Press, 2002).

816. Lawrence and Jewett, *The Myth of the American Superhero* p. 215.

817. Ibid., 214.

818. For a full description of the gameplay see Tim Bogenn and Rick Barba, *Grand Theft Auto: San Andreas: Official Strategy Guide* (Indianapolis, Indiana: Brady Games: Pearson Education, 2005). This is not a first person shooter perspective for the most part, though some weapons work in first-person view. Gameplay is also interspersed with cinematic segments where the player simply watches expository action.

819. San Andreas feels nation-like as it is comprised of three city environments: Los Santos (with a Los Angeles and housing projects ambience), San Fierro (a bayside city), and Las Venturas (reminiscent of Las Vegas) with interspaces comprised of the Badlands (countryside) and the Desert (ranches and dunes). CJ is a member of the Grove Street Families who strive for dominance over rival gangs, the Mafia, and corrupt officials.

820. Bartle, *Designing Virtual Worlds* p. 252.

821. Ibid., 474. Despite my argument that contemporary graphic interfaces still announce their own animated separation from the actual and that recognition of this counters immersion in the virtual, there are issues of virtual and real identity that are more complicated than that involved in first-person shooter games. Bartle asks the core question posed by virtual worlds: "Is identity unitary or multiple?" (Bartle, *Designing Virtual Worlds* p. 512.) A core reference on this issue is the empirical work by Sherry Turkel, *Life on the Screen* (New York: Simon and Schuster, 1995). Users experience credibility in simulations but user verisimilitude judgments are idiosyncratic. See Alexandre Francis and Mark Coutre, "Credibility of a Simulation-Based Virtual Laboratory: An Exploratory Study of Learner Judgments of Verisimilitude," *Journal of Interactive Learning Research* 14.4 (2003). The classic discussion of whether we are in a state of the posthuman, which is viewed as more complex than a simple virtual reality versus actual body divide—in N. Katherine Hayles, *How We Became Post-Human: Virtual Bodies in Cybernetics, Literature and Informatics* (Chicago: The University of Chicago Press, 1999)—still remains to be resolved. The contemporary existence of MMORPGs (massively multiplayer online-role-playing games), such as *Entropia* or *Second Life*, in which virtual capital made in online worlds (as players lead virtual lives) can be traded for real-world money is a real-life example of the complicated interface that exists between the virtual and the actual for players who have an online virtual identity and domicile in addition to the one they live offscreen. For a report on that phenomenon see Greg Bearup, "The Geek Australian Dream," *Sydney Morning Herald* October 14, 2006 and some photo case studies of online participants and their avatars see Robbie Cooper, *AlterEgo: Avatars and their Creators* (London: Chris Boot , 2007.) How far that virtuality actually morphs out of the actual into the virtual is clearly debatable. However, when, as reported in Bearup's article, there are

actual Third World gaming sweatshops where people are paid to play games and accumulate virtual profits to sell on e-Bay to Western players "too lazy, impatient or incompetent to acquire the required goods to advance through various levels in the game" (31), then immersion is far from a closed circle. Both the participation in real-world trading through the purchase of the ludic results of others by the player as a game tactic, and the decision to get someone else to play, which is a rejection of the parameters of the ludic virtual world, raises questions about the extent of encompassing immersion in the game. A British report detailing the intrusion of real-world crime in the form of money laundering, tax evasion, and child pornography into *Second Life* is a further reminder that "[t]here is nothing virtual about online crime." (Quoted in Ben Leapma, "Internet's Free World Attracts Dark Forces," *Sydney Morning Herald*, May 19–20, 2007: 18.) Such intrusions illustrate the existence of ways in which, as Martin Jay puts it, "the apparent self-sufficiency of the virtual universe may be disrupted." (See Jay, *Refractions of Violence* p. 131.) For a description of the characteristics of MMORPGS technologies that promote credibility inclusive of shared space, interface, and socialization see Betsy Book, "Moving Beyond the Game: Social Virtual Worlds," 2004, *Virtual Worlds Review*. Available: http://www.virtualworldsreview.com/papers/BBook_SoP2.pdf, October 15, 2006. For a list of virtual worlds online from 2003–06 by category plus links see Betsy Book, "Virtual Worlds List by Category," 2006, *Virtual Worlds Review*. Available: http://www.virtualworldsreview.com/info/categories.shtml, October 15, 2006.

822. Ibid., 318. Bartle cites more than one Web site that details the Cartoon Laws of Physics, including Paco Hope, "The Cartoon Laws of Physics," 2006, *The Funny Pages*. Available: http://funnies.paco.to/cartoon.html, October 10, 2006. One commonly used example is "All principles of gravity are negated by fear." It is in a related context that living an avatar life is also complicated by the MMORPG options having a fictional source to begin with; such as in the online game *Lord of the Rings: Shadows of AngMarch* For some fans, there are degrees of authenticity to be determined about avatar narratives of a known fictional world: "I know it is hard to judge a title before you play it but I feel like this won't feel like *real* [my italics] Lord of the Rings." (Quoted from Reuters, "Tolkien's Middle-earth Expands in Online Game," 2007, *Yahoo News*. Available: http://news,yahoo.com/nm/20070125/tc_nm/games_rings_dc_2, January 27, 2007.)

823. Quoted in Pip Cummings, "War of the Worlds," *Sydney Morning Herald* January 15–16, 2005: 6. As Steve Poole also observes, the purpose of video games is not simulation but gameplay and "underneath the flashy graphics, cinematic cut-scenes, real-time physics, mythological back stories, and everything else, a video game at bottom is still a highly artificial, purposely designed semiotic engine." (Quoted from Steven Poole, *Trigger Happy: The Inner Life of Videogames* (London: Fourth Estate, 2000), p. 214.) The player, while given choices, is confined within the parameters of that purpose built engine. (It is possible, of course, for gamers skilled enough to write additional coding to increase or change some choices in a game, which is possible with some games and encouraged by some game producers). For a discussion of current, experimental and projected technologies that bring animation onto the viewers side of the joystick and screen see Crawford, "The Digital Turn: Animation in the Age of Information Technologies."

824. John D. Anderson, *The Reality of Illusion: An Ecological Approach to Cognitive Film Theory* (Carbondale: Southern Illinois University Press, 1996), p. 121. Anderson's book has an extensive discussion of perceptions of such media frames in relation to film using cognitive film theory and the concept of viewing as a state of play.

825. Lawrence and Jewett, *The Myth of the American Superhero* p. 217.

826. Adam Sessler, *Doom Nation*, Bonus, DVD *Doom* Distant Planet Productions, Universal Pictures, 2006.

827. The third version of *Doom* made the largest advance in its graphical interface which, while it was more detailed than the original block-like graphics, for some players was less exciting as it slowed down the excitement of the original gameplay. The debate of the value of detailed graphics versus the cost to the needs of gameplay is an ongoing one amongst players and programmers. This debate suggests that graphical photorealism, while it may add to the aesthetics of play, is not the primary point of engagement with virtual reality games.

828. One need hardly add that transferring the trigger actions of gameplay to reality would lead to legal consequences.

829. The portrayal of stereotypically impossible exaggerations of the female body for marketing to male players in video games is perhaps the most convincing argument for such games creating fantasy worlds which are, in this respect at least, a masculine fantasy. For a discussion of the complex gender issues involved in videogaming, particularly from the point of view of female players and what they play (as opposed to what is marketed to them) see Justine Cassell and Henry Jenkins, *From Barbie to Mortal Kombat* (Cambridge: The MIT Press, 1999).

830. Lawrence and Jewett, *The Myth of the American Superhero* p. 217.

831. *Doom*, dir. Andrzeij Bartkowiak, prods. John Wells and Lorenzo di Bonaventura, (USA: Distant Planet Productions, Universal Pictures, 2005).

832. John Farhat, "First Person Shooter Sequence," Bonus, *Doom*, DVD Distant Planet Productions, Universal Pictures, 2006. As Farhat explains it on the DVD, the ratio is the height of the screen in relation to its width.

833. Henry Jenkins and Kurt Squire, "The Art of Contested Spaces," *Game On: The History and Culture of Videogames*, ed. Lucien King (London: Laurence King Publishing, 2002), p. 65.

834. Burnett, *How Images Think* p. 168.

835. Ibid., 169.

836. For Burnett, the contradiction at the heart of such simulations for the military was that the simulation had to follow the physics of shooting for training purposes, a real-world effect. At the same time it had to give consistent game rewards for engaging the enemy, which might not be the case in actual combat, and is thus a game effect.

837. King and Krzywinska, *Tomb Raiders and Space Invaders: Videogame Forms and Contexts* p. 200.

838. Ibid., 19.

839. Ndalianis, *Neo-Baroque Aesthetics and Contemporary Entertainment* p. 128.

840. Ibid., 129.

841. Ibid., 147.

842. Matt Groening, *The Simpsons*, 1989. For episode synopses of all 330 and more shows; links to discussion lists, articles, and interviews with actors and creators; character information; and all things Simpson, see alt.tv.simpsons, *The Simpsons Archive*, Home 2006. Available: www.snpp.com, September 24, 2006.

843. Pinsky, *The Gospel According to the Simpsons: The Spiritual Life of the World's Most Animated Family* p. 137. Pinsky notes that the show does not stop short of satirizing aspects of the sacred that are simplistic or hypocritical. The main vehicle for this are the characters of Ned Flanders, Homer's neighbor, and Reverend Lovejoy, the minister of the church the Simpson family attend.

844. Chris Turner, *Planet Simpson: How a Cartoon Masterpiece Defined a Generation* (Cambridge: Da Capo Press, 2004).

845. Bart's oppositional identity as Nietzschean hero of nihilistic chaos is noted by Mark T. Conard, "Thus Spake Bart: On Nietzsche and the Virtues of Being Bad," *The Simpsons and Philosophy: The D'oh! Of Homer*, eds. William Irwin, Mark T. Conard and Aeon J. Skoble , vol. 2, Popular Culture and Philosophy (Chicago, Illinois: Open Court, 2001).

846. Tony Russell DeMars, *From the Simpsons to the Bundys: A Critical Analysis of Disrespectful Discourse in Television Narratives*, Graduate Thesis, University of Southern Mississippi (Ann Arbor, Michigan: UMI Dissertation Services, 1996), p. 8.

847. "To riff on something is to begin from a basic premise—from the riff—and to build it out and up through wild new tangents into something unique and compelling." (See Turner, *Planet Simpson: How a Cartoon Masterpiece Defined a Generation* p. 27.) Turner notes the show's satirical and comedic taxonomy and the comedic ways in which it deconstructs authority but overestimates the ubiquity of its quotability as having global linguistic impact.

848. Turner, *Planet Simpson: How a Cartoon Masterpiece Defined a Generation* p. 25. Turner makes large claims for the show and its impact on the fans which, despite his own passionate fandom being an example, are difficult to sustain as a general claim about its audience: "the show began its quick transition from it's fans' favorite TV show to their central metaphorical framework for understanding modern life" (see p. 37). The show has certainly generated intense academic interest as a cultural icon. For a philosophical overview of the show as social and cultural commentary see William Irwin, Mark T. Conard, and J. Aeon Skoble, *The Simpsons and Philosophy: The D'oh! Of Homer*, Popular Culture and Philosophy, ed. William Irwin, vol. 2 (Chicago, Illinois: Open Court, 2001). It is possible for explanatory analysis of the show's social commentary to become reductive of its satirical humor. While Turner's analysis avoids that pitfall, there are those that do not, such as the overly literal Steven Keslowitz, *The World According to the Simpsons* (Naperville, Illinois: Source Books Inc., 2006).

849. It is important to note that animation, both 2D and CG deserve their own book and continuum of authenticity. To quote Paul Wells in his analysis of animation in *Animation: Genre and Authorship*: I am cognizant of the fact that "all animation may be placed within a continuum between *mimesis* and *abstraction*." See Wells, *Animation: Genre and Authorship* p. 5. Unfortunately, space does not permit that generic or historical discussion here. For a thorough history of animation that reveals the spatial range of two and three dimensionality and the movement towards hyperreal plausibility made possible by digital technologies see Jerry Beck, *Animation Art: From Pencil to Pixel, the History of Cartoon, Anime and CGI.* (New York: Harper Design International, 2004). For analysis with some history focusing on animation as an American phenomenon, see Paul Wells, *Animation and America* (Edinburgh: Edinburgh University Press, 2002). It has been noted that animation has origins in phantasmagoria entertainment in mass culture representation and technical innovation by Esther Leslie, *Hollywood Flatlands: Animation, Critical Theory and the Avante-Garde* (London: Verso, 2002). An older but workmanlike outline of the technological and industrial history of the industry which highlights the often forgotten fact when discussing the representational differences between limited and full 2D animation (and the technological achievements of pixilated 3D animation for that matter) that the descriptions used are definitions of style (with their own graphic requirements for representation) and are not definitions of narrative quality, see Furniss, *Art in Motion: Animation Aesthetics*. While published some time ago, a classic and useful history is to be found in Leonard Maltin, *Of Mice and Magic: A History of American Animated Cartoons* (New York: New American Library, 1987). It has

a good filmography by studio up to the date of publication and information on work done by minor studios that is often ignored elsewhere.

850. Deborah Knight, "Popular Parody: The Simpsons Meets the Crime Film," *The Simpsons and Philosophy: The D'oh! Of Homer*, eds. William Irwin, Mark T. Conard, and Aeon J. Skoble, vol. 2, Popular Culture and Philosophy (Chicago, Illinois: Open Court, 2001), p. 104.

851. Zemeckis, *Who Framed Roger Rabbit*.

852. Turner, *Planet Simpson: How a Cartoon Masterpiece Defined a Generation* p. 31.

853. Ibid., 29. As Turner points out, Springfield was also the name of the town in the 1950's family sitcom *Father Knows Best*. While the show's satire depends on the way it is unlike the traditional television sitcom, its satirical use of that form of narrative comes from its place in the developing history of that genre, which has become more politically aware over a period of decades. For a history of that increasingly subversive narrative in the sitcom genre, see Allan Neuwirth, *They'll Never Put That on the Air* (New York: Allworth Press, 2006).

854. H. Peter Steeves, "It's Just a Bunch of Stuff That Happened," *The Sitcom Reader: America Viewed and Skewed*, eds. Mary M. Dalton and Laura R. Linder (New York: State University of New York Press, 2005), p. 262.

855. Turner, *Planet Simpson: How a Cartoon Masterpiece Defined a Generation* p. 56.

856. "The Cartridge Family," 9.5. The title is a play on gun terminology and on the title of an earlier live action American sitcom *The Partridge Family*.

857. "Treehouse of Horror IX," 10.4.

858. Sweeps is the ratings period for American television. The reference to the crucifixion works on multiple satiric levels, inclusive of the way reality TV can trivialize anything, as well as drawing attention to the ridiculous insatiability of TV audiences for violence and the corporate mentality that will cross all boundaries of good taste to feed it. The comic freedom to use the crucifixion in that way undoubtedly owes a great deal to the groundwork laid by the Monty Python film, *The Life of Brian*. Who can ever forget the line "Crucifixion's a doddle." See *The Life of Brian*, dir. See Terry Jones, prod. John Goldstone (UK: Python Pictures and Handmade Films, 1979).

859. Turner, *Planet Simpson: How a Cartoon Masterpiece Defined a Generation* p. 32.

860. That children are a large part of the demographic which watch *The Simpsons*, and The Itchy and Scratchy violence within it is, of course, something the writers would be aware of and adds an ironic layer to the satire.

861. "Treehouse of Horror VI," 7.6.

862. Jones and Oliff, *Thinking Animation: Bridging the Gap Between 2D and CG* p. 165.

863. Zemeckis, *Who Framed Roger Rabbit*.

864. Jones and Oliff, *Thinking Animation: Bridging the Gap between 2D and CG* p. 196. In that context, animation techniques in 2D and CG such as motion blur (blurring of high speed motion which is more visible if the action is stop-framed) and squash and stretch (deforming an object to show weight or rigidity), while they are about approximating aspects of movement and solidity in actuality it is only in so far as is necessary to convince an audience of character design.

865. Allan Neuwirth, *Makin' Toons: Inside the Most Popular Animated TV Shows and Movies* (New York: Allworth Press, 2003), p. 121.

866. *Apocalypto*, dir. Mel Gibson, prods. Mel Gibson and Bruce Davey (USA: Icon Entertainment International and Buena Vista Pictures, 2006).

867. This opinion puts me in agreement with Stephen Prince's call for an increased focus in film theory on what viewers perceive on the screen when they watch digital images. Viewers judge authenticity by a range of textual cues which persuade them of textual credibility that are in turn related to their own real life experiences making the reception of any text a more complex matter than defining realism by improvements in technologically rendered detail. See Stephen Prince, "True Lies: Perceptual Realism, Digital Images and Film Theory," *The Film Cultures Reader*, ed. Graeme Turner (London: Routledge, 2002).

868. Poole, *Trigger Happy: The Inner Life of Videogames* p. 236.

869. *Monster House*, dir. Gil Kenan, prods. Jack Rapke and Steve Starkey (USA: Sony Pictures Entertainment, 2006).

870. It is interesting to note as a related point that, despite the extensive use of CG effects in *The Lord of the Rings* trilogy, the visual effects cinematographer on the films, Alex Funke, felt that miniature photography added something to cinematic illusion that was viewed as more realistic than CG and affected audience reception of verisimilitude: "At some subconscious level, viewers can tell when they're seeing real photography." (Quoted from Simon Gray, "Miniatures Add Grand Scale," p. 1, January 2004, *American Cinematographer*. Available: http://www.theasc.com/magazine/jan04/sub2/index.html, March 13, 2004.)

871. Roth is referring to his R-rated slash horror film *Hostel*. Quoted from Paul Byrnes, "A Shop of Horrors for All Backpackers," *Sydney Morning Herald* February 23, 2006: 14.

872. Pauline Kael, *Reeling* (London: Marion Boyars, 1977), p. 256.

873. Mark Ledbetter, *Victims and Postmodern Narrative or Doing Violence to the Body: An Ethic of Reading and Writing* (London: Macmillan Press, 1996), p. ix.

874. Peter Josyph, "Blood Music: Reading Blood Meridian," *Sacred Violence: A Reader's Companion to Cormac McCarthy*, eds. Wade Hall & Rick Wallach (El Paso: University of Texas, Texas Western Press, 1995), p. 184.

875. Kowalewski, *Deadly Musings: Violence and Verbal Form in American Fiction* p. 249.

876. Gary Maddox and Stephen Gibbs, "Just a Bloke Who Likes a Bit of Torture," *The Sydney Morning Herald* July 12, 2000: 21.

877. Ibid., p. 21.

878. Apart from his own writing, Read was available for consultation as he lives, postprison time, a reformed life.

879. Maddox and Gibbs, "Just a Bloke Who Likes a Bit of Torture," p. 21.

880. Ibid.

881. Ibid.

882. Gary Maddox, "Analyse This: My Life Is One Draft After Another," *Sydney Morning Herald* June 20, 2001: 21.

883. Ibid.

884. Roger Ebert, "Columbine Revisted," *Jerusalem Post* May 7, 2004: 3.

885. Gavin Smith, "Oliver Stone: Why Do I Provoke?" *Sight and Sound* IV.12 (1994): 12.

886. Scott Rankin, *Stickybricks*, Community Theatre, Big hArt, Sydney Festival, January 7–26, 2006, Sydney.

887. Justin Norrie and Les Kennedy, "Death in Housing Block Unnoticed by Neighbours Afraid to Go Out," *Sydney Morning Herald* February 14, 2006.

888. Quote is from the program notes, which was a series of cards with no page numbers or publishing details that could be cited. The quote is taken from the card titled "A director's note."

889. Program notes, "A director's note."

890. *The Last Horror Movie*, dir. Julian Richards, prod. Zorana Piggot, (USA: Bedford Entertainment Inc, 2003).

891. For a fascinating insight into why fans of the boxing film *Rocky* run the steps used to shoot one of the film's aspirational scenes see Michel Vitez, *Rocky Stories: Tales of Love, Hope and Happiness at America's Most Famous Steps* (Philadelphia: Paul Dry books, 2006).

892. G. J. Shaeffer and Sondra London, *Killer Fiction* (Venice, California: Feral House, 1997).

Bibliography

ABC News Special Report. September 11, 2001, 7:00 a.m. News and Public Affairs Collection, University of California Los Angeles Film and Television Archive, 2001.

Allan, Stuart. "News from Nowhere: Televisual News Discourse." *Approaches to Media Discourse*. Eds. Allan Bell and Peter Garrett. Oxford: Blackwell Publishers, 1998. pp. 105–41.

alt.tv.Simpsons. "The Simpsons Archive." Home 2006. Available: www.snpp.com. September 24, 2006.

American Academy of Pediatrics, The. "Media Violence." *Journal of the American Academy of Pediatrics* 95.6 (1995): 949–51.

Anastasia, George. *The Last Gangster: From Cop to Wise guy to FBI Informant: Big Ron Previte and the Fall of the American Mob*. New York: Regan Books, Harper Collins, 2004.

Anderson, John D. *The Reality of Illusion: An Ecological Approach to Cognitive Film Theory*. Carbondale: Southern Illinois University Press, 1996.

Andrejevic, Mark. *Reality TV: The Work of Being Watched*. Critical Media Studies Institutions, Politics, and Culture. Ed. Andrew Calabrese. Lanham: Rowman & Littlefield Publishers, Inc., 2004.

Andrew, Geoff. "Killing Joke." *Time Out* September 24–28, 1994: 24–26.

Apocalypto. 2006. Dir. Mel Gibson.

Arnold, Gary. "Cast in a New Light." *Insight On the News* 17.39 (2001): 27.

Arroya, Jose. "Mission Sublime." *Action Spectacle Cinema*. Ed. Jose Arroya. London: BFI Publishing, 2000. pp. 21–25.

Atkinson, Mike. "Delirious Inventions." *Action Spectacle Cinema*. Ed. Jose Arroyo. London: BFI Publishing, 2000. pp. 85–90.

Badley, Linda. *Film, Horror, and the Body Fantastic*. Westport, Connecticut: Greenwood Press, 1995.

Baiocchi, Gianpaolo. "Media Coverage of 9/11 in Brazil." *Television and New Media* 3.2 (2002): 183–89.

—. "Heroism Isn't a Hilton Ho and Tell." *Sydney Morning Herald* September 25–26, 2004, Weekend edn., sec. News Review: 37.

Baker, Rick, and Toby Russell. *The Essential Guide to Hong Kong Movies*. London: Eastern Heroes, 1994.

Bandy, Mary Lee, and Antonio Monda. *The Hidden God: Film and Faith*. New York: Museum of Modern Art, 2003.

Barker, Martin, and Julian Petley. *Ill-Effects: The Media/Violence Debate*. 2nd edn. London: Routledge, 2001.

Barsotti, Catherine M, and Robert K. Johnston. *Finding God in the Movies: 33 Films of Reel Faith*. Grand Rapids, Michigan: Baker Books, 2004.

Bartle, Richard A. *Designing Virtual Worlds*. Indianapolis: New Riders, 2004.

Barton, Laura. "The Man Who Rewrote His Life." Interview. *Sydney Morning Herald* October 7–8, 2006, Weekend edn., sec. Spectrum: 28–29.

Battis, Jes. *Chosen Families in Buffy, the Vampire Slayer and Angel*. Jefferson, NC: McFarland, 2005.

Baudrillard, Jean. *The Spirit of Terrorism and Other Essays*. Trans. Chris Turner. London: Verso, 2002.

—. *The Vital Illusion*. Ed. Julia Witwer. New York: Columbia University Press, 2000.

Bauer, Eric. "Sex, Violence and Spec-Scripts: Interview with Shane Black." *Creative Screenwriting* 3 (Winter). 3 (1996): 29–36.

Baumeister, Roy F. *Evil: Inside Human Violence and Cruelty*. New York: W.H. Freeman & Co., 1999.

Bawtree, Michael. *The New Singing Theatre: A Charter for the Music Theatre Movement*. Bristol: The Bristol Press, 1990.

Bearup, Greg. "The Geek Australian Dream." *Sydney Morning Herald* October 14, 2006, Weekend edn., sec. Good Weekend: 30+.

Beautiful Boxer. 2003. Dir. Ekachai Uekrongtham.

Beck, Jerry. *Animation Art: From Pencil to Pixel, the History of Cartoon, Anime and Cgi*. New York: Harper Design International, 2004.

Bell, Gail. *Shot*. Sydney: Picador, Pan Macmillan, 2003.

Bergesen, Albert J., and Andrew M. Greeley. *God in the Movies*. New Brunswick: Transaction Publishers, 2003.

Bernstein, Abbie. "Blonde Ambition." *Buffy the Vampire Slayer, Official Magazine* 8 June/July 2003: 18–22.

Biderman, Shai. "The Roar and the Rampage: A Tale of Revenge in *Kill Bill Volumes 1 and 2*." *Movies and the Meaning of Life: Philosophers Take on Hollywood*. Eds. Kimberly A. Blessing and Paul J. Tudico. Chicago, Illinois: Open Court, 2005. pp. 199–209.

Big Boss, The. 2005. Dir. Wei Lo.

Bilton, Michael. *Wicked Beyond Belief: The Hunt for the Yorkshire Ripper*. London: Harper Collins, 2003.

Bingham, Mike. *Suddenly One Sunday: The True Story of the Port Arthur Tragedy Based on Eyewitness Accounts*. Australia: Harper Collins, 1996.

Bird, Michael. "Film as Hierophany." *Religion in Film*. Eds. John May and Michael Bird. Knoxville: University of Tennessee Press, 1984. pp. 3–22.

Biskind, Peter. *Easy Rider's Raging Bulls: How the Sex 'N' Drugs 'N' Rock 'N' Roll Generation Saved Hollywood*. London: Bloomsbury, 1999.

Black, David A. *Law in Film: Resonance and Representation*. Urbana: University of Illinois Press, 1999.

Black, Joel. *The Aesthetics of Murder: A Study in Romantic Literature and Contemporary Culture*. Baltimore: The John Hopkins University Press, 1991.

Blackburn, Estelle. *Broken Lives*. Melbourne, Australia: Hardie Grant Books, 2002.

Blik, Anton. *Honor and Violence*. Cambridge: Polity, 2001.

Bogenn, Tim, and Rick Barba. *Grand Theft Auto: San Andreas: Official Strategy Guide*. Indianapolis, Indiana: Brady Games, Pearson Education, 2005.

Book, Betsy. "Moving Beyond the Game: Social Virtual Worlds." 2004. *Virtual Worlds Review*. Available: http://www.virtualworldsreview.com/papers/BBook_SoP2.pdf. October 15, 2006.

—. "Virtual Worlds List by Category." 2006. *Virtual Worlds Review*. Available: http://www.virtualworldsreview.com/info/categories.shtml. October 15, 2006.

Bordwell, David. *Figures Traced in Light: On Cinematic Staging*. Berkeley: University of California Press, 2005.

—. *Planet Hong Kong: Popular Cinema and the Art of Entertainment*. Cambridge, Massachusetts: Harvard University Press, 2000.

Bourden, Jerome. "Live Television Is Still Alive: On Television as an Unfulfilled Promise." *The Television Studies Reader*. Eds. Robert C. Allen and Annette Hill. London: Routledge, 2004. pp. 182–95.

Bowling for Columbine. 2002. Dir. Michael Moore.

"Bowling for Truth." Main 2004. *RichWatch*. Available: http://www.bowlingfortruth.com/. July 6, 2004.

Brandon, James. "It Seemed Clear: They Were Going to Kill Me." *Sydney Morning Herald* August 16, 2004, sec. Insight: 11.

Bredekamp, Horst, and Barbara Marie Stafford. "Hyperrealism: One Step Beyond." Interview. Magazine Archive. Visiting and Revisiting Art, etcetera, 6 (Spring) 2006. *Tate Online*. Available: http://www.tate.org.uk/tateetc/issue6/hyperrealism.htm. September 5, 2006.

Brenton, Sam, and Reuben Cohen. *Shooting People: Adventures in Reality TV*. London: Verso, 2003.

Breskin, Nicole. "Lighting up the Big Screen." *Jewish News* January 5, 2007, sec. Life: 8.

Bridge, The. 2006. Dir. Eric Steel.

Brown, Malcolm. "The Gas Did It: Bogle-Chandler Theory Blames Toxic Cloud." *Sydney Morning Herald* September 8, 2006, sec. News: 3.

Brown, Sheila. *Crime and Law in Media Culture*. Buckingham; Philadelphia: Open University Press, 2003.

Bruce, Jo, and Jason Rutter. "Spectacles of the Deathmatch: Character and Narrative in First-Person Shooters." *Screenplay: Cinema/Videogames/Interfaces*. Eds. Geoff King and Tanya Kryzwinska. London: Wallflower Press, 2002. pp. 66–80.

Bukataman, Scott. *Matters of Gravity: Special Effects and Supermen in the 20th Century*. Durham: Duke University Press, 2003.

Bunbury, Stephanie. "The Sound of No Hands Clapping." *Sydney Morning Herald* April 18, 2006, sec. News: 7.

Burnett, Ron. *How Images Think*. Cambridge, Massachusetts: MIT Press, 2004.

Burns, Ken. "Television and the War on Terrorism: The Artistic Community Responds." Panel Discussion 2002. Transcript. *Museum of Television and Radio*. Available: http://www.mtr.org/seminars/satellite/terrorism/terrorism5.htm. May 19, 2004.

Burr, Vivian. "Ambiguity and Sexuality in Buffy the Vampire Slayer: A Sartrean Analysis." *Sexualities* 6.3–4 (2003): 343–60.

Burton, Graeme. *Talking Television: An Introduction to the Study of Television*. London: Arnold, 2000.

Burton, John W. *Violence Explained: The Sources of Conflict, Violence and Crime and Their Prevention*. Manchester: Manchester University Press, 1997.

Byrnes, Paul. "Just Like a Rapper, This Doesn't Sing." *Sydney Morning Herald* January 19, 2006, sec. Arts and Entertainment: 15.

—. "A Shop of Horrors for All Backpackers." Review. *Sydney Morning Herald* February 23, 2006, sec. Arts and Entertainment: 14.

—. "Truth, Fiction and the Flight That Fell to Earth." *Sydney Morning Herald* August 10, 2006, sec. Film Guide: 14.

Calabresi, Massimo, Sam Dealey, and Stephan Faris. "The Tragedy of Sudan." *Time* October 4, 2004: 24+.

Capeci, Jerry. *Wiseguys Say the Darndest Things: The Quotable Mafia*. USA: Alpha, Penguin Group (USA) Inc., 2004.

Capote. 2005. Dir. Bennett Miller.

Capturing the Friedmans. 2003. Dir. Andrew Jarecki.

Carroll, Noel. "Non-Fiction Film and Postmodernist Skepticism." *Post-Theory: Reconstructing Film Studies*. Eds. David Bordwell and Noel Carroll. Wisconsin Studies in Film. Madison, Wisconsin: The University of Wisconsin Press, 1996. pp. 283–304.

Casetti, Francesco. *Inside the Gaze: The Fiction Film and Its Spectator*. Trans. Nell Andrew and Charles O'Brien. Bloomington: Indiana University Press, 1998.

Cassell, Justine, and Henry Jenkins. *From Barbie to Mortal Kombat*. Cambridge: The MIT Press, 1999.

Centre for Communication and Social Policy, University of Southern California, Santa Barbara. The Report of the *National Television Violence Study*. Sage Publications: Studio City, CA, 1996–97.

Chabrier, Rodolphe. "SFX Featurette": Extras: *Irréversible*. DVD Accent Film Entertainment, 2004.

Chan, Evans. "War and Images: 9/11/0, Susan Sontag, Jean Baudrillard, and Paul Virilio." September 5, 2003. *Film International* September. Available: http://www.filmint.nu/netonly/eng/warandimages/htm. May 24, 2004.

Chandler, Daniel. "Shaping and Being Shaped: Engaging with the Media." 1996. *CMC Magazine*. Available: http://www.december.com/cmc/mag/1996/chandler.html. June 17, 2004.

Chandler, Raymond. *The Simple Art of Murder*. Vintage Crime. New York: Vintage Books: Random House, 1988.

Chase, Alston. *Harvard and the Unabomber: The Education of an American Terrorist*. New York and London: W. W. Norton & Company, 2003.

Chase, David. *The Sopranos*. 1999–2007.

    1.1 Pilot: "The Sopranos." Writ. David Chase. Dir. David Chase. January 10, 1999.

    1.2 "46 Long." Writ. David Chase. Dir. David Chase. January 17, 1999.

    1.8 "The Legend of Tennessee Moltisanti." Writ. Frank Renzulli and David Chase. Dir. Tim Van Patten. February 28, 1999.

    2.1 "Guy Walks into a Psychiatrist's Office." Writ. Jason Cahill. Dir. Allen Coulter. January 16, 2000.

    2.4 "Commendatori." Writ. David Chase. Dir. Tim Van Patten. February 2, 2000.

    2.5 "Big Girls Don't Cry." Writ. Terence Winter. Dir. Tim Van Patten. February 13, 2000.

    2.7 "D-Girl." Writ. Todd A. Kessler. Dir. Allen Coulter. February 27, 2000.

    3.10 "To Save Us All from Satan's Power." Writ. Robin Green and Mitchell Burgess. April 29, 2001.

    5.1 "Two Tony's." Writ. David Chase and Terence Winter. Dir. Tim Van Patten. March 7, 2004.

    5.2 "Rat Pack." Writ. Matthew Weiner. Dir. Alan Taylor. March 14, 2004.

    5.4 "All Happy Families." Writ. Toni Kalem. Dir. Rodrigo Garcia. March 28, 2004.

5.5 "Sentimental Education." Writ. Matthew Weiner. Dir. Peter Bogdanovich. April 11, 2004.

5.10 "Cold Cuts." Writ. Robin Green and Mitchell Burgess. Dir. Mike Figgis. May 9, 2004.

5.12 "Longterm Parking." Writ. Terence Winter. Dir. Tim Van Patten. May 23, 2004.

5.13 "All Due Respect." Writ. David Chase, Robin Green, and Mitchell Burgess. Dir. John Patterson. June 6, 2004.

—. *Words into Pictures: Anatomy of a TV Drama: The Sopranos*. Rec 6 June 1999. Panel Discussion. VHS The Writer's Guild Foundation, Los Angeles, 1999.

Cherry, Brigid. "Refusing to Refuse to Look: Female Viewers of the Horror Film." *Horror, the Film Reader*. Ed. Mark Janovich. In Focus: Routledge Film Readers. London: Routledge, 2002. pp. 169–78.

Chinavoc.com. "Shaolin Kung Fu." Home 2007. Available: http://www.chinavoc.com/kungfu/index. asp. January 20, 2007.

Chivers, C. J. "September." *Esquire* 138.3 (2002): 144+.

Cho, Jaeho, Michael P. Boyle, Heejo Keum, Mark D. Shevy, Douglas M. McLeod, Dhavan V. Shah, Zhongdang Pan. "Media, Terrorism, and Emotionality: Emotional Differences in Media Content and Public Reactions to the September 11th Terrorist Attacks." *Journal of Broadcasting and Electronic Media,* 47.3 (2003): 309–27.

Citron, Stephen. *The Musical: From the Inside Out*. London: Hodder & Stoughton, 1991.

Clarke, Jason, and David T. Hardy. *Michael Moore Is a Big Fat Stupid White Man*. New York: ReganBooks, 2004.

Clarke, John and Andy Shea. *Touched by the Devil: Inside the Mind of the Australian Psychopath*. Sydney, Australia: Simon & Schuster, 2001.

Clennell, Andrew, Ben Cubby and Jonathan Pearlman. "Muslims Asked to Identify Attackers." *Sydney Morning Herald* January 27, 2006, sec. News: 3.

Clissold, Bradley D. "*Candid Camera* and the Origins of Reality TV: Contextualising a Historical Precedent." *Understanding Reality Television*. Eds. Su Holmes and Deborah Jermyn. London: Routledge, 2004. pp. 33–53.

Clover, Carol J. "Her Body, Himself: Gender in the Slasher Film." *Screening Violence*. Ed. Stephen Prince. New Brunswick, New Jersey: Rutgers University Press, 2000. pp. 125–74.

CNN Coverage of 9/11 (Paula Zahn Segments). Rec September 11, 2001. The Museum of Television and Radio, Los Angeles, 2001.

Coleman, Loren. *The Copycat Effect: How the Media and Popular Culture Trigger the Mayhem in Tomorrow's Headlines*. New York: Paraview Pocket Books, 2004.

Conard, Mark T. "Thus Spake Bart: On Nietzsche and the Virtues of Being Bad." *The Simpsons and Philosophy: The D'oh! Of Homer*. Eds. Mark T. Conard and Aeon J. Skoble William Irwin. Vol. 2. Popular Culture and Philosophy. Chicago, Illinois: Open Court, 2001. pp. 59–77.

Conrad, Peter. "The Art of Pain." *Observer* April 4, 2004, sec. Arts and Screen: 6.

Cook, James. W. *P.T. Barnum Reader: Nothing Else Like It in the Universe*. Urbana: University of Illinois Press, 2005.

Cooper, Robbie. *Alter Ego: Avatars and their Creators*. London: Chris Boot, 2007.

Corby, Stephen. "De-Capo-Tated." *Sunday Telegraph* April 16, 2006, Weekend edn., sec. 24/7 News in Review: 2.

Corley, Kathleen E., and Robert L. Webb. *Jesus and Mel Gibson's the Passion of the Christ: The Film, the Gospels and the Claims of History*. London: Continuum, 2004.

Corliss, Richard, and Simon Crittle. "The Last Don." *Time* March 4, 2004: 44+.

Corner, John. "Performing the Real: Documentary Diversions." *Television and New Media* 3.3 (August 2002): 255–69.

Cornford, Phillip. "Intrigue and Frailty on a Desert Highway." *Sydney Morning Herald* March 4–5, 2006, Weekend edn., sec. Spectrum, Review: 24.

Crawford, Alice. "The Digital Turn: Animation in the Age of Information Technologies." *Prime Time Animation: Television Animation and American Culture*. Eds. Carole A. Stabile and Mark Harrison. London: Routledge, 2003. pp. 110–30.

Creeber, Glen. "TV Ruined the Movies: Television, Tarantino and the Intimate World of the Sopranos." *This Thing of Ours: Investigating the Sopranos*. Ed. David Lavery. New York: Columbia University Press, 2002. pp. 124–34.

Crossan, John Dominic. "Hymn to a Savage God." *Jesus and Mel Gibson's the Passion of the Christ: The Film, the Gospel's and the Claims of History*. Eds. Kathleen E. Corley and Robert L. Webb. London: Continuum, 2004. pp. 8–27.

Crouching Tiger, Hidden Dragon (Wo Hu Cang Long). 2000. Dir. Li-Kong Hsu, Bill Kwong, and Ang Lee.

Crowther, Bruce. *Hollywood Faction: Reality and Myth in the Movies*. London: Columbus Books, 1984.

Cummings, Pip. "War of the Worlds." Cover Story. *Sydney Morning Herald* January 15–16, 2005, Weekend edn., sec. Icon: 6–7.

Curran, Ste. *Game Plan: Great Designs That Changed the Face of Computer Gaming*. Hove: RotoVision, 2004.

Dargis, Manhola. "Do You Like John Woo?" *Action Spectacle Cinema: A Sight and Sound Reader*. Ed. Jose Arroya. London: BFI Publishing, 2000. pp. 67–71.

Daugherty, Anne Millard. "Just a Girl: Buffy as Icon." *Reading the Vampire Slayer: An Unofficial Critical Companion to Buffy and Angel*. Ed. Roz Kaveny. London: Tauris Parke Paperbacks, 2002. pp. 148–65.

Davidson, Elise. "For Rhymes against Humanity." Review. *Sydney Morning Herald* January 13, 2006, sec. Metro: 7.

Davies, Anne. "Actor Poised to Follow in Reagan's Footsteps." *Sydney Morning Herald*, June 1, 2007, sec. World: 8.

Dekelb-Rittenhouse, Diane. "Sex and the Single Vampire: The Evolution of the Vampire Lothario and Its Representation in Buffy." *Fighting the Forces: What's at Stake in Buffy the Vampire Slayer*. Eds. Rhonda V. Wilcox and David Lavery. Lanham: Rowan & Littlefield, 2002. pp. 143–52.

DeMars, Tony Russell. *From the Simpsons to the Bundys: A Critical Analysis of Disrespectful Discourse in Television Narratives*. Graduate Thesis. University of Southern Mississippi. Ann Arbor, Michigan: UMI Dissertation Services. 1996.

Denver, John. "Introduction." *Legal Reelism: Movies as Legal Texts*. Ed. John Denver. Urbana: University of Illinois Press, 1996. pp. xi–xviii.

DeRosia, Margaret. "An Erotics of Violence: Masculinity and (Homo)Sexuality in Stanley Kubrick's *A Clockwork Orange*." *Stanley Kubrick's A Clockwork Orange*. Ed. Stuart Y. McDougal. Cambridge: Cambridge University Press, 2003. pp. 61–84.

Dershowitz, Alan M. "Life Is Not a Dramatic Narrative." *Law's Stories: Narrative and Rhetoric in the Law*. Eds. Peter Brooks and Paul Gewirtz. New Haven: Yale University Press, 1996. pp. 99–105.

Detweiler, Craig, and Barry Taylor. *A Matrix of Meanings: Finding God in Pop Culture*. Engaging Culture. Eds. William A. Dyrness and Robert K Johnston. Grand Rapids, Michigan: Baker Academic, 2003.

Die Hard. 1988. Dir. John McTiernan.

Doane, Mary Ann. "Film and the Masquerade: Theorising the Female Spectator." *Feminism and Film*. Ed. E. Ann Kaplan. Oxford Readings in Feminism. Oxford: Oxford University Press, 2000. pp. 418–36.

Donohue, Steve. "A Story Nets Could Not Overplay." *Multichannel News* September 17, 2001: 3.

Donohue, Steve, and Kent Gibbons. "Most Horrific Story of Our Time." *Multichannel News* September 17, 2001: 54.

Doom. 2005. Dir. Andrzeij Bartkowiak.

Dovey, Jon. *Freakshow: First Person Media and Factual Television*. London: Pluto Press, 2000.

Dow, David R. "Fictional Documentaries and Truthful Fictions: The Death Penalty in Recent American Film." *Constitutional Commentary* 17.3 (2000): 511–53.

Doyle, Peter. *City of Shadows: Sydney Police Photographs 1912–48*. Sydney: Historic Houses Trust, 2005.

Duffy, Michael. "Death in the Afternoon, Morning and Night." *Sydney Morning Herald* September 20–30, 2007, Weekend edn., sec. Spectrum: 28+.

Dunne, Stephen. "Flights of Fantasy." *Sydney Morning Herald* April 1–2, 2006, Weekend edn., sec. Spectrum: Special Promotion: 2–3.

Dyer, Richard. "Action!" *Action Spectacle Cinema: A Sight and Sound Reader*. Ed. Jose Arroya. London: BFI Publishing, 2000. pp. 17–21.

Ebert, Roger. "Bowling for Columbine." Movie Reviews 2002. *rogerebert.com*. Available: http://rogerebert.suntimes.com/apps/pbcs.dll/article?AID=/20021018/REVIEWS/210180303/1023. January 22, 2006.

—. "Columbine Revisited." Review. *Jerusalem Post* May 7, 2004, Weekend edn., sec. Billboard: 2.

Eckert, Penelope, and Sally McConnell-Ginet. *Language and Gender*. Cambridge: Cambridge University Press, 2003.

Edgar, David. "Rules of Engagement." Digital. October 22, 2005. *Guardian Unlimited*. Available: http://books.guardian.co.uk/review/story/0,12084,1596971,00.html. March 11, 2006.

Elber, Lynn. "Making the Dead." *Australian* September 4–5, 2004, Weekend edn., sec. View: R24–R25.

Elder, Robert K. *John Woo Interviews*. Conversations with Filmmakers. Ed. Peter Brunette. Jackson: University Press of Mississippi, 2005.

11'09'01: September 11: A Collective Film. 2002. Prod. Alain Brigand.

Enders, Jody. *Death by Drama and Other Medieval Urban Legends*. Chicago: University of Chicago Press, 2002.

Espenson, Jane. "Interview Succubus Club," Hour One. May 22, 2002. *slayage.com* Transcript: *rally@rallyvincent.com*. Available: http://www.slayage.com/news/020522-je_int.html. July 7, 2003.

Fargo. 1996. Dir. Joel Coen.

Farhat, John. "First Person Shooter Sequence". Bonus: *Doom*. DVD Distant Planet Productions, Universal Pictures, 2006.

Feuer, Jane. "The Self-Reflexive Musical and the Myth of Entertainment." *Film Genre Reader III*. Ed. Barry Keith Grant. Austin: University of Texas Press, 2003. pp. 457–71.

Fields, Ingrid Walker. "Family Values and Feudal Codes: The Social Politics of America's Twenty-First Century Gangster." *Journal of Popular Culture* 37.4 (2004): 611–33.

Fienberg, Daniel. "Thirst for Ice-T Quenched on New SVU." March 1, 2004. *Zap2it*: TV News. Available: http://tv.zap2it.com/tveditorial/tve_main/1,1002,271%7C86678%7C1%7C,00.html. December 7, 2005.

Film Force. "An Interview with Joss Whedon: The Creator of *Buffy, the Vampire Slayer* Discusses His Career." June 23, 2003. *IGN.com*. Available: http://filmforce.ign.com/articles/425/425492p1.html. June 28, 2003.

Fiske, John. *Television Culture*. London: Routledge, 1987.

Forkan, Jim. "Service Efforts Took Precedence." *Multichannel News* September 17, 2001: 4.

Forshey, Gerald E. *American Religious and Biblical Spectaculars*. Media and Society. Ed. J. Fred MacDonald. Westport, Connecticut: Praeger, 1992.

Foster, Anne. "Anne Foster Recalls Bob Edwards' Calming Voice." Voicemail Search Archive 2002. *The Sonic Memorial Project*. Available: http://sonicmemorial.org/sonic/public/archive.jsp. October 3, 2004.

Foster, Catherine. "Fight Coach Toils to Make Violent Scenes Bloody Good." Interview. *Boston Globe* August 5, 2005, 3rd edn.: D.6.

Foster, Susan L. "Textual Evidences: Organizing Dance's History." *Bodies of the Text*. Eds. Ellen W. Goellner and Jacqueline Shea Murphy. New Brunswick, New Jersey: Rutgers University Press, 1995. pp. 231–46.

Fowles, Jib. *The Case for Television Violence*. Thousand Oaks: Sage Publications Inc, 1999.

Francis, Alexandre, and Mark Coutre. "Credibility of a Simulation-Based Virtual Laboratory: An Exploratory Study of Learner Judgments of Verisimilitude." *Journal of Interactive Learning Research* 14.4 (2003): 439–64.

Fraser, Peter. *Images of the Passion: The Sacramental Mode in Film*. Westport, Connecticut: Praeger, 1998.

Fredriksen, Paula. *On the Passion of the Christ: Exploring the Issues Raised by the Controversial Movie*. Berkeley: University of California Press, 2006.

—. "Preface." *On the Passion of the Christ: Exploring the Issues Raised by the Controversial Movie*. Ed. Paula Fredriksen. Berkeley: University of California Press, 2006. pp. xi–xxiii.

—. "Gospel Truths." *On the Passion of the Christ: Exploring Issues Raised by the Controversial Movie*. Ed. Paula Fredriksen. Berkeley: University of California Press, 2006.

French, Karl. *Screen Violence*. London: Bloomsbury, 1996.

Fritz, Ben. "Viewer Beware." Column Archives November 19, 2002. *Spinsanity*: Countering Rhetoric With Reason. Available: http://www.spinsanity.org/columns/20021119.html. July 6, 2004.

Frow, John. "The Uses of Terror and the Limits of Cultural Studies." *Media International Australia Incorporating Culture and Policy* 2003.109 (2003): 14–21.

Furniss, Maureen. *Art in Motion: Animation Aesthetics*. London: John Libbey, 1998.

Gage, Caroline. "Bowling for Columbine: Michael Moore Off-Target." *Off Our Backs* January–February (2003): 51–54.

Gaines, Jane M. "Introduction: 'the Real Returns.'" *Collecting Visible Evidence*. Eds. Jane M. Gaines and Michael Renov. Vol. 6. Visible Evidence. Minneapolis: University of Minnesota Press, 1999. pp. 1–18.

Gang Tapes. 2002. Dir. Adam Ripp.

Gardaphe, Fred. "Fresh Garbage: The Gangster as Suburban Trickster." *A Sitdown with the Sopranos*. Ed. Regina Barrecca. New York: Palgrave, Macmillan, 2002. pp. 89–111.

Garner, Helen. *Joe Cinque's Consolation: A True Story of Death, Grief and the Law*. Sydney: Picador, Pan Macmillan Australia, 2004.

Gary, Jerome. *Master Seminar: Patti Jenkins, Steve Perry and Guy Livneh*. Rec January 28, 2004. Panel. American Film Institute, Los Angeles, 2004.

Get Rich or Die Tryin'. 2005. Dir. Jim Sheridan.

Gewirtz, Paul. "Victims and Voyeurs: Two Narrative Problems at the Criminal Trial." *Law's Stories: Narrative and Rhetoric in the Law*. Eds. Peter Brooks and Paul Gewirtz. New Haven: Yale University Press, 1996. pp. 135–61.

Gillespie, Angus Kress. "Professor Gillespie Remembers 9/11." Interview Search Archive 2002. *The Sonic Memorial Project*. Available: http://sonicmemorial.org/public/archive.jsp. October 3, 2004.

Gillings, Mark. "The Real, the Virtually Real, and the Hyperreal: The Role of VR in Archaeology." *Envisioning the Past: Archaeology and the Image*. Eds. Sam Smiles and Stephanie Moser. New Interventions in Art History. Oxford: Blackwell Publishing, 2005. pp. 223–39.

Giovanni, Nick. "To Be Black in America Is to Be Constantly at War." *Scars: American Poetry in the Face of Violence*. Ed. Cynthia Dubin Edelberg. Tuscaloosa, Alabama: University of Alabama Press, 1995. pp. 81–83.

Girard, Rene. "On Mel Gibson's *The Passion of the Christ*." 2004. *Anthropoetics* 10.1 (Spring/Summer). Available: http://www.anthropoetics.ucla.edu/ap1001/RGGibson.htm. September 5, 2006.

Gitlin, Todd. *Media Unlimited: How the Torrent of Images and Sounds Overwhelms Our Lives*. New York: Henry Holt and Company, 2002.

Glynn, Kevin. *Tabloid Culture: Trash Taste, Popular Power and the Transformation of American Television*. Durham: Duke University Press, 2000.

Godfather, The. 1972. Dir. Francis Ford Coppola.

Goellner, Ellen W. "Force and Form in Faulkner's *Light in August*." *Bodies of the Text: Dance as Theory, Literature as Dance*. Eds. Ellen W. Goellner and Jacqueline Shea Murphy. New Brunswick, New Jersey: Rutgers University Press, 1995. pp. 182–201.

Goldsworthy, Kerryn. *Helen Garner*. Australian Writers. Ed. Chris Wallace-Crabbe. Melbourne: Oxford University Press, 1996.

Goodman, Jonathan. *Tracks to Murder*. True Crime Series. Ed. Albert Borowitz. Kent and London: The Kent State University Press, 2005.

Goodman, Peter S. "Economists Say Movie Violence Might Temper the Real Thing." *New York Times*, January 7, 2008, sec. Business Day: C1+

Goodwin, Andrew. "TV News-Striking the Right Balance?" *Understanding Television*. Eds. Andrew Goodwin and Garry Whannel. London: Routledge, 1990. pp. 42–59.

Gourgouris, Stathis. "Enlightenment and Paranomia." *Violence, Identity and Self-Determination*. Eds. Hent de Vries and Samuel Weber. Stanford, California: Stanford University Press, 1997.

Gowers, Rebecca. *The Swamp Death: A True Tale of Victorian Lies and Murder*. London: Hamish Hamilton, 2004.

Grabe, Maria Elizabeth, Shuhua Zhou, and Brooke Barnett. "Explicating Sensationalism in Television News: Content and Bells and Whistles." *Journal of Broadcasting and Electronic Media* 45.4 (2001): 635–55.

Gracia, Jorge J. E. *Mel Gibson's Passion and Philosophy*. Popular Culture and Philosophy. Ed. William Irwin. Vol. 10. Chicago, Illinois: Open Court, 2004.

Graham, David John. "Redeeming Violence in the Films of Martin Scorsese." *Explorations in Theology and Film: Movies and Meaning*. Eds. Clive Marsh and Gaye Ortiz. Oxford: Blackwell Publishers, 1998. pp. 87–95.

Gray, Simon. "Miniatures Add Grand Scale." Page 1, January 2004. *American Cinematographer*. Available: http://www.theasc.com/magazine/jan04/sub2/index.html. March 13, 2004.

—. "Rebooting a Sci-Fi Spectacular." Index. June 2003. *American Cinematographer*. Available: http://www.theasc.com/magazine/june03/cover/index.html. March 13, 2004.

Gray, Timothy, M. "H'wood's Age of Innocence Is Over." *Variety* September 12, 2001, sec. Reel Life: 8.

Greene, Ray. "Counterpunch: 'Our' Violence Versus 'Theirs'." *Los Angeles Times* September 24, 2001, sec. Calender, Entertainment Desk: F7.

Greene, Richard, and Peter Vernezze. "The Sopranos and Philosophy: I Kill Therefore I Am." *Popular Culture and Philosophy*. Ed. William Irwin. Chicago, Illinois: Open Court, 2004. pp. 119–46.

Grenville, Kate, and Sue Woolfe. *Making Stories: How Ten Australian Novels Were Written*. Sydney: Allen & Unwin, 2001.

Grieg, Charlotte. *Evil Serial Killers: In the Minds of Monsters*. London: Capella, 2006.

Groening, Matt. *The Simpsons*. 1989.

> 7.9 "Treehouse of Horror VI." Writ. Donick Cary, Larry Doyle, and David X. Cohen. Dir. Steven Dean Moore. October 29, 1995.

> 9.5 "The Cartridge Family," Writ. John Swartzwelder. Dir. Pete Michels. November 2, 1997.

> 10.4 "Treehouse of Horror IX" Writ. Steve Tompkins, David X. Cohen, and John Swartzwelder. Dir. Bob Anderson. October 25, 1998.

Gross, Larry. "Big and Loud." *Action Spectacle Cinema: A Sight and Sound Reader*. Ed. Jose Arroyo. London: BFI Publishing, 2000. pp. 3–9.

Grossberg, Josh. "Law & Order Gets a Senator." August 28, 2002. *Eonline*. News. Available: http://www.eonline.com/News/Items/0,1,10454,00.html?newsrellink. December 12, 2004.

Grossman, Dave. *On Killing*. Boston: Little Brown, 1995.

Grossman, Dave, and Gloria DeGataetano. *Stop Teaching Our Kids to Kill: A Call to Action Against TV, Movie and Video Game Violence*. New York: Crown, 1999.

HaLevy, Ephraim. "Spielberg's Facts and Fiction." January 21, 2006. *Times Online*. Available: http://www.timesonline.co.uk/article/0923-2000576,00.html. January 21, 2006.

Hall, Sandra. "Tragedy as Tearjerker." *Sydney Morning Herald* September 30–October 1, 2006, Weekend edn., sec. Spectrum: 14.

Hall, Stuart. "Encoding/Decoding." *Media Texts: Authors and Readers*. Eds. David Graddol and Oliver Boyd-Barrett. Clevedon: Multilingual Matters and The Open University, 1994. pp. 200–11.

Hammond, Mary. "Monsters and Metaphors: *Buffy the Vampire Slayer* and the Old World." *Cult Television*. Eds. Sara Gwenllian-Jones and Roberta E. Pearson. Minneapolis: University of Minnesota Press, 2004. pp. 147–64.

Hammond, Stefan, and Mike Wilkins. *Sex and Zen & a Bullet in the Head: The Essential Guide to Hong Kong's Mind-Bending Films*. New York: Fireside: Simon & Shuster, 1996.

Hampe, Barry. *Making Documentary Films and Reality Videos: A Practical Guide to Planning, Filming, and Editing Documentaries of Real Events*. New York: Henry Hold and Company, 1997.

Haralovich, Mary Beth, and Michael W. Trosset. "Expect the Unexpected: Narrative Pleasure and Uncertainty Due to Chance in Survivor." *Reality TV: Remaking Television Culture*. Eds. Susan Murray and Laurie Ouellette. New York: New York University Press, 2004. pp. 288–302.

Hardy, David T. "Bowling for Columbine: Documentary or Fiction?" 2002. *hardylaw.net*. Available: http://www.hardylaw.net/Truth_About_Bowling.html. July 6, 2004.

Harkavy, Donna. "The Art of Bearing Witness." *The Culture of Violence*. Ed. Helaine Posner. Amherst: University Gallery, University of Massachusetts Amherst, 2002. pp. 19–26.

Hartcher, Peter. "Speed of Lies Equals the Ease of Acceptance." *Sydney Morning Herald* July 23, 2004, sec. Comment: 13.

Harvey, Paul. *The Condition of Postmodernity: An Enquiry Into the Origins of Cultural Change*. Oxford: Basil Blackwell, 1990.

Hawkes, Tim. "Lie Wrapped in Truth Is Still a Lie." *Sydney Morning Herald* April 28, 2006, sec. Comment: 13.

Hayles, N. Katherine. *How We Became Post-Human: Virtual Bodies in Cybernetics, Literature and Informatics*. Chicago: The University of Chicago Press, 1999.

Heffernan, Virginia. "Cut to the Chase." *Sydney Morning Herald* May 3, 2004, sec. The Guide: 5.

Heinecken, Dawn. *The Warrior Women: A Feminist Cultural Analysis of the New Female Body in Popular Media*. New York: Peter Lang, 2003.

Helfand, Jessica. *Screen: Essays on Graphic Design, New Media, and Visual Culture*. New York: Princeton Architectural Press, 2001.

Hewitt, Andrew. *Social Choreography: Ideology as Performance in Dance and Everyday Movement*. Durham: Duke University Press, 2005.

Higginbotham, Adam. "Blood on Their Hands." *Sydney Morning Herald* September 4, 2004, Weekend edn., sec. Good Weekend: 30+.

Hight, Craig. "'It Isn't Always Shakespeare, but It's Genuine': Cinema's Commentary on Documentary Hybrids." *Understanding Reality Television*. Eds. Su Holmes and Jermyn Deborah. London: Routledge, 2004. pp. 233–51.

Hill, Annette. *Shocking Entertainment: Viewer Response to Violent Movies*. Luton, United Kingdom: University of Luton Press, 1997.

Hines, Peter. "Our Fifteen Minutes Are Up." *Inside Film* 40.30–32 (2001–02): 30–35.

History of Violence, A. 2005. Dir. David Cronenberg.

Hoberman, J. "Made in Hollywood: How Movies Foretold the New Reality." *Village Voice* December 11, 2001, sec. Film: 109–10.

—. "Nietzsche's Boy." *Action Spectacle Cinema: A Sight and Sound Reader*. Ed. Jose Arroyo. London: BFI Publishing, 2000. pp. 28–34.

Hockensmith, Steve. "Dialogue with 'Buffy' Creator Joss Whedon." May 16, 2003. *Hollywood Reporter*. Available: http://story.news.yahoo.com/news?tmpl=story&u=/nm/20030520/en_nm/television_whedon_dc_1. May 16, 2003.

Hogue, Peter. "Documentaries as Movies." *Film Comment* 32.4 (1996): 56–60.

Hollywood, Amy. "Kill Jesus." *Mel Gibson's Bible: Religion, Popular Culture, and the Passion of the Christ*. Eds. Timothy K. Beale and Tod Linafelt. Afterlives of the Bible. Chicago: The University of Chicago Press, 2006. pp. 159–67.

Holmes, Su, and Deborah Jermyn. "Introduction: Understanding Reality TV." *Understanding Reality Television*. Eds. Su Holmes and Jermyn Deborah. London: Routledge, 2004. pp. 1–32.

Hope, Paco. "The Cartoon Laws of Physics." 2006. *The Funny Pages*. Available: http://funnies.paco.to/cartoon.html. October 10, 2006.

Hopkins, Susan. *Girl Heroes: The New Force in Popular Culture*. The Media Culture Series. Ed. McKenzie Wark. Sydney: Pluto Press Australia, 2002.

Horsley, Jake. *The Blood Poets: A Cinema of Savagery 1958–99*. Vol. 1: American Chaos: From Touch of Evil to The Terminator. Lanham: Scarecrow Press, Inc., 1999.

—. *The Blood Poets: A Cinema of Savagery 1958–99*. Vol. 2: Millennial Blues: From Apocalypse Now to The Matrix. Lanham: The Scarecrow Press, Inc., 1999.

Hughes, Lloyd. *The Rough Guide to Gangster Movies*. Rough Guides Reference. Ed. Mark Ellingham. London: Rough Guides Ltd., 2005.

Hunt, Leon. "'I Know Kung Fu!': The Martial Arts in the Age of Digital Reproduction." *Screenplay: Cinema/Videogames/Interfaces*. Eds. Geoff King and Tanya Krzywinska. London: Wallflower Press, 2002. pp. 194–205.

—. *Kung Fu Cult Masters: From Bruce Lee to Crouching Tiger*. London: Wallflower Press, 2003.

Hurley, Neil P. "Cinematic Transfigurations of Jesus." *Religion in Film*. Eds. John May and Michael Bird. Knoxville: University of Tennessee Press, 1984. pp. 61–78.

Hutchings, Peter J. *The Criminal Spectre in Law, Literature and Aesthetics*. London: Routledge, 2001.

Inness, Sherrie A. *Action Chicks: New Images of Tough Women in Popular Culture*. New York: Palgrave Macmillan, 2004.

Irréversible. 2002. Dir. Gaspar Noé.

Irwin, William. "Gibson's Sublime *Passion*: In Defense of the Violence." *Mel Gibson's Passion and Philosophy: The Cross, the Questions, the Controversy*. Ed. Jorge J.E. Gracia. Vol. 10. Popular Culture and Philosophy. Chicago, Illinois: Open Court, 2004. pp. 51–61.

—. *The Matrix and Philosophy: Welcome to the Desert of the Real*. Popular Culture and Philosophy. Vol. 3. Chicago, Ilinois: Open Court, 2002.

Irwin, William, Mark T. Conard, and J. Aeon Skoble. *The Simpsons and Philosophy: The D'oh! Of Homer*. Popular Culture and Philosophy. Ed. William Irwin. Vol. 2. Chicago, Illinois: Open Court, 2001.

Jaa, Tony. *Cast and Crew Interviews*. Documentary and Interviews: *Ong Bak*. Disc 2. Eastern Eye Asian Cinema. Madman Entertainment Pty. Ltd. DVD The AV Channel Pty. Ltd., 2003.

Jackson, Kenneth. "Kenneth Jackson Talks About 9/11." Part 2. Archive Interview December 11, 2001. *The Sonic Memorial Project*. Available: http://sonicmemorial.org/sonic/public/archive.jsp. September 28, 2004.

—. "Kenneth Jackson Talks About 9/11." Part 3. Archive Search Interview December 11, 2001. *The Sonic Memorial Project*. Available: http://sonicmemorial.org/sonic/public/archive.jsp. September 28, 2004.

Jacobs, Jason. "Gunfire." *Action Spectacle Cinema: A Sight and Sound Reader*. Ed. Jose Arroyo. London: BFI Publishing, 2000. pp. 9–16.

James, Caryn. "A Heart of Darkness Lurks Below." *Sydney Morning Herald* February 9, 2006, sec. Arts and Entertainment: 16.

Jancovich, Mark. *American Horror: From 1951 to the Present*. British Association for American Studies, Pamphlet 28. Staffordshire: Keele University Press, 1994.

Jarrar, Nada. "Betrayal but a Small Part of the Larger Deception." *Sydney Morning Herald* November 24, 2004, sec. Comment: 17.

Jay, Martin. *Refractions of Violence*. New York and London: Routledge, 2003.

Jenkins, Henry, and Kurt Squire. "The Art of Contested Spaces." *Game On: The History and Culture of Videogames*. Ed. Lucien King. London: Laurence King Publishing, 2002. pp. 64–75.

Jermyn, Deborah. "'This Is About Real People!': Video Technologies, Actuality and Affect in the Television Crime Appeal." *Understanding Reality Television*. Eds. Su Holmes and Deborah Jermyn. London: Routledge, 2004. pp. 71–90.

Johnson-Woods, Toni. *Big Bother: Why Did That Reality-TV Show Become Such a Phenomenon?* Brisbane: University of Queensland Press, 2002.

Johnston, Robert K. *Reel Spirituality: Theology and Film in Dialogue*. Engaging Culture. Eds. William A. Dyrness and Robert K. Johnston. Grand Rapids, Michigan: Baker Academic, 2000.

Jones, Angie, and Jamie Oliff. *Thinking Animation: Bridging the Gap Between 2D and CG*. Boston, MA: Thomson Course Technology, 2007.

Josyph, Peter. "Blood Music: Reading Blood Meridian." *Sacred Violence: A Reader's Companion to Cormac Mccarthy*. Eds. Wade Hall and Rick Wallach. El Paso: University of Texas, Texas Western Press, 1995.

Kael, Pauline. *Movie Love: Complete Reviews 1988–91*. New York: Plume, 1991.

—. *Reeling*. London: Marion Boyars, 1977.

Kalina, Paul. "An Image to Horrible to Bear." *Sydney Morning Herald* August 31, 2006, sec. Insight: 11.

Kaminsky, Stuart M. "Kung Fu Film as Ghetto Myth." *Journal of Popular Film* 3.2 (1974): 129–38.

—. *American Film Genres*. 2nd edn. Chicago: Nelson-Hall, 1984.

Kaplan, E. Ann. "Is the Gaze Male?" *Feminism and Film*. Ed. E. Ann Kaplan. Oxford Readings in Feminism. Oxford: Oxford University Press, 2000. pp. 119–38.

Keetley, Dawn. "Law & Order." *Prime Time Law: Fictional Television as Legal Narrative*. Eds. Robert M. Jarvis and Paul R. Joseph. Durham, North Carolina: Carolina Academic Press, 1998. pp. 33–53.

Kennedy, Rosanne. "The Dangerous Individual and the Social Body." *Thinking Through the Body of the Law*. Eds. Peng Cheah, David Fraser, and Judith Grbich. Sydney: Allen & Unwin, 1996. pp. 187–206.

Keslowitz, Steven. *The World According to the Simpsons*. Naperville, Illinois: Source Books, Inc, 2006.

Khouri, Norma. *Forbidden Love: A Harrowing True Story of Love and Revenge in Jordan*. Sydney: Bantam Books, 2003.

Kilday, Gregg. "No Escaping the Images." *The Hollywood Reporter* September 13, 2001: 1.

Kill Bill: Volume 1. 2003. Dir. Quentin Tarantino.

Kill Bill: Volume 2. 2004. Dir. Quentin Tarantino.

"Killing Her Way to Fame." *Time* February 18, 1991: 45.

King, Geoff, and Tanya Krzywinska. *Tomb Raiders and Space Invaders: Videogame Forms and Contexts*. London: I. B. Tauris, 2006.

King, Lucien. *Game On: The History and Culture of Videogames*. London: Laurence King Publishing, 2002.

Kipp, Jeremiah. "Lock and Load: Daniel Minehan Broadcasts *Series 7*." Archives 2001. *filmcritic.com*. Available: http://filmcritic.com/misc/emporium.nsf/84dbbfa4d710144986256c290016f76e/e8ef1 2d6a85001b588256a1200030bba?OpenDocument. July 9, 2004.

Kleinhams, Chuck, and Rick Morris. "Court TV: The Evolution of a Reality Format." *Reality TV: Remaking Television Culture*. Eds. Susan Murray and Laurie Ouellette. New York: New York University Press, 2004. pp. 157–75.

Klock, Geoff. *How to Read Superhero Comics and Why*. New York: Continuum, 2002.

Knight, Deborah. "Popular Parody: The Simpsons Meets the Crime Film." *The Simpsons and Philosophy: The D'oh! Of Homer*. Eds. William Irwin, Mark T. Conard, and Aeon J. Skoble. Vol. 2. Popular Culture and Philosophy. Chicago, Illinois: Open Court, 2001. pp. 93–107.

Knox, Malcolm. "For Khouri's Ally, It Was a Friendship Stronger Than Fiction." *Sydney Morning Herald* August 16, 2004, sec. News: 3.

—. "Her Life as a Fake: Bestseller's Lies Exposed." *Sydney Morning Herald* July 24, 2004, sec. News: 1.

—. "Khouri Lost for Words to Explain Book." *Sydney Morning Herald* August 5, 2004, sec. News: 3.

Knox, Malcolm, and Caroline Overington. "An Imaginary Life." *Sydney Morning Herald* July 31–August 1, 2004, Weekend edn., sec. News Review: 25.

Knox, Sara L. *Murder: A Tale of Modern American Life*. Durham: Duke University Press, 1998.

Kopel, Dave. "Bowling Truths: Michael Moore's Mocking." April 4, 2003. *National Review Online*. Available: http://www.nationalreview.com/kopel/kopel040403.asp. July 6, 2004.

Kowalewski, Michael. *Deadly Musings: Violence and Verbal Form in American Fiction*. Princeton, New Jersey: Princeton University Press, 1993.

Kremmer, Christopher, and Lisa Pryor. "Crime and Prejudice." *Sydney Morning Herald* August 5–6, 2006, Weekend edn., sec. News Review: 23+.

Lam, Miawling. "Creating a Big Song and Dance." *Sunday Telegraph* January 14, 2007, Weekend edn., sec. News: 20–21.

Lane, Phillip J. "The Existential Condition of Television Crime Drama." *Journal of Popular Culture* 34.4 (2001): 137–51.

Last Horror Movie, The. 2003. Dir. Julian Richards.

Lavery, David. "From Cinescape to Cyberspace: Zionists and Agents, Realists and Gamers in *the Matrix* and *Existenz*." *Journal of Popular Film and Television* 28.4 (2001): 150–57.

—. ed. *This Thing of Ours: Investigating the Sopranos*. Columbia: Wallflower, 2002.

—. ed. *Reading the Sopranos: Hit TV from HBO*. London: I. B. Tauris, 2006.

Lawrence, John Shelton, and Robert Jewett. *The Myth of the American Superhero*. Grand Rapids, Michigan: Cambridge, UK: William B. Eardmans Publishing Company, 2002.

Leapma, Ben. "Internet's Free World Attracts Dark Forces." *Sydney Morning Herald* May 19–20, 2007, Weekend edn., sec. World: 18.

Ledbetter, Mark. *Victims and Postmodern Narrative or Doing Violence to the Body: An Ethic of Reading and Writing*. London: Macmillan Press, 1996.

Lee, Ken-fang. "Far Away, So Close: Cultural Translation in Ang Lee's Crouching Tiger, Hidden Dragon." *Inter-Asia Cultural Studies* 4.2 (2003).

Lee, Patrick. "The Creators of Buffy Head Into Season Seven with a Lighter Heart." 2002. *scifi.com*. Available: http://www.scifi.com/sfw/issue282/interview.html. July 7, 2003.

Legge, Kate. "Hoaxer So Hard to Read." *Australian* July 31–August 1, 2004, Weekend edn., sec. The Nation: 1+.

Leitch, Thomas. *Crime Films*. Genres in American Cinema. Ed. Barry Keith Grant. Cambridge: Cambridge University Press, 2002.

Lekas, Michelle. "Ultrasound: The Feminine in the Age of Mechanical Reproduction." *Music and Cinema*. Eds. Caryl Flinn and David Neumeyer James Buhler. Hanover: Weslyan University Press, 2000. pp. 275–94.

Leonard, John. *Smoke and Mirrors*. New York: The New Press, 1997.

Leslie, Esther. *Hollywood Flatlands: Animation, Critical Theory and the Avante-Garde*. London: Verso, 2002.

Lesser, Wendy. *Pictures at an Execution*. Cambridge: Harvard University Press, 1993.

Lewis, Justin. "The Meaning of Real Life." *Reality TV: Remaking Television Culture*. Eds. Susan Murray and Laurie Oullette. New York: New York University Press, 2004. pp. 289–302.

Life of Brian, The. 1979. Dir. Terry Jones.

Lingis, Alphonso. *Body Transformations: Evolutions and Atavisms in Culture*. New York: Routledge, 2005.

Little, William G. "Jesus's Extreme Makeover." *Mel Gibson's Bible: Religion, Popular Culture, and the Passion of the Christ*. Eds. Timothy K. Beale and Tod Linafelt. Afterlives of the Bible. Chicago: The University of Chicago Press, 2006. pp. 169–76.

Mackendrick, Karen. "Embodying Transgression." *Of the Presence of the Body: Essays on Dance and Performance Theory*. Ed. Andre Lepecki. Middletown, Connecticut: Wesleyan University Press, 2004. pp. 140–56.

Maddox, Gary. "Analyze This: My Life Is One Draft after Another." Interview. *Sydney Morning Herald* June 20, 2001, sec. Metropolitan: 21.

—. "Da Vinci's Night a Lesson in Decorum." *Sydney Morning Herald* April 18, 2006, sec. News: 7.

—. "The Secret They'll Share With Everyone." *Sydney Morning Herald* April 18, 2006, sec. News: 7.

—. "Time to Face the Pain, Not Blame." *Sydney Morning Herald* August 19–20, 2006, Weekend edn., sec. Spectrum: 18–19.

Maddox, Gary, and Stephen Gibbs. "Just a Bloke Who Likes a Bit of Torture." *The Sydney Morning Herald* July 12, 2000, sec. Arts: 21.

Maher, Kevin. "What's Behind the Gore?" *Observer* January 12, 2003, sec. Review, Screen: 8.

Malcolm, Janet. *The Journalist and the Murderer*. London: Papermac, 1998.

Maltby, Richard. *Hollywood Cinema*. 2nd edn. Oxford: Blackwell, 2003.

—. "The Spectacle of Criminality." *Violence and American Cinema*. Ed. J. David Slocum. New York: Routledge, 2001. pp. 117–52.

Maltin, Leonard. *Of Mice and Magic: A History of American Animated Cartoons*. New York: New American Library, 1987.

Marquez, Jose. "Lights! Camera! Action!" *Mel Gibson's Bible: Religion, Popular Culture, and the Passion of the Christ*. Eds. Timothy K. Beale and Tod Linafelt. Afterlives of the Bible. Chicago: The University of Chicago Press, 2006. pp. 176–86.

Martin, Joel W., and Conrad E. Ostwalt Jr. *Screening the Sacred: Religion, Myth, and Ideology in Popular American Film*. Boulder, Colorado: Westview Press, 1995.

Mascaro, Thomas A. "The Network Executive Did It: Law & Order Indicts Network Programming Practices for Ethical Lapses in Reality TV." *Journal of Popular Film and Television*, 31.4 (2004): 149–58.

Matrix, The. 1999 . Dir. Andy Wachowski and Larry Wachowski.

Matrix: Reloaded, The. 2003. Dir. Andy Wachowski and Larry Wachowski.

Matrix: Revolutions, The. 2003. Dir. Andy Wachowski and Larry Wachowski.

McArthur, David L., Daniel Magana, Corinee Peek-Asa, and Jess F. Kraus. "Local Television News Coverage of Traumatic Deaths and Injuries." *The Western Journal of Medicine* 175.6 (2001): 380–84.

McCarthy, Terry. "Warning." *Time* March 19, 2001: 24+.

McCarty, John. *Bullets over Hollywood: The American Gangster Picture from the Silents to "the Sopranos."* Cambridge, MA.: Da Capo Press, 2004.

McClymont, Kate. "I Shot the Lotto Winner's Standover Man. Honest." *Sydney Morning Herald* December 11–12, 2004, Weekend edn., sec. News: 1.

McGeary, Johanna. "The Scandal's Growing Stain." *Time* May 17, 2004: 26+.

McKay, Esther. *Crime Scene: True Stories From the Life of a Forensic Investigator*. Melbourne: Viking, 2005.

McKee, Robert. *Story: Substance, Structure, Style, and the Principles of Screenwriting*. London: Methuen, 1999.

McMillin, Scott. *The Musical as Drama: A Study of the Principles and Conventions Behind Musical Shows from Kern to Sondheim*. Princeton and Oxford: Princeton University Press, 2006.

McQuail, Denis. *Mass Communication Theory: An Introduction*. 2nd edn. London: Sage, 1987.

Meisall, Louis K., and Linda Chase. *Photorealism at the Millennium*. Vol. 3. New York: Harry N. Abrams Inc., 2002.

Menon, Vinay. "The Eternal Buffy." May 17, 2003. *Toronto Star*. Available: http://www.thestar.com/NASApp/cs/ContentServer?pagename=thestar/Layout/Article_Type1&c=Article&cid=1052251582169&call_pageid=968867495754&col=969483191630. May 18, 2003.

Miles, Margaret R. *Seeing and Believing: Religion and Values in the Movies*. Boston: Beacon Press, 2002.

Miller, Frank. *Batman: The Dark Knight Returns*. New York: DC Comics, 2002.

Miller, John. *The Real Deal, Documentaries, Special Features, the Sopranos: The Complete Second Season*. Disc 3. DVD HBO Home Video, 2000.

Miller, William Ian. *Faking It*. Cambridge: Cambridge University Press, 2003.

Mills, Jane. *The Money Shot: Cinema, Sin and Censorship*. Sydney: Pluto Press Australia, 2001.

Mitchell, Edward. "Apes and Essences: Some Sources of Significance in the American Gangster Film." *Film Genre Reader III*. Ed. Barry Keith Grant. Austin: University of Texas Press, 2003. pp. 219–28.

Mitchell, Susan. *All Things Bright and Beautiful: Murder in the City of Light*. Australia: Macmillan, 2004.

Monster. 2003. Dir. Patti Jenkins.

Monster House. 2006. Dir. Gil Kenan.

Moore, Michael. "How to Deal with the Lies and the Lying Liars When They Lie About *Bowling for Columbine*." 2003. *Michael Moore.com*. Available: http://www.michaelmoore.com/words/wackoattacko/. November 24, 2004.

Moran, James M. *There's No Place Like Home Video*. Visible Evidence. Eds. Faye Ginsburg, Jane Gaines, and Michael Renov. Minneapolis: University of Minnesota Press, 2002.

Morse, Margaret. "News as Performance: Image as Event." *The Television Studies Reader*. Eds. Robert C. Allen and Annette Hill. London: Routledge, 2004. pp. 209–25.

Moses, Alexa. "Beating About the Bush." *Sydney Morning Herald* July 2, 2004, sec. Metro: 3.

Moss, Linda. "Entertainment Nets Turned to News." *Multichannel News* September 17, 2001: 4.

Muller, Judy, Shane Black, Manhola Dargi, Leslie Dixon, Buffy Shutt, and Courtney Valenti. *Words into Pictures: Chick Flick Versus Dick Flick*. Panel Discussion. VHS The Writer's Guild Foundation, Los Angeles, 1999.

Mulvey, L. "Visual Pleasure and Narrative Cinema." *Feminism and Film.* Ed. E. Ann Kaplan. Oxford Readings in Feminism. Oxford: Oxford University Press, 2000. pp. 34–47.

Munich. 2005. Dir. Steven Spielberg.

Murch, Walter. *In the Blink of an Eye: A Perspective on Film Editing.* 2nd edn. Los Angeles: Silman-James Press, 2001.

Murdoch, Lindsay, and Liz Gooch. "Family Begs Outback Killer to Reveal Body." *Sydney Morning Herald* December 15, 2005, sec. News: 7.

Murphy, Kerry. *TV Land: Australia's Obsession with Reality Television.* Milton: John Wiley & Sons Australia, Ltd., 2006.

Murray, Madeleine. "Cover Boys." *Sydney Morning Herald* December 29, 2005, sec. Summer Herald: 17–18.

Murray, Steve, and Phil Kloer. "Buffy's Deep Inner Meaning." May 17, 2003. *TheState.com.* Available: http://www.thestate.com/mid/thestate/5878387.htm. July 14, 2003.

Murray, Susan. "'I Think We Need a New Name for It:' The Meeting of Documentary and Reality TV." *Reality TV: Remaking Television Culture.* Eds. Susan Murray and Laurie Ouellette. New York: New York University Press, 2004. pp. 40–55.

Natoli, Joseph. *Memory's Orbit: Film and Culture 1999–2000.* The Suny Series in Postmodern Culture. Ed. Joseph Natoli. Albany: State University of New York Press, 2003.

Ndalianis, Angela. *Neo-Baroque Aesthetics and Contemporary Entertainment.* Media in Transition. Ed. David Thorburn. Cambridge, Massachusetts: The MIT Press, 2004.

Neroni, Hilary. "The Men of Columbine: Violence and Masculinity in American Culture." *Journal for the Psychoanalysis of Culture & . . .* 5(Fall).2 (2000): 256–62.

—. *The Violent Woman: Femininity, Narrative, and Violence in Contemporary American Culture.* Suny Series in Feminist Criticism and Theory. Ed. Michelle A. Masse. New York: State University of New York Press, 2005.

Neuwirth, Allan. *Makin' Toons: Inside the Most Popular Animated TV Shows and Movies.* New York: Allworth Press, 2003.

—. *They'll Never Put That on the Air.* New York: Allworth Press, 2006.

Newfield, Jack. "An Interview with Michael Moore." 1998. *Tikkun,* Nov–December Available: http://www.findarticles.com/p/articles/mi_m1548/is_n6_v13/ai_21248742. July 6, 2004.

Newseum. "Today's Front Pages: The Story Behind the News." September 12, 2001. Available: http://www.newseum.org/frontpages/index.htm. October 11, 2004.

Nichols, Bill. *Blurred Boundaries: Questions of Meaning in Contemporary Culture.* Bloomington and Indianapolis: Indiana University Press, 1994.

9/11: The Falling Man. 2006. Dir. Henry Singer.

Norrie, Justin, and Les Kennedy. "Death in Housing Block Unnoticed by Neighbours Afraid to Go Out." *Sydney Morning Herald* February 14, 2006, sec. News: 5.

Noxon, Marni. "Interview in Watch with Wanda: Grill, Gossip and Gripe." March 29, 2002. *Eonline.com.* Available: http://www.eonline.com/Gossip/Wanda/Archive2002/020329b.html. July 14, 2003.

O'Rourke, William. *What We Saw: How September 11 Looked on TV.* Archive Search 2001. Commonweal Magazine October 26, 2001/CXXVIII.18. Available: http://www.commonwealmagazine.org/article.php?id_article=352. January 24, 2006.

O'Donnell, Mick. *Mercy: In Pursuit of the Truth About the Death of Yvonne Gilford.* Pymble, N.S.W.: Harper Collins, 1999.

O'Hare, Kate. "'Buffy' Relationship Tips into Domestic Violence." February 8, 2002. *Psi Fi*. Available: http://pub128.ezboard.com/fpsififrm55.showMessage?topicID=42.topic. July 9, 2003.

Oliver, M. B. "Portrayals of Crime, Race, and Aggression in "Reality-Based" Police Shows: A Content Analysis." *Journal of Broadcasting and Electronic Media* 38 (1994): 179–92.

Overbey, Karen Eileen, and Lahney Preston-Matto. "Staking in Tongues: Speech Act as Weapon in Buffy." *Fighting the Forces: What's at Stake in Buffy the Vampire Slayer*. Eds. Rhonda V. Wilcox and David Lavery. Lanham: Rowan & Littlefield, 2002. pp. 73–84.

Overington, Caroline. "As Not Seen on TV: Non-Existent Crime Script Overturns Murder Sentence." *Sydney Morning Herald* January 8–9, 2004, Weekend edn., sec. News: 3.

Palmer, Jerry. *Thrillers: Genesis and Structure of a Popular Genre*. London: Edward Arnold, 1978.

Paoli, Letizia. *Mafia Brotherhoods: Organized Crime, Italian Style*. Oxford: Oxford University Press, 2003.

Papke, David Ray. "Myth and Meaning: Francis Ford Coppola and Popular Response to the Godfather Trilogy." *Legal Reelism: Movies as Legal Texts*. Ed. John Denver. Urbana: University of Illinois Press, 1996. pp. 2–22.

Paradise Lost: The Child Murders at Robin Hood Hills/Paradise Lost 2: Revelations. 2005. Dirs: Joe Berlinger and Bruce Sinofsky.

Passion of the Christ, The. 2004. Dir. Mel Gibson.

Pattie, David. "Mobbed Up: The Sopranos and the Modern Gangster Film." *This Thing of Ours: Investigating the Sopranos*. Ed. David Lavery. New York: Columbia University Press, 2002. pp. 135–45.

Pavlus, John. "A Bride Vows Revenge." October 2003. *American Cinematographer*. Available: http://www.theasc.com/magazine/oct03/cover/index.html. March 13, 2004.

Pearlman, Jonathan. "Anything but Child's Play." *Sydney Morning Herald* February 3, 2006, sec. Insight: 9.

Pediatrics, American Academy of. "Media Violence." *Journal of the American Academy of Pediatrics* 95.6 (1995): 949–51.

Pemberton, Patrick S. "Watching the Detectives." *Australian* September 25–26, 2004, Weekend edn., sec. View: R24–R25.

Pender, Patricia. "I'm Buffy and You're . . . History: The Postmodern Politics of Buffy." *Fighting the Forces: What's at Stake in Buffy the Vampire Slayer*. Eds. Rhonda V. Wilcox and David Lavery. Lanham: Rowan & Littlefield, 2002. pp. 35–44.

Petersen, George. "Building Character Through Violence: A One-Two Punch." *Creative Screenwriting* 3.1 (Summer) (1996): 107–17.

Petrie Jnr, Dan. *Guns Don't Kill People Writers Do*. Video. Words into Pictures. Writers Foundation, Los Angeles, 1999.

Phillips, Lyn. *Flirting with Danger: Young Women's Reflections on Sexuality and Domination*. New York: New York University Press, 2000.

Pierson, Michele. *Special Effects: Still in Search of Wonder*. Film and Culture. Ed. John Belton. New York: Columbia University Press, 2002.

Pinkaew, Prachya. *Ong Bak*. Eastern Eye Asian Cinema, Sahamongkol Film International. Madman Entertainment Pty. Ltd. DVD. The AV Channel Pty. Ltd., Thailand, 2003.

Pinsky, Mark. I. *The Gospel According to Disney: Faith, Trust and Pixie Dust*. Louisville: John Knox Press, 2004.

—. *The Gospel According to the Simpsons: The Spiritual Life of the World's Most Animated Family.* Louisville: John Knox Press, 2001.

Plantinga, Carl. R. *Rhetoric and Representation in Nonfiction Film.* Cambridge Studies in Film. Eds. William Rothman and Dudley Andrew. Cambridge: Cambridge University Press, 1997.

Poole, Steven. *Trigger Happy: The Inner Life of Videogames.* London: Fourth Estate, 2000.

Potter, W. James. *On Media Violence.* Thousand Oaks: Sage Publications Inc., 1999.

Poynting, Scott, Greg Noble, Paul Tabarl, and Jock Collins. *Bin Laden in the Suburbs: Criminalising the Arab Other.* Sydney Institute of Criminology Series. Eds. Chris Cunneen, Mark Findley, and Julie Stubbs . Sydney: Sydney Institute of Criminology, 2004.

Prince, Stephen. "The Aesthetic of Slow-Motion Violence in the Films of Sam Peckinpah." *Screening Violence.* Ed. Stephen Prince. New Brunswick, New Jersey: Rutgers University Press, 2000. pp. 175-201.

—. *Classical Film Violence: Designing and Regulating Brutality in Hollywood Cinema 1930–68.* New Brunswick, New Jersey: Rutgers University Press, 2003.

—. "True Lies: Perceptual Realism, Digital Images and Film Theory." *The Film Cultures Reader.* Ed. Graeme Turner. London: Routledge, 2002. pp. 115–28.

Probst, Christopher. *Welcome to the Machine.* Page 1, April 1999. American Cinematographer. Available: http://www.theasc.com/magazine/apr99/matrix/pg1.htm. March 13, 2003.

Projansky, Sarah. *Watching Rape: Film and Television in Post-Feminist Culture.* New York: London: New York University Press, 2001.

Pyle, Forest. "Making Cyborgs, Making Humans: Of Terminators and Blade Runners." *Film Theory Goes to the Movies.* Eds. Jim Collins, Hilary Radner, and Ava Preacher Collins. AFI Film Readers. New York: Routledge, 1993. pp. 227–41.

Rand-Kirshner, Rebecca. *Life as the Big Bad: A Season Six Overview.* Special Features: Buffy The Vampire Slayer. Disc 6. Collectors Edition. DVD Twentieth Century Fox Home Entertainment, 2003.

Rankin, Scott. *Stickybricks.* Community Theatre. Big hART, Sydney Festival, January 7–26, 2006.

Ratboy. "TV to Go." *Film West* Winter. 46 (2001): 64–65.

Raw Deal: A Question of Consent. 2002. Dir. Billy Corben. DVD.

Read, Jacinda. *The New Avengers: Feminism, Femininity and the Rape-Revenge Cycle.* Manchester: Manchester University Press, 2000.

Reeves, Byron, and Clifford Nass. *The Media Equation: How People Treat Computers, Television, and New Media Like Real People and Places.* Stanford, California: CSLI Publications, 1996.

Reid, Craig D. "Fighting Without Fighting: Film Action Fight Choreography." *Film Quarterly* 47.2. Winter (1993–94): 30–35.

Renov, Michael. "Documentary Horizons: An Afterforward." *Collecting Visible Evidence.* Visible Evidence. Eds. Jane M. Gaines and Michael ReNovember Vol. 6. Minneapolis: University of Minnesota Press, 1999. pp. 313–25.

—. *The Subject of Documentary.* Visible Evidence. Eds. Michael Renov, Faye Ginsburg, and Jane Gaines. Vol. 16. Minneapolis: University of Minnesota Press, 2004.

Report, Staff. "The Paths of Destruction." *Time* 158.12 (2001): 32.

Reser, Joseph P., and Steven Muncer. "Sense-Making in the Wake of September 11: A Network Analysis of Lay Understandings." *British Journal of Psychology* 95 (2004): 283–96.

Reuters. "A Marine Takes Aim and Shoots His Prisoner Dead." *Sydney Morning Herald* November 17, 2004, sec. Front Page: 1.

—. "Tolkien's Middle-earth Expands in Online Game." 2007. *Yahoo News*. Available: http://news,yahoo. com/nm/20070125/tc_nm/games_rings_dc_2. January 27, 2007.

Reynolds, Richard. *Superheroes: A Modern Mythology*. London: B. T. Batsford Ltd, 1992.

Rhodes, Gary D. "Mockumentaries and the Production of Realist Horror." *Post Script* 21.13 (2002): 46–62.

Rhys, Gwynneth. "Why Spike as Rapist Feels Like Character Rape to Me or, Seeing Red over Seeing Red." 2002. *Chez Gwyn*. Available: http://www.drizzle.com/~gwyneth/morestuff/spike.html. July 20, 2003.

Rich, B. Ruby. "After the Fall: Cinema Studies Post-9/11." *Cinema Journal* 43.2 (2004): 109–15.

—. "Day of the Woman." Features, June 2004. *Sight and Sound*. Available: http://www.bfi.org.uk/ cgi-bin/wac.cgi/http://www.bfi.org.uk/sightandsound/2004_06/killbill.php. June 17, 2004.

Ritchie, Ruth. "Truths Are Still Simple." *Sydney Morning Herald* September 9–10, 2006, Weekend edn., sec. Spectrum: 10.

Rittikrai, Panna. *Cast and Crew Interviews*. Documentary and Interviews: *Ong Bak*. Disc 2. DVD Eastern Eye Asian Cinema, 2003.

Rize. 2005. Dir. David La Chapelle.

Robinson, Lillian S. *Wonder Women: Feminisms and Superheroes*. London: Routledge, 2004.

Rock, The. "Fight the Good Fight." Special Features: *Walking Tall*. DVD MGM Home Entertainment, 2005.

Ronson, Jon. "The Egos Have Landed." Features. *Sight and Sound* November 2002. British Film Institute. Available: http://www.bfi.org.uk/sightandsound/feature/37. June 6, 2004.

Rose, Charlie. *Interview with the Coen Brothers*. Special Features: *Fargo*. DVD Gold Edition, MGM Home Entertainment, 2005.

Rotten Tomatoes. The Passion of the Christ. Reviews 2006. Available: http://www.rottentomatoes.com/ m/passion_of_the_christ. September 5, 2006.

Rushdie, Salman. "Reality TV: A Dearth of Talent and the Death of Morality." *Guardian* June 9, 2001: 12.

Ruth, David E. *Inventing the Public Enemy: The Gangster in American Culture, 1918–34*. Chicago: The University of Chicago Press, 1996.

Ryan, Marie-Laure. *Narrative as Virtual Reality: Immersion and Interactivity in Literature and Electronic Media*. Parallax: Revisions of Culture and Society. Eds. Gerald Prince and Wendy Steiner Stephen G. Nichols. Baltimore: The Johns Hopkins University Press, 2001.

Sandars, Diana. "From the Warehouse to the Multiplex: Techno and Rave Culture's Reconfiguration of Late 1990's Sci-Fi Spectacle as Musical Performance." July 29, 2005. *Screening the Past*. 18. Available: http://www.latrobe.edu.au/screeningthepast/firstrelease/fr_18/DSfr18a.html. April 13, 2006.

Schaffer, Bill. "Just Like a Movie: September 11 and the Terror of Moving Images." Archive 2001. *Senses of Cinema* 17. Nov–December Available: http://www.sensesofcinema.com/contents/01/17/ symposium/schaffer.html. September 9, 2004.

Schager, Nicholas. *Movie Review: Irréversible*. 2003. *filmcritic.com*. Available: http://filmcritic.com/ misc/emporium.nsf/84dbbfa4d710144986256c290016f76e/d792dfcead7fd85888256cc700167826 ?OpenDocument&Highlight=0,Irreversible. January 28, 2004.

Schechner, Richard. *Performance Theory*. Revised edn. London: Routledge Classics, 2003.

Schickel, Richard. "The Alternate Realities of Hot Documentaries: Three Non-Fiction Films Are Attracting Lots of Attention This Summer—Maybe for the Wrong Reason." *Time* 162.2 (2003): 67.

—. "Spielberg Takes on Terror." *Time* December 12, 2005: 64.

Schilt, Paige. "Media Whores and Perverse Media: Documentary Film Meets Tabloid TV in Nick Broomfield's *Aileen Wournos: The Selling of a Serial Killer*." *Velvet Light Trap* 45. Spring (2000): 50–61.

Schmid, David. *Natural Born Celebrities: Serial Killers in American Culture*. Chicago: The University of Chicago Press, 2005.

Schrader, Paul, and Kevin Jackson. *Schrader on Schrader*. London: Faber and Faber, 2004.

Schudson, Michael. *The Sociology of News*. Contemporary Societies. Ed. Jeffrey C. Alexander. New York: W. W. Norton & Company, 2003.

Schulenburg, Caroline. "Dying to Entertain: Violence on Prime Time Broadcast Television 1998–2006. Parents Television Council. 2007. *parentstv.org*. Available: http://www.parents.org/PTC?publications/reports/violencestudy/exsummary.asp January 28, 2007.

Schwartz, Jeffrey. *Minnesota Nice: A Documentary*. Rec 2005. Special Features: *Fargo* DVD Gold Edition, MGM Home Entertainment, 2003.

Scott, A. O. "True Horror: When Movie Violence Is Random." *New York Times* March 23, 2003, sec. Week in Review Desk; 4: 2.

Seaton, Jean. *Carnage and the Media: The Making and Breaking of News About Violence*. London: Allen Lane, 2005.

Seay, Chris, and Greg Garrett. *The Gospel Reloaded: Exploring Spirituality and Faith in the Matrix*. Colorado Springs: Pinon, 2003.

Selling of a Serial Killer. 1992. Dir. Nick Broomfield.

Seltzer, Mark. *Serial Killers: Death and Life in America's Wound Culture*. New York: Routledge, 1998.

Series 7: The Contenders. 2001. Dir. Daniel Minehan.

Sessler, Adam. *Doom Nation*. Bonus. DVD *Doom* Distant Planet Productions, Universal Pictures, 2006.

Setlove, Richard. "Woo: Getting Kicks from Action Pix." *Variety* November 18–24, 1996, New York edn.: 25.

Shadoian, Jack. *Dreams and Dead Ends: The American Gangster Film*. 2nd edn. Oxford: Oxford University Press, 2003.

Shaeffer, G. J., and Sondra London. *Killer Fiction*. Venice, CA: Feral House, 1997.

Shalbak, Ihab. "The False Identity That Helped Provide a Moral Case for War." *Sydney Morning Herald* 2004, sec. Comment: 15.

Sharrett, Christopher. *Mythologies of Violence in Postmodern Media*. Detroit: Wayne State University Press, 1999.

Sheedy, Chris. "The Real CSI." *Sydney Morning Herald* September 8, 2004, sec. Radar: 4.

Sherwin, Richard K. "Framed." *Legal Reelism: Movies as Legal Texts*. Ed. John Denver. Urbana: University of Illinois Press, 1996. pp. 70–94.

Shilling, Chris. *The Body in Culture, Technology and Society*. Theory, Culture and Society. Ed. Mike Featherstone. London: Sage Publications, 2005.

Simon, Bob, Rick Berke, Ari Fleischer, Paul Freidman, Jay M. Parker, and Norman Pearlstine. "Television and the War on Terrorism: The War Abroad: The U.S. Perspective." 2002. Panel

Transcript. *Museum of Radio and Television*. Available: http://www.mtr.org/seminars/satellite/terrorism/terror2trans.htm. May 19, 2004.

Simpson, Roger. "Journalism and Trauma: A Long Overdue Conjunction." *Nieman Reports* 58.2 (2004): 77+.

Six Reasons. *Gang Tapes*. Special Features: The Making of Gang Tapes. DVD Lions Gate Entertainment, 2004.

Sklar, Robert. *Movie-Made America: A Cultural History of American Movies*. Revised edn. New York: Vintage Books: Random House Inc., 1994.

Skoble, J. Aeon. "Superhero Revisionism in *Watchmen* and *the Dark Knight Returns*." *Superheroes and Philosophy: Truth, Justice and the Socratic Way*. Eds. Tom Morris and Matt Morris. Chicago, Illinois: Open Court, 2005. pp. 29–41.

Slotkin, Richard. *Regeneration Through Violence: The Mythology of the American Frontier, 1600–1860*. Middletown, Connecticut: Wesleyan University Press, 1973.

Smith, Gavin. "Oliver Stone: Why Do I Provoke?" *Sight and Sound* IV.12 (1994): 8–12.

Sobchack, Vivian. "Bringing It All Back Home: Family Economy and Generic Exchange." *American Horrors*. Ed. Gregory A. Waller. Urbana and Chicago: University of Illinois Press, 1987. pp. 175–95.

—. "Toward a Phenomenology of Nonfictional Film Experience." *Collecting Visible Evidence*. Visible Evidence. Eds. Jane M. Gaines and Michael Renov. Vol. 6. Minneapolis: University of Minnesota Press, 1999. pp. 241–54.

Soden, Gary. *Falling*. New York: W. W. Norton & Company, 2003.

Sonic Memorial Project, The. Home Page. 2002. National Public Radio. Available: www.sonicmemorial.org. October 3, 2004.

Sontag, Susan. *Regarding the Pain of Others*. New York: Farrar Straus and Giroux, 2003.

Spah, Victoria. *Buffy Dialogue Database*. 2003. Available: http://vrya.net/bdb/quips/php. June 30, 2003 Transcripts.

Sparks, Colin. "The Global, the Local and the Public Sphere." *The Television Studies Reader*. Eds. Robert C. Allen and Annette Hill. London: Routledge, 2004. pp. 139–50.

Spence, Edward. "Stranger Than Fiction: The Fabrication of Fact." *Sydney Morning Herald* January 16, 2006, sec. Comment: 9.

Spence, Louise. "In Focus: Teaching 9/11." *Cinema Journal* 43.2 (2004): 90–91.

St. John, Warren. "What Men Want: Neanderthal TV." December 11, 2005. *nytimes.com*. Available: http://www.nytimes.com/2005/12/11/fashion/sundaystyles/11MEN.html?pagewanted=print. December 15, 2005.

Stacey, Jackie. "Desperately Seeking Difference." *Feminism and Film*. Ed. E. Ann Kaplan. Oxford Readings in Feminism. Oxford: Oxford University Press, 2000. pp. 450–65.

Staff Report. "If You Want to Humble an Empire." *Time* 158.12 (2001): 32–42.

Stanko, Elizabeth. "Naturalising Danger: Women, Fear and Personal Safety." *Dangerous Offenders: Punishment and Social Order*. Eds. Mark Brown and John Pratt. London: Routledge, 2000. pp. 147–63.

Stapleton, Christopher, Charles Hughes, Michael Moshall, Pauluis Micikevicius, Marty Altman. "Applying Mixed Reality Entertainment." December 2002. *Computer.org*. Available: http://www.computer.org/computer/homepage/1202/entertainment. June 22, 2004.

States, National Commission on Terrorist Attacks Upon the United. *The 9/11 Commission Report: Final Report of the National Commission on Terrorist Attacks Upon the United States*. Authorised edn. New York: W. W. Norton & Company, 2004.

Steele, Bruce C. "The Making of a Monster." *Advocate* March 2, 2004: 36–45.

Steeves, H. Peter. "It's Just a Bunch of Stuff That Happened." *The Sitcom Reader: America Viewed and Skewed*. Eds. Mary M. Dalton and Laura R. Linder. New York: State University of New York Press, 2005. pp. 261–71.

Stein, Joel. "The New Quiz Show Scandal: Reality Television." *Los Angeles Times* December 5, 2004, sec. Laptop L.A.: M1.

Stone, Bryan P. *Faith and Film: Theological Themes at the Cinema*. St. Louis, Missouri: Chalice Press, 2000.

Stott, Sian. "Film-Makers on Film: Joss Whedon: Joss Whedon Talks to Siân Stott About Vincent Minnelli's Brigadoon (1954)." Arts Home. March 4, 2006. *film.telegraph*. Available: http://www.telegraph.co.uk/arts/main.jhtml?xml=/arts/2006/03/04/bffmof04.xml&menuId=564&sSheet=/arts/2006/03/04/ixfilmmain.html. March 4, 2006.

Strathern, Andrew, and Pamela J. Stewart. "Introduction: Terror, the Imagination, and Cosmology." *Terror and Violence: Imagination and the Unimaginable*. Eds. Andrew Strathern, Pamela J. Stewart, and Neil L. Whitehead . London: Pluto Press, 2006. pp. 1–39.

Strick, Phillip. "The Matrix." *Action Spectacle Cinema: A Sight and Sound Reader*. Ed. Jose Arroya. London: Bfi Publishing, 2000. pp. 259–61.

Study, National Television Violence. *National Television Violence Study*. Studio City, CA, 1996, 1997.

Symonds, Gwyn. "'Bollocks!': Spike Fans and Reception of Buffy the Vampire Slayer." 2003. *Refractory: A Journal of Entertainment Media*. 2. March 2003. Available: http://www.refractory.unimelb.edu.au//journalissues/vol2/gwynsymonds.htm. July 5, 2003.

—. "'Not Taking It Personally': Performing the Teacher's "Role" and Responding to Challenging Behaviors." *Australasian Journal of Special Education* 27.1 (2003): 29–45.

—. "Playing More Soul Than Is Written: James Marsters' Performance of Spike and the Ambiguity of Evil in Sunnydale." 2005. *Slayage: The Online International Journal of Buffy Studies* 16: March Available: http://www.slayageonline.com/essays/slayage16/Symonds.htm. January 28, 2007.

—. "Show Business or Dirty Business: The Theatrics of Mafia Narrative and Empathy for the Last Mob Boss Standing in *the Sopranos*." *Reading the Sopranos: Hit TV from HBO*. Ed. David Lavery. Reading Contemporary Television. London and New York: I. B. Tauris, 2006. pp. 127–37.

—. "'Solving Problems with Sharp Objects': Female Empowerment, Sex and Violence in Buffy, the Vampire Slayer." 2004. *Slayage: The Online International Journal of Buffy Studies*, 11/12: April Available: http:www.slayageonline.com/essays/slayage11_12/Symonds.htm. January 28, 2007.

—. "The Superhero Versus the Troubled Teen: Parenting Conner and the Fragility of Family in *Angel*." *Super/Heroes: From Hercules to Superman*. Eds. Wendy Haslem, Angela Ndalianis, and Chris Mackie. Washington: New Academia Publishing, 2007.

Taliaferro, Charles. "The Focus of *the Passion* Puts the Person of Jesus out of Focus." *Mel Gibson's Passion and Philosophy: The Cross, the Questions, the Controversy*. Ed. Jorge J. E. Gracia. Vol. 10. Popular Culture and Philosophy. Chicago, Illinois: Open Court, 2004. pp. 40–49.

Tarantino, Quentin. *The Making of Kill Bill Volume 2*. Special Features: Kill Bill. Vol. 2. DVD Buena Vista Home Entertainment.

Taubin, Amy. "The Allure of Decay." *Action Spectacle Cinema: A Sight and Sound Reader*. Ed. Jose Arroyo. London: BFI Publishing, 2000. pp. 150–55.

Taylor, S. Caroline. *Court Licensed Abuse: Patriarchal Lore and the Legal Response to Intrafamilial Sexual Abuse of Children*. New Literacies and Digital Epistemologies. Eds. Colin Lankshear, Knobel Michele, and Peters Michael. Vol. 11. New York: Peter Lang, 2004.

Tejada-Flores, Miguel, Wes Craven, Rusty Cardieff, Steven Gaydes, Debra Hill, and Neal Moritz. *Words Into Pictures: I Know What You Screamed Last Summer*. Panel Discussion. VHS The Writer's Guild Foundation, Los Angeles, 1999.

Telford, William R. "Jesus Christ Movie Star: The Depiction of Jesus in the Cinema." *Explorations in Theology and Film: Movies and Meaning*. Eds. Clive Marsh and Gaye Ortiz. Oxford: Blackwell Publishers, 1998. pp. 115–39.

Teo, Stephen. *Hong Kong Cinema: The Extra Dimensions*. London: BFI Publishing, 1997.

Thin Blue Line, The. 1988. Dir. Errol Morris.

Thomas, Gordon. "We Know Where You Live." *Sydney Morning Herald* January 14–15 2006, Weekend edn., sec. News Review: 25.

Thompson, Jim. "Just a Girl: Feminism, Postmodernism and *Buffy the Vampire Slayer*." 2003. *Refractory: A Journal of Entertainment Media*. 2. March 2003. Available: http:www.sfca.unimelb.edu.au/refractory/journalissues/vol2/jimthompson.htmn. June 23, 2003.

Tiffin, John. "Introduction." *Hyperreality: Paradigm for the Third Millennium*. Eds. John Tiffin and Nobuyoshi Terashima. London: Routledge, 2001. pp. xv–xvi.

Times, New York, and Agence France Press. "Execution Prompts Children's Hangings." *Sydney Morning Herald* January 6–7, 2007, Weekend edn., sec. World: 9.

Today in L.A: NBC New Special Report. Rec September 11, 2001, 5: 52 a.m. News and Public Affairs Collection. University of California Los Angeles Film and Television Archive, Los Angeles, 2001.

Topel, Fred. *Charlize Theron Interview: Portraying Monster Aileen Wournos*. Action-Adventure Movies 2005. About Inc. Available: http://actionadventure.about.com/cs/weeklystories/a/aa121903.htm. January 13, 2005.

—. *Ending Buffy: Talking About the Buffy Series Finale*. Action Adventure Movies 2003. About.com. Available: http://actionadventure.about.com/cs/weeklystories/a/aa041903.htm#b. July 7, 2003.

Tulloch, John. *Watching Television Audiences: Cultural Theories & Methods*. London: Arnold, 2000.

Tung, Charlene. "Embodying an Image: Gender, Race, and Sexuality in *La Femme Nikita*." *Action Chicks: New Images of Tough Women in Popular Culture*. Ed. Sherrie A. Inness. New York: Palgrave Macmillan, 2004. pp. 95–121.

Turkel, Sherry. *Life on the Screen*. New York: Simon and Schuster, 1995.

Turner, Chris. *Planet Simpson: How a Cartoon Masterpiece Defined a Generation*. Cambridge: Da Capo Press, 2004.

TV.com. "Law & Order Episode Guide." Season Episodes 2006. Available: http://www.tv.com/law-and-order/show/180/episode_guide.html. January 22, 2006.

Vankin, Jonathan, and John Whalen. *Based on a True Story: Fact and Fantasy in 100 Movies*. Chicago: Chicago Review Press, 2005.

Verghis, Sharon. "Collaboration Sets Off Motion Senses." *Sydney Morning Herald* August 10, 2004, sec. Metropolitan: 15.

—. "Not Another Terrorist Movie." *Sydney Morning Herald* August 19–20, 2006, Weekend edn., sec. Spectrum: 19.

Vint, Sherryl. "Killing Us Softly: A Feminist Search for the "Real" Buffy. March 2001. *Slayage: The International Online Journal of Buffy Studies* 2. Available: http://www.slayageonline.com/essays/ slayage5/vint.htmn. January 28, 2007.

Virilio, Paul. *Ground Zero*. Trans. Chris Turner. London: New York: Verso, 2002.

—. *The Vision Machine*. Trans. Julie Rose. Perspectives. Eds. Colin MacCabe and Paul Willemen. Bloomington: Indiana University Press and BFI Publishing, 1996.

Wainwright, Robert. "The Case for the Prosecution." *Sydney Morning Herald* September 9–10, 2006, Weekend edn., sec. News Review: 29.

Waldon, Steven, and Selma Milovanovic. "Gangster Who Nursed Sick Mother, Found God and Loved a Laugh." *Sydney Morning Herald* February 11–12, 2006, Weekend edn., sec. News: 9.

Waldren, Murray, and Tony Koch. "Honor Kill Book's Shelf Life Runs Out." *Australian* July 27, 2004, sec. The Nation: 3.

Walker, Joseph S. "Cunnilingus and Psychiatry Have Brought Us to This: Livia and the Logic of Falsehoods in the First Season of the Sopranos." *This Thing of Ours: Investigating the Sopranos*. Ed. David Lavery. New York: Columbia University Press, 2002. pp. 109–21.

Wallace, Natasha. "Teenager Gets 24 Years for Merciless Rape." *Sydney Morning Herald* December 23–25, 2004, Weekend edn., sec. News: 5.

Warshaw, Robert. *The Immediate Experience*. New York: Atheneum, 1974.

Weber, Samuel. *Theatricality as Medium*. New York: Fordham University Press, 2004.

Weiner, Susan. "True Crime: Fact, Fiction and the Law." *Legal Studies Forum* 17.3 (1993): 275–88.

Weld, George. "9.11 (1)." Journal 2001. *Like An Orb*. Available: http://www.likeanorb.com/wtc/index. php?Number=1. January 26, 2006.

—. "Before." Journal 2001. *Like An Orb*. Available: http://www.likeanorb.com/wtc/before/index. php?Number=0. October 19, 2004.

Wells, Dominic. "It's Life Jim." *Time Out* December 17–31, 1997: 22–23.

Wells, Paul. *Animation and America*. Edinburgh: Edinburgh University Press, 2002.

—. *Animation: Genre and Authorship*. Short Cuts. Ed. Maureen Furniss. London: Wallflower, 2002.

Whedon, Joss. Creator and Exec. Prod. *Buffy, the Vampire Slayer*. 1997–2003.

    1.11 "Out of Mind, Out of Sight (Invisible Girl)." Writ. Joss Whedon, Ashley Gable, and Thomas A. Swyden. Dir. Reza Badiyi. May 10, 1997.

    1.12 "Prophecy Girl." Writ. Joss Whedon. Dir. Joss Whedon. June 2, 1997.

    2.4 "Inca Mummy Girl." Writ. Matt Kiene and Joe Reinkemeyer. Dir. Ellen S. Pressman. October 6, 1997.

    2.10 "What's My Line, Part 2." Writ. Marti Noxon. Dir. David Semel. November 24, 1997.

    2.11 "Ted." Writ. David Greenwalt and Joss Whedon. Dir. Bruce Seth Green. December 8, 1997.

    2.18 "Killed by Death. Writ. Rob Des Hotel and Dean Batali. Dir. Bruce Seth Green. March 3, 1998.

    2.19 "I Only Have Eyes for You." Writ. Marti Noxon. Dir. James Whitmore Jnr. April 28, 1998.

    3.9 "The Wish." Writ. Marti Noxon. Dir. David Greenwalt. December 8, 1998.

    3.10 "Amends." Writ. Joss Whedon. Dir. Joss Whedon. December 15, 1998.

    3.12 "Helpless." Writ. David Fury. Dir. James A. Contner. January 19, 1999.

    3.13 "The Zeppo." Writ. Dan Vebber. Dir. James Whitmore Jnr. January 26, 1999.

    4.2 "Living Conditions." Writ. Marti Noxon. Dir. David Grossman. October 12, 1999.

    4.6 "Wild at Heart." Writ. Marti Noxon. Dir. David Grossman. November 9, 1999.

4.8   "Pangs." Writ. Jane Espenson. Dir. Michael Lang. November 23, 1999.

5.1   "Buffy vs Dracula." Writ. Marti Noxon. Dir. David Grossman. September 26, 2000.

5.10   "Into the Woods." Writ. Marti Noxon. Dir. Marti Noxon. December 19, 2000.

5.22   "The Gift." Writ. Joss Whedon. Dir. Joss Whedon. May 21, 2001.

6.1   "Bargaining, Part 1." Writ. Marti Noxon and David Fury. Dir. David Grossman. October 2, 2001.

6.5   "Life Serial." Writ. David Fury and Jane Espenson. Dir. Nick Marck. October 23, 2001.

6.7   "Once More, with Feeling." Writ. Joss Whedon. Dir. Joss Whedon. November 6, 2001.

6.9   "Smashed." Writ. Drew Z. Greenberg. Dir. Turi Meyer. November 20, 2001.

6.10   "Wrecked." Writ. Marti Noxon. Dir. David Solomon. November 27, 2001.

6.11   "Gone." Writ. David Fury. Dir. David Fury. January 8, 2002.

6.13   "Dead Things." Writ. Steven S. DeKnight. Dir. James A. Contner. February 5, 2002.

6.15   "As You Were." Writ. Douglas Petrie. Dir. Douglas Petrie. February 26, 2002.

6.18   "Entropy." Writ. Drew Z. Greenberg. Dir. James A. Contner. April 30, 2002.

6.19   "Seeing Red." Writ. Steven S. DeKnight. Dir. Michael Gershman. May 7, 2002.

6.22   "Grave." Writ. David Fury. Dir. James A. Contner. May 21, 2002.

7.1   "Lessons." Writ. Joss Whedon. Dir. David Solomon. September 24, 2002.

7.2   "Beneath You." Writ. Douglas Petrie. Dir. Nick Marck. October 1, 2002.

7.5   "Selfless." Writ. Drew Goddard. Dir. David Solomon. October 22, 2002.

7.8   "Sleeper." Writ. David Fury and Jane Espenson. Dir. Alan J. Levi. November 19, 2002.

7.9   "Never Leave Me." Writ. Drew Goddard. Dir. David Solomon. November 26, 2002.

7.22   "Chosen." Writ. Joss Whedon. Dir. Joss Whedon. May 20, 2003.

—. "10 Questions for Joss Whedon." Readers Opinions 2003. *New York Times.* May 16, 2003. Available: http://www.nytimes.com/2003/05/16/readersopinions/16WHED.html?ex=1058068800&en=f8e6a8f6097acef9&ei=5070. May 18, 2003.

—. *Behind the Scenes of Buffy, the Vampire Slayer.* Panel Discussion, June 18, 2002. Academy of Television Arts and Sciences. Special Features: Season 6. Collectors Edition, Season 6, Disc 3. DVD Twentieth Century Fox Home Entertainment, 2003.

Whitlock, Gillian. "Tainted Testimony: The Khouri Affair." *Australian Literary Studies* 21.4 (2004): 165–78.

Who Framed Roger Rabbit. 1988. Dir. Frank Marshall.

Wilcox, Rhonda V. "Every Night I Save You: Buffy, Spike, Sex and Redemption." May 5, 2002. *Slayage: The International Online Journal of Buffy Studies.* Available: http://www.slayageonline.com/essays/slayage5/wilcox.htm. January 28, 2007.

—. *Why Buffy Matters: The Art of Buffy the Vampire Slayer.* London: I. B. Tauris, 2006.

Wilkinson, Marian. "The Darkest Hours." *Sydney Morning Herald* July 24–25, 2004, Weekend edn., sec. News Review: 29.

Williams, Sue. "Selections from the Exhibition." *The Culture of Violence.* Ed. Helaine Posner. Amherst: University of Massachusetts Amherst, 2002. pp. 53–86.

Wilshire, Peter. "Presentation and Representation in Michael Moore's Bowling for Columbine." *Australian Screen Education* Summer.35 (2004): 91–95.

Wilson, Peter. "Thanks for the Memories." *Weekend Australian.* February 2–3, 2008, sec. Inquirer: 23.

Wilson, Steve. "Laugh, Spawn of Hell, Laugh." *Reading the Vampire Slayer: An Unofficial Critical Companion to Buffy and Angel*. Ed. Roz Kaveney. London: Tauris Park Paperbacks, 2002. pp. 78–97.

Wisker, Gina. "Vampires and Schoolgirls: Highschool Hijinks on the Hellmouth in Buffy the Vampire Slayer." March 2, 2001. *Slayage: The International Online Journal of Buffy Studies* March. Available: http://slayageonline.com/essays/slayage2/wisker.htm. January 28, 2003.

Wolf, Dick. *Law and Order: Crime Scenes*. New York: Barnes & Noble, 2007.

—. Exec. Prod. *Law & Order*. 1990

Wood, Aylish. "The Collapse of Reality and Illusion in *the Matrix*." *Action and Adventure Cinema*. Ed. Yvonne Tasker. London: Routledge, 2004. pp. 119–29.

Wood, Robin. "Burying the Undead: The Use and Obsolescence of Count Dracula." *The Dread of Difference: Gender and the Horror Film*. Ed. Barry Keith Grant. Austin: University of Texas Press, 1996. pp. 364–78.

—. "An Introduction to the American Horror Film." *Planks of Reason: Essays on the Horror Film*. Ed. Barry Keith Grant. Metuchen, New Jersey: Scarecrow Press, 1984. pp. 164–200.

Wright, Gerard. "A Drunk, Angry Bigot: Mel's Mouth Proves His Most Lethal Weapon." *Sydney Morning Herald* July 31, 2006, sec. Front Page: 1–2.

—. "Have I Got a Story for You." *Sydney Morning Herald,* January 14–15, 2006, Weekend edn., sec. News Review: 23.

—. "You're Not a Jew, Are You?" *Sydney Morning Herald* August 5–6, 2006, Weekend edn., sec. News Review: 25.

Wyndham, Susan. "On Death and Madness." *Sydney Morning Herald* August 9, 2004, sec. Insight: 15.

—. "Undercover: Forbidden but Not Forgotten." *Sydney Morning Herald* June 17–18, 2006, Weekend edn., sec. Spectrum: 30.

X-Men: The Last Stand. 2006. Dir. Brett Ratner.

Yacowar, Maurice. "The Bug in the Rug: Notes on the Disaster Genre." *Film Genre Reader III*. Ed. Barry Keith Grant. Austin: Texas University Press, 2003. pp. 277–95.

—. *The Sopranos on the Couch: Analyzing Television's Greatest Series*. Expanded edn. New York: Continuum, 2003.

Zani, Steven J. "Traumatic Disaster and Titanic Recuperation." *Journal of Popular Film and Television* 31.3 (2003): 125–31.

Zavodny, John. "I Am Jack's Wasted Life: *Fight Club* and Personal Identity." *Movies and the Meaning of Life: Philosophers Take on Hollywood*. Eds. Kimberly A. Blessing and Paul J. Tudico. Chicago, Illinois: Open Court, 2005. pp. 47–60.

Zimmerman, Patricia R. *States of Emergency: Documentaries, Wars, Democracies*. Visible Evidence. Eds. Michael Renov, Faye Ginsburg, and Jane Gaines. Vol. 7. Minneapolis: University of Minnesota Press, 2000.

Zimring, Franklin, E. *American Youth Violence*. Studies in Crime and Public Policy. Ed. Michael Tonry and Norval Morris. New York: Oxford University Press, 1998.

Zizek, Slavoj. *Welcome to the Desert of the Real*. London: Verso, 2002.

Zuidervaart, Lambert. *Artistic Truth: Aesthetics, Discourse, and Imaginative Disclosure*. Cambridge: Cambridge University Press, 2004.

Index